Lecture Notes in Computer Science 3573

Commenced Publication in 1973
Founding and Former Series Editors:
Gerhard Goos, Juris Hartmanis, and Jan van Leeuwen

W0225617

Lecture Notes in Computer Science

Sandro Etalle (Ed.)

Logic Based Program Synthesis and Transformation

14th International Symposium, LOPSTR 2004
Verona, Italy, August 26 – 28, 2004
Revised Selected Papers

 Springer

Volume Editor

Sandro Etalle
University of Twente
Distributed and Embedded System Group
P.O. Box 217, 7500 AE Enschede, The Netherlands
E-mail: s.etalle@utwente.nl

Library of Congress Control Number: 2005927904

CR Subject Classification (1998): F.3.1, D.1.1, D.1.6, D.2.4, I.2.2, F.4.1

ISSN   0302-9743
ISBN-10   3-540-26655-0 Springer Berlin Heidelberg New York
ISBN-13   978-3-540-26655-6 Springer Berlin Heidelberg New York

Springer is a part of Springer Science+Business Media

springeronline.com

© Springer-Verlag Berlin Heidelberg 2005
Printed in Germany

Typesetting: Camera-ready by author, data conversion by Scientific Publishing Services, Chennai, India
Printed on acid-free paper   SPIN: 11506676   06/3142   5 4 3 2 1 0

Preface

This volume contains a selection of the papers presented at LOPSTR 2004, the 14th International Symposium on Logic-Based Program Synthesis and Transformation.

The aim of the LOPSTR series is to stimulate and promote international research and collaboration on logic-based program development. The workshop is open to contributions in logic-based program development in any language paradigm. This year, LOPSTR put extra emphasis on the field of verification by incorporating the VCL (Verification in Computational Logic) workshop.

LOPSTR 2004 took place in Verona, Italy, and was co-located with the International Static Analysis Symposium (SAS 2004), the ACM SIGPLAN 2004 Workshop on Partial Evaluation and Semantics Based Program Manipulation (PEPM 2004), and the 6th ACM-SIGPLAN International Conference on Principles and Practice of Declarative Programming (PPDP 2004).

Past workshops were held in Manchester (UK), Louvain-la-Neuve (Belgium), Pisa (Italy), Arnhem (the Netherlands), Stockholm (Sweden), Leuven (Belgium), Venice (Italy), London (UK), Paphos (Cyprus), Madrid (Spain) and Uppsala (Sweden). Since 1994 the proceedings have been published in the Springer LNCS series.

We received 23 *full paper submissions* (1 from Australia, 3 from the US, 4 from Asia, 3 from Africa, 11 from Europe[1], and one Spain–US cooperation), and 11 *extended abstract submissions* (1 from Israel, 1 from Africa, one US–Spain cooperation, and the others were from Europe[2]). We accepted for presentation 11 full papers and 8 extended abstracts. This volume contains a selection consisting of the 11 full papers and of the full version of 6 of the extended abstracts.

I would like to express my gratitude to the authors of the papers, the reviewers, and in particular to the members of the Program Committee, for their invaluable help.

My warmest thanks also go to Roberto Giacobazzi – who was extremely generous and efficient in organizing the event – and to the members of the Organizing Committee. In particular Fausto Spoto and Samir Genaim made my life very easy by managing the webserver, also during holidays. Finally, I would like to thank Eugenio Moggi and the chairs of the other events (David Scott Warren of PPDP, Nevin Heintze and Peter Seztof of PEPM, and Roberto Giacobazzi of SAS) for the pleasant and stimulating cooperation.

March 2005   Sandro Etalle

---

[1] Of which 2 from Spain, 2 from Germany, 2 from Denmark, and the others were from other countries or were cooperation between different countries.

[2] All extended abstract submissions came from different countries or from combinations of countries.

Organization

Program Chair

Sandro Etalle   University of Twente, The Netherlands.

Program Committee

Gilles Barthe   INRIA Sophia-Antipolis, France
Annalisa Bossi   University of Venice, Italy
Maurice Bruynooghe   University of Leuven, Belgium
Francisco Bueno   Technical University of Madrid, Spain
Giorgio Delzanno   University of Genova, Italy
Tom Ellman   Vassar College, USA
Sandro Etalle   University of Twente, The Netherlands
Norbert Fuchs   University of Zürich, Switzerland
Gopal Gupta   University of Texas at Dallas, USA
Patricia M. Hill   University of Leeds, UK
Kung-Kiu Lau   University of Manchester, UK
Fabio Martinelli   IIT-CNR, Italy
Alberto Pettorossi   University of Rome "Tor Vergata", Italy
Andreas Podelski   Max Planck Institute for Computer Science, Germany
C.R. Ramakrishnan   SUNY at Stony Brook, USA
Abhik Roychoudhury   National University of Singapore, Singapore
Wim Vanhoof   University of Namur, Belgium
Germán Vidal   Technical University of Valencia, Spain

Additional Referees

Chiara Braghin   Nicoletta Cocco   Maurizio Gabbrielli
Irina Mariuca Gheorghita   Dilian Gurov   Florian Kammueller
Andrew Ireland   Gebriele Lenzini   Ajay Mallya
Alberto Momigliano   Bert van Nuffelen   Claudio Ochoa
Mario Ornaghi   Vajirapan Panumong   Maurizio Proietti
Alessandro Provetti   Femke van Raamsdonk   Tamara Rezk
Sabina Rossi   Andrey Rybalchenko   Luke Simon
Josep Silva   Jan-Georg Smaus   Joost Vennekens

Sponsoring Institution

The Association for Logic Programming
University of Verona

Table of Contents

Program Development

Termination

Program Development and Synthesis

Searching Semantically Equivalent Code Fragments in Logic Programs

Wim Vanhoof

Institut d'Informatique,
University of Namur, Belgium
wva@info.fundp.ac.be

Abstract. In this work, we devise an analysis that searches for semantically equivalent code fragments within a given logic program. The presence of duplicated code (or functionality) is a primary indication that the design of the program can be improved by performing a so-called refactoring transformation. Within the framework of our analysis, we formally characterize three situations of duplicated functionality and their associated refactorings: the extraction of a duplicated goal into a new predicate, the removal of equivalent predicates and the generalization of two predicates into a higher-order predicate. The resulting analysis detects in a completely automatic way what program fragments are suitable candidates for the considered refactoring transformations.

1   Introduction

Program refactoring is the process of systematically changing the structure of a program without changing its semantics. The goal of refactoring is to improve the design of the code after it has been written, in order to facilitate maintenance (including further development) of the software. Emerged from the OO and XP communities [5], program refactoring has recently gained attention in the fields of functional [8] and logic programming [14]. Within the software engineering community, the process of refactoring is considered important and has been identified as central to software development and maintenance [6, 5].

At the basis of the refactoring process is a *catalogue* of available source-to-source transformations – the so-called *refactorings*. For each refactoring, a set of conditions is specified under which the transformation is correct in the sense that it preserves the semantics of the program. The activity of refactoring consists then in repeatedly searching through the source code, looking for a code fragment of which the design could be improved by a particular refactoring from the catalogue. The particular refactoring is subsequently applied, and the whole process is repeated. Although each transformation can have an impact (positive or negative) on the performance of the program, the primary aim of each transformation is to improve the readability and maintainability of the code. In the context of logic programming, which we pursue in this paper, typical examples of refactorings are the elimination of unreachable predicates (i.e. dead code

S. Etalle(Ed.): LOPSTR 2004, LNCS 3573, pp. 1–18, 2005.

elimination), removing duplicated predicates, adding or (re)moving predicate arguments, extracting new predicates etc. See [5] for an overview of refactoring in general and [14] for an overview of available refactorings in logic programming.

Refactoring is basically a manual process that is performed by the programmer. Nevertheless, the need for automation is recognized [5, 8, 11] due to the time-consuming and error-prone nature of the refactoring activity. Automation (or at least partial automation) can be achieved on several levels. On one level, we can design tools that aid the developer with *performing* a particular refactoring on a selected fragment of source code (including the verification of the correctness conditions). An example of such a tool is the Refactoring Browser [11] that was developed for Smalltalk. On another level, one could employ program analysis tools to aid the developer with *identifying* in the program opportunities for refactoring, as such (partially) automating the search for which transformations to apply to which code fragments. It is at the latter level that our current work is situated.

Identifying where to perform (a particular) refactoring is in itself a non-trivial and creative process. Nevertheless, the primary indication for when to perform refactoring [5] is the presence of duplicated code (or better: duplicated functionality). Let us, by means of introduction, consider a number of typical situations that illustrate how functionality can be duplicated in a logic program. First, *goals* can be duplicated within a program. Assume for example we have a program in which we encounter, in two different clauses (a) and (b) the following subgoals:

```
...                       ...
X = (A-B),                Data = (Left-Right),
reverse(A,Ar),            reverse(Right,RR),
reverse(B,Br),            reverse(Left,LR),
...                       ...
       (a)                       (b)
```

Although the two goals are textually different, it is obvious that they both are meant to perform the same computation, i.e. they apply the `reverse/2` predicate to both elements of a given pair. A typical refactoring that removes this kind of goal duplication is *predicate extraction*: the duplicated goal is made the body of a newly created predicate and each occurrence of the goal is replaced by a call to the new predicate. The above code could for example be transformed into

```
...                              ...
retrieve_and_reverse(X,Ar,Br),   retrieve_and_reverse(Data,LR,RR),
...                              ...
         (a)                               (b)
```

in combination with the newly defined predicate

```
retrieve_and_reverse((A-B),AR,BR):- reverse(A,AR), reverse(B,BR).
```

A second, more extreme case of code duplication is the presence in the program of two or more predicates that essentially specify the same relation, as in the following example.

```
append([],L,L).
append([X|Xs],Y,[X|Zs]):- append(Xs,Y,Zs).

concat(L,[],L).
concat([E|Zs],[E|Es],Y):-concat(Zs,Es,Y).
```

Intuitively it is clear that the two predicates define the same relation, where one argument is the concatenation of the two others. The duplication can be removed by the *remove duplicate predicates* refactoring that consists in deleting one of both predicate definitions and replacing each call to it by a call to the remaining predicate. In the example above, one could delete the definition of concat/3 and subsequently replace every call concat(t_1,t_2,t_3) with a call append(t_2,t_3,t_1).

As a third case, we consider predicates that do not implement the same relation, but nevertheless share a common functionality. Consider as a typical example the following definitions.

```
rev_all([],[]).
rev_all([X|Xs],[Y|Ys]):- reverse(X,Y), rev_all(Xs,Ys).

add1_and_sqr([],[]).
add1_and_sqr([X|Xs],[Y|Ys]):- N is X + 1, Y is N*N, add1_and_sqr(Xs,Ys).
```

Such definitions implement two different relations: rev_all reverses all the elements of an input list, while add1_and_sqr transforms each element x of an input list into $(x+1)^2$. They nevertheless have a common core and if we assume a language with higher-order capabilities (as for example in [15]), one can extract the common functionality into a map/3 predicate

```
map([],_,[]).
map([X|Xs],P,[Y|Ys]):- P(X,Y), map(Xs,Ys).
```

and replace every call of the form rev_all(t_1,t_2) by a call

```
map(t1,lambda([X,Y],reverse(X,Y)),t2)
```

and every call add1_and_sqr(t_3,t_4) by

```
map(t3,lambda([X,Y],(N is X+1, Y is N*N)),t4).
```

In this work, we define a simple yet powerful analysis that basically computes for a given definite logic program sets of code fragments that are "semantically equivalent". We use the notion of semantic equivalence to denote different code fragments that implement the same functionality in the sense outlined above. Note that the analysis is nontrivial and goes further than a simple syntactic comparison of goals: as shown by the examples, it needs to deal with renamed variables, differently ordered literals, renamed predicates and permutated predicate arguments. We furthermore characterize each of the above illustrated cases of duplicated functionality within the formal framework of our analysis. As a result, we obtain an analysis that identifies in a straightforward way those code fragments in a program that are suitable candidates for refactoring using one of the considered transformations: the extraction of goals into a new predicate, the removal of duplicated predicates and the introduction of higher-order predicates. The analysis is completely automatic and is, to the best of our knowledge, the first to support the programmer in finding candidate code fragments for this kind of refactorings.

2   Preliminaries

In what follows, we assume the reader to be familiar with the basic logic programming concepts as they are found, for example, in [1, 9]. We restrict ourselves to definite programs. In particular, we consider a program to be defined as a set of clauses of the form $H \leftarrow B_1, \ldots, B_n$ with H an atom and $B_1, \ldots, B_n$ a conjunction of atoms. We assume that clauses are in a normal form such that each atom is of the form: $p(X_1, \ldots, X_n)$, $X = Y$ or $X = f(X_1, \ldots, X_n)$ (with $X, Y, X_1, \ldots, X_n$ different variables). Moreover, in this normal form every clause defining a predicate p/n has the same head atom $p(X_1, \ldots, X_n)$. Given a predicate p/n, we denote with $head(p/n)$ the (identical) head atom of every clause that defines p/n. Given a particular clause c, we denote with $body(c)$ the conjunction of atoms that constitutes the body of the clause. For any syntactic entity E (be it a term, atom, goal or clause), we use $vars(E)$ to denote the set of variables occurring in E. As usual, a *substitution* is defined as a finite mapping from distinct variables to terms. A *variable renaming* is a bijective mapping from variables onto variables. For any mapping $f : X \mapsto Y$, we denote with $f_{|D}$ the restriction of the mapping to the domain $D \subseteq X$. The inverse of any mapping f is denoted by f^{-1}. We use the notation $\{x_1/y_1, \ldots, x_n/y_n\}$ to explicitly represent a mapping $f : X \mapsto Y$ with $dom(f) = \{x_1, \ldots, x_n\}$ and $y_i = f(x_i) \ \forall i$.

We define the meaning of a program P by means of its fixed point semantics $\mathcal{F}(P)$ which was introduced in [4]. Let H_V denote the non-ground Herbrand Base; that is the set of all atoms modulo variance. For a given program P, $\mathcal{F}(P)$ is then defined as the least fixed point of a non-ground T_P operator

$$T_P(I) = \left\{ H\theta \left| \begin{array}{l} \exists H \leftarrow B_1, \ldots, B_n \in P, \\ \exists A_1, \ldots, A_n \text{ renamed apart variants of atoms in } I, \\ \exists \theta = mgu((A_1, \ldots, A_n), (B_1, \ldots, B_n)) \end{array} \right. \right\}$$

for $I \subseteq H_V$. The fixed point semantics of a program P is equivalent with the operational semantics [4, 2], in the sense that it characterizes the *set* of computed answer substitutions. Indeed, the set of computed answers associated to a goal $(B_1, \ldots, B_n)$ equals the set

$$\{\theta \mid (A_1, \ldots, A_n) \in \mathcal{F}(P) \text{ and } \theta = mgu((A_1, \ldots, A_n), (B_1, \ldots, B_n))\}.$$

Note that by choosing the fixed point semantics to define the meaning of a program, we make abstraction of a concrete search strategy and selection rule.

In what follows we assume that clauses are numbered. We furthermore assume that every atom in the program text is identified by a unique *program point* which we will represent by a pair of natural numbers (k, i) where k denotes the number of the clause of the atom and i denotes the position of the atom within the clause body. We define a *code fragment* as a set of program points occurring within a single clause. The *size* of a code fragment φ is defined as the number of program points occurring in φ. Throughout the text, we will represent a code fragment symbolically by using the Greek letter φ. If B denotes an atom, we will often use $B \in \varphi$ as shorthand notation for "let B be the atom associated to a program point $a \in \varphi$". Likewise, we will often leave the program points implicit and simply regard a code fragment φ as a (multi)set of atoms $\varphi = \{B_1, \ldots, B_n\}$.

Example 1. Reconsider the definitions of append/3 and concat/3 from the introduction, but now in normal form.

```
(1) append(X,Y,Z):- X = [], Z = Y.
(2) append(X,Y,Z):- X = [Xe|Xs], Z = [Xe|Zs], append(Xs,Y,Zs).
(3) concat(A,B,C):- B = [], A = C.
(4) concat(A,B,C):- A = [Be|As], B = [Be|Bs], concat(As,Bs,C).
```

If we assume that within a clause atoms are numbered from 1, the code fragment $\varphi_1 = \{(1, 1), (1, 2)\}$ denotes the set of atoms $\{X = [], Z = Y\}$ in the first clause, whereas the code fragment $\varphi_2 = \{(4, 1), (4, 3)\}$ denotes the set of atoms $\{A = [Be|As], concat(As, Bs, C)\}$ in clause (4). As shorthand notation, we write $\varphi_1 = \{X = [], Z = Y\}$ and $\varphi_2 = \{A = [Be|As], concat(As, Bs, C)\}$.

A code fragment is a syntactic entity, referring to a subset of the body atoms in a clause in the program P. Nevertheless, a code fragment can be interpreted as a goal, with an associated set of computed answers in $\mathcal{F}(P)$, by considering the set of atoms as if it was a conjunction. Consequently, we will define two code fragments to be semantically equivalent if and only if their associated sets of computed answers are identical under a variable renaming. Formally:

Definition 1. *Let P be a definite program. Let $\{B_1, \ldots, B_n\}$ and $\{B'_1, \ldots, B'_n\}$ be two sets of atoms corresponding to two code fragments φ and φ' in P. We say that φ and φ' are semantically equivalent if and only if there exists a variable renaming $\rho : vars(\{B_1, \ldots, B_n\}) \mapsto vars(\{B'_1, \ldots, B'_n\})$ such that*

$$\{A_1, \ldots, A_n\} \subseteq \mathcal{F}(P) \text{ with } \theta = mgu((A_1, \ldots, A_n), (B_1, \ldots, B_n))$$

if and only if

$$\{A'_1, \ldots, A'_n\} \subseteq \mathcal{F}(P) \text{ with } \theta' = mgu((A'_1, \ldots, A'_n), (B'_1, \ldots, B'_n))$$

with for each $x \in vars(\{B_1, \ldots, B_n\}) : \rho(\theta(x)) = \theta'(\rho(x))$ and for each $y \in vars(\{B'_1, \ldots, B'_n\}) : \rho^{-1}(\theta'(y)) = \theta(\rho^{-1}(y))$.

Conforming with the use of the fixed point semantics, the definition of semantic equivalence abstracts from a particular execution strategy: for two code fragments to be semantically equivalent, it suffices that the set of computed answers associated to one fragment is a renaming of the other. The fact that we formulate semantic equivalence at the level of the computed answers allows us to consider calls to different predicates as semantically equivalent, as the following example demonstrates.

Example 2. Consider the definitions of append/3 and concat/3 from before. The code fragments $\varphi = \{append(X_1, X_2, X_3)\}$ and $\varphi' = \{concat(Y_1, Y_2, Y_3)\}$ are semantically equivalent due to the existence of the variable renaming $\rho :$ $vars(\varphi) \mapsto vars(\varphi')$ defined as $\{(X_1, Y_2), (X_2, Y_3), (X_3, Y_1)\}$. Indeed, one can verify that for any atom $append(X_1, X_2, X_3)\{X_1/t_1, X_2/t_2, X_3/t_3\} \in \mathcal{F}(P)$, there exists an atom $concat(Y_1, Y_2, Y_3)\{Y_1/t'_1, Y_2/t'_2, Y_3/t'_3\} \in \mathcal{F}(P)$ such that $\rho(t_1) = t'_2$, $\rho(t_2) = t'_3$ and $\rho(t_3) = t'_1$ and that likewise $\rho^{-1}(t'_1) = t_3$, $\rho^{-1}(t'_2) = t_1$ and $\rho^{-1}(t'_3) = t_2$.

3   Computing Semantically Equivalent Code Fragments

In this section we discuss how one can compute, for a program P, an approximation of the sets of semantically equivalent code fragments in P. It follows immediately from Definition 1 that if the set of atoms associated to a code fragment φ is a renaming of the set of atoms associated to another code fragment φ', then the two code fragments are semantically equivalent. This observation motivates the definition of a k-isomorphism as follows.

Definition 2. *Let c and c' be clauses in P and $k \in \mathbb{N}$. A k-isomorphism (between c and c') is a 4-tuple $\langle \varphi, \varphi', \beta, \rho \rangle$ where φ is a code fragment of size k in c, φ' a code fragment of size k in c' and $\rho : vars(\varphi) \mapsto vars(\varphi')$ a variable renaming and $\beta : \varphi \mapsto \varphi'$ a bijective mapping such that:*

- *$\forall A \in \varphi : \rho(A) = \beta(A)$, and*
- *$\forall A' \in \varphi' : \rho^{-1}(A') = \beta^{-1}(A')$.*

Informally, a k-isomorphism defines a unique mapping between two sets of k atoms such that one set is a renaming of the other. Whenever the size of a k-isomorphism has no importance, we will drop the k and simply talk about an isomorphism. We also say that the code fragments φ and φ' are (β,ρ)-isomorphic (or simply isomorphic) if and only if there exists an isomorphism $\langle \varphi, \varphi', \beta, \rho \rangle$. The set of all isomorphisms is denoted by Iso.

Example 3. Consider the definitions of append/3 and concat/3 as in Example 1. Let $\varphi = \{(2, 1), (2, 2)\}$ (i.e. the code fragment comprising the set of atoms $\{X = [Xe|Xs], Z = [Xe|Zs]\}$) in clause (2) and $\varphi' = \{(4, 1), (4, 2)\}$ (i.e. comprising the set of atoms $\{A = [Be|As], B = [Be|Bs]\}$) in clause (4). Then there exist two 2-isomorphisms between φ and φ', namely $\langle \varphi, \varphi', \beta_1, \rho_1 \rangle$ and $\langle \varphi, \varphi', \beta_2, \rho_2 \rangle$ with

$$\beta_1 = \{(2, 1)/(4, 1), (2, 2)/(4, 2)\}$$
$$\rho_1 = \{X/A, Xe/Be, Xs/As, Z/B, Zs/Bs\}$$

and

$$\beta_2 = \{(2, 1)/(4, 2), (2, 2)/(4, 1)\}$$
$$\rho_2 = \{X/B, Xe/Be, Xs/Bs, Z/A, Zs/As\}$$

Hence, the first isomorphism in this example maps the first atom of clause (2) onto the first atom of clause (4), whereas the second isomorphism maps the first atom of clause (2) onto the second atom of clause (4), etc.

We introduce the following notion to express that there exists a *partial* isomorphism between two code fragments.

Definition 3. *Given two code fragments φ and φ', we say that φ and φ' are (β, ρ)-isomorphic modulo (φ_m, φ'_m) if and only if there exists an isomorphism $\langle (\varphi \setminus \varphi_m), (\varphi' \setminus \varphi'_m), \beta, \rho \rangle$.*

Example 4. Reconsider the definitions of append/3 and concat/3 as in Example 1. Let φ and φ' denote respectively the set of all body atoms of clauses (2) and (4), that is $\varphi = \{(2,1),(2,2),(2,3)\}$ and $\varphi' = \{(4,1),(4,2),(4,3)\}$. If we take β_1 and ρ_1 as in Example 3, we have that φ and φ' are (β_1, ρ_1)-isomorphic modulo $(\{(2,3)\}, \{(4,3)\})$.

Note that it follows from Definitions 2 and 3 that in an expression of the form "φ and φ' are isomorphic modulo (φ_m, φ'_m)" the isomorphic parts, i.e. $\varphi \setminus \varphi_m$ and $\varphi' \setminus \varphi'_m$, are of equal size but the non-isomorphic parts can have different sizes. An important observation is that any k-isomorphism, for a value $k > 1$, is constructed from smaller isomorphisms. The following definition states the conditions under which two isomorphisms can be combined into a single isomorphism:

Definition 4. *Let c and c' denote two clauses in a definite program P, and let $\langle \varphi_1, \varphi'_1, \beta_1, \rho_1 \rangle$ and $\langle \varphi_2, \varphi'_2, \beta_2, \rho_2 \rangle$ denote respectively a k-isomorphism and an l-isomorphism between c and c'. If*

$$\beta_1 \cup \beta_2 : \varphi_1 \cup \varphi_2 \mapsto \varphi'_1 \cup \varphi'_2$$

is a bijective mapping and

$$\rho_1 \cup \rho_2 : vars(\varphi_1 \cup \varphi_2) \mapsto vars(\varphi'_1 \cup \varphi'_2)$$

a variable renaming, then the two isomorphisms are said to be compatible *and there exists a single m-isomorphism $\langle \varphi_1 \cup \varphi_2, \varphi'_1 \cup \varphi'_2, \beta_1 \cup \beta_2, \rho_1 \cup \rho_2 \rangle$ with $m = k + l - \#(\varphi_1 \cap \varphi_2)$. Otherwise the two isomorphisms are said to be* incompatible.

Intuitively, two isomorphisms between clauses c and c' are compatible if the following holds: 1) if an atom in $body(c)$ is mapped by both isomorphisms, it is mapped onto the same atom in $body(c')$, and 2) both variable renamings can be combined into a single variable renaming.

Example 5. Reconsider the definitions of append/3 and concat/3 as in Example 1. The following two 1-isomorphisms

$$I_1 = \langle \{(2,1)\}, \{(4,1)\}, \{(2,1)/(4,1)\}, \{X/A, Xe/Be, Xs/As\} \rangle$$
$$I_2 = \langle \{(2,2)\}, \{(4,2)\}, \{(2,2)/(4,2)\}, \{Z/B, Xe/Be, Zs/Bs\} \rangle$$

(mapping, respectively, the first atom in clause (2) onto the first atom in clause (4) and the second atom in clause (2) onto the second atom in clause (4)) are compatible. Combining them results in the isomorphism $\langle \varphi, \varphi', \beta_1, \rho_1 \rangle$ from Example 3.

Example 6. Suppose we have clauses c and c' with the sets of atoms $\{X = [Xe|Xs], Xs = [Xe|Ys]\} \subseteq body(c)$ and $\{A = [Ae|As], B = [Ae|Bs]\} \subseteq body(c')$. Then the 1-isomorphisms mapping respectively $X = [Xe|Xs]$ onto $A = [Ae|As]$ and $Xs = [Xe|Ys]$ onto $B = [Ae|Bs]$ are incompatible since their renamings cannot be combined due to the conflict between Xs/As and Xs/B.

Definition 4 suggests a way of constructing (k-)isomorphisms. Indeed, any k-isomorphism between c and c' can be constructed by combining k compatible 1-isomorphisms between c and c'. Hence, one could first construct the set of 1-isomorphisms, and then repeatedly combine these in order to construct larger isomorphisms. Computing the set of all 1-isomorphisms between clauses c and c' is straightforward and of complexity $O(n^2)$ with n the total number of atoms in c and c'. Although exhaustively combining the 1-isomorphisms is a complete method (and thus guaranteed to find *all* isomorphisms that exist between a pair of clauses), it requires to consider every subset of 1-isomorphisms and hence is of exponential complexity ($O(2^m)$ with m the number of 1-isomorphisms between c and c'). However, we can easily compute a partitioning of the set of 1-isomorphisms between c and c' into sets of compatible 1-isomorphisms with the following characteristic: all 1-isomorphisms within a single set are compatible (hence they can be combined into a single isomorphism) but the isomorphisms resulting from different sets are mutually incompatible. The following algorithm computes such a partitioning for given clauses c and c' and has a worst-case complexity of $O(m^2)$ with m the number of 1-isomorphisms involved.

Algorithm 3.1
Input: clauses c and c'
Output: a set of mutually incompatible isomorphisms[1]
    Let S_0 be the set of all 1-isomorphisms between c and c'.
    return combine(S_0)
    where combine:$\mathcal{P}(Iso) \mapsto \mathcal{P}(\mathcal{P}(Iso))$ is defined as follows:

$$\text{combine}(S) = \text{select } \gamma \in S$$
$$\text{let } C = \{\gamma' \mid \gamma' \in (S \setminus \{\gamma\}) \text{ and } \gamma' \text{ incompatible with } \gamma\}$$
$$\text{return combine}(C) \cup \{\{\gamma\} \cup E \mid E \in \text{combine}(S \setminus (\{\gamma\} \cup C))\}$$

The algorithm proceeds by selecting a 1-isomorphism γ in S and partitioning the remaining 1-isomorphisms into those incompatible with γ (the set C) and those compatible with γ (the set $S \setminus C$). Each of these sets is then recursively partitioned and γ is added to each element in the partitioning of $(S \setminus C)$. Note that the algorithm is non-deterministic and does by no means try to find a partitioning that includes the best (or the largest) isomorphism. It nevertheless guarantees that the resulting isomorphisms are mutually incompatible. Hence, they cannot be combined into a larger isomorphism and thus we can hope that

---

[1] Technically, the algorithm outputs sets of compatible 1-isomorphisms that can hence be combined into a single isomorphism. The resulting isomorphisms are however mutually incompatible.

the resulting partition contains an isomorphism that is "sufficiently large" for the purpose at hand. Moreover, the algorithm *can* be steered towards "large" solutions by refining the "select $\gamma \in S$ operation, for example making sure that a γ is selected with a minimal number of incompatibilities (worst-case complexity $O(m^3)$).

4 Finding Duplicated Functionality

We will now proceed with characterizing within the framework of our analysis the three common cases of functionality duplication that we encountered in the introduction. Doing so renders each case recognizable by automatic analysis.

4.1 Case 1: Duplicated Goals

The existence of an isomorphism between two code fragments renders the code fragments semantically equivalent and hence candidates for extraction into a new predicate. Recall however that a code fragment identifies an arbitrary subset of the body atoms of a clause. Hence for a code fragment to be replaceable by a predicate call, the corresponding atoms must be "connected" in the sense that there should be no mutual data flow dependency between an atom in the code fragment and an atom outside the code fragment.

Definition 5. *Let DF_P be the dataflow graph of a program P, that is DF_P is a graph (V, E) with V the set of program points defined in P and E the set of edges defined as $E = \{(v, v')|v, v' \in V$ and the atoms identified by v and v' belong to a single clause and share a variable\}. A code fragment φ is connected if and only if $\forall a, a' \in \varphi$, it holds that for each path $\langle a, b_1, \ldots, b_n, a' \rangle \in DF_P$: $b_i \in \varphi$, $\forall i \in \{1, \ldots, n\}$.*

Example 7. Consider the conjunction

$$\ldots, \text{X = [A|As], As = [B|Bs], plus(A,B,Sum)}, \ldots$$

that is meant to compute the sum of the first two elements of a list in X. The code fragment comprising only the first and third atom , i.e. $\varphi = \{X = [A|As], plus(A, B, Sum)\}$, is *not* connected since there is a mutual data flow dependency between φ and the remaining atom $As = [B|Bs]$ (due to the variables As and B that are both shared by this atom and φ).

If a code fragment φ is connected, it can be replaced by a call to a new predicate that is defined by a single clause with the body φ. The arguments passed to the newly defined predicate are all variables that are shared by φ and some atom outside φ. We will denote this set of variables by $exvars(\varphi)$.

Definition 6. *Let φ be a code fragment in a program P. Then $exvars(\varphi) = vars(\varphi) \setminus \{x \mid x$ is shared by φ and some atom $A \notin \varphi$ belonging to the same clause as $\varphi\}$.*

In general, a code fragment can be duplicated several times in a program. We introduce the notion of an *extraction* to denote a set of non-overlapping isomorphic connected code fragments.

Definition 7. *A* k-extraction *E* *is a set of connected code fragments of size* k *with for all* $\varphi, \varphi' \in E$:

1. *φ is k-isomorphic to φ', and*
2. *$\varphi \neq \varphi' \Rightarrow \varphi \cap \varphi' = \emptyset$.*

As with the isomorphisms, we will drop the k in case the size of the code fragments in the extraction is not important. Since the code fragments in an extraction are connected, mutually isomorphic and no two code fragments overlap, they can all be replaced by a call to the same (new) predicate.

Remains to discuss how one can actually compute an extraction. First, computing *all* extractions in a program P is again computationally unfeasible. However, one can compute an extraction in a straightforward way, starting from a given set of isomorphisms.

Algorithm 4.2
Input: a program P and a mapping $\mu : Clause \times Clause \mapsto \mathcal{P}(Iso)$
Output: a set of extractions S
  Let $S \leftarrow \emptyset$

repeat
  select two clauses c and c'
  select an isomorphism $\langle \varphi_1, \varphi_2, \beta, \rho \rangle \in \mu(c, c')$
  if there exists an extraction $E \in S$ and a code fragment $\varphi \in E$
    such that $\#(\varphi_1 \cap \varphi) \geq \epsilon$ for some $\epsilon \in \mathbb{N}$
  then
    downsize each code fragment in E such that it is isomorphic with $\varphi \cap \varphi_1$
    add $\beta_{|\varphi_1 \cap \varphi}(\varphi_1)$ to E
  else
    let $S \leftarrow S \cup \{ \{\varphi_1, \varphi_2\} \}$
until all combinations of clauses c,c' have been selected.

Algorithm 4.2 constructs a set of extractions from a mapping between clause pairs and isomorphisms as for example the one computed by Algorithm 3.1. Starting from an empty set of extractions, the algorithm repeatedly selects an isomorphism $\langle \varphi_1, \varphi_2, \beta, \rho \rangle$ from the mapping, and checks whether one of the involved code fragments, say φ_1, sufficiently overlaps with a code fragment (φ) in one of the extractions (E) under construction. If this is the case, the code fragments in E are all downsized in such a way that they remain mutually isomorphic with $\varphi \cap \varphi_1$ and subsequently the code fragment $\beta_{|\varphi \cap \varphi_1}(\varphi_1) \subseteq \varphi_2$ (i.e. the accordingly downsized code fragment φ_2 from the selected isomorphism) is added to E. If it is not the case, a new extraction is created containing the two code fragments $\{\varphi_1, \varphi_2\}$.

Again, the algorithm is non-deterministic. The quality of the resulting extraction is determined by the mapping μ and the particular isomorphism that is selected from the set $\mu(c, c')$. It should be noted that producing "high quality" extraction is a non-trivial task, in particular since the definition of "high quality" may depend on the application at hand. Characteristics that are likely be taken into account are the number of code fragments in the extraction, the size of the code fragments in the extraction and the number of non-overlapping extractions found. Developing heuristics to search for extractions is an interesting topic for further research.

4.2   Case 2: Duplicated Relations

As a second case, we consider the detection of duplicated relations. Relations p/n and q/n are duplicates if and only if a call of the form $p(X_1, \ldots, X_n)$ is semantically equivalent to a call $q(Y_1, \ldots, Y_n)$. From Definition 1, it follows that a sufficient condition for two predicates to be equivalent is that their definitions are isomorphic, modulo a permutation of their arguments.

Definition 8. *Given two predicates p/n and q/n, we define an* argument permutation *between p/n and q/n as a bijective mapping $\pi : \{1, \ldots, n\} \mapsto \{1, \ldots, n\}$.*

Note that an argument permutation π between p/n and q/n induces a unique variable renaming from the arguments of a call $C_p = p(X_1, \ldots, X_n)$ to the arguments of a call $C_q = q(Y_1, \ldots, Y_n)$, which we will denote by $ren_\pi(C_p, C_q)$. Formally, this renaming is defined by

$$ren_\pi(C_p, C_q) = \{X_1/Y_{\pi(1)}, \ldots, X_n/Y_{\pi(n)}\}$$

for $C_p = p(X_1, \ldots, X_n)$ and $C_q = q(Y_1, \ldots, Y_n)$.

Example 8. Consider the argument permutation $\pi : \{(1,2), (2,3), (3,1)\}$ between append/3 and concat/3 as they are defined before. Informally, this mapping maps the first two arguments of append to the last two arguments of concat and the third argument of append to the first argument of concat. The induced renaming from a call $append(X, Y, Z)$ to a call $concat(A, B, C)$ is then

$$ren_\pi(append(X, Y, Z), concat(A, B, C)) = \{X/B, Y/C, Z/A\}.$$

Our definition of isomorphism basically defines two code fragments as isomorphic if and only if one is a renaming of the other. Consequently, using this definition alone we are unable to conclude the definition of two recursive predicates to be isomorphic. To deal with recursiveness, we introduce the notion of a *pseudo-isomorphism*, that associates a set of recursive calls in a clause with a set of recursive calls in another clause.

Definition 9. *Let c be a clause in the definition of a predicate p/n and c' a clause in the definition of a predicate q/n and $k \in \mathbb{N}$. A pseudo k-isomorphism (between c and c') is a triplet $\langle \varphi_1, \varphi_2, \beta \rangle$ where φ_1 is a code fragment of size k in c such that every atom in φ_1 is a recursive call (to p/n) and φ_2 a code fragment of size k in c' such that every atom in φ_2 is a recursive call (to q/n), $p \neq q$ and $\beta : \varphi_1 \mapsto \varphi_2$ is a bijective mapping.*

Like with regular k-isomorphisms, we say that two code fragments φ_1 and φ_2 are β-pseudo isomorphic (or pseudo-isomorphic w.r.t. β) iff $\langle \varphi_1, \varphi_2, \beta \rangle$ is a pseudo isomorphism. From Definition 9, it follows that there exists a pseudo 1-isomorphism between every pair of recursive calls. Note that a pseudo k-isomorphism can only exist between two clauses that each contain at least k

recursive calls. Also note that, contrary to a regular isomorphism, a pseudo isomorphism only provides a mapping between the individual recursive calls in the two clauses, it does not require the atoms to be renamings.

Example 9. Reconsider the definitions of append/3 and concat/3 from example 1, in addition with the following definition for a predicate funnyappend/3 that is basically equal to append except for the recursive call in which the first two arguments are exchanged (from [3]).

```
(5) funnyappend(D,E,F):- D = [], F = E.
(6) funnyappend(D,E,F):- D = [De|Ds], F=[De|Fs], funnyappend(E,Ds,Fs).
```

We have the following pseudo 1-isomorphisms:

$$\langle\{(2,3)\},\{(4,3)\},\beta_1\rangle \text{ with } \beta_1 = \{(2,3)/(4,3)\}$$
$$\langle\{(2,3)\},\{(6,3)\},\beta_2\rangle \text{ with } \beta_2 = \{(2,3)/(6,3)\}$$
$$\langle\{(4,3)\},\{(6,3)\},\beta_3\rangle \text{ with } \beta_3 = \{(4,3)/(6,3)\}$$

mapping the recursive calls between, respectively, append and concat, append and funnyappend, and concat and funnyappend.

Note that the concepts of isomorphism and pseudo-isomorphism are orthogonal, in the sense that two program points belonging to different predicates cannot be both isomorphic and pseudo isomorphic. We combine the notions of isomorphism and pseudo isomorphism to define an isomorphism between two predicate definitions, which is a sufficient condition so that two predicates can be regarded as duplicates.

Definition 10. *Given two predicates p/n and q/n that are defined respectively by the sets of clauses $\{c_1,\ldots,c_m\}$ and $\{c'_1,\ldots,c'_m\}$. Let $H_p = head(p/n)$ and $H_q = head(q/n)$. The predicate definitions for p/n and q/n are isomorphic if there exists a bijective mapping $\kappa : \{c_1,\ldots,c_m\} \mapsto \{c'_1,\ldots,c'_m\}$ and an argument permutation π between p/n and q/n such that for each pair of corresponding clauses c_i and $\kappa(c_i)$ holds that*

1. *$body(c_i)$ and $body(\kappa(c_i))$ are (β_i,ρ_i)-isomorphic modulo (φ_i,φ'_i)*
2. *φ_i and φ'_i are pseudo isomorphic w.r.t. some β_i^r*
3. *$\rho_i \cup \rho_i^r$, the latter defined as*

$$\rho_i^r = \bigcup_{B\in\varphi_i} \{ren_\pi(B,\beta_i^r(B))\}$$

is a variable renaming and $ren_\pi(H_p,H_q) \subseteq \rho_i \cup \rho_i^r$.

First, the mapping κ associates each clause of p/n with a unique corresponding clause in q/n. The use of κ allows to take any ordering of the clauses of p/n and q/n into account. In the examples, however, we will often leave κ implicit and simply assume that the i'th clause of p/n corresponds to the i'th clause of q/n. The definition states a number of sufficient conditions that must hold between each pair of corresponding clauses in p/n and q/n so that the relations p/n and q/n are duplicates. Firstly, there must exist a partial isomorphism between the two clause bodies and, secondly, the code fragments that are not isomorphic must be pseudo isomorphic – meaning that they both contain an equal number of recursive calls. Thirdly, the union of the variable renaming from the isomorphism and the renamings induced by the chosen argument permutation π between each pair of corresponding recursive calls must (1) itself be a renaming, and (2) include the variable renaming induced by π between the heads of the clauses. This third condition guarantees that there is a one-to-one mapping (namely $\rho_i \cup \rho_i^r$) between the variables of both clauses and that corresponding variables are found in the corresponding argument positions in the heads of the predicates as in each recursive call.

Example 10. Consider once more the definitions of append/3 and concat/3 from Example 1. Take the argument permutation π and its induced renaming between the heads of the predicates $\rho_h = \{X/B, Y/C, Z/A\}$ from Example 8 . We have that

- the body of the first clause of append/3 and the body of the first clause of concat/3 are isomorphic w.r.t. the variable renaming $\rho_1 = \{X/B, Y/C, Z/A\}$. It follows immediately that $\rho_h \subseteq \rho_1$.
- the bodies of clauses (2) and (4) are (β_2, ρ_2)-isomorphic modulo the code fragments $(\{(2,3)\}, \{(4,3)\})$, with β_2 and ρ_2 as in Example 3. Moreover, the code fragment $\{(2,3)\}$ is pseudo isomorphic with $\{(4,3)\}$) (see Example 9). The renaming induced by π between these recursive calls is $\rho^r = \{Xs/Bs, Y/C, Zs/As\}$ and we can verify that

$$\rho_2 \cup \rho^r = \{X/B, Xe/Be, Xs/Bs, Z/A, Zs/As, Y/C\}$$

is a variable renaming and that $\rho_h \subseteq (\rho_2 \cup \rho^r)$.

Hence, the definitions of append/3 and concat/3 are isomorphic according to Definition 10 with respect to the argument permutation π.

Consider, by means of counterexample, the definitions of the append/3 and funnyappend/3 predicates from examples 1 and 9. One can easily verify that there does not exist an argument permutation π such that

$$ren_\pi(append(X, Y, Z), funnyappend(D, E, F))$$
$$\subseteq$$
$$ren_\pi(append(Xs, Y, Zs), funnyappend(E, Ds, Fs))$$

and consequently, the third condition of Definition 10 can never be satisfied.

4.3   Case 3: Duplicated Common Functionality

It can occur that two or more predicates do not define exactly the same relation but still are similar enough such that one can extract the common functionality into a *higher-order* predicate. Each call to one of the original predicates is then replaced by a call to the higher-order predicate, with as an additional parameter a lambda expression defining the functionality that was specific to the original predicate. A typical example is the abstraction of the rev_all/2 and add1_and_sqr/2 predicates from the introduction into the well-known map/3 predicate. Our framework enables to formulate a set of conditions for this transformation to be applicable in terms of (pseudo) isomorphisms as follows.

Definition 11. *Given two predicates p/n and q/n that are defined respectively by the sets of clauses $\{c_1, \ldots, c_m\}$ and $\{c'_1, \ldots, c'_m\}$. Let $H_p = head(p/n)$ and $H_q = head(q/n)$. The predicates p/n and q/n can be generalized into a higher-order predicate if here exists a bijective mapping $\kappa : \{c_1, \ldots, c_m\} \mapsto \{c'_1, \ldots, c'_m\}$ and an argument permutation π between p/n and q/n such that for each pair of corresponding clauses c_i and $\kappa(c_i)$ holds that*

1. *$body(c_i)$ and $body(\kappa(c_i))$ are (β_i, ρ_i)-isomorphic modulo (φ_i, φ'_i)*
2. *φ_i and φ'_i are β_i^r-pseudo isomorphic modulo (ψ_i, ψ'_i)*
3. *$\rho_i \cup \rho_i^r$, the latter defined as*

$$\rho_i^r = \bigcup_{B \in (\varphi_i \setminus \psi_i)} \{ren_\pi(B, \beta^r(B))\}$$

   is a variable renaming and $ren_\pi(H_p, H_q) \subseteq \rho_i \cup \rho_i^r$.
4. *there exists a bijective mapping $\nu : exvars(\psi_i) \mapsto exvars(\psi'_i)$ such that $\forall x \in exvars(\psi_i) : (\rho_i \cup \rho_i^r)(x) = \nu(x)$*

   Moreover, $\{\psi_1, \ldots, \psi_m\}$ and $\{\psi'_1, \ldots, \psi'_n\}$ are extractions.

The situation characterized in Definition 11 is rather similar to the situation that characterizes duplicated relations (Definition 10) with the exception that each clause within an associated clause pair can have a part of its body (the code fragments ψ_i in p/n and ψ'_i in q/n) that is *not* involved in a (pseudo) isomorphism. To be eligible for higher-order generalization, each such ψ_i in the definition of p/n must be connected and mutually isomorphic, that is $\{\psi_1, \ldots, \psi_m\}$ must be an extraction. This guarantees that each ψ_i can be replaced by a call to the *same* predicate. The same conditions must hold on the code fragments $\{\psi'_1, \ldots, \psi'_m\}$ in the definition of q/n. The fourth condition guarantees that both extractions $\{\psi_1, \ldots, \psi_m\}$ and $\{\psi'_1, \ldots, \psi'_m\}$ can be abstracted into a single higher-order call.

Example 11. Reconsider the definitions of rev_all/3 and add1_and_sqr/3 from the introduction. It can be easily verified that the unifications in both definitions are isomorphic and that the recursive calls are pseudo-isomorphic. The considered argument permutation is the identity permutation and the renaming is the identify renaming. Hence, the only non (pseudo) isomorphic parts are $\psi = \{reverse(X, Y)\}$ in rev_all/3 and $\psi' = \{N \ is \ X + 1, Y \ is \ N * N\}$ in add1_and_sqr/3. We can verify that $exvars(\psi) = \{X, Y\} = exvars(\psi')$ and hence both code fragments can be replaced by a single higher-order call of the form $P(X, Y)$.

5   Discussion and Related Work

In this work, we have given a formal characterization of a number of different but related situations in which functionality is duplicated within a logic program. The presence of duplicated functionality is the number one indication that a refactoring should be performed [5] in order to improve the design of the code. Refactoring as a software engineering technique has been studied mainly in the context of object oriented programming [5] but has more recently gained some attention in the functional [8] and logical paradigms [14]. These works concentrate on the transformational aspects of refactoring and they define a catalogue of suitable transformations and the conditions under which they can safely be applied. Automatic support is provided in the form of tools that aid the programmer at performing a particular transformation but the decision where and when to refactor is left to the programmer. By searching for duplicated functionality, our analysis attempts to automate the search for refactoring opportunities in a logic programming context. To the best of our knowledge, our work is the first to provide 1) a formal characterization of the envisaged refactoring opportunities based on the notion of semantic equivalence and 2) an analysis that effectively computes sets of semantically equivalent code fragments within a logic program. The analysis is completely automatic and its results give the programmer an indication as where to perform the considered refactoring. Moreover, the analysis provides sufficient information such that the corresponding refactoring could be applied automatically (although user input may still be required in order to give suitable names to the newly introduced predicates etc.).

Computing code fragments with identical behaviour has been considered before. The work of [18] represents programs by a so-called program representation graph and gives an algorithm that partitions this graph into program components that exhibit identical execution behaviours. The language considered is imperative without procedures or functions and with only scalar variables and constants. The work is in particular targeted towards finding semantic and textual differences between two versions of the *same* program [7, 17]. In more recent work, [16] also considers the task of analyzing two *related* imperative programs to determine the behavioral differences between them. The latter technique concentrates on situations where the structural differences between the programs is small. Also related is work on parametrised string matching as for example in the MOSS system [13], which aims at finding near-duplication in software and which is mainly used for detecting plagiarism in programming classes. Whether and how the fingerprinting technique of [13] can be applied in our current setting is an interesting topic of further research.

Our notion of a k-isomorphism, that we use to approximate the notion of semantic equivalence between code fragments, does not take control dependencies between the atoms into account. This is in accordance with the chosen semantics and allows much liberty in matching code fragments as isomorphisms can be constructed between (parts of) two conjunctions, also if the order of the atoms is different. While this liberty in matching is definitely an advantage in order to find as much isomorphisms as possible, it renders the search process computationally heavier and may require to impose extra conditions on the isomorphisms found before they can be used for refactoring. One such condition is the connectedness condition – see example 7 – necessary for transforming a code fragment into a call to a newly defined predicate. Taking control dependencies into account during matching can narrow the search space, and may be necessary when one wants to adopt our techniques to find isomorphisms between fragments of programs in which the order of the atoms *is* important. This issues arises when one wants to preserve the order in which answers are found by a particular execution mechanism or when one wants to deal with more involved programming constructs such as if-then-else or with the non-logical aspects of a language like Prolog. We believe that our basic framework can be easily extended to take control structures into account. One possibility in this direction would be matching program representations that include data and control information, such as e.g. [19].

We have given a concrete algorithm to compute a set of isomorphisms within a given program. The algorithm is rather naive and simply computes an arbitrary set of isomorphisms, rather than trying to find an "optimal" set of isomorphisms. As a proof of concept, we have implemented the algorithm (and the tests to detect duplicated functionality) in Prolog. Preliminary experiments show that the sets of isomorphisms resulting from Algorithm 3.1 are sufficiently good to handle (in a completely automatic way) the examples that are presented in the paper. Moreover, the implementation demonstrates that the technique is computationally feasible. As an indication, consider the analysis of a 258-line Prolog source file (which is part of the implementation of the analyzer) that contains 384 atoms divided over 25 predicates. Computing the set of all 1-isomorphism (1399 in total) is the most expensive operation and takes 47.03 seconds on a 700Mhz Pentium III. Subsequently computing μ by Algorithm 3.1 takes 7.45 seconds. Although time-consuming, these computations need to be performed only once. The subsequent searches for duplicated functionality all use the computed mapping μ as a starting point. The maximum time that was registered for comparing two predicates in search for duplicated relations was 0.02 seconds, the mean time 0.006 seconds.

We believe that our analysis provides a solid base to automate (the search for) a number of important refactoring opportunities. Interesting topics for further research include the development of heuristics to guide the search for "good" isomorphisms and extractions, rather the arbitrary ones computed by Algorithms 3.1 and 4.2. Also, the incorporation of control dependencies between atoms and clauses would render the technique useful for more involved languages like Prolog and Mercury, and might help to narrow the search space of possible isomorphisms. In our current setting, a code fragment is restricted to a set of atoms where all atoms belong to a single clause. By removing this restriction, and allowing a code fragment to include sets of atoms in different clauses, one could possibly use the resulting analysis to steer a number of more involved transformations like folding [10] and to automate the introduction of new program constructs, such as the logic loop of [12].

Acknowledgements

The author would like to thank the LOPSTR participants for providing interesting comments and remarks. The author would also like to thank John Gallagher for pointing out some interesting relations with other work and the anonymous referees for providing constructive remarks.

References

1. K. R. Apt. Logic programming. In J. van Leeuwen, editor, *Handbook of Theoretical Computer Science, Volume B, Formal Models and Semantics*, pages 493–574. Elsevier Science Publishers B.V., 1990.
2. A. Bossi, M. Gabbrielli, G. Levi, and M. Martelli. The S-semantics approach: Theory and applications. *Journal of Logic Programming*, 19/20:149–197, 1994.
3. Maurice Bruynooghe, Michael Leuschel, and Kostis Sagonas. A polyvariant binding-time analysis for off-line partial deduction. In Chris Hankin, editor, *Proceedings of the European Symposium on Programming (ESOP'98)*, volume 1381 of *Lecture Notes in Computer Science*, pages 27–41. Springer-Verlag, 1998.
4. M. Falaschi, G. Levi, M. Martelli, and C. Palamidessi. Declarative modeling of the operational behaviour of logic programs. *Theoretical Computer Science*, 69:289–318, 1989.
5. M. Fowler, K. Beck, J. Brant, W. Opdyke, and D. Roberts. *Refactoring: Improving the Design of Existing Code*. Objet Technology Series. Addison-Wesley, 1999.
6. W. G. Griswold and D. Notkin. Program restructuring as an aid to software maintenance. Technical report, Seattle, WA, USA, August 1990.
7. Susan Horwitz. Identifying the semantic and textual differences between two versions of a program. *ACM SIGPLAN Notices*, 25(6):234–245, 1990.
8. H. Li, C. Reinke, and S. Thompson. Tool support for refactoring functional programs. In J. Jeuring, editor, *ACM SIGPLAN 2003 Haskell Workshop*. Association for Computing Machinery, 2003.
9. J. W. Lloyd. *Foundations of Logic Programming*. Springer-Verlag, 1987.
10. A. Pettorossi and M. Proietti. Transformation of logic programs: Foundations and techniques. *Journal of Logic Programming*, 19/20:261–320, 1994.
11. Don Roberts, John Brant, and Ralph E. Johnson. A refactoring tool for Smalltalk. *Theory and Practice of Object Systems (TAPOS)*, 3(4):253–263, 1997.
12. Joachim Schimpf. Logical loops. In *International Conference on Logic Programming*, volume 2401 of *Lecture Notes in Computer Science*, pages 224–??, 2002.
13. S. Schleimer, D.S. Wilkerson, and A. Aiken. Winnowing: local algorithms for document fingerprinting. In *Proceedings of the 2003 ACM SIGMOD international conference on Management of Data*, San Diego, CA, 2003.
14. T. Schrijvers, A. Serebrenik, and B. Demoen. Refactoring logic programs. Technical Report CW 373, Department of Computer Science, K.U.Leuven, 2003.
15. D. H. D. Warren. Higher-Order Extensions to Prolog: Are They Needed? volume Machine Intelligence 10, pages 441–454. Ellis Horwood, Chichester, England, 1982.
16. J. Winstead and D. Evans. Towards differential program analysis. 2002.

17. Wuu Yang. Identifying syntactic differences between two programs. *Software Practice and Experience*, 21(7):739–755, 1991.
18. Wuu Yang, Susan Horwitz, and Thomas Reps. Detecting program components with equivalent behaviors. Technical Report CS-TR-1989-840, University of Wisconsin, Madison, 1989.
19. J. Zhao, J. Cheng, and K. Ushijima. Program dependence analysis of concurrent logic programs and its applications. In *1996 International Conference on Parallel and Distributed Systems (ICPADS '96)*, Tokyo,Japan, 1996.

Determinacy Analysis for Logic Programs Using Mode and Type Information

P. López-García[1], F. Bueno[1], and M. Hermenegildo[1,2]

[1] School of Computer Science,
Technical University of Madrid (UPM)
[2] Depts. of Comp. Science and El. and Comp. Eng.,
U. of New Mexico (UNM)
{pedro.lopez, bueno, herme}@fi.upm.es

Abstract. We propose an analysis for detecting procedures and goals that are deterministic (i.e. that produce at most one solution), or predicates whose clause tests are mutually exclusive (which implies that at most one of their clauses will succeed) even if they are not deterministic (because they call other predicates that can produce more than one solution). Applications of such determinacy information include detecting programming errors, performing certain high-level program transformations for improving search efficiency, optimizing low level code generation and parallel execution, and estimating tighter upper bounds on the computational costs of goals and data sizes, which can be used for program debugging, resource consumption and granularity control, etc. We have implemented the analysis and integrated it in the *CiaoPP* system, which also infers automatically the mode and type information that our analysis takes as input. Experiments performed on this implementation show that the analysis is fairly accurate and efficient.

Keywords: Determinacy Inference, Program Analysis, Modes, Types.

1   Introduction

Knowing that certain predicates are deterministic for a given class of calls has a number of interesting applications in program debugging, verification, transformation, and optimization. By a predicate being deterministic we mean that it produces at most one solution. It is also interesting to detect predicates whose clause tests are mutually exclusive (which implies that at most one of their clauses will succeed) even if they are not deterministic because they call other predicates that can produce more than one solution.

Perhaps the most important application of compile-time determinacy information is in the context of program development. If we assume that the programmer has indicated that certain predicates should be deterministic for certain calling patterns (using suitable assertions as those used in Ciao [14]. Mercury [25], or HAL [7]) and a predicate is determined to be non-deterministic in one of those cases then, clearly, a compile-time error has been detected and can be reported [14, 12]. This is quite useful since certain classes of programming

S. Etalle(Ed.): LOPSTR 2004, LNCS 3573, pp. 19–35, 2005.

errors often result in turning predicates intended to be deterministic into non-deterministic ones. Also, in addition to detecting programming errors at compile time, determinacy inference can obviously be used to *verify* (i.e., prove correct) such determinacy assertions [14].

Determinacy information can also be used for performing low-level optimizations [21, 25] as well higher-level program transformations for improving search efficiency. In particular, literals can be reordered so that deterministic goals are executed ahead of possibly non-deterministic goals where possible, improving the efficiency of parallel search [24]. Determinacy information is also very useful during program specialization. In addition, the implementation of (and-)parallelism is greatly simplified in presence of determinacy information: knowing that a goal is deterministic allows one to eliminate significant run-time overhead (due to *markers*) [11] and, in addition, performing data parallelism transformations [13].

Finally, determinacy (and mutual exclusion) information can be used to estimate much tighter upper bounds on the computational costs of goals [5]. Since it is generally not known in advance how many of the solutions generated by a predicate will be demanded, a conservative upper bound on the computational cost of a predicate can be obtained by assuming that all solutions are needed, and that all clauses are executed (thus the cost of the predicate is assumed to be the sum of the costs of all of its clauses). It is straightforward to take mutual exclusion into account to obtain a more precise estimate of the cost of a predicate, using the maximum of the costs of mutually exclusive groups of clauses. Moreover, knowing that all literals in a clause will produce at most one solution allows one to assume that an upper bound on the cost of the clauses is the sum of the cost of all literals in it, which simplifies the cost estimation (as explained in [5]). These upper bounds can be used for improved granularity control of parallel tasks [20] and for better performance/complexity debugging and verification of programs [14].

In this paper we propose a method whereby, given (upper approximations of) mode and type information, we can detect procedures and goals that are deterministic (i.e., that produce at most one solution), or predicates whose clause tests are mutually exclusive, even if they are not deterministic because they call other predicates that can produce more than one solution (i.e. that are not deterministic).

There has been much interest on determinacy detection in the literature (see [15] and its references), using several different forms of determinism. The line of work closest to ours starts with [6], in which functional computations are detected and exploited. However, the notion of mutual exclusion in this work is not based on constraint satisfaction. This concept is used in the analysis presented in [4], where, nonetheless, no algorithms are defined for the detection of mutual exclusion. The cut is not taken into account, either. In [10] a combined analysis of modes, types, and determinacy is presented, as well as in the more accurate [2]. As we will show, our analysis improves on these proposals.

Several programming systems also make use of determinacy, e.g., Mercury [25, 12] and HAL [7]. The Mercury and HAL systems allow the programmer to declare that a predicate will produce at most one solution, and attempts to verify this with respect to the Herbrand terms with equality tests. As far as we know, both systems use the same analysis [12], which does not handle disequality constraints on the Herbrand domain. Nor does it handle arithmetic tests, except in the context of the if-then-else construct. As such, it is considerably weaker than the approach described here. Also, our approach does not require any annotations from programmers, since the types and modes on which it is based are *inferred* (in our case by *CiaoPP* [14]).

2   Modes, Types, Tests, and Mutual Exclusion

We assume an acquaintance with the basic notions of logic programming. In order to reason about determinacy, it is necessary to distinguish between unification operations that act as tests (and which may fail), and output unifications that act as assignments (and always succeed). To this end, we assume that mode information is available, as a result of a previous analysis, i.e., for each unification operation in each predicate, we know whether the operation acts as a test or creates an output binding. Note that this is weaker than most conventional notions of moding in that it does not require input arguments to be completely ground, and allows an output argument to occur as a subterm of an input argument.

We also assume that type information is available, generally also as the result of a previous analysis. A type refers to a set of terms, and can be denoted by using several type representations (e.g. *type terms* and *regular term grammars* as in [3], or *type graphs* as in [16] or simply predicates as in the Ciao system). We include below the definitions of *type term*, *type rule*, and *deterministic type rule* from [3], for a better understanding of the algorithms that we have developed, and in order to make this paper more self-contained.

We assume the existence of an infinite set of *type symbols* (each type symbol refers to a set of terms, i.e., to a type). There are two special type symbols: μ, that represents the type of the entire Herbrand universe and the type symbol ϕ, that represents the empty type.

Definition 1. [Type term] A *type term* is defined inductively as follows:

1. A constant symbol is a type term.
2. A variable is a type term.
3. A type symbol is a type term.
4. If f is a n-ary function symbol, and each ω_i is a type term, then $f(\omega_1, \ldots, \omega_n)$ is a type term.

A *pure type term* is a variable-free type term. A *logical term* is a type-symbol-free type term. ∎

In this paper, we refer to *logical terms* as *Herbrand terms*. Note that according to this definition, all type symbols are type terms, however, the converse is not true.

There is a distinguished non-empty finite subset of the set of type symbols called the set of *base type symbols*. The set of Herbrand terms represented by a base type symbol is called a *base type*. For example, the set of all constant symbols that represent integer numbers is a base type represented by the base type symbol *integer*.

Definition 2. [Type rule] A *type rule* is an expression of the form $\alpha \to \Upsilon$, where α is a type symbol, and Υ is a set of pure type terms.   ∎

Example 1. The following type rule defines the type symbol *intlist*, that denotes the set of all lists of integer numbers:

$$intlist \to \{[\,], [integer|intlist]\} \qquad \qquad \square$$

Definition 3. A (non-base) type symbol α, is *defined* in, or by, a set of type rules T if there exists a type rule $(\alpha \to \Upsilon) \in T$.   ∎

Definition 4. A pure type term ω is *defined* by a set of type rules T if each type symbol in ω is either μ, ϕ, a base type symbol, or a (non-base) type symbol defined in T.   ∎

We assume that for each type rule $(\alpha \to \Upsilon) \in T$ it holds that each element (i.e. pure type term) of Υ is defined in T, and that each type symbol defined in T has *exactly* one defining type rule in T.

Definition 5. [Deterministic type rule] A type rule $\alpha \to \Upsilon$ is *deterministic* if no element of Υ is a type symbol and there is no pair of pure type terms $\omega_1, \omega_2 \in \Upsilon$, such that $\omega_1 \neq \omega_2$, $\omega_1 = f(\omega_1^1, \ldots, \omega_n^1)$, and $\omega_2 = f(\omega_1^2, \ldots, \omega_n^2)$.   ∎

For instance, the type rule in Example 1 is deterministic. The class of types that can be described by deterministic type rules is the same as the class of *tuple-distributive regular types* [3]. Additional background on type-related issues may be found in [3, 16].

For concreteness, the determinacy analysis we describe is based on *regular types* [3], which are specified by *regular term grammars* in which each type symbol has exactly one defining *type rule*, although it can easily be generalized to other type systems.

Let type[q] denote the type of each predicate q in a given program. In this paper, we are concerned exclusively with "calling types" for predicates —in other words, when we say "*a predicate p in a program P has type* type[p]", we mean that in any execution of the program P starting from some class of queries of interest, whenever there is a call $p(\bar{t})$ to the predicate p, the argument tuple $\bar{t}$ in the call will be an element of the set denoted by type[p].

A *primitive test* is an "atom" whose predicate is a built-in such as the unification or some arithmetic predicate ($<, >, \leq, \geq, \neq$, etc.) which acts as a "test" (note that with our assumptions of having available both mode and type information for each variable in a program, it is straightforward to identify primitive tests in a program). We define a *test* to be either a primitive test, or a conjunction $\tau_1 \wedge \tau_2$, or a disjunction $\tau_1 \vee \tau_2$, or a negation $\neg\tau_1$, where τ_1 and τ_2 are tests.

We denote the Herbrand Universe (i.e., the set of all ground terms) as $\mathcal{H}$, and the set of n–tuples of elements of $\mathcal{H}$ as $\mathcal{H}^n$. Given a (finite) set of variables $V = \{x_1, \ldots, x_n\}$, a *type assignment* ρ over V is a mapping from V to a set of types, written as $(x_1 : \omega_1, \ldots, x_n : \omega_n)$, where $\rho(x_i) = \omega_i$, for $1 \leq i \leq n$, and ω_i is a (nonempty) type representation (a type term in the algorithms that we present). Given a term t and a type representation ω, in an abuse of terminology we say that $t \in \omega$, meaning that t belongs to the set of terms denoted by ω.

We now define some notions related to clause tests and determinacy. Where necessary to emphasize the input test in a clause (i.e. the conjunction of primitive tests in the body), we will write the clause in "guarded" form, as:

$$p(x_1, \ldots, x_n) :- \mathit{input\_tests}(x_1, \ldots, x_n) \,\|\, Body.$$

As an example, consider a predicate defined by the clauses:

$$abs(X, Y) :- X \geq 0 \,\|\, Y = X.$$
$$abs(Y, Z) :- Y < 0 \,\|\, Z = -Y.$$

Assume we know that this predicate will always be called with its first argument bound to an integer. Obviously, for any particular call, only one of the tests '$X \geq 0$' or '$X < 0$' will succeed (i.e. the tests are mutually exclusive).

Fundamental to our approach to detecting determinacy is the notion of tests being "exclusive" w.r.t. a type assignment:

Definition 6. Two tests $\tau_1(\bar{x})$ and $\tau_2(\bar{x})$ are *exclusive* w.r.t. a type assignment $\bar{x} : \bar{\omega}$, if for every $\bar{t} \in \bar{\omega}$, $\bar{x} = \bar{t} \wedge \tau_1(\bar{x}) \wedge \tau_2(\bar{x})$ is unsatisfiable. ∎

Definition 7. Let $C_1, \ldots, C_n$, $n > 0$, be a sequence of clauses, with input tests $\tau_1(\bar{x}), \ldots, \tau_n(\bar{x})$ respectively. Let ρ be a type assignment. We say that $C_1, \ldots, C_n$ is *mutually exclusive* w.r.t. ρ if either, $n = 1$, or, for every pair of clauses C_i and C_j, $1 \leq i, j \leq n$, $i \neq j$, $\tau_i(\bar{x})$ and $\tau_j(\bar{x})$ are exclusive w.r.t. ρ. ∎

Consider a predicate p defined by n clauses $C_1, \ldots, C_n$, with input tests $\tau_1(\bar{x}), \ldots, \tau_n(\bar{x})$ respectively:

$$p(\bar{x}) :- \tau_1(\bar{x}) \,\|\, Body_1.$$
$$\ldots$$
$$p(\bar{x}) :- \tau_n(\bar{x}) \,\|\, Body_n.$$

We assume, without loss of generality, that each $\tau_i(\bar{x})$ is a conjunction of primitive tests (note that it is always possible to obtain an equivalent sequence of clauses where disjunctions have been removed).

Suppose that the predicate p has type type[p]: in the interest of simplicity, we sometimes say that the predicate p is mutually exclusive w.r.t. the type type[p] (or simply say that the predicate p is mutually exclusive) if the sequence of clauses $C_1, \ldots, C_n$ defining p is mutually exclusive w.r.t. the type assignment $\bar{x} : $ type[p]. Given a call c to predicate p in the body of a clause, we also say that c is mutually exclusive if p is. Note that if the predicate p is mutually exclusive, then at most one of its clauses will succeed for any call $p(\bar{t})$, with $\bar{t} \in \bar{\omega}$.

3   Determinacy Analysis

In this section we explain our algorithm for detecting predicates and goals that are deterministic (i.e., that produce at most one solution). Before introducing our algorithm, we give some instrumental definitions. We define the "calls" relation between predicates in a program as follows: p calls q, written $p \rightsquigarrow q$, if and only if a literal with predicate symbol q appears in the body of a clause defining p. Let $\rightsquigarrow^*$ denote the reflexive transitive closure of $\rightsquigarrow$. The following result shows the importance of mutual exclusion information for detecting determinacy:

Theorem 1. A predicate p in the program is deterministic if, for each predicate q such that $p \rightsquigarrow^* q$, q is mutually exclusive.

Proof. Assume that p is not deterministic, i.e., there is a goal $p(\bar{t})$, with $\bar{t} \in \text{type}[p]$, which is not deterministic. It is a straightforward induction on the number of resolution steps to show that there is a q such that $p \rightsquigarrow^* q$ and q is not mutually exclusive. ∎

Our algorithm for detecting determinacy consists on first determining which predicates are mutually exclusive (which is in fact the complex part, and is explained in detail in Section 4). Then, inferring determinacy is straightforward: from Theorem 1, analysis of determinacy reduces to the determination of reachability in the call graph of the program. In other words, a predicate p is deterministic if there is no path in the call graph of the program from p to any predicate q that is not mutually exclusive. It is straightforward to propagate this reachability information in a single traversal of the call graph in reverse topological order. The idea is illustrated by the following example.

Example 2. Consider the following predicate taken from a quicksort program:

```
qs(X1,X2)  :- X1 = []   ‖ X2 = [].
qs(X1,X2)  :- X1 = [H|L] ‖ part(H,L,Sm,Lg),
   qs(Sm,Sm1), qs(Lg,Lg1), app(Sm1,[H|Lg1],X2).
```

Assume that it has been inferred that qs/2 will be used with mode (in, out) and type (intlist, -), and assume we have already shown that part/4 and app/3 are mutually exclusive w.r.t. the types (integer, intlist, -, -) and (intlist, intlist, -) inferred for their body literals in the recursive clause above. The input tests for the sequence of clauses of qs/2 are X1 = [] , X1 = [H|L], which are mutually exclusive w.r.t. the type intlist, which means that at most one head unification will succeed for qs/2. It follows that a call to qs/2 with the first argument bound to a list of integers is deterministic, in the sense that at most one of the clauses of qs/2 will succeed, and if it does, it succeeds only once (thus, at most, only one solution will be produced). □

4   Checking Mutual Exclusion

Our approach to the problem of determining whether two tests $\tau_1(\bar{x})$ and $\tau_2(\bar{x})$ are *exclusive* w.r.t. a type assignment $\bar{x} : \bar{\omega}$, consists of partitioning the test

$\tau_1(\bar{x}) \wedge \tau_2(\bar{x})$ such that tests in different resulting partitions involve different constraint systems, and then applying to each partition an algorithm specific to the corresponding constraint system that checks mutual exclusion. In this paper we consider two commonly encountered constraint systems: Herbrand terms with equality and disequality tests, on variables with *tuple-distributive regular types* [3] (i.e., as mentioned in Section 2, types which are specified by regular term grammars in which each type symbol has exactly one defining type rule and each type rule is *deterministic*); and for linear arithmetic tests on integer variables.

4.1   Checking Mutual Exclusion in the Herbrand Domain

We present a decision procedure for checking mutual exclusion of tests that is inspired by a result, due to Kunen [17], that the emptiness problem is decidable for Boolean combinations of (notations for) certain "basic" subsets of the Herbrand universe of a program. It also uses straightforward adaptations of some operations described by Dart and Zobel [3].

The reason the mutual exclusion checking algorithm for Herbrand is as complex as it is, is that we want a *complete* algorithm for equality and disequality tests. It is possible to simplify this considerably if we are interested in equality tests only. Before describing the algorithm, we introduce some definitions and notation.

We use the notions (to be defined later in this section) of *type-annotated term*, and in general *elementary set*, as representations which denote some subsets of $\mathcal{H}^n$ (for some $n \geq 1$). These subsets can be, for example, the set of n-tuples for which a test succeeds, or a "calling type" for a predicate p (i.e. the set denoted by type[p]). Given a representation S (elementary set or type-annotated term), $Den(S)$ refers to the subset of $\mathcal{H}^n$ denoted by S.

Definition 8. [type-annotated term] A *type-annotated term* is a pair $M = (\bar{t}_M, \rho_M)$, where $\bar{t}_M$ is a tuple of terms, and ρ_M is a type assignment. A type-annotated term $(\bar{t}_M, \rho_M)$ denotes the set of all the ground terms $\bar{t}_M\theta$, where θ is some substitution, such that $x\theta \in \rho_M(x)$ for each variable in $\bar{t}_M$.   ∎

Given a type-annotated term $(\bar{t}, \rho)$, the tuple of terms $\bar{t}$ can be regarded as a Herbrand term (i.e. a type-symbol-free type term) and ρ can be considered to be a *type substitution* [1], so that, if we apply this type substitution to $\bar{t}$, we get a pure type term (a variable-free type term). This is useful for defining the "intersection" and "inclusion" operations over type-annotated terms (that we define later) using the algorithms described by Dart and Zobel [3] for performing these operations over pure type terms. When we have a type-annotated term $(\bar{t}, \rho)$ such that $\rho(x) = \mu$ for each variable x in $\bar{t}$, we omit the type assignment ρ for brevity and use the tuple of terms $\bar{t}$ (recall that μ denotes the type of the entire Herbrand universe). Thus, a tuple of terms $\bar{t}$ with no associated type

---

[1] A type substitution is similar to a substitution that maps variables to type terms. A detailed definition of type substitutions is given in [3].

assignment can be regarded as a type-annotated term which denotes the set of all ground instances of $\bar{t}$.

Definition 9. [elementary set] An elementary set is defined as follows:

- Λ is an elementary set, and denotes the empty set (i.e., $Den(\Lambda) = \emptyset$);
- a type-annotated term $(\bar{t}, \rho)$ is an elementary set; and
- if A and B are elementary sets, then $A \otimes B$, $A \oplus B$ and $comp(A)$ are elementary sets that denote, respectively, the sets of (tuples of) terms $Den(A) \cap Den(B)$, $Den(A) \cup Den(B)$, and $\mathcal{H}^n \setminus Den(A)$. ∎

We define the following relations between elementary sets: $A \sqsubseteq B$ iff $Den(A) \subseteq Den(B)$. $A \sqsubset B$ iff $Den(A) \subset Den(B)$. $A \simeq B$ iff $Den(A) = Den(B)$.

We define below two particular classes of elementary sets, namely, *cobasic sets* and *minsets*, which are suitable representations of tests for the algorithms that we present in this paper. A test $\tau(\bar{x})$ that is a conjunction of unification and disunification tests, is represented as a minset that denotes the set of ground instances of $\bar{x}$ (i.e., subsets of $\mathcal{H}^n$, assuming that $\bar{x}$ is a n-tuple) for which the test succeeds. In Figure 1 we will provide the *test2minset* function, which gives the minset representation of a test. A disunification test is represented by a cobasic set (which denotes the complementary set of a subset of $\mathcal{H}^n$).

Definition 10. [cobasic set] A cobasic set is an elementary set of the form $comp(\bar{t})$, where $\bar{t}$ is a tuple of terms (recall that $\bar{t}$ is in fact a type-annotated term $(\bar{t}, \rho)$ such that $\rho(x) = \mu$ for each variable x in $\bar{t}$). ∎

Definition 11. [minset] A *minset* is either Λ or an elementary set of the form $A \otimes comp(B_1) \otimes \cdots \otimes comp(B_n)$, for some $n \geq 0$, where A is a tuple of terms, $comp(B_1), \ldots, comp(B_n)$ are cobasic sets, and for all $1 \leq i \leq n$, $B_i = A\theta_i$ and $A \not\sqsubseteq B_i$ for some substitution θ_i (i.e. $B_i \sqsubset A$). ∎

For brevity, we write a minset of the form $A \otimes comp(B_1) \otimes \cdots \otimes comp(B_n)$ as A/C, where $C = \{comp(B_1), \ldots, comp(B_n)\}$. We also denote the tuple of terms of a cobasic set $Cob \equiv comp(B)$ as $\bar{t}_{Cob}$, i.e. $\bar{t}_{Cob} \equiv B$.

Example 3. We define some examples of type-annotated terms A, B, and C as follows: $A = ((x, y), (x : \alpha_1, y : \alpha_2))$, where $\alpha_1 \rightarrow \{f(\mu)\}$, and $\alpha_2 \rightarrow \{g(\mu), h(\mu)\}$; B is the type-annotated term such that $\bar{t}_B \equiv (f(z), w)$ and $\rho_B \equiv (z : \mu, w : \alpha_2)$ (note that A and B denote the same subset of $\mathcal{H}^n$, i.e., $Den(A) = Den(B)$); C is the type-annotated term with $\bar{t}_C \equiv (f(v_1), g(v_2), v_3, v_4, f(a), f(v_5), v_6)$ and $\rho_C \equiv (v_1 : \mu, v_2 : list, v_3 : \alpha_2, v_4 : \alpha_3, v_5 : \alpha_3, v_6 : list)$, where $\alpha_3 \rightarrow \{a, b\}$ and $list \rightarrow \{[\,], [\mu|list]\}$. □

Definition 12. [type-annotated term instance] Let A and B be two type-annotated terms. We say that A is an instance of B if $A \sqsubset B$ and there is a substitution θ such that $\bar{t}_A = \bar{t}_B\theta$. ∎

$test2minset(\tau)$:

Input: a conjunction of unification and disunification tests τ. We assume that τ is of the form $E \wedge D_1 \wedge \cdots \wedge D_n$, where E is the conjunction of all unification tests of τ (i.e., a system of equations) and each D_i a disunification test (i.e., a disequation).

Output: a minset S representing the test τ (i.e., the set of tuples of terms $Den(S)$ is equal to the set of solutions of τ).

    1. Let θ be the substitution associated with the solved form of E (this can be computed by using the techniques of Lassez et al. [18]).

    2. Let θ_i, for $1 \le i \le n$, be the substitution associated with the solved form of $E \wedge N_i$, where N_i is the negation of D_i.

    3. $S = A \otimes comp(B_1) \otimes \cdots \otimes comp(B_n)$, where $A = (\bar{x})\theta$ and $B_i = (\bar{x})\theta_i$, for $1 \le i \le n$.

Fig. 1. Definition of the function *test2minset*

Let τ_1 and τ_2 be tests which are conjunctions of unification and disunification tests, and ρ a type assignment. Let M be a type-annotated term representing the type assignment ρ. Let S_i be a minset representing τ_i, for $i = 1, 2$, the function *test2minset*, defined in Figure 1, gives the minset representation of a test, i.e., $S_i = test2minset(\tau_i)$.

We have that τ_1 and τ_2 are exclusive w.r.t. ρ if and only if $M \otimes S_1 \otimes S_2 \simeq \Lambda$. Let S be the minset resulting of computing $S_1 \otimes S_2$ (this intersection can be trivially defined in terms of most general unifiers of the tuples of terms composing the minsets S_1 and S_2). Then, the fundamental problem is to devise an algorithm to test whether $M \otimes S \simeq \Lambda$, where M is a type-annotated term and S a minset. The algorithm that we propose is given by the boolean function $empty(M, S)$. Due to space limitations, we provide a high level description of this function. A detailed algorithm for its implementation can be found in [19].

- First, perform the "intersection" of M and the tuple of terms A of the minset S (we assume that $S = A/C$). Let R denote this intersection (i.e. $M \otimes A$). For example, assume that M denotes $((X), (X : list))$ and S denotes $(X3)/\{comp([\,]), comp([X1|X2])\}$. In this case, A denotes the tuple of terms $(X3)$ and C denotes the set of cobasic sets $\{comp([\,]), comp([X1|X2])\}$. Thus, the "intersection" of M and A is the type-annotated term $((X4), (X4 : list))$ (denoted by R).

- If R is empty (i.e., $R \simeq \Lambda$), or A is "included" in R (i.e. $A \sqsubseteq R$), then it can be reported that $M \otimes S \simeq \Lambda$ (the "inclusion" operation can be defined by using a straightforward adaptation of the function $subset_T(\omega_1, \omega_2)$ described in [3], that determines whether the type denoted by a pure type term is a subset of the type denoted by another). In our example, none of these conditions hold (recall that the tuple of terms $(X3)$ represents the type-annotated term $((X3), (X3 : \mu))$).

- Otherwise, the problem is reduced to checking whether $R/C \simeq \Lambda$.

- This way, if R is "included" in some tuple of terms of some cobasic set in C, then it can be reported that $R/C \simeq \Lambda$.
- Otherwise, it means that R is "too big", and thus, it is "expanded" to a set of "smaller" type-annotated terms (with the hope that each of them will be "included" in the tuple of terms of some cobasic set in C). This way, the initial problem is reduced to a set of subproblems, one subproblem for each element in the set of "smaller" type-annotated terms to which R has been "expanded". This holds in the example, where the type-annotated term $((X4), (X4 : list))$ is "expanded" to a set of two "smaller" type-annotated terms $\{R_1, R_2\}$ where R_1 denotes $(([X5|X6]), (X5 : \mu, X6 : list))$ and R_2 denotes $(([\ ]), \emptyset)$ ($\emptyset$ denotes an empty type assignment, since $([\ ])$ has no variables). Then, two subproblems arise:
  - Checking whether $R_1/C \simeq \Lambda$, which holds because $(([X5|X6]), (X5 : \mu, X6 : list))$ is "included" in $(([X1|X2]))$ (the tuple of terms of the cobasic set $comp([X1|X2])$); and
  - Checking whether $R_2/C \simeq \Lambda$ is empty, which also holds because $(([\ ]), \emptyset)$ is "included" in the tuple of terms of the cobasic set $comp([\ ])$.
- Thus, it can be concluded that $R/C \simeq \Lambda$ and hence $M \otimes S \simeq \Lambda$.

In [19] conditions are defined for ensuring that type-annotated terms are not infinitely expanded, and hence ensuring termination. Intuitively, these conditions are based on detecting and removing "useless" cobasic sets from C, and also on expanding the type-annotated term R into type-annotated terms whose depth is bounded (it is always possible to detect when it is not necessary to expand type-annotated terms to more than a "decision depth" in order to solve the corresponding subproblem). We say that a cobasic set Cob is "useless" whenever if $R/(C - \{Cob\}) \not\simeq \Lambda$, then $R/C \not\simeq \Lambda$. For example, if the tuple of terms of a cobasic set Cob in C is "disjoint" with R, then it is useless. This way, if C becomes empty, then $R/C \not\simeq \Lambda$.

4.2   Checking Mutual Exclusion in Linear Arithmetic Over Integers

In this section, we give an algorithm for checking whether two linear arithmetic tests $\tau_i(\bar{x})$ and $\tau_j(\bar{x})$ are exclusive w.r.t. the type assignment of integer to each variable in $\bar{x}$. This amounts to determining whether $(\exists \bar{x})(\tau_i(\bar{x}) \wedge \tau_j(\bar{x}))$ is unsatisfiable.

The system $\tau_i(\bar{x}) \wedge \tau_j(\bar{x})$ can be transformed into disjunctive normal form as:

$$(\tau_i(\bar{x}) \wedge \tau_j(\bar{x})) = \bigvee_{k=1}^{n} \bigwedge_{l=1}^{m} \phi_{kl}(\bar{x})$$

where each of the tests $\phi_{kl}(\bar{x})$ is of the form $\phi_{kl}(\bar{x}) \equiv a_0 + a_1 x_1 + \cdots + a_p x_p \; \textcircled{?} \; 0$, with $\textcircled{?} \in \{=, <, \leq, >, \geq\}$. For doing this transformation, note that a test of the form $\sum_{i=0}^{p} a_i x_i \neq 0$ can be written in terms of two tests involving the operators '$>$' and '$<$':

$$(\sum_{i=0}^{p} a_i x_i > 0) \vee (\sum_{i=0}^{p} a_i x_i < 0)$$

The resulting system, transformed to disjunctive normal form, defines a set of integer programming problems: the answer to the original mutual exclusion problem is "yes" if and only if none of these integer programming problems has a solution. Since a test can give rise to at most finitely many integer programming problems in this way, it follows that the mutual exclusion problem for linear integer tests is decidable.

Since determining whether an integer programming problem is solvable is NP-complete [9], it is straightforward to show that the mutual exclusion problem for linear arithmetic tests over the integers is co-NP-hard. It should be noted, however, that the vast majority of arithmetic tests encountered in practice tend to be fairly simple: our experience has been that tests involving more than two variables are rare. The solvability of integer programs in the case where each inequality involves at most two variables, i.e., is of the form $ax + by \leq c$, can be decided efficiently in polynomial time by examining the loops in a graph constructed from the inequalities [1]. The integer programming problems that arise in practice, in the context of mutual exclusion analysis, are therefore efficiently decidable.

The ideas explained in this section for linear arithmetic over integers extend directly to linear tests over the reals, which turn out to be computationally somewhat simpler.

4.3   Checking Mutual Exclusion: Putting It All Together

Consider a predicate p defined by n clauses $C_1, \ldots, C_n$, with input tests $\tau_1(\bar{x}), \ldots, \tau_n(\bar{x})$ respectively:

$p(\bar{x}) :- \tau_1(\bar{x}) \, [\![\, Body_1.$

. . .

$p(\bar{x}) :- \tau_n(\bar{x}) \, [\![\, Body_n.$

Assume that the predicate p has type type$[p]$. We also assume, without loss of generality, that each $\tau_i(\bar{x})$ is a conjunction of primitive tests (see Section 2).

In order to check whether the predicate p is mutually exclusive (i.e. its clauses are mutually exclusive w.r.t. the type assignment $\bar{x} :$ type$[p]$) we need to solve the problem of determining whether a pair of tests $\tau_i(\bar{x})$ and $\tau_j(\bar{x})$, $1 \leq i, j \leq n$, $i \neq j$, are exclusive w.r.t. $\bar{x} :$ type$[p]$. Let ρ be the type assignment $\bar{x} :$ type$[p]$. Consider the type assignment ρ written as a type-annotated term M, and consider each $\tau_i(\bar{x})$ written as $\tau_i^H \wedge \tau_i^A$, where τ_i^H and τ_i^A are a conjunction of primitive unification and arithmetic tests respectively (i.e., we write arithmetic tests after unification tests). Consider also each τ_i^H written as a minset D_i (the function *test2minset*, defined in Figure 1, gives the minset representation of a test). We have that the pair of tests $\tau_i(\bar{x})$ and $\tau_j(\bar{x})$, are exclusive w.r.t. ρ if:

1. $M \otimes D_i \otimes D_j \simeq \Lambda$ (this can be checked as explained in Section 4.1), or
2. $M \otimes D_i \otimes D_j \not\simeq \Lambda$ and $\tau_i^A \theta_i \wedge \tau_j^A \theta_j$ is unsatisfiable, where θ_i (resp. θ_j), is the most general unifier of the tuple of terms of D_{ij} and D_i (resp. D_j), and D_{ij} is the minset intersection of D_i and D_j. That is, if $D_i \equiv A_i/B_i$, $D_j \equiv A_j/B_j$, and $D_{ij} \equiv A_{ij}/B_{ij}$, then $\theta_i = mgu(A_i, A_{ij})$, $A_{ij} \equiv A_i \theta_i$,

$\theta_j = mgu(A_j, A_{ij})$, $A_{ij} \equiv A_j\theta_j$ (note that there exists a substitution μ_{ij}, such that $\mu_{ij} = mgu(A_i, A_j)$). We use the algorithm described in Section 4.2 for checking whether $\tau_i^A\theta_i \wedge \tau_j^A\theta_j$ is unsatisfiable.

Example 4. Let p be the predicate `partition/4` from the familiar quicksort program. Let $X = [\,]$, $(X = [H|L] \wedge H > Y)$, $(X = [H|L] \wedge H \leq Y)$ be the sequence of tests for the clauses in p and let ρ be $(X : intlist, Y : integer)$, where $intlist \rightarrow \{[\,], [integer|intlist]\}$. In this case, we have that M is $((X,Y), (X : intlist, Y : integer))$. $\tau_1(\bar{x}) \equiv X = [\,]$, $\tau_2(\bar{x}) \equiv X = [H|L] \wedge H > Y$, and $\tau_3(\bar{x}) \equiv X = [H|L] \wedge H \leq Y$. $\tau_1(\bar{x})$ can be written as $\tau_1^H \wedge \tau_1^A$, where $\tau_1^H \equiv X = [\,]$ and $\tau_1^A \equiv true$. Similarly, $\tau_2^H \equiv X = [H|L]$ and $\tau_2^A \equiv H > Y$, and $\tau_3^H \equiv X = [H|L]$ and $\tau_3^A \equiv H \leq Y$. $D_1 \equiv ([\,], Y)$, $D_2 \equiv ([H|L], Y)$, and $D_3 \equiv ([H|L], Y)$. We have that `partition/4` is mutually exclusive because: $M \otimes D_i \otimes D_j \simeq \Lambda$, for $i = 1$ and $j \in \{2, 3\}$, and (although $M \otimes D_2 \otimes D_3 \not\simeq \Lambda$), we have that $H > Y \wedge H \leq Y$ is unsatisfiable (note that $D_{2,3} \equiv ([H|L], Y)$, and θ_2 and θ_3 are the identity). $\square$

4.4   Checking Mutual Exclusion: Dealing with the Cut

The presence of the pruning operator (cut) in the clauses of a program can help the detection of mutual exclusion of clauses. In order to take the cut into account, we simply redefine the concept of mutually exclusive clauses given in Definition 7 as follows:

Definition 13. Let $C_1, \ldots, C_n$, $n > 0$, be a sequence of clauses, with input tests $\tau_1, \ldots, \tau_n$ respectively. Let ρ be a type assignment. We say that $C_1, \ldots, C_n$ is *mutually exclusive* w.r.t. ρ if either, $n = 1$, or, for every pair of clauses C_i and C_j, $1 \leq i, j \leq n$, $i \neq j$:

1. C_i has a cut and and $i < j$, or
2. C_j has a cut and and $j < i$, or,
3. $\tau_i(\bar{x})$ and $\tau_j(\bar{x})$ are exclusive w.r.t. ρ. ∎

We also have to take into account that the pruning operator introduces implicit tests. Consider a predicate p defined by n clauses $C_1, \ldots, C_n$, with input tests $\tau_1(\bar{x}), \ldots, \tau_n(\bar{x})$ respectively:

$$p(\bar{x}) :- \tau_1(\bar{x}) \,\|\, Body_1.$$
$$\ldots$$
$$p(\bar{x}) :- \tau_n(\bar{x}) \,\|\, Body_n.$$

Let I be the set of indexes k of clauses C_k which have a cut and are before the clause C_i (i.e. $k < i$). Let τ_k^b be the test (conjunction of tests) that is before the cut in clause C_k (i.e. $\tau_k \equiv \tau_k^b \wedge \tau_k^a$, where τ_k^a is the test that is after the cut in clause C_k).

Now, instead of considering the test τ_i, for $1 \leq i \leq n$, in Definition 13, we take the test τ_i^c defined as follows:

$$\tau_i^c = \begin{cases} \tau_i & \text{if } I = \emptyset \\ (\bigwedge_{k \in I} \neg \tau_k^b) \wedge \tau_i & \text{otherwise.} \end{cases}$$

Note that the introduction of the negation in the tests τ_i^c is not a problem, since it is always possible to reduce the problem of determining whether a pair of tests τ_i^c and τ_j^c are exclusive w.r.t. a given type assignment, to one o more exclusion subproblems where the pair of tests involved in each subproblem are conjunctions of primitive tests (transforming tests to disjunctive normal form).

5   Improving Determinacy Analysis Using Cut

The presence of the pruning operator in the clauses of a program not only improves detection of mutual exclusion, but it can also help in the overall process of detecting deterministic predicates. Besides helping the detection of mutual exclusion of clauses (as we have seen before), it can also improve the propagation algorithm given in Section 3. Assume that we would like to infer that a predicate p is deterministic. Consider any clause defining p in which one or more cuts appear, and any body literals that appear to the left of the rightmost cut in that clause. Those literals are not required to be deterministic (we say that a literal with predicate symbol q is deterministic if q is). In other words, in Theorem 1, we can use a restricted definition $(\leadsto_r)$ of the "call" relation $(\leadsto)$ between predicates in a program, defined as follows: $p \leadsto_r q$, if and only if a literal with predicate symbol q appears in the body of a clause defining p, and there is no cut to the right of this literal in the clause. Similarly, $\leadsto_r^*$ denotes the reflexive transitive closure of $\leadsto_r$.

6   A Prototype Implementation

In order to evaluate the effectiveness and efficiency of our approach to determinacy analysis we have constructed a relatively complete prototype which performs such analysis in an automatic way. The system takes Prolog programs as input,[2] which include a module definition in the standard way. In addition, the types and modes of the arguments of exported predicates are either given or obtained from other modules during modular type and mode analysis (including the intervening type definitions). The system uses the *CiaoPP* PLAI analyzer to derive mode information, using, for the reported experiments, the Sharing+Freeness domain [22], and an adaptation of Gallagher's analysis to derive the types of predicates [8]. The resulting type- and mode-annotated programs are then analyzed using the algorithms presented for Herbrand and linear arithmetic tests.

Herbrand mutual exclusion is checked by a naive direct implementation of the analyses presented. Testing of mutual exclusion for linear arithmetic tests is implemented directly using the Omega test [23]. This test determines whether

---

[2] In fact, the input language currently supported includes also a number of extensions —such as functions or feature terms— which are translated by the first (expansion) passes of the Ciao compiler to clauses, possibly with cut.

there is an integer solution to an arbitrary set of linear equalities and inequalities, referred to as a problem.

We have tested the prototype first on a number of simple standard benchmarks, and then on more complex ones. The latter are taken from those used in the cardinality analysis of Braem *et al.* [2], which is the closest related previous work that we are aware of. In the case of *Kalah*, we have inserted the missing cuts as is also done in [2], to make the comparison meaningful. Some relevant results of these tests are presented in Table 1. **Program** lists the program names, **N** the number of predicates in the program, **D** the number of predicates detected by the analysis as deterministic, **M** the number of predicates whose tests are mutually exclusive, **C** the number of deterministic predicates detected in [2], $\mathbf{T}_D$ the time required by the determinacy analysis (Ciao version 1.9p111 and CiaoPP-0.8, on a medium-loaded Pentium IV Xeon 2.0Ghz, 1Gb of RAM memory, running Red Hat Linux 8.0, and averaging several runs, eliminating the best and worst values), $\mathbf{T}_M$ the time required to derive the modes and types, and $\mathbf{T}_T$ the total analysis time (all times are given in milliseconds). Averages (per predicate in the case of analysis time) are also provided in the last row of the table.

Table 1. Accuracy and efficiency of the determinacy analysis (times in mS)

Program	N	D (%)	M (%)	C	$\mathbf{T}_D$	$\mathbf{T}_M$	$\mathbf{T}_T$
Hanoi	2	2 (100)	2 (100)	N/A	69	79	148
Fib	1	1 (100)	1 (100)	N/A	39	19	58
Mmatrix	3	3 (100)	3 (100)	N/A	89	79	168
Tak	1	1 (100)	1 (100)	N/A	49	29	78
Subs	1	1 (100)	1 (100)	N/A	70	19	89
Reverse	2	2 (100)	2 (100)	N/A	39	19	58
Qsort	3	3 (100)	3 (100)	3 (100)	50	69	119
Qsort2	5	5 (100)	5 (100)	5 (100)	99	70	169
Queens	6	3 (50)	5 (83)	2 (33)	99	59	158
Gabriel	20	6 (30)	11 (55)	4 (20)	360	279	639
Kalah	44	40 (91)	42 (95)	40 (91)	1110	3589	4699
Plan	16	8 (50)	12 (75)	3 (19)	459	949	1408
Credit	25	18 (72)	21 (84)	16 (64)	1209	359	1568
Pg	10	6 (60)	9 (90)	6 (60)	440	209	649
Mean	–	71%	85%	61%	30 (/p)	42 (/p)	72 (/p)

The results are quite encouraging, showing that the developed analysis is fairly accurate. The analysis is more powerful in some cases than the cardinality analysis [2], and at least as accurate in the others. It is pointed out in [2] that determinacy information can be improved by using a more sophisticated type domain. This is also applicable to our analysis, and the types inferred by our system are similar to those used in [2]. The determinacy analysis times are also encouraging, despite the currently relatively naive implementation of the system (for example, the call to the omega test is done by calling an external process).

The overall analysis times are also reasonable, even when including the type and mode analysis times, which are in any case very useful in other parts of the compilation process.

7   Conclusions

We have proposed an analysis for detecting procedures and goals that are deterministic (i.e. that produce at most one solution), or predicates whose clause tests are mutually exclusive, even if they are not deterministic (because they call other predicates which are nondeterministic). This approach has advantages w.r.t. previous approaches in that it provides an algorithm for detecting mutual exclusion and it handles disequality constraints on the Herbrand domain and arithmetic tests.

We have implemented the proposed analysis and integrated it into the *CiaoPP* system, which also infers automatically the mode and type information that the proposed analysis takes as input. The results of the experiments performed on this implementation show that the analysis is fairly accurate and efficient, providing more accurate or similar results, regarding accuracy, than previous proposals, while offering substantially higher automation, since typically no information is needed from the user.

Acknowledgments

This work has been supported in part by the European Union IST program under contracts IST-2001-38059 "ASAP", by MCYT project TIC 2002-0055 "CUBICO", by FEDER infrastructure project UNPM-E012, and by the Prince of Asturias Chair in Information Science and Technology at the University of New Mexico. We would also like to thank the anonymous reviewers for their useful comments on earlier versions of the paper.

References

1. B. Aspvall and Y. Shiloach. A polynomial time algorithm for solving systems of linear inequalities with two variables per inequality. In *Proc. 20th ACM Symposium on Foundations of Computer Science*, pages 205–217, October 1979.
2. C. Braem, B. Le Charlier, S. Modart, and P. Van Hentenryck. Cardinality analysis of prolog. In *Proc. International Symposium on Logic Programming*, pages 457–471, Ithaca, NY, November 1994. MIT Press.
3. P.W. Dart and J. Zobel. A Regular Type Language for Logic Programs. In *Types in Logic Programming*, pages 157–187. MIT Press, 1992.
4. S. Dawson, C.R. Ramakrishnan, I.V. Ramakrishnan, and R.C. Sekar. Extracting Determinacy in Logic Programs. In *1993 International Conference on Logic Programming*, pages 424–438. MIT Press, June 1993.
5. S.K. Debray and N.W. Lin. Cost analysis of logic programs. *ACM Transactions on Programming Languages and Systems*, 15(5):826–875, November 1993.

6. S.K. Debray and D.S. Warren. Functional computations in logic programs. *ACM Transactions on Programming Languages and Systems*, 11(3):451–481, 1989.
7. B. Demoen, M. Garcia de la Banda, W. Harvey, K. Marriott, and P. Stuckey. An overview of HAL. In *PPCP'99: Principles and Practice of Constraint Programming*, pages 174–178, 1999.
8. J.P. Gallagher and D.A. de Waal. Fast and precise regular approximations of logic programs. In Pascal Van Hentenryck, editor, *Proc. of the 11th International Conference on Logic Programming*, pages 599–613. MIT Press, 1994.
9. M.R. Garey and D.S. Johnson. *Computers and Intractability: A Guide to the Theory of NP-Completeness*. W.H. Freeman, New York, 1979.
10. Roberto Giacobazzi and Laura Ricci. Detecting determinate computations by bottom-up abstract interpretation. In *Symposium proceedings on 4th European symposium on programming*, pages 167–181. Springer-Verlag, 1992.
11. G. Gupta, E. Pontelli, K. Ali, M. Carlsson, and M. Hermenegildo. Parallel Execution of Prolog Programs: a Survey. *ACM Transactions on Programming Languages and Systems*, 23(4):472–602, July 2001.
12. F. Henderson, Z. Somogyi, and T. Conway. Determinism analysis in the Mercury compiler. In *Proc. Australian Computer Science Conference*, pages 337–346, Melbourne, Australia, January 1996.
13. M. Hermenegildo and M. Carro. Relating Data–Parallelism and (And–) Parallelism in Logic Programs. *The Computer Languages Journal*, 22(2/3):143–163, July 1996.
14. M. Hermenegildo, G. Puebla, F. Bueno, and P. López-García. Program Development Using Abstract Interpretation (and The Ciao System Preprocessor). In *10th International Static Analysis Symposium (SAS'03)*, number 2694 in LNCS, pages 127–152. Springer-Verlag, June 2003.
15. P.M. Hill and A. King. Determinacy and determinacy analysis. *Journal of Programming Languages*, 5(1):135–171, December 1997.
16. G. Janssens and M. Bruynooghe. Deriving Descriptions of Possible Values of Program Variables by means of Abstract Interpretation. *Journal of Logic Programming*, 13(2 and 3):205–258, July 1992.
17. K. Kunen. Answer Sets and Negation as Failure. In *Proc. of the Fourth International Conference on Logic Programming*, pages 219–228, Melbourne, May 1987. MIT Press.
18. J.-L. Lassez, M. Maher, and K. Marriott. Unification Revisited. In J. Minker, editor, *Foundations of Deductive Databases and Logic Programming*, pages 587–626. Morgan Kaufman, 1988.
19. P. López-García, F. Bueno, and M. Hermenegildo. Towards Determinacy Analysis for Logic Programs Using Mode and Type Information. Technical Report CLIP4/2005.0, Technical University of Madrid (UPM), School of Computer Science, UPM, April 2005.
20. P. López-García, M. Hermenegildo, and S.K. Debray. A Methodology for Granularity Based Control of Parallelism in Logic Programs. *Journal of Symbolic Computation, Special Issue on Parallel Symbolic Computation*, 22:715–734, 1996.
21. J. Morales, M. Carro, and M. Hermenegildo. Improving the Compilation of Prolog to C Using Moded Types and Determinism Information. In *Proceedings of the Sixth International Symposium on Practical Aspects of Declarative Languages*, number 3507 in LNCS, pages 86–103, Heidelberg, Germany, June 2004. Springer-Verlag.
22. K. Muthukumar and M. Hermenegildo. Combined Determination of Sharing and Freeness of Program Variables Through Abstract Interpretation. In *1991 International Conference on Logic Programming*, pages 49–63. MIT Press, June 1991.

23. W. Pugh. A Practical Algorithm for Exact Array Dependence Analysis. *Communications of the ACM*, 35(8):102–114, August 1992.
24. V. Santos-Costa, D.H.D. Warren, and R. Yang. Andorra-I: A Parallel Prolog System that Transparently Exploits both And- and Or-parallelism. In *Proceedings of the 3rd. ACM SIGPLAN Symposium on Principles and Practice of Parallel Programming*, pages 83–93. ACM, April 1991. SIGPLAN Notices vol 26(7), July 1991.
25. Z. Somogyi, F. Henderson, and T. Conway. The execution algorithm of Mercury: an efficient purely declarative logic programming language. *JLP*, 29(1–3), October 1996.

Mechanical Verification of Automatic Synthesis of Fault-Tolerant Programs[1]

Sandeep S. Kulkarni, Borzoo Bonakdarpour, and Ali Ebnenasir

Department of Computer Science and Engineering,
Michigan State University,
48824 East Lansing, Michigan, USA
{sandeep, borzoo, ebnenasi}@cse.msu.edu
http://www.cse.msu.edu/~{sandeep,borzoo,ebnenasi}

Abstract. Fault-tolerance is a crucial property in many systems. Thus, mechanical verification of algorithms associated with synthesis of fault-tolerant programs is desirable to ensure their correctness. In this paper, we present the mechanized verification of algorithms that automate the addition of fault-tolerance to a given fault-intolerant program using the PVS theorem prover. By this verification, not only we prove the correctness of the synthesis algorithms, but also we guarantee that any program synthesized by these algorithms is correct by construction. Towards this end, we formally define a uniform framework for formal specification and verification of fault-tolerance that consists of abstract definitions for programs, specifications, faults, and levels of fault-tolerance, so that they are independent of platform and architecture. The essence of synthesis algorithms involves fixpoint calculations. Hence, we also develop a reusable library for fixpoint calculations on finite sets in PVS.

Keywords: Fault-tolerance, PVS, Program synthesis, Program transformation, Mechanical verification, Theorem proving, Addition of fault-tolerance.

1   Introduction

Fault-tolerance is a necessity in most computer systems and, hence, one needs strong assurance of fault-tolerance properties of a given system. Mechanical verification of such systems is one way to get a strong form of assurance. The related work in the literature has focused on verification of concrete fault-tolerant programs. For example, Owre et al [1] present a survey on formal verification of a fault-tolerant digital-flight control system. Mantel and Gärtner verify the correctness of a fault-tolerant broadcast protocol [2]. Qadeer and Shankar [3] mechanically verify the self-stability property of Dijkstra's mutual exclusion token

---

[1] This work was partially sponsored by NSF CAREER CCR-0092724, DARPA Grant OSURS01-C-1901, ONR Grant N00014-01-1-0744, NSF grant EIA-0130724, and a grant from Michigan State University.

S. Etalle(Ed.): LOPSTR 2004, LNCS 3573, pp. 36–52, 2005.

ring algorithm [4]. Kulkarni, Rushby, and Shankar [5] verify the same algorithm by exploiting the theory of detectors and correctors [6].

While the verifications performed in [1,2,3,5] enable us to gain confidence in the programs being verified, it is difficult to extend these verifications to other programs. A more general approach, therefore, is to verify algorithms that generate fault-tolerant programs.

With this motivation, in this paper, we focus on the problem of *verifying algorithms that synthesize fault-tolerant programs*. With such verification, we are guaranteed that all the programs generated by the synthesis algorithms indeed satisfy their fault-tolerance requirements. Towards this end, we verify the transformation algorithms presented by Kulkarni and Arora [7,8] using the PVS theorem prover. The algorithms in [7,8], focus on the problem of transforming a given fault-intolerant program to a fault-tolerant program. To verify these algorithms, first, we model a framework for fault-tolerance in PVS. This framework consists of definitions for programs, specifications, faults, and levels of fault-tolerance. Then, we verify that the programs synthesized by the algorithms are indeed fault-tolerant. By this verification, we ensure that any program synthesized by these algorithms is also correct by construction and, hence, there is no need to verify the individual synthesized programs.

We note that the algorithms in [7,8], are the basis for their extensions to deal with simultaneous occurrence of multiple faults from different types [9] and for synthesizing distributed programs [10,11]. Thus, the specification and verification of transformation algorithms in [7,8] is reusable in developing specification and verification of algorithms in [10,11,9]. Since fixpoint calculation is at the heart of the synthesis algorithms, we also develop a library for fixpoint calculations on *finite sets* in PVS. This library is reusable for other purposes that involve fixpoint calculations as well [2].

Contributions of the paper. The contributions of this paper are as follows: (1) We verify the correctness of the synthesis algorithms in [7,8]. Thus, not only we ensure their correctness but also we guarantee that any program synthesized by the algorithms is also correct by construction. (2) We provide a foundation for formal specification and verification of later research work that are extensions of [7,8]. (3) We develop a reusable library in PVS for fixpoint calculations on finite sets.

Organization of the paper. The organization of the paper is as follows: We provide the formal definitions of programs, specifications, faults, and fault-tolerance in Section 2. Using these definitions, we formally state the problem of mechanical verification of synthesis of fault-tolerant programs in Section 3. In Section 4, first, we develop a theory for fixpoint calculations on finite sets. Then, based on the definitions in Section 2 and our fixpoint calculation library, we formally specify the synthesis algorithms proposed in [7,8] in PVS. In Section 5,

---

[2] The URL http://www.cse.msu.edu/~borzoo/pvs contains the PVS specifications and formal proofs.

we present the verification of algorithms. Finally, we make concluding remarks and discuss future work in Section 7.

2   Modeling a Fault-Tolerance Framework

In this section, we give formal definitions for programs, specifications, faults, and fault-tolerance. The programs are specified in terms of their state space and their transitions. The definition of specifications is adapted from Alpern and Schneider [12]. The definitions of faults and fault-tolerance are adapted from Arora and Gouda [13] and Kulkarni [6]. We also discuss how we model the definitions in PVS in an abstract way, so that they are independent of any particular program. We note that in describing this model, due to space limitation, we omit the proofs of certain simple judgements and lemmas

2.1   Program

A program p is a finite set of transitions in its state space. In our framework, the notion of state is abstract. Hence, in PVS, we model state by an UNINTER-PRETED TYPE [3]. Likewise, a transition is modeled as an ordered pair of states, which is also an uninterpreted type. We also assume that the number of states and transitions are finite. The state space of p, S_p, is the set of all possible states of p. In PVS, we model the state space by the finite *fullset* over states. We define the following JUDGEMENT to avoid getting repetitive type-checking proof obligations from the PVS type-checker:

Judgement 2.1: S_p has type of finite set.
We model program, p, by a subset of $S_p \times S_p$. A state predicate of p is a subset of S_p. In PVS, we model a state predicate, StatePred, as a finite set over states. The type Action denotes finite sets of transitions. A state predicate S is closed in the program p iff for all transitions (s_0, s_1) in p, if $s_0 \in S$ then $s_1 \in S$. Hence, we define closure as follows: $closed(S, p) = (\forall s_0, s_1 \mid (s_0, s_1) \in p : (s_0 \in S \Rightarrow s_1 \in S))$. A sequence of states, $\langle s_0, s_1, ... \rangle$, is a computation of p iff any pair of two consecutive states is a transition in p. We formalize this by a DEPENDENT TYPE[4] as follows:

$$Computation(p) : TYPE =$$
$$\{c : sequence[state] \mid (\forall i \mid i \geq 0 : (c_i, c_{i+1}) \in p)\}$$

where $sequence[state] : \mathbb{N} \to state$ and p is any finite set of type Action. A computation prefix is a finite sequence of states, where the first j steps are transitions in the given program:

---

[3] Uninterpreted types support abstraction by providing a means of introducing a type with a minimum of assumptions on the type and imposing almost no constraints on an implementation of the specification [14].

[4] In PVS specification language, a type may be defined in terms of an earlier defined type [14].

$$prefix(p,j) : TYPE = \{c : sequence[state] \mid (\forall i \mid i < j : (c_i, c_{i+1}) \in p)\}$$

We deliberately model computation prefixes by infinite sequences of which only a finite part is used. This is due to the fact that using finite sequences in PVS is not very convenient and the type checker generates several proof obligations whenever finite sequences are used.

The projection of program p on state predicate S consists of transitions of p that start in S and end in S, denoted as $p \mid S$. Similar to the notion of program, we model projection of p on S by a finite set of transitions: $p \mid S = \{(s_0, s_1) \mid (s_0, s_1) \in p \ \wedge \ (s_0, s_1 \in S)\}$.

2.2   Specification

The specification consists of a safety specification and a liveness specification. The safety specification is specified as a set of *bad transitions*. Thus, for program p, its safety specification is a subset of $S_p \times S_p$. Hence, we can model the safety specification by a finite set of transitions, called *spec*. We explain the liveness issue in Section 2.3.

Given program p, state predicate S, and specification *spec*, we say that p satisfies its specification from S iff (1) S is closed in p, and (2) every computation of p that starts in a state where S is true, does not contain a transition in *spec*. If p does not satisfy its specification from S, we say p violates its specification. If p satisfies specification from S and $S \neq \{\}$, we say that S is an invariant of p. Since we do not deal with a specific program, in PVS, we model an invariant by an arbitrary state predicate that is closed in p.

2.3   Faults and Fault-Tolerance

The faults that a program is subject to are systematically represented by a finite set of transitions. A class of fault f for program p is a subset of $S_p \times S_p$. A computation of program p in presence of faults f is an infinite sequence of states where either a transition of p or a transition of f occurs at every step. Hence, we model computation of program in presence of faults as $c : Computation(p \cup f)$.

We say that a state predicate T is an f-span (read as fault-span) of p from S iff the following two conditions are satisfied: (1) $S \Rightarrow T$, and (2) T is closed in $p \cup f$. Thus, we model fault-span in PVS as follows: $FaultSpan(T, S, p \cup f) = ((S \subseteq T) \wedge (closed(T, p \cup f)))$. Observe that for all computations of p that start at states where S is true, T is a boundary in the state space of p up to which (but not beyond which) the state of p may be perturbed by the transitions in f. Hence, we define the different levels of fault-tolerance based on the behavior of the fault-tolerant program in its fault-span.

We say that p is failsafe f-tolerant (read as fault-tolerant) to its specification from S iff two conditions hold: (1) p satisfies its specification from S, and (2) there exists T such that T is an f-span of p from S, and no prefix of a computation of $p \cup f$ that starts in T has a transition in *spec*.

We say that p is masking f-tolerant (read as fault-tolerant) to its specification from S iff the following conditions hold: (1) p satisfies its specification from S, and (2) there exists T such that T is an f-span of p from S, no prefix of a computation of $p \cup f$ that starts in T has a transition in *spec*, and every computation of $p \cup f$ that starts from a state in T contains a state of S.

In [7,8], the liveness specification is modeled implicitly. Specifically, for fail-safe fault-tolerance, the requirement is that the fault-tolerant program does not *deadlock* in the absence of faults. And, for masking fault-tolerance, the requirement is that the fault-tolerant program does not deadlock even in the presence of faults. A program deadlocks in state s_0 iff $\forall s_1 \mid s_1 \in S : (s_0, s_1) \notin p$.

There is an additional type of tolerance in [7,8], *nonmasking*, where after the occurrence of faults, eventually the program recovers to its invariant. However, the safety specification may be violated during recovery. We omit the discussion of nonmasking tolerance, as the algorithm for this case is straightforward; it suffices to add one step recovery from all states reached in the presence of faults. However, in [15], the author presents formal specification and verification of synthesis of nonmasking fault-tolerance.

3   Problem Statement

In this section, we recall (from [7,8]) the problem of automatic synthesis of fault-tolerance. As described in Section 2, the fault-intolerant program p is specified in terms of its state space S_p, its transitions, p, and its invariant, S. The specification provides a set of bad transitions (that should not occur in program computation). The faults, f, are specified in terms of a finite set of transitions. Likewise, the fault-tolerant program p' is specified in terms of its state space S_p, its set of transitions, say p', its invariant, S', its specification, *spec*, and the type of fault-tolerance it provides.

The transformation problem is as follows (this definition will be instantiated in the obvious way depending upon the level of tolerance):

The Transformation Problem
Given p, S, *spec*, and f such that p satisfies *spec* from S.
Identify p' and S' such that:
$$S' \subseteq S$$
$$(p'|S') \subseteq (p|S')$$
p' is f-tolerant to *spec* from S'

We now explain the reasons behind the first two conditions briefly:

- If S' contains states that are not in S then, in the absence of faults, p' will include computations that start outside S and hence, p' contains new behaviors in the absence of faults. Therefore, we require that $S' \subseteq S$.
- Regarding the transitions of p and p', we focus only on the transitions of $p'|S'$ and $p|S'$. If $p'|S'$ contains a transition that is not in $p|S'$, p' can use this transition in a new computation in the absence of faults and hence, we require that $p'|S' \subseteq p|S'$.

Soundness. An algorithm for the transformation problem is sound iff for any given input, its output, namely p' and S', satisfies the transformation problem.

Our goal is to mechanically verify that the proposed algorithms in [7,8] are indeed sound. In other words, based on the definitions in Section 2, we show that the algorithms in [7,8] satisfy the transformation problem.

4   Description and Specification of Synthesis Algorithms

In this section, we describe the synthesis algorithms in [7,8] and explain how we formally specify them in PVS. As mentioned in Section 2, we are interested in two levels of fault-tolerance: failsafe and masking. The essence of adding failsafe and masking fault-tolerance to a given fault-intolerant program is recalculation of the invariant of the fault-intolerant program which in turn involves calculating the fixpoint of a formula. More specifically, we calculate fixpoint of a given formula to (i) calculate the set of states from where safety may be violated by faults alone; (ii) remove the set of states from where closure of fault-span is violated by fault transitions, and (iii) remove deadlock states that occur in a given set of states.

The $\mu-$calculus theory of the PVS prelude contains general definitions of the standard fixpoint calculation, however, it is not convenient to use that theory in the context of our problem. This is due to the fact that this library focuses on infinite sets and is not specialized to account for the properties of functions used in the synthesis of fault-tolerant programs. By contrast, we find that by customizing the theory to the properties of functions used in the synthesis of fault-tolerant programs, we can simplify the verification of the synthesis algorithms. Hence, in Section 4.1, we develop a theory for fixpoint calculations on *finite sets* that is reusable elsewhere. Based on the definitions in Section 4.1, we model the synthesis algorithms for addition of failsafe and masking tolerance in sections 4.2 and 4.3 respectively.

4.1   Specification of Fixpoint Calculation for Finite Sets

In this section, we describe how we formally specify fixpoint calculation for finite sets in PVS. A fixpoint of a function $f : X \to X$ is any value $x_0 \in X$ such that $f(x_0) = x_0$. In other words, further application of f does not change its value. A function may have more than one fixpoint. The least upper bound of fixpoints is called the *smallest fixpoint* and the greatest lower bound of fixpoints is called the *largest fixpoint*. In our context, the functions whose fixpoint is calculated demonstrate certain characteristics. Hence, as described above, we focus on customizing the fixpoint theory based on these characteristics.

In the context of finite sets, domain and range of f, X, are both finite sets of finite sets. Throughout this section and in Section 5.1, the variables i, j, k range over natural numbers. The variable x is any finite set of any uninterpreted type. Variable b is any member of such finite set.

One type of functions used in synthesis of fault-tolerance is a decreasing function for which the largest fixpoint is calculated. Towards this end, we start from an *initial set* and at each step of calculation, we remove a subset of the initial set that has a certain property. Thus, the type DecFunc is the type of functions g, such that $g : \{A : finiteset\} \rightarrow \{B : finiteset \mid B \subseteq A\}$. In other words, for all finite sets x, $g(x) \subseteq x$. With such a decreasing function, we define $Dec(i, x)(g)$ to formalize the recursive behavior of the largest fixpoint calculation. $Dec(i, x)(g)$ keeps removing the elements of the initial set, x, that the function g of type DecFunc returns at every step:

$$Dec(i, x)(g) = \begin{cases} Dec(i - 1, x)(g) - g(Dec(i - 1, x)(g)) & \text{if } i \neq 0; \\ x & \text{if } i = 0 \end{cases}$$

Finally, we define the largest fixpoint as follows:

$$LgFix(x)(g) = \{b \mid \forall k : b \in Dec(k, x)(g))\}$$

Our goal is to prove the following property of largest fixpoint based on our definitions: $g(LgFix(x)(g)) = \emptyset$.

Remark. The above definition of fixpoint is somewhat non-traditional. We find that this definition assists in verification of the synthesis algorithms. For example, we apply this fixpoint calculation for removing deadlock states where $g(x)$ denotes the deadlock states in set x. After calculating the largest fixpoint, we need to show that no deadlock states remain in the set x. Thus, we should show that $g(LgFix(x)) = \emptyset$. Moreover, if $g(LgFix(x)) = \emptyset$ then $\forall i : Dec(i, LgFix(x)) = LgFix(x)$.

The second type of fixpoint used in synthesis of fault-tolerance is an increasing function for which the smallest fixpoint is calculated. Towards this end, we start from an *initial set* and at each step, we add a set that is disjoint from the initial set. Thus, the type IncFunc is the type of functions r such that $r : \{A : finiteset\} \rightarrow \{B : finiteset \mid A \cap B = \emptyset\}$. In other words, for all finite sets x, $x \cap r(x) = \emptyset$. With such an increasing function, we define $Inc(i, x)(r)$ to formalize the recursive behavior of the smallest fixpoint calculation. $Inc(i, x)(r)$ keeps adding elements to the initial set, x, that the function r of type IncFunc returns at every step:

$$Inc(i, x)(r) = \begin{cases} Inc(i - 1, x)(r) \cup r(Inc(i - 1, x)(r)) & \text{if } i \neq 0; \\ x & \text{if } i = 0 \end{cases}$$

Finally, we define the smallest fixpoint as follows:

$$SmFix(x)(r) = \{b \mid \exists k : b \in Inc(k, x)(r)\}$$

Our goal is to prove the following property of smallest fixpoint:

$$r(SmFix(x)(r)) = \emptyset$$

4.2   Specification of the Synthesis of Failsafe Tolerance

The essence of adding failsafe tolerance is to remove the states from where safety may be violated by one or more fault transitions. We reiterate the algorithm *Add_failsafe* (from [7,8]) in Figure 1.

Throughout this section and Sections 4.3, 5.2 and 5.3, the variables x, s, s_0, s_1 range over states. The variables i, j, k, m range over natural numbers. The variable X ranges over StatePred and the variable Z ranges over Action. As defined in Section 3, p and p' are respectively fault-intolerant and fault-tolerant programs, S and S' are respectively invariants of fault-intolerant and fault-tolerant programs, T is fault-span, f is the finite set of faults, and *spec* is the finite set of bad transitions that represents the safety specification.

Add_failsafe(p, f : transitions, S : state predicate, *spec* : specification)
{
$\quad$ $ms := smallestfixpoint(X = X \cup \{s_0 \mid (\exists s_1 :$
$\quad\quad\quad\quad\quad\quad\quad\quad\quad (s_0, s_1) \in f) \quad \wedge \quad (s_1 \in X \vee (s_0, s_1)$ violates $spec) \}$;
$\quad$ $mt := \{(s_0, s_1) : ((s_1 \in ms) \vee (s_0, s_1)$ violates $spec) \}$;
$\quad$ $S' := $ ConstructInvariant($S - ms, p - mt$);
$\quad$ if ($S' = \{\}$) declare no failsafe f-tolerant program p' exists;
$\quad$ else $p' := $ ConstructTransitions($p - mt, S'$)
}

ConstructInvariant(S : state predicate, p : transitions)
// Returns the largest subset of S such that computations of p
$\quad\quad\quad\quad\quad\quad\quad\quad$ within that subset are infinite
$\quad$ return $largestfixpoint(X = (X \cap S) - \{s_0 \mid (\forall s_1 : s_1 \in X : (s_0, s_1) \notin p)\}$

ConstructTransitions(p : transitions, S : set of states)
$\quad$ { return $p - \{(s_0, s_1) : s_0 \in S \ \wedge \ s_1 \notin S\}$ }

Fig. 1. The synthesis algorithm for adding failsafe tolerance

In order to construct ms, the set of states from where safety can be violated by one or more fault transitions, first, we define $msInit$ as the finite set of states from where safety can be violated by a *single* fault transition. Note that $(s_0, s_1) \in spec$ means violation of the safety specification. Formally,

$$msInit : StatePred = \{s_0 \mid \exists s_1 : (s_0, s_1) \in f \wedge (s_0, s_1) \in spec\}$$

Now, we define a function, $RevReachStates$, that calculates a state predicate from where states of another finite set, rs, are reachable by fault transition. Formally,

$$RevReachStates(rs : StatePred) : StatePred =$$
$$\{s_0 \mid \exists s_1 : s_1 \in rs \wedge (s_0, s_1) \in f \wedge s_0 \notin rs\}$$

The following judgement helps the PVS type checker in discharging later proof obligations:

Judgement 4.1 : $RevReachStates$ has type of IncFunc.
We use the definition of smallest fixpoint in Section 4.1 to define the state predicate ms. Towards this end, we instantiate the initial set with $msInit$, and the r function with $RevReachStates$:

$$ms : StatePred = SmFix(msInit)(RevReachStates)$$

Then, we define the finite set of transitions, mt, that must be removed from p. These transitions are either transitions that may lead a computation to reach a state in ms or transitions that directly violate safety:

$$mt : Action = \{(s_0, s_1) \mid (s_1 \in ms \vee (s_0, s_1) \in spec)\}$$

The algorithm *Add_failsafe* removes the set ms from the invariant of the fault-intolerant program S. However, this removal may create **deadlock states**. The set of deadlock states in ds of program Z is denoted as follows:

$$DeadlockStates(Z)(ds : StatePred) : StatePred =$$
$$\{s_0 \mid s_0 \in ds : (\forall s_1 \mid s_1 \in ds : (s_0, s_1) \notin Z)\}$$

Judgement 4.2: $DeadlockStates(Z)$ has type of DecFunc.

We construct the invariant of the fault-tolerant program by removing the deadlock states to ensure that computations of fault-tolerant program are infinite (cf. Section 2.3). In general, we define $ConstructInvariant$ using largest fixpoint of a finite set X, that removes deadlock states of a given state predicate X:

$$ConstructInvariant(X, Z) : StatePred = LgFix(X)(DeadlockStates(Z))$$

The formal definition of the invariant of fault-tolerant program is as follows:

$$S' : StatePred = ConstructInvariant(S - ms, p - mt)$$

Finally, we construct the finite set of transitions of fault-tolerant program by removing the transitions that violate the closure of S':

$$p' : Action = p - mt - \{(s_0, s_1) \mid ((s_0, s_1) \in (p - mt)) \wedge (s_0 \in S' \wedge s_1 \notin S')\}$$

4.3   Specification of the Synthesis of Masking Tolerance

In this section, we describe how we formally specify the addition of masking fault-tolerance to a given program p. We reiterate the algorithm *Add_masking* (from [7,8]) in Figure 2. Note that we extensively *reuse* the formal definitions developed in Section 4.2 to model *Add_masking*.

```
Add_masking(p, f : transitions, S : state predicate, spec : specification)
{
    ms := smallestfixpoint(X  =  X ∪ {s₀ | (∃s₁ :
                           (s₀, s₁) ∈ f)   ∧    (s₁ ∈ X ∨ (s₀, s₁) violates spec) };
    mt := {(s₀, s₁) : ((s₁ ∈ ms) ∨ (s₀, s₁) violates spec) };
    S₁ := ConstructInvariant(S − ms, p − mt);
    T₁ := true − ms;
    repeat
        T₂, S₂ := T₁, S₁;
        p₁ := p|S₂ ∪ {(s₀, s₁) : s₀ ∉ S₂ ∧ s₀ ∈ T₂ ∧ s₁ ∈ T₂} − mt;
        T₁ := ConstructFaultSpan(T₂ − {s : S₁ is not reachable from s in p₁ }, f);
        S₁ := ConstructInvariant(S₂ ∧ T₁, p₁);
        if (S₁ = {} ∨ T₁ = {})
            declare no masking f-tolerant program p′ exists;
            exit
    until (T₁ = T₂ ∧ S₁ = S₂);

    For each state s : s ∈ T₁ :
        Rank(s) = length of the shortest computation prefix of p₁
                  that starts from s and ends in a state in S₁;
        p′ := {(s₀, s₁) : ((s₀, s₁) ∈ p₁) ∧ (s₀ ∈ S₁ ∨ Rank(s₀) > Rank(s₁))};
        S′ := S₁;
        T′ := T₁
}
ConstructFaultSpan(T : state predicate, f : transitions)
// Returns the largest subset of T that is closed in f.
{
    return largestfixpoint(X = (X ∩ T) − {s₀ : (∃s₁ : (s₀, s₁) ∈ f  ∧  s₁ ∉ X)})
}
```

Fig. 2. The synthesis algorithm for adding masking tolerance

As mentioned in Section 2, in addition of masking fault-tolerance, the requirement for preserving the liveness properties of a program is that the fault-tolerant program does not deadlock even in the presence of faults and it should recover to the invariant after a finite number of steps while preserving safety. Hence, we assume that the number of occurrences of faults in a computation is finite by an axiom in our PVS specification. This is the only axiom used in our work.

Axiom 4.3 : $\forall p : \forall c(p \cup f) : (\exists\, n \mid n \geq 0 : (\forall j \mid j \geq n : (c_j, c_{j+1}) \in p))$.

The main difficulty in formalizing *Add_masking* algorithm is modeling the repeat-until loop (cf. Figure 2).We model the algorithm in three phases: initialization, identifying the loop invariant, and termination conditions. This loop invariant includes two properties (1) the intermediate invariant at the start of the loop is a subset of S, the invariant of the fault-intolerant program, and (2) the intersection of ms and the intermediate fault-span at the start of the loop is the empty set. Hence, in Section 5.3, to verify the algorithm, first, we show these properties for the initial guess of invariant and fault-span. Then, we show that if these properties hold at the start of an iteration, they hold at the start of the subsequent iteration as well.

Initialization: To model the part of *Add_masking* before the loop, we define S_{init} and T_{init} as follows:

$$S_{init} : StatePred = ConstructInvariant(S - ms, p - mt)$$
$$T_{init} : StatePred = S_p - ms$$

The loop invariant: Now, we model the repeat-until loop. The value of the intermediate invariant (respectively, fault-span) at the start of the loop is S_2 (respectively, T_2). We recalculate the invariant and fault-span in the loop. Let the new values be S_1 and T_1 respectively. Now, we define S_1 and T_1 in terms of (arbitrary predicates) S_2 and T_2.

1. We define an intermediate program p_1 as follows. We require that for a transition (s_0, s_1) in p_1, the following conditions are satisfied: (1) if $s_0 \in S_2$ then $s_1 \in S_2$, (2) if $s_0 \in T_2$ then $s_1 \in T_2$. Moreover, p_1 does not contain any transition in mt. Formally

   $S_2 : StatePred$
   $T_2 : StatePred$
   $p_1 : Action = (p \mid S_2 \cup TS) - mt$, where
   $TS : StatePred = \{(s_0, s_1) \mid s_0 \notin S_2 \;\wedge\; s_0 \in T_2 \;\wedge\; s_1 \in T_2\}$

2. To formally specify construction of T_1, we first define the finite set of states from where closure of T_2 may be violated. Formally,

   $TNClose(X : StatePred) : StatePred =$
   $\qquad \{s_0 \mid \exists s_1 : s_0 \in X \;\wedge\; (s_0, s_1) \in f \;\wedge\; s_1 \notin X\}$.

   Then, we define the finite set of states from where S_2 is reachable. Formally,

   $TReach : StatePred = \{s \mid s \in T_2 \wedge reachable(S_2, T_2, p_1, s)\}$ where
   $reachable(S_2, T_2, p_1, s) : StatePred =$
   $\qquad \exists c(p_1) : ((s \in T_2) \;\wedge\; (s = c_0) \;\wedge\; \exists j : c_j \in S_2)$.

We now define $ConstructFaultspan$ as the largest subset of $TReach$ that is closed in f. Formally,

$T_1 = ConstructFaultspan(TReach)$, where
$ConstructFaultspan(X : StatePred) = LgFix(X)(TNClose)$

3. Since S_1 is a subset of T_1, we model the recalculation of invariant as follows:

$S_1 : StatePred = ConstructInvariant(S_2 \cap T_1)(p_1)$

Termination of the loop: We formalize the termination condition of the loop in the verification phase. More specifically, we prove that provided $(S_1 = S_2) \wedge (T_1 = T_2)$ is true, p_1 is failsafe and provides potential recovery from every state in fault-span.

5   Verification of the Synthesis Algorithms

In this section, we verify the soundness of the synthesis algorithms based on the formal specification in Section 4.

5.1   Verification of the Fixpoint Theory

In order to verify the soundness of the synthesis algorithms, we first prove the properties of fixpoint calculations (cf. Section 4.1) in theorems 5.4 and 5.5. Due to space limitation, we only state the theorems and we refer the reader to [15] for detailed formal proofs.

Theorem 5.4: Application of function g on the largest fixpoint of a finite set returns the empty set. Formally, $g(LgFix(x)(g)) = \emptyset$.

Theorem 5.5: $r(SmFix(x)(r)). = \emptyset$

5.2   Verification of the Synthesis of Failsafe Tolerance

In order to verify the soundness of $Add\_failsafe$ algorithm, we now prove that the synthesized program, p', satisfies the three conditions of the transformation problem stated in Section 3. More specifically, in Theorems 5.7 and 5.8, we prove the correctness of the first two conditions of the transformation problem. Then, in the remaining theorems, we show that the program synthesized by $Add\_failsafe$ is indeed failsafe fault-tolerant.

Observation 5.6: $S' \cap ms = \emptyset$.
Proof. After expanding the definition of S', $ConstructInvariant$, and $LgFix$, we need to prove: $\forall x : (\forall k : \ x \in Dec(k, S - ms)(DeadlockStates(p - mt)) \implies x \notin ms$. By instantiating k with 0, propositional simplification discharges the observation.   □

Theorem 5.7: $S' \subseteq S$.
Proof. Our strategy to prove this theorem is based on the fact that S' is made out of S by removing some states. After expanding the definition of S',

$ConstructInvariant$, and $LgFix$, we need to prove:

$\forall k : (\forall x : (x \in Dec(k, S - ms)(DeadlockStates(p - mt)) \Longrightarrow x \in S))$.

Towards this end, first, we instantiate k with zero. Then, after expanding the definitions, we need to prove $\forall x : (x \in S - ms \Longrightarrow x \in S)$, which is trivially true. □

Theorem 5.8: $p'|S' \subseteq p|S'$.

Theorem 5.9: S' is closed in p'. Formally, $closed(S', p')$.

Lemma 5.10: $\forall(s_0, s_1) : ((s_0, s_1) \in f \wedge s_1 \in ms) \Longrightarrow s_0 \in ms$.

Proof. The GRIND strategy discharges this lemma and theorems 5.8 and 5.9. □

Lemma 5.11: $DeadlockStates(p - mt)(S') = \emptyset$.

Proof. First, we expand the definitions of S' and $ConstructInvariant$. Then, we need to prove: $DeadlockDtates(p - mt)(LgFix(S - ms)(DeadlockStates(p - mt))) = \emptyset$. Using Theorem 5.4, we instantiate x with $LgFix(S - ms)$, and g with $DeadlockStates(p - mt)$ to complete the proof. □

Theorem 5.12: All computations of p' that start from a state in S' must be infinite. Formally, $DeadlockStates(p')(S') = \emptyset$.

Proof. In Lemma 5.11, we showed that all computations of $p - mt$ that start from a state in S' are infinite. Now we need to show that all the computations of $p - mt$ after removing the transitions that violate the closure of S' are still infinite. Obviously, removal of such transitions does not have anything to do with deadlock states, because the source of a transition that violates the closure must have been removed during the removal of deadlock states. Hence, the verification is only a sequence of expansions and propositional simplifications. □

Remark. Note that Theorem 5.12 is one of the instances where formalization of the fixpoint in Section 4.1 is used. More specifically, $DeadlockStates(p')(S')$ denotes the deadlock states in S' using program p'. We repeatedly remove these deadlock states. Hence, once the fixpoint is reached, there are no deadlock states.

Lemma 5.13: In the presence of faults, no computation prefix of failsafe tolerant program that starts from a state in S', reaches a state in ms. Formally,

$\forall j : (\forall c : prefix(p' \cup f, j) \mid c_0 \in S' : \forall k \mid k < j : c_k \notin ms)$.

Proof. After eliminating the universal quantifier on $c(p' \cup f)$ by skolemization, we proceed by induction on k. In the base case, $k = 0$, we need to prove $c_0 \in S' \Longrightarrow c_0 \notin ms$. The base case can be discharged using Observation 5.6. In induction step, we need to prove $(\forall n \mid n < j : (c_n, c_{n+1}) \in p' \cup f) \Longrightarrow (\forall k \mid k < j : c_k \notin ms \Rightarrow c_{k+1} \notin ms)$. From Lemma 5.10, we know that if the destination of a fault transition , (s_0, s_1), is in ms, then the source, s_0, is in ms as well. This means that if s_0 is not in ms then s_1 is not in ms either. We know that $c_k \notin ms$ and, hence, based on Lemma 5.10, $c_{k+1} \notin ms$. □

Theorem 5.14: Any prefix of any computation of failsafe tolerant program in the presence of faults that starts in S' does not violate safety. Formally,

$\forall j : \forall (c : prefix(p' \cup f), j \mid c_0 \in S') : \forall k \mid k < j : (c_k, c_{k+1}) \notin spec.$

Proof. In Lemma 5.13, we proved that no computation prefix of $p' \cup f$ that starts from a state in S' never reaches a state in ms. In addition, p' does not contain any transition that is in $spec$. Thus, a computation prefix of $p' \cup f$ that starts from a state in S' does not contain a transition in $spec$.   □

5.3   Verification of the Synthesis of Masking Tolerance

We verify the algorithm $Add\_masking$ based on the three phases that we modeled the algorithm in Section 4.3. More specifically, first, we show these properties for the initial guess of invariant and fault-span. Then, we show that if these properties hold at the start of an iteration, they hold at the start of the subsequent iteration as well:

Properties of initial values for the invariant and fault-span: Similar to Observation 5.6 and Theorem 5.7, we can prove the following theorems; note that these theorems show that the initial values of the invariant and fault-span satisfy the loop invariant:

Observation 5.15: $T_{init} \cap ms = \emptyset$.

Theorem 5.16: $S_{init} \subseteq T_{init}$.

Theorem 5.17: $S_{init} \subseteq S$.

Properties of the loop invariant: Similar to the verification of $Add\_failsafe$, we prove that the synthesized masking tolerant program satisfies the transformation problem by stating and proving a series of theorems and intermediate lemmas. First, we show the loop invariant, i.e., we show that if S_2 and T_2 satisfy the loop invariant then so do S_1 and T_1 (cf. Theorem 5.18). Then, we state and prove additional theorems about S_1 and T_1. Proofs of Theorems 5.18-5.21 are similar to the proofs of corresponding theorems in the verification of failsafe. Hence, we omit these proofs.

Theorem 5.18: $((T_2 \cap ms = \emptyset) \Rightarrow (T_1 \cap ms = \emptyset)) \land ((S_2 \subseteq S) \Rightarrow (S_1 \subseteq S))$

Theorem 5.19: $S_1 \subseteq T_1$.

Theorem 5.20 : $(p_1|S_2 \subseteq p|S_2) \Rightarrow (p_1|S_1 \subseteq p|S_1)$.

Theorem 5.21: $DeadlockStates(p_1)(S_1) = \emptyset$.

Theorem 5.22: The recalculated fault-span is closed in f. Formally, $closed(T_1, f)$.

Proof: The proof is similar to proof of Lemma 5.11. We know that $T_1 = ConstructFaultSpan(...) = LgFix(...)$. Using Theorem 5.4, in the definition of $LgFix$, we instantiate X with $TReach$, and g with $TNClose$ to complete the proof.   □

Properties at the termination of the loop: As mentioned in Section 4.3, we prove that provided $(S_1 = S_2) \land (T_1 = T_2)$ is true, p_1 is failsafe and provides potential recovery from every state in fault-span.

Theorem 5.23: $(S_1 = S_2) \Rightarrow closed(S_1, p_1)$.

Proof: Based on the fact that S_2 is closed in p_1 by construction, when $S_1 = S_2$, p_1 is closed in S_1 as well. Hence, by replacing S_1 by S_2, we complete the proof. ☐

Theorem 5.24: Any prefix of any computation of the masking tolerant program in the presence of faults does not violate safety. Formally, $((S_1 = S_2) \land (T_1 = T_2)) \Rightarrow \forall j : (\forall c : prefix(p_1 \cup f, j) \mid c_0 \in T_1 : \forall k \mid k < j : (c_k, c_{k+1}) \notin spec)$.
Proof: Proof is similar to proof of Theorem 5.14. ☐

Theorem 5.25: $(T_1 = T_2) \Rightarrow closed(T_1, p_1 \cup f)$.
Proof: Based on the fact that T_2 is closed in p_1 by construction, when $T_1 = T_2$, T_1 is closed in p_1 as well. From Theorem 5.22, we also know that $closed(T_1, f)$. Thus, using Theorem 5.22 and by replacing T_1 by T_2, we complete the proof. ☐

Theorem 5.26: After termination of the loop, for any state in fault-span, T_1, there exists a computation of p_1 that starts from that state and reaches the invariant, S_1. Formally,
$$((S_1 = S_2) \land (T_1 = T_2)) \Rightarrow (\forall s \mid s \in T_1 : reachable(S_1, T_1, p_1, s)).$$
Proof: First, we use Axiom 4.3 to show that there exists a suffix for every computation of $p_1 \cup f$ that contains no transition in f. After replacing T_1 and S_1 by T_2 and S_2 in the deducing part, we need to prove $\forall s \mid s \in T_1 : reachable(S_2, T_2, p_1, s)$. By expanding the definitions of T_1, $ConstructFaultSpan$, and $LgFix$ respectively, we need to prove:
$$\forall k : (s \in Dec(k, TReach)(TClose)) \Longrightarrow reachable(S_2, T_2, p_1, s)$$
By instantiation of k with 0, the **GRIND** strategy discharges the theorem. ☐

Finally, the fault-tolerant program, p' is obtained by removing cycles in p_1 that occur in states in $T_1 - S_1$. Hence, we can easily extend the theorems 5.20-5.25 to show that they hold for program p' as well. Moreover, in Theorem 5.26, the fact that the shortest path from a state in T_1 to a state in S_1 is preserved, and p' does not create deadlock states can be used to show that every computation of p' eventually reaches a state in S_1. For reasons of space, we omit the discussion of these proofs.

6   Discussion

Related work. In [16], Emerson and Clarke propose an algorithm that synthesizes a program from its temporal logic specification. Since then, other algorithms have been proposed in the literature [17,18,19]. In the previous work prior to [7], the input to synthesis algorithms is either an automaton or temporal logics specification and any modification in the specification requires synthesizing the new program from scratch. In contrast, the algorithms in [7] reuse the fault-intolerant program to synthesize the fault-tolerant version. This reusability helps to improve the time complexity to some extent. Thus, the algorithms proposed in [7] seem to be suitable candidates for practical implementation purposes. In [20], the authors introduce a set of heuristics for synthesizing distributed fault-tolerant programs in polynomial time. Based on the heuristics, Ebnenasir and Kulkarni have developed a tool for synthesizing fault-tolerant programs [11]. Therefore, by formal verification of the algorithms in [7], we gain more confidence on their practical implementations as well.

Advantages of mechanical verification of algorithms for the synthesis of fault-tolerant algorithms. Fault-tolerant systems are often in need of strong assurance. Mechanical verification is a reliable way to ensure that the fault-tolerance requirements of a system are met. We find that verification of algorithms for synthesis of fault-tolerance is a systematic and abstract way for formal verification of fault-tolerance.

High level of abstraction. The algorithms presented in [7] make no assumptions about the properties of the system, except that they have finite state space. This high level of abstraction enables the algorithms to be applicable to synthesize both finite state hardware and software systems. Our focus on formal verification of such abstract algorithms makes it possible to extend our work to verify other algorithms that are based on the ones in [7] for any system regardless of the platform and architecture. In addition, having the developed specification and verification in this paper, we can easily verify the extensions of the algorithms in [10, 20, 9] by reusing the specification developed in this paper.

Correctness of synthesized programs. Another advantage of verifying a synthesis algorithm rather than individual fault-tolerant programs is to guarantee that any synthesized program by the algorithm is correct by construction. This advantage makes us free from verification of individual synthesized programs.

Reusability of formal proofs. Although most of the related work on formal verification of fault-tolerance [1, 2, 3, 5] provide confidence in correctness of their concerns, reusing the formal proof of one, in verification of others is not quite convenient. Manual reusability of formal proofs is the first step to develop proof strategies. As an illustration, in Section 5.3, we showed how we manually reused the formal proofs of *Add_failsafe* to verify the soundness of *Add_masking*.

7   Conclusion and Future Work

In this paper, we focused on the problem of verifying transformation algorithms that generate fault-tolerant programs that are correct by construction. We considered two types of fault-tolerance properties, *failsafe* and *masking*. We would like to note that we have also verified the algorithm for synthesizing *nonmasking* fault-tolerant programs where the program recovers to states from where its specification is satisfied although safety may be violated during recovery [15].

The algorithms verified in this paper synthesize programs in the high atomicity model, where a process can read and write all variables in an atomic step. In [7, 8], authors have presented a non-deterministic algorithm for designing distributed programs. We have also verified that algorithm using PVS [15].

Since we focus on verification of the transformation algorithms, we note that our results ensure that the programs synthesized using these algorithms indeed satisfy their required fault-tolerance properties. Thus, our approach is more general than verifying a particular fault-tolerant program. Also, to verify the algorithms that synthesize failsafe and masking fault-tolerant programs, we developed a fixpoint library for finite sets. This library is expected to be applicable elsewhere.

In a broader context, the verification of the algorithms considered in this paper will assist us in verifying several other transformations. For example, in [9], the authors extend the algorithms in [7,8] to deal with multiple classes of faults. The algorithms in [7,8] have also been used to synthesize fault-tolerant distributed programs. As an illustration, we note that the algorithms in [20,10, 11] that are extensions of the algorithms in [7,8] have been used to synthesize solutions for several fault-tolerant programs including, Byzantine agreement, consensus, token ring, and alternating bit protocol. Thus, the theories developed in this paper are directly applicable to verify the transformation algorithms in [20,10,11,9] as well.

Our experience shows that significant number of proofs were reused. For instance, we manually reused proofs of failsafe tolerance to verify the soundness of synthesized masking tolerant programs. We expect to reuse many of the theorems and proofs in future verifications as well. Therefore, as a future work, one can develop *proof strategies* based on our experience in reusability of proofs.

References

1. Sam Owre, John Rushby, Natarajan Shankar, and Friedrich von Henke. Formal verification for fault-tolerant architectures: Prolegomena to the design of PVS. *IEEE Transactions on Software Engineering*, 21(2):107–125, February 1995.
2. Heiko Mantel and Felix C.Gärtner. A case study in the mechanical verification of fault-tolerance. Technical Report TUD-BS-1999-08, Department of Computer Science, Darmstadt University of Technology, 1999.
3. S. Qadeer and N. Shankar. Verifying a self-stabilizing mutual exclusion algorithm. In David Gries and Willem-Paul de Roever, editors, *IFIP International Conference on Programming Concepts and Methods (PROCOMET '98)*, pages 424–443, Shelter Island, NY, June 1998. Chapman & Hall.
4. E. W. Dijkstra. Self-stabilizing systems in spite of distributed control. *Communications of the ACM*, 17(11), 1974.
5. S. S. Kulkarni, J. Rushby, and N. Shankar. A case-study in component-based mechanical verification of fault-tolerant programs. *Proceedings of the 19th IEEE International Conference on Distributed Computing Systems Workshop on Self-Stabilization (WSS'99) Austin, Texas, USA*, pages 33–40, June 1999.
6. S. S. Kulkarni. *Component-based design of fault-tolerance*. PhD thesis, Ohio State University, 1999.
7. S. S. Kulkarni and A. Arora. Automating the addition of fault-tolerance. *Formal Techniques in Real-Time and Fault-Tolerant Systems*, 2000.
8. S. S. Kulkarni and A. Arora. Automating the addition of fault-tolerance. Technical Report MSU-CSE-00-13, Department of Computer Science and Engineering, Michigan State University, East Lansing, Michigan, 2001.
9. S. S. Kulkarni and A. Ebnenasir. Automated synthesis of multitolerance. IEEE Conference on Dependable and Network Systems *(DSN'04)*, 2004.

10. S. S. Kulkarni and A. Ebnenasir. Enhancing the fault-tolerance of nonmasking programs. *International Conference on Distributed Computing Systems*, 2003.
11. A. Ebnenasir and S. S. Kulkarni. A framework for automatic synthesis of fault-tolerance. http://www.cse.msu.edu/ sandeep/software/Code/synthesis-framework/.
12. B. Alpern and F. B. Schneider. Defining liveness. *Information Processing Letters*, 21:181–185, 1985.
13. A. Arora and M. G. Gouda. Closure and convergence: A foundation of fault-tolerant computing. *IEEE Transactions on Software Engineering*, 19(11):1015–1027, 1993.
14. S. Owre, N. Shankar, J. M. Rushby, and D. W. J. Stringer-Calvert. *PVS Language Reference, Version 2.4*. Computer Science Laboratory, SRI International, Menlo Park, CA, December 2001. URL: http://pvs.csl.sri.com/manuals.html.
15. Borzoo Bonakdarpour. Mechanical verification of automatic synthesis of fault-tolerant programs. Master's thesis, Michigan State University, 2004.
16. E.A. Emerson and E.M. Clarke. Using branching time temporal logic to synthesis synchronization skeletons. *Science of Computer Programming*, 2(3):241–266, 1982.
17. Z. Manna and P. Wolper. Synthesis of communicating processes from temporal logic specifications. *ACM Transactions on Programming Languages and Systems*, 6(1):68–93, 1984.
18. O. Kupferman and M.Y. Vardi. Synthesizing distributed systems. In *Proc. 16th IEEE Symp. on Logic in Computer Science*, July 2001.
19. P. Attie and E. Emerson. Synthesis of concurrent systems with many similar processes. *ACM Transactions on Programming Languages and Systems*, 20(1):51–115, 1998.
20. S. S. Kulkarni, A. Arora, and A. Chippada. Polynomial time synthesis of Byzantine agreement. *Symposium on Reliable Distributed Systems*, 2001.

Fully Automatic Binding-Time Analysis for Prolog[*]

Stephen-John Craig[1], John P. Gallagher[2], Michael Leuschel[1],
and Kim S. Henriksen[2]

[1] Department of Electronics and Computer Science,
University of Southampton, Highfield,
Southampton, SO17 1BJ, UK
{sjc02r, mal}@ecs.soton.ac.uk
[2] Department of Computer Science,University of Roskilde,[**]
P.O. Box 260, D-4000 Roskilde, Denmark
{jpg, kimsh}@ruc.dk

Abstract. Offline partial evaluation techniques rely on an annotated version of the source program to control the specialisation process. These annotations guide the specialisation and ensure the termination of the partial evaluation. We present an algorithm for generating these annotations automatically. The algorithm uses state-of-the-art termination analysis techniques, combined with a new type-based abstract interpretation for propagating the binding types. This algorithm has been implemented as part of the LOGEN partial evaluation system, along with a graphical annotation visualiser and editor, and we report on the performance of the algorithm for a series of benchmarks.

1 Introduction

The offline approach to specialisation has proven to be very successful for functional and imperative programming, and more recently for logic programming.

Most offline approaches perform a *binding-time analysis* (BTA) prior to the specialisation phase. Once this has been performed, the specialisation process itself can be done very efficiently [20] and with a predictable outcome.

Compared to online specialisation, offline specialisation is in principle less powerful (as control decisions are taken by the BTA *before* the actual static input is available), but much more efficient (once the BTA has been performed). This makes offline specialisation very useful for compiling interpreters [19], a key application of partial evaluation. However, up until now, no automatic BTA for logic programs has been fully implemented (though there are some partial implementations, discussed in Section 7), requiring users to manually annotate

---

[*] Work supported in part by European Framework 5 Project ASAP (IST-2001-38059).
[**] Roskilde authors supported in part by the IT-University of Copenhagen.

S. Etalle(Ed.): LOPSTR 2004, LNCS 3573, pp. 53–68, 2005.

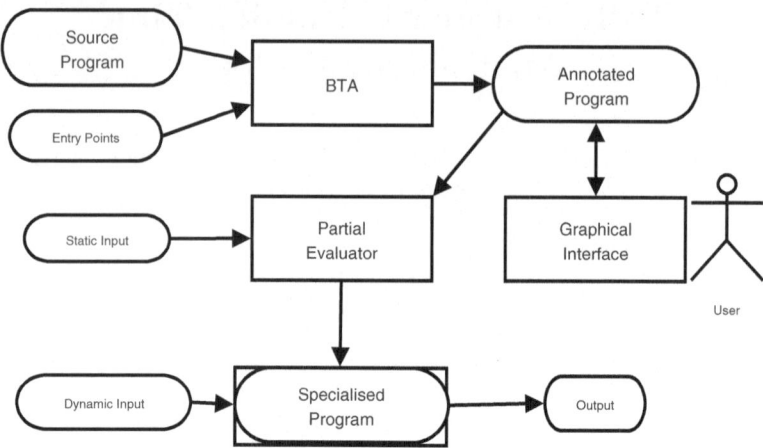

Fig. 1. The role of the BTA for offline specialisation using LOGEN

the program. This is an error-prone process, and requires considerable exper-
tise. Hence, to make offline specialisation accessible to a wider audience, a fully
automatic BTA is essential.

In essence, a *binding-time analysis* does the following: given a program and
a description of the input available for specialisation, it approximates all values
within the program and generates annotations that steer the specialisation process. The partial evaluator (or the compiler generator generating the specialised
partial evaluator) then uses the generated annotated program to guide the specialisation process. This process is illustrated in Fig. 1. The figure also shows
our new graphical editor which allows a user to inspect the annotations and fine
tune them if necessary.

To guide our partial evaluator the binding-time analysis must provide *binding
types* and *clause annotations*, which will now be described.

Binding Types
Each argument of a predicate in an annotated program is given a *binding type*
by means of *filter declarations*. A binding type indicates something about the
structure of an argument at specialisation time. The basic binding types are
usually known as *static* and *dynamic* defined as follows.

- **static:** The argument is definitely known at specialisation time;
- **dynamic:** The argument is possibly unknown at specialisation time.

We will see in Section 3 that more precise binding types can be defined by
means of regular type declarations, and combined with basic binding types.
For example, an interpreter may use an environment that is a partially static
data structure at partial evaluation time. To model the environment, e.g., as a
list of static names mapped to dynamic variables we would use the following
definition:

```
:- type binding = static / dynamic.
:- type list_env = [] ; [binding | list_env].
```

Through the filter declarations we associate binding types with arguments of particular predicates, as in the following example (taken from the inter_binding benchmark to be discussed in Section 6):

```
:- filter int(static, (type list_env), dynamic).
```

The filter declarations influence *global control*, since *dynamic* parts of arguments are generalised away (that is, replaced by fresh variables) and the known, *static* parts are left unchanged. They also influence whether arguments are "filtered out" in the specialised program. Indeed, static parts are already known at specialisation time and hence do not have to be passed around at runtime.

Clause Annotations

Clause annotations indicate how each call in the program should be treated during specialisation. Essentially, these annotations determine whether a call in the body of a clause is performed at specialisation time or at run time. Clause annotations influence the *local control* [22]. For the LOGEN system [20] the main annotations are the following.

- **Unfold:** The call is unfolded under the control of the partial evaluator. The call is replaced with the predicate body, performing all the needed substitutions
- **Memo:** The call is not unfolded, instead the call is generalised using the filter declaration and specialised independently
- **Call:** The call is fully executed without further intervention
- **Rescall:** The call is left unmodified in the residual code

2   Algorithm Overview

Implementing a fully automatic BTA is a challenging task for several reasons. First, the binding type information about the static and dynamic parts of arguments has to be propagated all throughout the program. Second, on has to decide how to treat each body call in the program. This has to be guided by termination issues (avoiding infinite unfolding) but also safety issues (avoiding calling built-ins that are not sufficiently instantiated). Furthermore, the decisions made about how to treat body calls in turn affect the propagation of the binding types, which in turn affect how body calls are to be treated. In summary, we need

- a precise way to propagate binding types, allowing for new types and partially static data,
- a way to detect whether the current annotations ensure safety and termination at specialisation time,
- and an overall algorithm to link the above two together.

Also, in case the current annotations do not ensure termination we need a way to identify the body calls that are causing the (potential) non-termination in order to update the annotations. For this we had to implement our own termination analyzer, based on the binary clause semantics [9]. To achieve a precise propagation of binding types we have used a new analysis framework [13] based on regular types and type determinization.

We now outline the main steps of our overall BTA algorithm depicted in Fig. 2. The input to the algorithm consists of a program, a set of binding types, and a filter declaration giving binding types to the entry query (the query with respect to which the program is to be partially evaluated). The core of the algorithm is a loop which propagates the binding types from the entry query with respect to the current clause annotations (step 1), generates the abstract binary program (steps 2 and 3) and checks for termination conditions (step 4).

If a call is found to be unsafe at step 4 (e.g. might not terminate) the annotations are modified accordingly. Initially, all calls are annotated as *unfold* (or *call* for built-ins), with the exception of imported predicates which are annotated as *rescall* (step 0). Annotations can be changed to *memo* or *rescall*, until termination is established. Termination of the main loop is ensured since there is initially only a finite number of *unfold* or *call* annotations, and each iteration of the loop eliminates one or more *unfold* or *call* annotation.

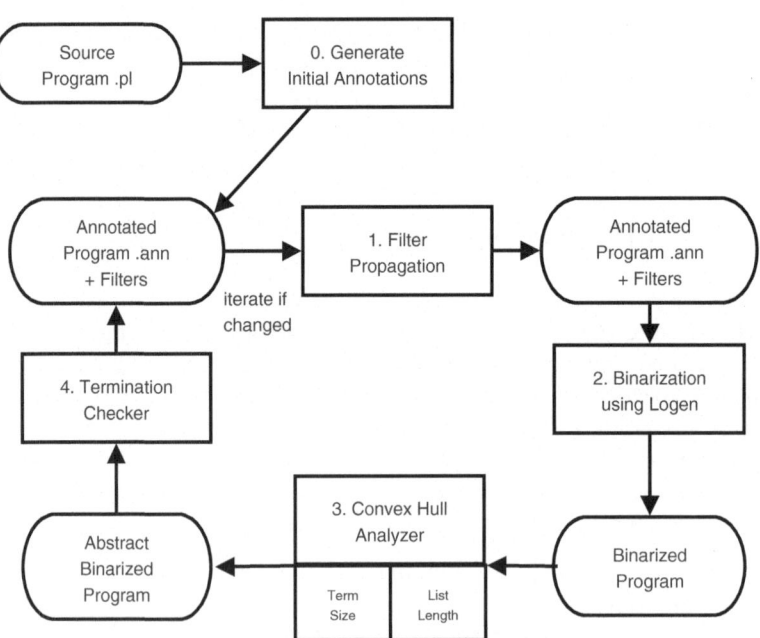

Fig. 2. Overview of the BTA algorithm

The decision on how to annotate calls to built-in predicates cannot be handled by the termination checker, but is guided by a definition of the allowed calling patterns, with respect to the given set of binding types. For instance, considering simple binding types *static* and *dynamic*, the call X > Y can be executed only when both X and Y are static, whereas the call X is Y can be executed where Y is static but X is dynamic (either known or unknown). Some built-ins have more than one allowed calling pattern; for example functor(T,F,N) can be executed if either T is static or both F and N are static. Whenever the binding types for a call to a built-in predicate do not match one of the allowed calling patterns, the call is marked *rescall*. Thus if no calling patterns are supplied for some built-in, then all calls to that built-in will be annotated *rescall*.

3   Binding Type Propagation

The basis of the BTA is a classification of arguments using abstract values. In this section we explain how to obtain such a classification for a given program and initial goal. Our method is completely independent of the actual binding types, apart from requiring that they should include the type *dynamic*. Usually *static* and *nonvar* are also included. A *binding-time division* is a set of filter declarations of the form $p(t_1, \ldots, t_n)$, where p/n is a program predicate and $t_1, \ldots, t_n$ are binding types. For the purpose of explanation we consider here only *monovariant* binding-time divisions, namely those in which there is not more than one filter declaration for each predicate. However, the algorithm has been extended to *polyvariant* binding-time divisions, which allow several filter declarations for each predicate.

A binding-time division defines the binding types occurring in each predicate call in an execution of the program for a given initial goal. This information in turn is used when determining which calls to unfold and which to keep in the residual programs. A binding-time division should be *safe* in the sense that every possible concrete call is described by some filter declaration in it.

The use of *static-dynamic* binding types was introduced for functional programs, and has been used in BTAs for logic programs [23]. However, a simple classification of arguments into "fully known" or "totally unknown" is often unsatisfactory in logic programs, where partially unknown terms occur frequently at runtime, and would prevent specialisation of many "natural" logic programs such as the vanilla meta-interpreter [15, 21] or most of the benchmarks from the DPPD library [18].

We outline a method of describing more expressive binding types and propagating them. The analysis framework is described elsewhere [13]. In this framework, modes (or "binding times") such as *static* and *dynamic* can be freely mixed with binding *types* such as lists.

Regular Binding Types
A regular type t is defined by a rule $t = f_1(t_{1,1}, \ldots, t_{1,m_1}); \ldots; f_n(t_{n,1}, \ldots, t_{n,m_n})$ where $f_1, \ldots, f_n$ are function symbols (possibly not distinct) and for all $1 \leq i \leq n$ and $1 \leq j \leq m_i$, m_i is the arity of f_i, and $t_{i,j}$ are regular types. The

interpretation of such rules is well understood in the framework of regular tree grammars or finite tree automata [10].

Instantiation modes including *static, dynamic* and *nonvar* can be coded as regular types, for a fixed signature. For example, if we assume that the signature is $\{[], [.|.], s, 0, v\}$ with the usual arities, then the definitions of the types *ground term (static), non-variables (nonvar)* and *any term (dynamic)* are as follows.

$$static = 0; []; [static|static]; s(static)$$
$$nonvar = 0; []; [dynamic|dynamic]; s(dynamic)$$
$$dynamic = 0; []; [dynamic|dynamic]; s(dynamic); v$$

The constant v is a distinguished constant not occurring in programs or goals. Note that v is not included in the types *static* and *nonvar*. Therefore any term of type *dynamic* is possibly a variable.

In addition to modes, regular types can describe common data structures. The set of all lists, for instance, is given as $list = []; [dynamic|list]$. We can describe the set of lists of list by the type $listlist = []; [list|listlist]$. Program-specific types such as the type of environments are also regular types.

$$binding = static/dynamic$$
$$list\_env = []; [binding|list\_env]$$

Type Determinization

We take a given set of regular types, and transform them into a set of *disjoint* regular types. This process is called *determinization* and is a standard operation on finite tree automata [10]. A set of disjoint types is represented by a set of type rules of the form $t = f_1(t_{1,1}, \ldots, t_{1,m_1}); \ldots; f_n(t_{n,1}, \ldots, t_{n,m_n})$ as before, but with the added condition that there are no two rules having an occurrence of the same term $f_i(t_{i,1}, \ldots, t_{i,m_i})$. Such a set of rules corresponds to a bottom-up deterministic finite tree automata [10]. The inclusion of the type *dynamic* ensures that the set of rules is *complete*, that is, that every term is a member of exactly one of the disjoint types.

For example, given the types *dynamic, static, nonvar* and *list* as shown above, determinization yields definitions of the disjoint sets of terms, which are (1) non-ground, non-variable non-lists, (2) non-ground lists, (3) ground lists, (4) variables and (5) ground non-lists. The rules defining these disjoint types are typically hard to read and would be difficult to write directly. For example, naming the above 5 types $q_1, \ldots, q_5$ respectively, the type rule for non-ground lists is $q_2 = [q_1|q_2]; [q_2|q_2]; [q_3|q_2]; [q_4|q_2]; [q_5|q_2]; [q_2|q_3]; [q_1|q_3]; [q_4|q_3]$. A more compact representation is actually used [13].

Types are abstractions of terms, and can be used to construct a domain for abstract interpretation [4, 7, 8, 16]. The advantage of determinized types is that we can propagate them more precisely than non-disjoint types. Overlapping types tend to lose precision. Suppose t_1 and t_2 are not disjoint; then terms that are in the intersection can be represented by both t_1 and t_2 and hence the two types will not be distinguishable wherever terms from the intersection can arise. In effect, a set of disjoint types contains, in such cases, separate types representing $t_1 \cap t_2$, $t_1 \setminus t_2$ and $t_2 \setminus t_1$. In the worst case, it can thus be seen that there is an exponential number of disjoint types for a given set of types. In practice, many of the intersections and set complements are empty and we find usually that the number of disjoint types is similar to the number of given types. Thus with disjoint types, we can obtain a more accurate representation of the set of terms that can appear in a given argument position, while retaining the intuitive, user-oriented notation of arbitrary types. In fact, the type declarations of LOGEN can be used without modification to construct an abstract domain.

The rules for a complete set of disjoint types define a *pre-interpretation* of the signature Σ, whose domain is the set of disjoint types. An abstract interpretation based on this pre-interpretation gives the least model over the domain [2, 3, 12]. This yields success patterns for each program predicate, over the disjoint types. That is, each predicate p/n has a set of possible success patterns $\{p(t_1^1, \ldots, t_n^1); \ldots; p(t_1^m, \ldots, t_n^m)\}$. A set of accurate call patterns can be computed from the model and an initial typed goal. We use the "magic-set" approach to obtain the calls, as described by Codish and Demoen [6]. This yields a set of "call patterns" for each predicate, say $\{p(s_1^1, \ldots, s_n^1); \ldots; p(s_1^k, \ldots, s_n^k)\}$. (Note that we could use a top-down analysis framework, but for analyses based on pre-interpretations, this would give exactly the same results).

Finally the filter for p/n derived from the set of calls is obtained by collecting all the possible types for each argument together. The set of call patterns $\{p(s_1^1, \ldots, s_n^1); \ldots; p(s_1^k, \ldots, s_n^k)\}$ yields the filter $p(\{s_1^1, \ldots, s_1^k\}, \ldots, \{s_n^1, \ldots, s_n^k\})$. For displaying to the user, if required, these filters can be translated back to a description in terms of the original types, rather than the disjoint types.

Analysing Annotated Programs

The standard methods for computing an abstract model and abstract call patterns have to be modified in our procedure, since some body calls may be marked as *memo* or *rescall*. That is, they are not to be unfolded but rather kept in the specialised program. This obviously affects propagation of binding types, since a call annotated as memo or rescall cannot contribute any answer bindings.

When building the abstract model of a program, we simply delete memo-ed and rescall-ed calls from the program, as they cannot contribute anything to the model. Let C be a conjunction of calls; then denote by $\overline{C}$ the conjunction obtained by deleting memo-ed and rescall-ed atoms from C. Let P be an annotated program; then we compute the success patterns for the program $\overline{P} = \{H \leftarrow \overline{B} \mid H \leftarrow B \in P\}$.

When deriving a call pattern, say for atom B_j in clause $H \leftarrow B_1, \ldots, B_j, \ldots$, we ignore the answers to memo-ed and rescall-ed calls occurring in $B_1, \ldots, B_{j-1}$. That is, we consider the clause $H \leftarrow \overline{B_1, \ldots, B_{j-1}}, B_j, \ldots$, when computing the calls to B_j.

4   Termination Checking

Without proper annotations in the source program, the specialiser may fail to terminate. There are two reasons for nontermination:

- **Local Termination:** Unfolding an unsafe call may fail to terminate or provide infinitely many answers.
- **Global Termination:** Even if local termination is ensured, the specialisation may still fail to terminate if it attempts to build infinitely many specialised versions of some predicate for infinitely many different static values.

We do not discuss global termination in this paper. We approach the *local termination* problem using the *binary clause semantics* [9], a representation of a program's computations that makes it possible to reason about loops and hence termination.

Binary Clause Semantics

Informally, the binary clause semantics of a program P is the set of all pairs of atoms (called binary clauses) $p(\bar{X})\theta \leftarrow q(\bar{t})$ such that p is a predicate, $p(\bar{X})$ is a most general atom for p, and there is a finite derivation (with leftmost selection rule) $\leftarrow p(\bar{X}), \ldots, \leftarrow (q(\bar{t}), Q)$ with computed answer substitution θ. In other words a call to $p(\bar{X})$ is followed some time later by a call to $q(\bar{t})$, computing a substitution θ.

We modify the semantics to include *program point* information for each call in the program. A clause $p(ppM, \bar{X})\theta \leftarrow q(ppN, \bar{t})$ details that the call $p(\bar{X})$ at program point ppM is followed sometime later by a call to $q(\bar{t})$ at program point ppN, computing a substitution θ. This extra precision is required to correctly identify the actual unsafe call.

To create the binary clause semantics we specialise a modified vanilla interpreter with respect to our source program. This allows us to easily adapt the semantics for the annotations by changing the rules of the interpreter.

For example, take the classic append program shown in Fig. 3. The transformation to binary clause semantics is shown in Fig. 4. The first clause represents a loop from the call app([A|B], C, [A|D]) at program point 0 back to itself with the arguments app(B, C, D), the second clause represents an infinite number of possible loops through the same point.

```
app([], B, B).
app([A|As], B, [A|Cs]) :- app(As, B, Cs).
```

Fig. 3. The append program

```
bin_solve_atom__2(0, app([A|B], C, [A|D]), app(B, C, D)).
bin_solve_atom__2(0, app([A|B], C, [A|D]), app(E, F, G)) :-
        bin_solve_atom__2(0, app(B, C, D), app(E, F, G)).
```

Fig. 4. The binary clause version of append from Fig. 3

Convex Hull Abstraction

The binary semantics is in general infinite, but we make a safe approximation of the set of binary clauses using abstract interpretation. We use a domain of convex hulls We use a domain of convex hulls (the convex hull analyser used in our implementation is derived from ones kindly supplied by Genaim and Codish [14]] and by Benoy, King and Mesnard [1]) to abstract the set of binary clauses with respect to a selected norm.

Our implementation currently uses two norms, term size as defined in Eq. 1 and list length as defined in Eq. 2. The use of only two norms effectively restricts ourcurrent implementation to handle only list-processing examples effectively; we are extending the system to derive the norms automatically from the propagated binding types, using techniques described in the literature [17, 27].

$$|t|_{term} = \begin{cases} 1 + \sum_{i=1}^{n} |t_i|_{term} & \text{if } t = f(t_1, ..., t_n) \\ 0 & otherwise \end{cases} \tag{1}$$

$$|t|_{list} = \begin{cases} 1 + |ts|_{list} & \text{if } t = [t|ts] \\ 0 & otherwise \end{cases} \tag{2}$$

Using such an abstraction, we obtain a finite set of binary clauses and a set of constraints representing a linear relationship between the sizes of the respective concrete arguments. Fig. 5 is the binary clause program for append, Fig. 4, abstracted using the domain of convex hulls with respect to the list norm.

```
bin_solve_atom(0, app(A,B,C), app(D,E,F)) :-
        [A = 1 + D, B = E, C = 1 + F,  D > = 0, E >= 0, F >= 0]
```

Fig. 5. Abstract Convex Hull of Fig. 4 using List norm

Checking Termination Criteria

In particular, loops are represented by binary clauses with the same predicate occurring in the head and body. Termination proofs require that for every abstract binary clause between p and p (at the same program point) there is a strict reduction in the size for some *rigid* argument. An argument is rigid if all of its instances have the same size with respect to the selected norm. We detect rigidity by examining the filters derived for the arguments, as illustrated below.

The constraints shown in Fig. 5 show a decrease in the first ($A = 1 + D$) and third argument ($C = 1 + F$). Given the initial filter declaration:

```
:- filter app(type list(dynamic), dynamic, dynamic).
```

The first argument is rigid with respect to the list norm, so termination is proven for this loop providing these binding types. If the filter specified was:

```
:- filter app(dynamic,type list(dynamic), dynamic).
```

Then the call would have to be marked unsafe and would be changed from **unfold** to **memo**, as there is no strict decrease in any rigid arguments.

5   Example

We demonstrate the binding-time analysis using the transpose example shown in Fig. 6. The program takes a matrix, represented as a list of lists, and transposes the rows and columns.

```
/* Created by Pylogen */
/* file: transpose.pl */
transpose(Xs,[]) :-  nullrows(Xs).
transpose(Xs,[Y|Ys]) :-   makerow(Xs,Y,Zs), transpose(Zs,Ys).

makerow([],[],[]).
makerow([[X|Xs]|Ys],[X|Xs1],[Xs|Zs]) :-  makerow(Ys,Xs1,Zs).

nullrows([]).
nullrows([[]|Ns]) :-  nullrows(Ns).
```

Fig. 6. Program for transposing a matrix

The initial filter declaration, providing the binding types of the entry point is :- filter transpose((type list(dynamic)), dynamic). The first argument is a list of *dynamic* elements, the length of the list will be known but the individual elements will not be known at specialisation time. The second argument is fully *dynamic*; it will not be given at specialisation time. All calls in the program are initially annotated as unfold. Using this initial annotation and the entry types for transpose we propagate the binding types throughout the program. The resultant binding types are shown in Fig. 7. The list structure has been successfully propagated through the clauses of the program.

The next stage of the algorithm looks for possibly non-terminating loops in the annotated program. The result is shown in Fig. 8. The binary clause representation of the program has been abstracted with respect to the list norm over the domain of convex hulls. Termination of each of the loops in Fig. 8 must show a strict decrease in any rigid argument. Based on the propagated binding types only the first argument of each predicate is rigid with respect to the list norm. The predicate makerow/3 has a strict decrease $(A=1.0+D)$, nullrows/1 also has a strict decrease $(A=1.0+B)$ but the recursive call to transpose has no decrease in a rigid argument and is unsafe.

```
:- filter   transpose((type list(dynamic)), dynamic).
:- filter   makerow((type list(dynamic)), dynamic, dynamic).
:- filter   nullrows((type list(dynamic))).
```

Fig. 7. Propagated filters for Fig. 6 using the initial filter transpose((type list(dynamic)), dynamic)

```
bin_solve_atom(3, makerow(A,B,C), makerow(D,E,F)) :-
        [A=1.0+D,D>=0.0,B=1.0+E,E>=0.0,C=1.0+F,F>=0.0].
bin_solve_atom(4, nullrows(A), nullrows(B)) :-
        [A=1.0+B,B>=0.0].
bin_solve_atom(2, transpose(A,B), transpose(C,D)) :-
        [B>D,C>=0.0,D>=0.0,A=C,B=1.0+D].


%% Loop at program point 2 is unsafe (transpose/2)
```

Fig. 8. Binary clause representation of Fig.6 abstracted over the domain of convex hulls with respect to the list norm

```
logen(transpose, transpose(A,[])) :-
        logen(unfold, nullrows(A)).
logen(transpose, transpose(A,[B|C])) :-
        logen(unfold, makerow(A,B,D)),
        logen(memo, transpose(D,C)).
logen(makerow, makerow([],[],[])).
logen(makerow, makerow([[A|B]|C],[A|D],[B|E])) :-
        logen(unfold, makerow(C,D,E)).
logen(nullrows, nullrows([])).
logen(nullrows, nullrows([[]|A])) :-
        logen(unfold, nullrows(A)).

:- filter    makerow((type list(dynamic)), dynamic, dynamic).
:- filter    nullrows((type list(dynamic))).
:- filter    transpose((type list(dynamic)), dynamic).
```

Fig. 9. Annotated version of Transpose from Fig. 6

Marking the offending unsafe call as *memo* removes the potential loop and further iterations through the algorithm produce no additional unsafe calls. The final output of the BTA algorithm is shown in Fig. 9.

6   Experimental Results

The automatic binding-time analysis detailed in this paper is implemented as part of the LOGEN partial evaluation system. The system has been tested using benchmarks derived from the DPPD benchmark library [18]. The figures in Table 1 present the timing results[1] from running the BTA on an unmodified program given an initial filter declaration. These benchmark examples along

---

[1] The execution time for the Original and Specialised code is based on executing the benchmark query 20,000 times on a 2.4Ghz Pentium with 512Mb running SICStus Prolog 3.11.1. The specialisation times for all examples was under 10ms.

Table 1. Benchmark Figures for Automatic Binding-Time Analysis

Benchmark	BTA	Original	Specialised	Relative Time
combined	3220ms	110ms	30ms	0.27
inter binding	1380ms	60ms	10ms	0.17
inter medium	1440ms	140ms	10ms	0.07
inter simple	2670ms	80ms	30ms	0.38
match	400ms	90ms	70ms	0.78
regexp	780ms	220ms	60ms	0.28
transpose	510ms	80ms	10ms	0.13

with the PYLOGEN system, shown in Fig. 10, can be downloaded from LOGEN website[2].

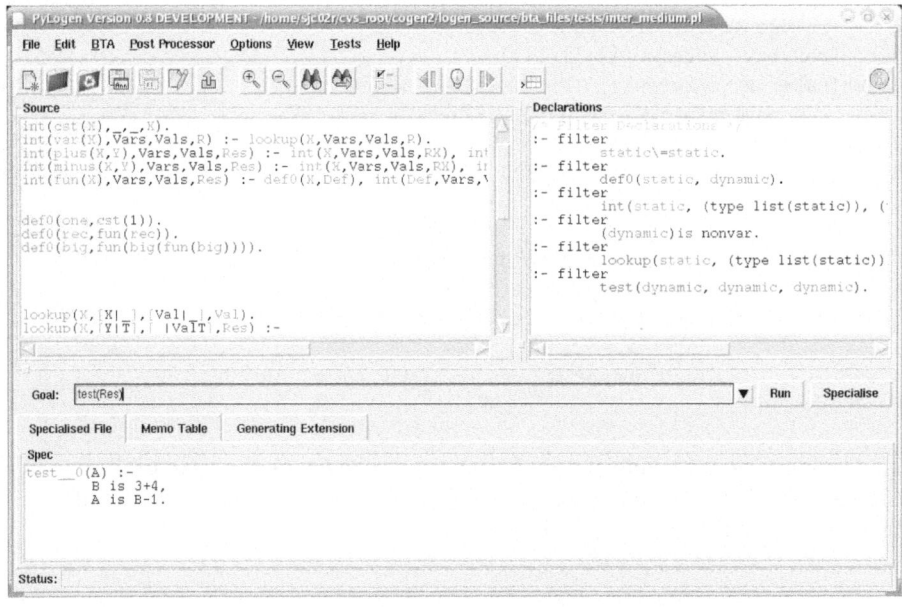

Fig. 10. Snapshot of a PYLOGEN session

- **combined** - A test case combining the inter medium, inter simple and regular expression interpreters.
- **inter binding** - An interpreter using a partially static data structure for an environment. In this example we combine the list and term norms.

---

[2] http://www.asap.soton.ac.uk/logen

- **inter medium** - An interpreter with the environment split into two separate lists, one for the static names the other for the dynamic values.
- **inter simple** - A simple interpreter with no environment, but contains a selection of built-in arithmetic functions.
- **match** - A string pattern matcher.
- **regexp** - An interpreter for regular expressions.
- **transpose** - A matrix transpose program.

7   Related Work and Conclusion

To the best of our knowledge, the first binding-time analysis for logic programming is [5]. The approach of [5] obtains the required annotations by analysing the behaviour of an *online* specialiser on the subject program. Unfortunately, the approach was overly conservative. Indeed, [5] decides whether or not to unfold a call based on the original program, not taking current annotations into account. This means that a call can either be completely unfolded or not at all. Also, the approach was never fully implemented and integrated into a partial evaluator.

In Section 6 of [20] a more precise BTA has been presented, which has been partially implemented. It is actually the precursor of the BTA here. However, the approach was not fully implemented and did not consider the issue of filter propagation (filters were supposed to be correct). Also, the identification of unsafe calls was less precise as it did not use the binary clause semantics with program points (i.e., calls may have been classified as unsafe even though they were not part of a loop).

[26] is probably the most closely related work to ours. This work has a lot in common with ours, and we were unaware of this work while developing our present work.[3] Let us point out the differences. Similar to [20], [26] was not fully implemented (as far as we know, based on the outcome of the termination analysis, the user still had to manually update the annotations by hand) and also did not consider the issue of filter propagation. Also, [26] cannot handle the `nonvar` annotation (this means that, e.g., it can only handle the vanilla interpreter if the call to the object program is fully static). However, contrary to [20], and similar to our approach, [26] does use the binary clause semantics. It even uses program point information to identify non-terminating calls. However, we have gone one step further in using program point information, as we will only look for loops from one program point back to itself. Take for example the following program:

```
p(a) :- q(a).          q(a) :- q(b).          q(b) :- q(b).
```

Both our approach and [26] will mark the call `q(a)` as unfoldable and the call `q(b)` in clause 3 as unsafe. However, due to the additional use of program points,

---

[3] Thanks for reviewers of LOPSTR'04 for pointing this work out to us.

we are able to mark the call q(b) in clause 2 as unfoldable (as there is no loop from that program point back to itself), whereas we believe that [26] will mark it as unsafe. We believe that this extra precision may pay off for interpreters. Finally, due to the use of our meta-programming approach we can handle the full LOGEN annotations (such as call, rescall, resif,...) and can adapt our approach to compute memoisation loops and tackle global termination.

The papers [24, 25, 28] describe various BTAs for Mercury, even addressing issues such as modularity and higher-order predicates. An essential part of these approaches is the classification of unifications (using Mercury's type and mode information) into tests, assignments, constructions and deconstructions. Hence, these works cannot be easily ported to a Prolog setting, although some ideas can be found in [28].

Currently our implementation guarantees correctness and termination at the local level, and correctness but not yet termination at the global level. However, the framework can very easily be extended to ensure global termination as well. Indeed, our binary clause interpreter can also compute memoisation loops, and so we can apply exactly the same procedure as for local termination. Then, if a memoised call is detected to be unsafe we have to mark the non-decreasing arguments as dynamic. Finally, as has been shown in [11], one can actually relax the strict decrease requirement for global termination (i.e., one can use $\leq$ rather than $<$), provided so-called "finitely partitioning" norms are used.

Acknowledgements. Thanks to Dan Elphick for his work on the Python mode for Logen.

References

1. F. Benoy, A. King, and F. Mesnard. Computing Convex Hulls with a Linear Solver. *Theory and Practice of Logic Programming*, January 2004.
2. D. Boulanger and M. Bruynooghe. A systematic construction of abstract domains. In B. Le Charlier, editor, *Proc. First International Static Analysis Symposium, SAS'94*, volume 864 of *Springer-Verlag Lecture Notes in Computer Science*, pages 61–77, 1994.
3. D. Boulanger, M. Bruynooghe, and M. Denecker. Abstracting s-semantics using a model-theoretic approach. In M. Hermenegildo and J. Penjam, editors, *Proc. 6th International Symposium on Programming Language Implementation and Logic Programming, PLILP'94*, volume 844 of *Springer-Verlag Lecture Notes in Computer Science*, pages 432–446, 1994.
4. M. Bruynooghe and G. Janssens. An instance of abstract interpretation integrating type and mode inferencing. In R. Kowalski and K. Bowen, editors, *Proceedings of ICLP/SLP*, pages 669–683. MIT Press, 1988.
5. M. Bruynooghe, M. Leuschel, and K. Sagonas. A polyvariant binding-time analysis for off-line partial deduction. In C. Hankin, editor, *Proceedings of the European Symposium on Programming (ESOP'98)*, LNCS 1381, pages 27–41. Springer-Verlag, April 1998.

6. M. Codish and B. Demoen. Analysing logic programs using "Prop"-ositional logic programs and a magic wand. In D. Miller, editor, *Proceedings of the 1993 International Symposium on Logic Programming, Vancouver.* MIT Press, 1993.

7. M. Codish and B. Demoen. Deriving type dependencies for logic programs using multiple incarnations of Prop. In B. Le Charlier, editor, *Proceedings of SAS'94, Namur, Belgium,* 1994.

8. M. Codish and V. Lagoon. Type dependencies for logic programs using ACI-unification. *Theoretical Computer Science,* 238(1-2):131–159, 2000.

9. M. Codish and C. Taboch. A semantic basic for the termination analysis of logic programs. *The Journal of Logic Programming,* 41(1):103–123, 1999.

10. H. Comon, M. Dauchet, R. Gilleron, F. Jacquemard, D. Lugiez, S. Tison, and M. Tommasi. *Tree Automata Techniques and Applications.* http://www.grappa.univ-lille3.fr/tata, 1999.

11. S. Decorte, D. De Schreye, M. Leuschel, B. Martens, and K. Sagonas. Termination analysis for tabled logic programming. In N. Fuchs, editor, *Proceedings of the International Workshop on Logic Program Synthesis and Transformation (LOPSTR'97),* LNCS 1463, pages 111–127, Leuven, Belgium, July 1998.

12. J. Gallagher, D. Boulanger, and H. Sağlam. Practical model-based static analysis for definite logic programs. In J. W. Lloyd, editor, *Proc. of International Logic Programming Symposium,* pages 351–365, 1995.

13. J. P. Gallagher and K. Henriksen. Abstract domains based on regular types. In V. Lifschitz and B. Demoen, editors, *Proceedings of the International Conference on Logic Programming (ICLP'2004),* volume 3132 of *LNCS.* Springer Verlag, 2004.

14. S. Genaim and M. Codish. Inferring termination conditions of logic programs by backwards analysis. In *International Conference on Logic for Programming, Artificial intelligence and reasoning,* volume 2250 of *Springer Lecture Notes in Artificial Intelligence,* pages 681–690, 2001.

15. P. Hill and J. Gallagher. Meta-programming in logic programming. In D. M. Gabbay, C. J. Hogger, and J. A. Robinson, editors, *Handbook of Logic in Artificial Intelligence and Logic Programming,* volume 5, pages 421–497. Oxford Science Publications, Oxford University Press, 1998.

16. K. Horiuchi and T. Kanamori. Polymorphic type inference in prolog by abstract interpretation. In *Proc. 6th Conference on Logic Programming,* volume 315 of *Springer-Verlag Lecture Notes in Computer Science,* pages 195–214, 1987.

17. V. Lagoon, F. Mesnard, and P. J. Stuckey. Termination analysis with types is more accurate. In C. Palamidessi, editor, *Proceedings of Logic Programming, 19th International Conference, ICLP 2003,* volume 2916 of *Springer-Verlag Lecture Notes in Computer Science,* pages 254–268, 2003.

18. M. Leuschel. The ECCE partial deduction system and the DPPD library of benchmarks. Obtainable via http://www.ecs.soton.ac.uk/~mal, 1996-2002.

19. M. Leuschel, S.-J. Craig, M. Bruynooghe, and W. Vanhoof. Specializing interpreters using offline partial deduction. In M. Bruynooghe and K.-K. Lau, editors, *Program Development in Computational Logic,* LNCS 3049, pages 341–376. Springer-Verlag, 2004.

20. M. Leuschel, J. Jørgensen, W. Vanhoof, and M. Bruynooghe. Offline specialisation in Prolog using a hand-written compiler generator. *Theory and Practice of Logic Programming,* 4(1):139–191, 2004.

21. B. Martens and D. De Schreye. Two semantics for definite meta-programs, using the non-ground representation. In K. R. Apt and F. Turini, editors, *Meta-logics and Logic Programming,* pages 57–82. MIT Press, 1995.

22. B. Martens and J. Gallagher. Ensuring global termination of partial deduction while allowing flexible polyvariance. In L. Sterling, editor, *Proceedings ICLP'95*, pages 597–613, Kanagawa, Japan, June 1995. MIT Press.
23. T. Mogensen and A. Bondorf. Logimix: A self-applicable partial evaluator for Prolog. In K.-K. Lau and T. Clement, editors, Logic Program Synthesis and Transformation. *Proceedings of LOPSTR'92*, pages 214–227. Springer-Verlag, 1992.
24. W. Vanhoof. Binding-time analysis by constraint solving: a modular and higher-order approach for Mercury. In M. Parigot and A. Voronkov, editors, *Proceedings of LPAR'2000*, LNAI 1955, pages 399–416. Springer-Verlag, 2000.
25. W. Vanhoof and M. Bruynooghe. Binding-time analysis for Mercury. In D. De Schreye, editor, *Proceedings of the International Conference on Logic Programming ICLP'99*, pages 500–514. MIT Press, 1999.
26. W. Vanhoof and M. Bruynooghe. Binding-time annotations without binding-time analysis. In R. Nieuwenhuis and A. Voronkov, editors, *Logic for Programming, Artificial Intelligence, and Reasoning, 8th International Conference*, LNCS 2250, pages 707–722. Springer-Verlag, 2001.
27. W. Vanhoof and M. Bruynooghe. When size does matter. In A. Pettorossi, editor, *Logic Based Program Synthesis and Transformation, 11th International Workshop, LOPSTR 2001*, Springer-Verlag Lecture Notes in Computer Science, pages 129–.147, 2001.
28. W. Vanhoof, M. Bruynooghe, and M. Leuschel. Binding-time analysis for Mercury. In M. Bruynooghe and K.-K. Lau, editors, *Program Development in Computational Logic*, LNCS this Volume. Springer-Verlag, 2004.

Logical Mobility and Locality Types

Jonathan Moody

Carnegie Mellon University
jwmoody@cs.cmu.edu

Abstract. We present a type theory characterizing the mobility and
locality of program terms in a distributed computation. The type theory of our calculus is derived from logical notions of necessity ($\Box A$) and
possibility ($\Diamond A$) of the modal logic $S4$ via a Curry-Howard style isomorphism. Logical worlds are interpreted as sites for computation, accessibility corresponds to dependency between processes at those sites.
Necessity ($\Box A$) describes terms of type A which have a structural kind
of mobility or location-independence. Possibility ($\Diamond A$) describes terms
of type A located somewhere, perhaps at a remote site. The modalities
$\Box$ and $\Diamond$ are defined in a clean, orthogonal manner, leading to a simple account of mobility and higher-order functions. For illustration, we
assume an execution environment with each location distinguished by a
mutable store. Here modal types ensure that store addresses never es-
cape from the location where they are defined, eliminating a source of
runtime errors. We speculate as to other advantages or trade-offs of this
disciplined style of distributed programming.

1 Introduction and Motivation

We claim that modal logic with necessity ($\Box A$) and possibility ($\Diamond A$) can serve
as the basis of a *location-aware* type theory for distributed computation. We
present a statically typed calculus derived from a natural deduction formulation
of $S4$ modal logic — derived, in the sense that programs correspond to proof
terms, and types to propositions. The modal propositions $\Box A$ ("mobile A") and
$\Diamond A$ ("remote A") capture spatial properties of terms relevant to distributed
computation. Mobility and locality are explicitly recognized, but the particular
locations involved remain abstract.

We then give an operational interpretation compatible with the intuition that
types $\Box A$ and $\Diamond A$ denote mobility and locality, respectively. Our operational
model assumes a number of definite locations (computation sites) distinguished
by fixed resources, as well as some indefinite or interchangeable locations. We
consider mutable stores as an example of a fixed resource. To illustrate this application, we consider an extension of the pure $S4$ theory with mutable references
and a simple form of effect typing.

The logical reading of the typing rules leads naturally to the following operational interpretation: $\Box$ elimination spawns a freely mobile term of type $\Box A$ for
evaluation at an arbitrary, indefinite location, and $\Diamond$ elimination sends a mobile

S. Etalle(Ed.): LOPSTR 2004, LNCS 3573, pp. 69–84, 2005.

fragment of code to a definite location where a remote resource of type $\Diamond A$ resides. Our intuitions are validated when we show type safety for the semantics. Only terms known to be portable (free of store dependencies) are moved between locations.

While it is desirable to insulate the programmer from the details of scheduling and communication in a distributed program, spatial considerations are entwined with certain language constructs at the level of implementation. A memory address or file handle, for example, is meaningful only at a particular machine. Implementation techniques such as remote references (proxy objects) and a clever marshalling scheme allow a language designer to conceal these exceptional cases. But this has costs in terms of complexity and performance. Rather, we choose to consider programs based on a simpler kind of mobility. The type theory of $S4$ is a static characterization of this class of programs — those that respect the locality of fixed resources without recourse to runtime mechanisms for creating and managing remote references.

In this work, we focus on the logical origins of mobility and locality, presenting the type theory, and exploring its application to distributed programming. But it is important to note that, from an *operational* perspective, the behaviors we describe are not novel. Our process spawning model is similar to futures of Multilisp [13], and jumping (or something similar) is a feature of many mobile process calculi such as Mobile Ambients [6], DPI [9], and others [19, 17]. Jagannathan [10] calls it a "communication-passing" style. In section 6, we discuss other distributed calculi, their approach to modeling locations, and their static type theories (if any). Most closely related are calculi due to Jia and Walker [12, 11], and Murphy *et. al* [21, 22]. These authors give a distributed interpretation to the modalities $\Box A$ and $\Diamond A$ — one based on $S5$ semantics (as opposed to $S4$). Though the methodologies are similar, the calculus derived from $S4$ is qualitatively different, both in terms of execution model and the programming discipline it imposes.

In section 2 we present an overview of the logical foundations of the type theory, referring to prior work [18]. We then define the calculus and its type system in section 3, justifying the typing rules by reference to logical meanings of $\Box$ and $\Diamond$. In section 4, we give an operational semantics and prove its type safety. In sections 5 and 6 we reflect on the programming discipline of mobility and locality types and how this solution is related to others. Proofs and some remarks on our examples are available in a companion technical report [16].

2   Logical Preliminaries

Modal logic is built on a foundational assumption that truth is "localized". The Kripke semantics for a classical modal logic ascribes to each world w a local valuation function $V_w(A_0)$ for the atomic propositions. Thus proposition A_0 may be true at world w but false at w'. This localized conception of truth is what gives modal logic the capacity to describe distributed computation. In a constructive formulation, we no longer have localized truth valuations, but proofs of a certain form may be portable, establishing the truth of A in the context of assumptions true at any accessible world. Others proofs may be tied to a particular world. When removed from that local context, they no longer establish truth of A.

The types, syntax, and static semantics of our calculus are derived from a constructive formalization of modal logic developed by Pfenning and Davies [18]. This was chosen over other intuitionistic formalisms, such as Simpson's [20], since proof reduction and substitution have simple explanations, and the logic does not rely on explicit reasoning about worlds and accessibility. The Pfenning/Davies formalism is based on three primitive judgments on A, a proposition: A true, meaning that A is locally true "here"; A valid, meaning that A true holds in *every* accessible world; and A poss, meaning that A true holds in *some* accessible world. Validity (A valid) is also commonly referred to as necessary truth. These judgments and the propositions $A \to B$ (implication), $\Box A$ (necessity), and $\Diamond A$ (possibility) are defined in relationship to one another, culminating in a natural deduction system for a modal logic supporting axioms characteristic of constructive S4. The primary judgments are $\Delta; \Gamma \vdash A$ true and $\Delta; \Gamma \vdash A$ poss, where Δ are assumptions of the form A_i valid, and Γ are assumptions A_i true.

The intuition behind our application of modal logic to distributed programming is the following: If, following the Curry-Howard approach, we interpret propositions as types and proofs as programs, it is also quite natural to interpret the logical worlds as sites for computation. Proofs of validity (A valid) correspond to mobile, portable terms. And proofs of possibility (A poss) correspond to computations that produce a term in some definite, perhaps remote, location. An extended discussion of the background and logical motivation of the calculus can be found in the technical report [15].

3   Modal Type Theory and Calculus

The syntax of terms M and types A is given in figure 1. We call the fragment with types $A \to B$, $\Box A$ and $\Diamond A$ the core calculus. To support interesting examples, we include several extensions: generic effectful computation characterized by the monadic type $\bigcirc A$, and mutable references ref A as store-effects. We also assume a set of base types nat, bool, 1 (unit type), *etc.*

Corresponding to the judgments A true and A poss of the modal deduction system, we have typing judgments $M : A$ and $M \div A$, respectively. To characterize local, effectful computations we add a third form of judgment $M \rightsquigarrow A$. We summarize the typing judgments and their informal readings:

Judgment	Significance
$\Delta; \Gamma \vdash M : A$	M has type A here (local pure term)
$\Delta; \Gamma \vdash M \rightsquigarrow A$	M produces result of type A here (local effects)
$\Delta; \Gamma \vdash M \div A$	M produces result somewhere (non-localized comp.)

The hypothetical form(s) $\Delta; \Gamma \vdash M : A$, *etc.* are made in the context of some mobile variables u :: $A \in \Delta$, corresponding to assumptions A valid, and local

	Types (A, B)	Syntactic Forms (M, N)
Local	$A \to B$ $1, \mathtt{bool}, \mathtt{nat}$	$\mathtt{x} \mid \lambda \mathtt{x}{:}A\,.\,M \mid M\,N$ $() \mid \mathtt{true} \mid \mathtt{false} \mid$ (defn. elided...)
Spatial	$\Box A$ $\Diamond A$	$\mathtt{u} \mid \mathtt{box}\,M \mid \mathtt{let\,box}\,\mathtt{u} = M\,\mathtt{in}\,N$ $\mathtt{dia}\,M \mid \mathtt{let\,dia}\,\mathtt{x} = M\,\mathtt{in}\,N$
Effects	$\bigcirc A$ $\mathtt{ref}\,A$	$\mathtt{comp}\,M \mid \mathtt{let\,comp}\,\mathtt{x} = M\,\mathtt{in}\,N$ $\mathtt{ref}\,M \mid \,!M \mid M := N$

Fig. 1. Types and terms of the modal calculus

variables $\mathtt{x} : A \in \Gamma$ corresponding to assumptions A true. The typing rules are presented in figure 2.

Locations are implicit in the local context Γ, in the following sense: $\Delta; \Gamma \vdash M : A$ means M has type A *in a location where* local bindings for Γ are available. Thus certain forms of judgment have a special significance. $\Delta; \cdot \vdash M : A$, means that $M : A$ *any* place via weakening on Γ. This form of typing derivation corresponds to a proof of A valid in the deduction system. By analogy, $\Delta; \mathtt{x} : B \vdash M \div A$, means that $M \div A$ holds *in a location where* $\mathtt{x} : B$.

3.1 Spatial Content of Typing

Neither the deductive formalism [18] nor the typing rules involve locations explicitly, but a few of the typing rules nonetheless have spatial content, by virtue of interaction between the local context Γ, and judgments $M : A$, $M \div A$, *etc.* For example, rule $\Box I$ states that mobile terms are those which depend only on other mobile terms in Δ. Effects are prohibited under $\mathtt{box}\,M$ by requiring $M : A$.[1] The elimination form allows us to bind such a term to $\mathtt{u} :: A$ in Δ. Such variables have a scope extending beyond the confines of a single location, so it is essential that only mobile values be bound to $\mathtt{u} :: A$.

$$\frac{\Delta; \cdot \vdash M : A}{\Delta; \Gamma \vdash \mathtt{box}\,M : \Box A}\ \Box I \qquad \frac{\Delta; \Gamma \vdash M : \Box A \quad \Delta, \mathtt{u} :: A; \Gamma \vdash N : B}{\Delta; \Gamma \vdash \mathtt{let\,box}\,\mathtt{u} = M\,\mathtt{in}\,N : B}\ \Box E$$

The rule $\bigcirc E$ describes binding the result of a local computation $M : \bigcirc A$ to a local variable $\mathtt{x} : A$. Of course, some variables in Γ could be bound to values dependent on prior effects. Under the assumption that effects are not destructive, it is sound to retain the local context Γ in typing $\Delta; \Gamma, \mathtt{x} : A \vdash N \leadsto B$.

$$\frac{\Delta; \Gamma \vdash M : \bigcirc A \quad \Delta; \Gamma, \mathtt{x} : A \vdash N \leadsto B}{\Delta; \Gamma \vdash \mathtt{let\,comp}\,\mathtt{x} = M\,\mathtt{in}\,N \leadsto B}\ \bigcirc E$$

---

[1] This might be weakened to allow some benign, non-observable classes of effects, but executing I/O effects at an arbitrary location leads to unpredictable behavior.

$$\text{Mobile Context} \quad \Delta ::= \cdot \mid \Delta, \mathsf{u}{::}A$$
$$\text{Local Context} \quad \Gamma ::= \cdot \mid \Gamma, \mathsf{x}{:}A$$

$\boxed{\Delta; \Gamma \vdash M : A}$

$$\frac{}{\Delta; \Gamma, \mathsf{x} : A, \Gamma' \vdash \mathsf{x} : A} \; hyp \qquad \frac{}{\Delta, \mathsf{u} :: A, \Delta'; \Gamma \vdash \mathsf{u} : A} \; hyp^*$$

$$\frac{\Delta; \Gamma, \mathsf{x} : A \vdash M : B}{\Delta; \Gamma \vdash \lambda \mathsf{x}{:}A.\, M : A \to B} \to I \qquad \frac{\Delta; \Gamma \vdash M : A \to B \quad \Delta; \Gamma \vdash N : A}{\Delta; \Gamma \vdash M\,N : B} \to E$$

$$\frac{\Delta; \cdot \vdash M : A}{\Delta; \Gamma \vdash \mathsf{box}\, M : \Box A} \; \Box I \qquad \frac{\Delta; \Gamma \vdash M : \Box A \quad \Delta, \mathsf{u} :: A; \Gamma \vdash N : B}{\Delta; \Gamma \vdash \mathsf{let\, box\, u} = M \,\mathsf{in}\, N : B} \; \Box E$$

$$\frac{\Delta; \Gamma \vdash M \mathbin{\sim} A}{\Delta; \Gamma \vdash \mathsf{comp}\, M : \bigcirc A} \; \bigcirc I \qquad \frac{\Delta; \Gamma \vdash M \div A}{\Delta; \Gamma \vdash \mathsf{dia}\, M : \Diamond A} \; \Diamond I$$

$\boxed{\Delta; \Gamma \vdash M \mathbin{\sim} A}$

$$\frac{\Delta; \Gamma \vdash M : A}{\Delta; \Gamma \vdash M \mathbin{\sim} A} \; comp \qquad \frac{\Delta; \Gamma \vdash M : \bigcirc A \quad \Delta; \Gamma, \mathsf{x} : A \vdash N \mathbin{\sim} B}{\Delta; \Gamma \vdash \mathsf{let\, comp\, x} = M \,\mathsf{in}\, N \mathbin{\sim} B} \; \bigcirc E$$

$$\frac{\Delta; \Gamma \vdash M : A}{\Delta; \Gamma \vdash \mathsf{ref}\, M \mathbin{\sim} \mathsf{ref}\, A} \; talloc \qquad \frac{\Delta; \Gamma \vdash M : \Box A \quad \Delta, \mathsf{u} :: A; \Gamma \vdash N \mathbin{\sim} B}{\Delta; \Gamma \vdash \mathsf{let\, box\, u} = M \,\mathsf{in}\, N \mathbin{\sim} B} \; \Box E_c$$

$$\frac{\Delta; \Gamma \vdash M : \mathsf{ref}\, A}{\Delta; \Gamma \vdash\, !M \mathbin{\sim} A} \; tget \qquad \frac{\Delta; \Gamma \vdash M : \mathsf{ref}\, A \quad \Delta; \Gamma \vdash N : A}{\Delta; \Gamma \vdash M := N \mathbin{\sim} 1} \; tset$$

$\boxed{\Delta; \Gamma \vdash M \div A}$

$$\frac{\Delta; \Gamma \vdash M : A}{\Delta; \Gamma \vdash M \div A} \; poss \qquad \frac{\Delta; \Gamma \vdash M : \Diamond A \quad \Delta; \mathsf{x} : A \vdash N \div B}{\Delta; \Gamma \vdash \mathsf{let\, dia\, x} = M \,\mathsf{in}\, N \div B} \; \Diamond E$$

$$\frac{\Delta; \Gamma \vdash Q \mathbin{\sim} A}{\Delta; \Gamma \vdash Q \div A} \; poss' \qquad \frac{\Delta; \Gamma \vdash M : \Box A \quad \Delta, \mathsf{u} :: A; \Gamma \vdash N \div B}{\Delta; \Gamma \vdash \mathsf{let\, box\, u} = M \,\mathsf{in}\, N \div B} \; \Box E_p$$

$$\frac{\Delta; \Gamma \vdash M : \bigcirc A \quad \Delta; \Gamma, \mathsf{x} : A \vdash N \div B}{\Delta; \Gamma \vdash \mathsf{let\, comp\, x} = M \,\mathsf{in}\, N \div B} \; \bigcirc E_p$$

Fig. 2. Typing rules for the core modal calculus extended with effects. Allocation, dereference, update of reference cells are considered effectful computations. Rules for base types, other type constructors, *etc.* are omitted since they are orthogonal and defined in the usual ways under local term typing ($\Delta; \Gamma \vdash M : A$). The diagram illustrates subsumptions between the judgments (*poss*, *poss'* and *comp*)

Finally, $\Diamond E$ describes the binding of a remote term value to a local variable x : A. For this to be sound, it must be the case that the continuation $\Delta; x : A \vdash N \div B$ be well-formed at the remote location. This is ensured by restricting the local context to a single binding x : A available at some remote location. The $\Diamond I$ rule allows us to encapsulate a term $M \div A$ as a remote term $\Diamond A$.

$$\frac{\Delta; \Gamma \vdash M \div A}{\Delta; \Gamma \vdash \mathsf{dia}\, M : \Diamond A} \Diamond I \qquad \frac{\Delta; \Gamma \vdash M : \Diamond A \quad \Delta; x : A \vdash N \div B}{\Delta; \Gamma \vdash \mathsf{let}\, \mathsf{dia}\, x = M \,\mathsf{in}\, N \div B} \Diamond E$$

3.2   Examples

The definition of $\Box A$ (mobility) is orthogonal to the rest of the type constructors; even lexically scoped closures of type nat $\rightarrow$ nat can be mobile $\Box$(nat $\rightarrow$ nat). This is more powerful than ad-hoc restrictions on mobility based on the form of types.

```
let plusk : □nat -> □(nat -> nat) =
  (λ x : □ nat .
    let box k = x in
      box (λ y : nat . y + k))
(* incr a mobile function *)
let box incr :: nat -> nat = plusk (box 1)
```

Moving the closure representation of incr is sound since we know the free variable k :: nat in box $(\lambda y{:}nat\,.\,y + k)$ is bound to a mobile value.

Mobile terms (box $M : \Box A$) are Γ-closed and free of local dependencies. They can be evaluated at *any* location without regard to local resources. The elimination form let box u = box M in N spawns M for evaluation in an independent process (at an arbitrary location). It is straightforward to introduce parallelism with box and let box. Consider the Fibonacci function, implemented in a recursive fashion:

```
let fib : □nat -> nat =
    mfix f . λ bn .
        let box n = bn in
      if n < 2 then n
          else let box f1 = box f (box (n-1)) in
        let box f2 = box f (box (n-2)) in
              f1 + f2
in fib (box 5)
```

Here the definition of f must itself be mobile, since f occurs under box. The typing rule for mobile fixpoint mfix requires that the body be Γ-closed analogous to the rule $\Box I$. Fixpoint operators are described formally in a companion technical report [16].

Values of type $\Diamond A$ can be used to model locations with special roles during computation. Type A describes the resource/interface provided by that site. Non-trivial values of this type must be obtained through a primitive binding mechanism. We can form a term $\mathtt{dia}\,M : \Diamond A$ in the source language, but M is only "remote" in a trivial sense.

```
(* rqueue : ◇({insert:nat->○unit, ...}) *)
let rqueue = bind_queue ... in

(* insert (x : □nat) into rqueue *)
let box v = x in
let dia q = rqueue in (* jump to queue location *)
  let comp () = q.insert v in
  ...
```

The actual location of `rqueue` is hidden by the type constructor $\Diamond$, so the binding mechanism is free to choose which location will provide the service. Our type discipline requires that the code sent to the remote location be free of any dependence on local bindings in Γ with the exception of q itself, which can be bound upon arrival. See [16] for further discussion of primitive remote resources.

4   Operational Interpretation

4.1   Model of Locations

We now formalize the operational semantics in a way that is consistent with the logical readings of $\Box A$ and $\Diamond A$ described above. The semantics should reflect clearly the spatial distribution of program fragments, so that communication (movement) of terms is evident. To this end we introduce processes $\langle l : M \rangle$ consisting of a term M labeled uniquely by l. The semantics should also represent concretely the distinguishing features of each location. In this instance, locations are distinguished by a store H mapping addresses a to values. Finally, processes are placed in structured configurations C that reflect the relationships between processes, stores, and other processes. See figure 3.

The notation $[H \vDash P]$ represents a collection of processes P executing inside a definite location under the store H. Some processes have no definite location, only a placement $\langle l : M \rangle \lhd C$ relative to other processes C. If one thinks of processes as worlds of a Kripke model, the connective $\lhd$ can be viewed as an assertion of accessibility. For example, $[H \vDash P] \lhd C$ means that processes C are accessible from P.

$$
\begin{array}{rl}
\text{Store} & H ::= \cdot \mid H[a \mapsto \overline{V}] \\[2mm]
\text{Co-located Processes} & P ::= \cdot \mid P, \langle l : M \rangle \\[1mm]
\text{Configuration} & C ::= \cdot \mid \langle l : M \rangle \lhd C \mid [H \vDash P] \lhd C
\end{array}
$$

Fig. 3. Runtime Structures: processes, stores, and configurations

$$\text{Runtime Term} \quad M, N ::= \ldots \mid l \mid @l \mid a$$

$$\text{Mobile Context} \quad \Delta ::= \cdot \mid \Delta, \mathtt{u} :: A \mid \Delta, l :: A$$

$$\text{Local Context} \quad \Gamma ::= \cdot \mid \Gamma, \mathtt{x} : A \mid \Gamma, a : A \mid \Gamma, @l : A$$

$$\frac{\Delta = \Delta_1, l :: A, \Delta_2}{\Delta; \Gamma \vdash l : A} \; res \qquad \frac{\Gamma = \Gamma_1, @l : A, \Gamma_2}{\Delta; \Gamma \vdash @l \div A} \; loc \qquad \frac{\Gamma = \Gamma_1, a : A, \Gamma_2}{\Delta; \Gamma \vdash a : \mathtt{ref}\, A} \; addr$$

$$\boxed{\Delta \vdash^c C : \Gamma}$$

$$\frac{\Delta; \cdot \vdash M : A \quad \Delta, l :: A \vdash^c C : \Gamma}{\Delta \vdash^c \langle l : M \rangle \lhd C : \Gamma} \; indef \qquad \frac{}{\Delta \vdash^c \cdot : \cdot} \; none$$

$$\frac{\Delta \vdash^c C : \Gamma \quad \Delta; \Gamma \vdash^s H : \Gamma^H \quad \Delta; \Gamma, \Gamma^H \vdash^c P : \Gamma'}{\Delta \vdash^c [H \vDash P] \lhd C : \Gamma', \Gamma} \; location$$

$$\boxed{\Delta; \Gamma \vdash^c P : \Gamma'}$$

$$\frac{\Delta; \Gamma \vdash^c P : \Gamma' \quad \Delta; \Gamma \vdash M \div A}{\Delta; \Gamma \vdash^c P, \langle l : M \rangle : \Gamma', @l : A} \; proc \qquad \frac{}{\Delta; \Gamma \vdash^c \cdot : \cdot} \; empty$$

$$\boxed{\Delta; \Gamma \vdash^s H : \Gamma'}$$

$$\Delta; \Gamma \vdash^s H : \Gamma' \iff \forall a \in \mathrm{Dom}(H \cup \Gamma') \, . \; \Delta; \Gamma, \Gamma' \vdash H(a) : \Gamma'(a)$$

Fig. 4. Runtime terms, generalized typing contexts, and configuration typing

We permit process labels and store addresses in terms at runtime. Process labels occur in two forms: l and $@l$. Both refer to a process $\langle l : M \rangle$ but l denotes the result value of a mobile process and $@l$ denotes the value "at" process l (which may not be mobile). Typing contexts Δ and Γ are generalized to account for labels and addresses. We provide typing rules for these new syntactic forms in figure 4.

A configuration C is well-formed iff $\cdot \vdash^c C : \Gamma$. That is, all processes in C are well-formed, and the processes P at definite locations $[H \vDash P]$ have types given by Γ. See figure 4 for the definition. There are subsidiary judgments for typing stores $\Delta; \Gamma \vdash^s H : \Gamma'$, and co-located processes $\Delta; \Gamma \vdash^c P : \Gamma'$. The label-binding structure of a configuration is determined by accessibility ($\lhd$). The form $\langle l : M \rangle \lhd C$ binds $l :: A$ in the subsequent portion C. The form $[H \vDash P] \lhd C$ binds the labels $l_i : A_i$ due to C in the processes P. Local store addresses a defined by H are also bound in P.

4.2   Substitution and Values

We adopt the definitions of substitution from Pfenning and Davies [18] with trivial extensions to account for labels and store addresses. There are multiple forms of substitution, two of which are relevant here. $[\![M/\mathtt{u}]\!]$ is the substitution of a mobile term for u and $[M/\mathtt{x}]$ is substitution of a local term for $\mathtt{x}$. They are defined in the usual compositional way, avoiding variable capture. Labels and store addresses denote syntactically closed terms, so $[\![M/\mathtt{u}]\!]@l = @l$, for example. Because of this, we can say that substitution acts *locally* (within a single process). Variables of the two sorts have different typing properties so the relevant substitution properties are subtly different.

Lemma 1 (Substitution Properties).

$$\Delta; \cdot \vdash M : A \;\wedge\; \Delta, \mathtt{u} :: A, \Delta'; \Gamma \vdash N : B \;\implies\; \Delta, \Delta'; \Gamma \vdash [\![M/\mathtt{u}]\!]N : B$$
$$\Delta; \cdot \vdash M : A \;\wedge\; \Delta, \mathtt{u} :: A, \Delta'; \Gamma \vdash N \backsim B \;\implies\; \Delta, \Delta'; \Gamma \vdash [\![M/\mathtt{u}]\!]N \backsim B$$
$$\Delta; \cdot \vdash M : A \;\wedge\; \Delta, \mathtt{u} :: A, \Delta'; \Gamma \vdash N \div B \;\implies\; \Delta, \Delta'; \Gamma \vdash [\![M/\mathtt{u}]\!]N \div B$$

$$\Delta; \Gamma \vdash M : A \wedge \Delta; \Gamma, \mathtt{x} : A, \Gamma' \vdash N : B \;\implies\; \Delta; \Gamma, \Gamma' \vdash [M/\mathtt{x}]N : B$$
$$\Delta; \Gamma \vdash M : A \wedge \Delta; \Gamma, \mathtt{x} : A, \Gamma' \vdash N \backsim B \;\implies\; \Delta; \Gamma, \Gamma' \vdash [M/\mathtt{x}]N \backsim B$$
$$\Delta; \Gamma \vdash M : A \wedge \Delta; \Gamma, \mathtt{x} : A, \Gamma' \vdash N \div B \;\implies\; \Delta; \Gamma, \Gamma' \vdash [M/\mathtt{x}]N \div B$$

Proof: straightforward, by induction on the typing derivation for N. The property is established for derivations of $N : B$ first, then $N \backsim B$ assuming the former case, then $N \div B$ assuming substitution properties hold in both the former cases. □

Substitutions $[\![M/\mathtt{u}]\!]N$ and $[M/\mathtt{x}]N$ are only properly defined for terms M satisfying $M : A$. For example, $[\![\mathtt{let\,dia\,x} = M \mathtt{\,in\,} N/\mathtt{u}]\!]$ is undefined. Terms $M \backsim A$ and $M \div A$ have different logical properties which are not respected by ordinary substitution. Special forms of substitution can be defined for these cases (see [18]), but our operational semantics is designed so that only $[\![M/\mathtt{u}]\!]N$ and $[M/\mathtt{x}]N$ are required.

The values of the calculus are as follows, eliding values of base type which are standard. Local values correspond to the typing judgment $\Delta; \Gamma \vdash V : A$ (or $V \backsim A$). General values correspond to $\Delta; \Gamma \vdash V^* \div A$.

Local Value $V ::= \mathtt{x} \;|\; \mathtt{u} \;|\; \lambda \mathtt{x}{:}A.\,M \;|\; \mathtt{box}\,M \;|\; \mathtt{dia}\,M \;|\; \mathtt{comp}\,M \;|\; a \;|\; \ldots$

Value $V^* ::= @l \;|\; V$

To achieve more concurrency, we treat labels l as pseudo-values, though they can be reduced further by synchronizing on the result of process l. We use the notation $\overline{V}$ to denote local value *or* label l.

4.3   Reduction Rules

We use evaluation context notation to specify where reduction steps may occur inside of terms; $\mathcal{R}[\,N\,]$ denotes a term decomposed into context $\mathcal{R}[\;]$ and subterm N. Any well-formed term has one or more decompositions. Non-uniqueness arises from the treatment of labels r. Pseudo-values $\overline{V}$ occur throughout the definition of contexts and redices, so $M = l\,N$ is decomposed as either $\mathcal{R} = [l]\,N$ (function position) or $\mathcal{R} = l\,\mathcal{R}'$ (argument position).

We present the reduction rules $C \implies C'$ in a way that elides unchanged, irrelevant parts of the configuration. For example, the rule $\langle l : M \rangle \implies \langle l : M' \rangle$ applies to any single process, in a definite location $[H \models \ldots]$ or not. See figure 5.

Eval. Ctxt. $\mathcal{R} ::= [\,] \mid \mathcal{R}\,N \mid \overline{V}\,\mathcal{R} \mid \mathtt{let\,box\,u} = \mathcal{R}\,\mathtt{in}\,N$
$\mid \mathtt{let\,dia\,x} = \mathcal{R}\,\mathtt{in}\,N \mid \mathtt{let\,dia\,x} = \mathtt{dia}\,\mathcal{R}\,\mathtt{in}\,N$
$\mid \mathtt{let\,comp\,x} = \mathcal{R}\,\mathtt{in}\,N \mid \mathtt{let\,comp\,x} = \mathtt{comp}\,\mathcal{R}\,\mathtt{in}\,N$
$\mid \mathtt{ref}\,\mathcal{R} \mid !\mathcal{R} \mid \mathcal{R} := N \mid a := \mathcal{R}$

---

letbox $\langle l_1 : \mathcal{R}[\,\mathtt{let\,box\,u} = \mathtt{box}\,M\,\mathtt{in}\,N\,]\rangle \Longrightarrow \langle l_2 : M\rangle \lhd \langle l_1 : \mathcal{R}[\,[\![l_2/u]\!]N\,]\rangle$
(where l_2 **fresh**)

syncr $\langle l_2 : \overline{V}\rangle \lhd \ldots \langle l_1 : \mathcal{R}[\,l_2\,]\rangle \Longrightarrow \langle l_2 : \overline{V}\rangle \lhd \ldots \langle l_1 : \mathcal{R}[\,\overline{V}\,]\rangle$

syncl $\langle l_1 : \mathcal{R}[\,\mathtt{let\,dia\,x} = \mathtt{dia}\,(@l_2)\,\mathtt{in}\,N\,]\rangle \lhd \ldots [H \vDash \langle l_2 : \overline{V}\rangle]$
$\Longrightarrow \langle l_1 : @l_3\rangle \lhd \ldots [H \vDash \langle l_2 : \overline{V}\rangle, \langle l_3 : \mathcal{R}[\,[\overline{V}/x]N\,]\rangle]$
(where l_3 **fresh**)

resolve $\langle l_1 : \mathcal{R}[\,\mathtt{let\,dia\,x} = \mathtt{dia}\,(@l_2)\,\mathtt{in}\,N\,]\rangle \lhd \ldots \langle l_2 : @l_3\rangle$
$\Longrightarrow \langle l_1 : \mathcal{R}[\,\mathtt{let\,dia\,x} = \mathtt{dia}\,(@l_3)\,\mathtt{in}\,N\,]\rangle \lhd \ldots \langle l_2 : @l_3\rangle$

letdia $\langle l_1 : \mathcal{R}[\,\mathtt{let\,dia\,x} = \mathtt{dia}\,\overline{V}\,\mathtt{in}\,N\,]\rangle$
$\Longrightarrow \langle l_1 : \mathcal{R}[\,[\overline{V}/x]N\,]\rangle$

---

letcomp $H \vDash \langle l : \mathcal{R}[\,M\,]\rangle \quad\Longrightarrow H \qquad \vDash \langle l : \mathcal{R}[\,[\overline{V}/x]N\,]\rangle$
(where $M = \mathtt{let\,comp\,x} = \mathtt{comp}\,\overline{V}\,\mathtt{in}\,N$)

alloc $H \vDash \langle l : \mathcal{R}[\,\mathtt{ref}\,\overline{V}\,]\rangle \Longrightarrow H[a \mapsto \overline{V}] \vDash \langle l : \mathcal{R}[\,a\,]\rangle$
(where a **fresh**)

get $H \vDash \langle l : \mathcal{R}[\,!a\,]\rangle \quad\Longrightarrow H \qquad \vDash \langle l : \mathcal{R}[\,H(a)\,]\rangle$

set $H \vDash \langle l : \mathcal{R}[\,a := \overline{V}\,]\rangle \Longrightarrow H[a \mapsto \overline{V}] \vDash \langle l : \mathcal{R}[\,(\,)\,]\rangle$

---

app $\langle l : \mathcal{R}[\,(\lambda x{:}A\,.\,M)\,\overline{V}\,]\rangle \Longrightarrow \langle l : \mathcal{R}[\,[\overline{V}/x]M\,]\rangle$
$\ldots \Longrightarrow \ldots$

Fig. 5. Reduction rules, organized by category. There are spatial reductions associated with the modalities which allow interaction between processes, as well as pure and effectful local reductions

The most revealing reduction rules are those governing $\Box$ and $\Diamond$ introduction and elimination. This is where the *spatial* content of the calculus is found, and our semantics permits creation and interaction between processes in these rules. To reduce $(\mathtt{let\,box\,u} = \mathtt{box}\,M\,\mathtt{in}\,N)$, we spawn an independent process l_2 to carry out the evaluation of subterm M. The spawned process l_2 is placed outside of a definite location, reflecting the fact that M may be evaluated *anywhere*. The rule *syncr* allows retrieving the mobile result value of such a process. Reducing $(\mathcal{R}[\,\mathtt{let\,dia\,x} = \mathtt{dia}\,@l_2\,\mathtt{in}\,N\,])$ involves sending $\mathcal{R}[\,]$ and N to the specific location where $\langle l_2 : \overline{V}\rangle$ resides. Notice that the value $\overline{V}$ is never moved outside $[H \vDash \ldots]$, though it is duplicated in the fresh process l_3. Rule *resolve* allows traversing chains of indirection to locate a remote value, and *letdia* covers the trivial case of a local term.

There are also pure and effectful local reduction steps. The local reductions involve only one process, and, in the latter case, the local store H. Reductions associated with additional base types, products $(A \times B)$, sums $(A + B)$, *etc.* would be in this family.

4.4   Properties

Type preservation and progress theorems hold for our semantics; mobility $(\Box A)$ and locality $(\Diamond A)$ types ensure that our distributed programs are safe. This would be unremarkable but for the presence of certain localized terms in our semantics — the store addresses a. The criterion for well-formed configurations specifies that addresses bound by store H only occur in processes P inside the definite location $[H \vDash P]$. The modal type discipline ensures that programs respect the locality of store addresses.

For well-formed decompositions $\mathcal{R}[M]$, there is an inversion lemma which allows us to conclude M is also well-formed. This is a standard property for evaluation contexts, but in our case M might satisfy more than one of the three typing judgments. Some decompositions are ruled out by typing, $\mathcal{R}[M] : B$ and $M \sim A$, for example, are incompatible.

Lemma 2 (Context Typing Inversion).

$$\Delta; \Gamma \vdash \mathcal{R}[M] : B \implies \exists A . \Delta; \Gamma \vdash M : A$$
$$\Delta; \Gamma \vdash \mathcal{R}[M] \sim B \implies \exists A . \Delta; \Gamma \vdash M : A \ \lor \ \Delta; \Gamma \vdash M \sim A$$
$$\Delta; \Gamma \vdash \mathcal{R}[M] \div B \implies \exists A . \Delta; \Gamma \vdash M : A \ \lor \ \Delta; \Gamma \vdash M \sim A \ \lor \ \Delta; \Gamma \vdash M \div A$$

Proof: Each is proved in order, assuming the prior one(s) hold. Individually, we proceed by induction on evaluation contexts. For each form of context, we can invert to the relevant typing rule or a subsumption rule (*comp, poss,* or *poss'*) applies.   □

Under certain conditions, a context $\mathcal{R}[\ ]$ can be moved from one environment to another because its constituent subterms are Γ-closed. That is, $\mathcal{R}[\ ]$ may be independent of local bindings and mobile, just as a term M encapsulated as box M is mobile.

Lemma 3 (Mobile Continuations). *Assume a context $\mathcal{R}[\ ]$ such that $\Delta; \Gamma \vdash M \div A \implies \Delta; \Gamma \vdash \mathcal{R}[M] \div B$ (for any M). Then $\Delta, \Delta'; \Gamma' \vdash N \div A \implies \Delta, \Delta'; \Gamma' \vdash \mathcal{R}[N] \div B$ (for any Δ', Γ', and N).*

Proof: by induction on the structure of $\mathcal{R}$. Due to typing, the only possibility is $\mathcal{R} = \mathtt{let\,dia\,x_1 = dia}\,\mathcal{R}'\,\mathtt{in}\,N_1$. By inversion on typing we can apply the IH to $\mathcal{R}'$. Also by inversion, $\Delta; \mathsf{x}_1 : A_1 \vdash N_1 \div B$. The conclusion follows by Δ-weakening and the $\Diamond E$ typing rule.   □

Theorem 1 (Type Preservation). *If $\vdash^c C : \Gamma$ and $C \implies C'$ then $\vdash^c C' : \Gamma'$ for some Γ' which extends Γ.*

Proof: by cases on derivation of $C \implies C'$, using the definition of $\vdash^c C : \Gamma$, inversion on typing derivations, and substitution properties. In the critical cases where fragments of the program move from one process to another, these mobile terms, values, or contexts remain well-formed via weakening (of Δ and/or Γ). See the companion technical report [16] for selected cases. $\square$

To establish progress, we first enumerate the redices of the semantics and give a decomposition lemma. The category $\langle localredex \rangle$ corresponds to local reduction rules. But note that reducing l or $\mathtt{let\ dia}\,x = \mathtt{dia}\,@l\ \mathtt{in}\,N$ requires interaction with other processes.

Definition 1 (Redex and Local Redex).

$$\langle redex \rangle ::= l \mid \mathtt{let\ dia}\,x = \mathtt{dia}\,@l\ \mathtt{in}\,N \mid \langle localredex \rangle$$
$$\langle localredex \rangle ::= (\lambda x{:}A\,.\,M)\,\overline{V} \mid \mathtt{let\ box}\,u = \mathtt{box}\,M\ \mathtt{in}\,N$$
$$\mid\ \mathtt{let\ dia}\,x = \mathtt{dia}\,\overline{V}\ \mathtt{in}\,N \mid \mathtt{let\ comp}\,x = \mathtt{comp}\,\overline{V}\ \mathtt{in}\,N$$
$$\mid\ \mathtt{ref}\,\overline{V} \mid !a \mid a := \overline{V}$$

Lemma 4 (Decomposition). *Well-formed terms M are either values, or can be decomposed as $\mathcal{R}[N]$ where N is of the form $\langle redex \rangle$.*

$$\Delta; \Gamma \vdash M : B \implies M = V \quad \vee \quad \exists \mathcal{R}\,.\,M = \mathcal{R}[\langle redex \rangle]$$
$$\Delta; \Gamma \vdash M \sim B \implies M = V \quad \vee \quad \exists \mathcal{R}\,.\,M = \mathcal{R}[\langle redex \rangle]$$
$$\Delta; \Gamma \vdash M \div B \implies M = V^* \quad \vee \quad \exists \mathcal{R}\,.\,M = \mathcal{R}[\langle redex \rangle]$$

Proof: Each is proved in order, assuming the prior one(s) hold. The proof is by induction on typing derivations. If M is a value V (or $M = V^*$), we are done. Otherwise, M is a redex in the empty context (trivial decomposition), or we invert the relevant typing rule and proceed by induction on a typing subderivation to show that M has a non-trivial decomposition. $\square$

Theorem 2 (Progress). *If $\vdash^c C : \Gamma$ then either (1) there exists C' such that $C \implies C'$ or (2) C is terminal (all processes contain V^*).*

Proof: Generalize the statement as follows: If $\Delta \vdash^c C : \Gamma$ then (1) $C \implies C'$ or (2) C is terminal or (3) C has a process $\langle l : \mathcal{R}[l'] \rangle$ blocked on label $l' :: A \in \Delta$. The proof is by induction on derivations and relies on case analysis and the decomposition lemma. The main progress theorem is an instance where C is closed ($\Delta = \cdot$), so case (3) is vacuous. See [16] for details. $\square$

5   Consequences of Modal Types

Adherence to a theoretical definition of mobility and locality imposes a certain programming discipline. It is difficult to justify our choice of $S4$ as *the singular* theory of mobility and locality for distributed programming. However, we can point out the consequences of adopting $S4$ and identify situations in which such a discipline is advantageous.

In the first place, $S4$ gives us a clean, *static* definition of mobility independent of the dynamic one. It is embodied in the judgment $\Delta; \cdot \vdash M : A$ (and the variation $\Delta; x{:}A \vdash M \div B$) which requires a mobile term be Γ-closed (or nearly so). Without this condition, the simple copying interpretation of mobility (rules *letbox*, *syncr*, *syncl*) is wrong! To repair this, we could handle store addresses as a special case. But runtime mobility would then *mean* different things for different types, indicating that something is perhaps amiss — that there is a distinction between terms we failed to recognize. The type discipline of $S4$ allows us to recognize this early, during typechecking. For example:

```
(* Incorrect *)                 (*Correct (explicit duplication)*)
let comp xr = comp ref 0 in     let comp xr = comp ref 0 in
                                let comp n = comp !xr in
                                let box u = marsh n in
let dia _ = someplace in        let dia _ = someplace in
                                  let comp xr' = comp ref u in
  let comp y = comp !xr in       let comp y = comp !xr' in
 ...                             ...
```

The incorrect code refers to a local value xr inside mobile code, while the correct version explicitly duplicates the reference cell as xr' in the new location. The function marsh : nat → □nat is assumed to convert a natural number to its mobile representation. While the example above is trivial, the type theory also accounts for structured data and higher-order functions.

Secondly, there are consequences linked to the particular choice of $S4$ modal logic. The character of $S4$ comes from an assumption that accessibility between worlds is reflexive and transitive. In practice, this means that distance (number of hops) is irrelevant. This is reflected in both the type theory and the semantics of our calculus. For example: $\langle l_1 : V \rangle \lhd \langle l_2 : l_1 \rangle \lhd \langle l_3 : l_2 \rangle \implies \langle l_1 : V \rangle \lhd \langle l_3 : l_1 \rangle$ via rule *syncr*. However, there is no requirement that accessibility be symmetric. But why should *direction* matter? Essentially this means that programs execute without introducing 2-way interdependence between processes/locations. This is advantageous when one considers garbage collection of processes or store locations. With cycles among locations allowed, distributed garbage collection becomes quite difficult to implement efficiently.

If, on the other hand, symmetry is explicitly recognized (as it is in the logic $S5$), certain new programming idioms become admissible. [21, 12] Some of these involve a mobility by-remote-reference interpretation.[2] This second kind of mobility introduces interdependencies among locations. So it seems that the type discipline of $S4$, though not the only way to define mobility and locality, describes a simpler kind of distributed programming which is likely to be efficiently implementable.

---

[2] The detailed reasons behind this claim are beyond the scope of this paper, but the interested reader should compare our interpretation of values of type $\Diamond A$ to those in an $S5$-based calculus such as [21].

6   Related Work

There are many prior foundational calculi which have a distributed operational interpretation. Most notably the Pi-calculus [14] and offspring. Pi-calculus processes interact by communicating names over named channels. Locations are thought of as implicit in the connectivity of processes. And names, the only form of resource, do not have a definite location or fixed scope (due to scope-extrusion). Thus locations in the Pi-calculus have no fixed properties or identity. Our approach differs in that we focus on describing locations and their distinguishing properties.

Various proposed calculi have added explicit locations to the Pi-calculus. Examples are the DPI calculus of Hennessy *et. al* [9] and *lsdπ* by Ravara, Matos, *et. al* [19]. These calculi allow some channel names to be declared fixed to a location, while others follow the laws of scope extrusion. DPI has a type system that tracks the locality of channel names, and associates each location with a set of resources (names) bound in that location. The Klaim calculus is also based on localized resources (multiple tuple spaces). De Nicola, *et. al* give a type system for Klaim [17] that checks process behaviors against administratively granted capabilities.

The ambient calculus [6] proposed by Cardelli and Gordon is a more radical departure, replacing channels with ambients $n[\ ]$. Ambients are places which may contain other ambients and running processes. They also serve as locations in which fragments of the program exchange messages. Cardelli and Gordon [8, 7] and Caires and Cardelli [2, 3] have developed an ambient logic with modal operators to characterize the location structure and behavior of ambient calculus programs. In their work, accessibility is interpreted as containment of ambients, $\square\Psi$ requires all sub-locations satisfy Ψ, and $\Diamond\Psi$ requires that some sub-location satisfy Ψ. As with names in the Pi-calculus, untyped ambients have no fixed locality or scope; in the absence of a specification, nested ambients may move freely in and out of other ambients in response to actions of the running program. Cardelli, Ghelli, and Gordon also developed a static type system for ambients [4, 5] which restricts ambient mobility. But their notion of mobility is quite different from the one we derived from logical necessity. An ambient characterized as immobile may be nested inside a mobile one, for example.

Modal logics should be referred to in the plural, because there are several different ways to define the meaning of $\square A$ and $\Diamond A$. Following a similar intuition, others have derived distributed calculi from $S5$ or $S5$-like hybrid logics. $S5$ is distinguished from $S4$ by the assumption that accessibility between worlds is symmetric, in addition to reflexive and transitive. The Lambda 5 calculus of Murphy, Crary, Harper, and Pfenning [21, 22] is derived from pure $S5$. And Jia and Walker's λ_{rpc} language [12, 11] is based on a $S5$-like hybrid logic with spatial types $A@w$ and $n[A]$ (absolute and relative locations) in addition to the pure modalities $\square A$ and $\Diamond A$. Both type theories are based in a formalism with explicit worlds; the programmer specifies directly where all fragments of the program are evaluated. This is qualitatively different than our $S4$ calculus, in which boxed terms are evaluated at any indefinite location. In some ways, $S5$ allows a programmer to do more than $S4$. For the most part, this is explained by the axiom schemas (5) $\Diamond A \rightarrow \square\Diamond A$ and (5') $\Diamond\square A \rightarrow \square A$. Axiom (5) represents the ability to make (references to) remote terms mobile, and (5') the ability to return a mobile term which happens to be remote. Both can be given a safe and sensible semantics, but there are costs to be weighed. For example, supporting (5) complicates storage management in a distributed implementation, since mobile remote references to arbitrary local values can be created. The $S4$ type theory defines mobility and locality in a minimal way without invoking this capability.

In [1] Borghuis and Feijs present a language based on a single $\Box^o$ modality. However, their operational interpretation of this modality is not based on the spatial interpretation of $\Box$ that we adopt. Rather $\Box^o(A \to B)$ represents location o's knowledge of how to transform a value of type A to one of type B. The calculus allows composing services and applying them to values, which are all assumed to be mobile.

7   Conclusions

While $S4$ does not lead to the most computationally powerful distributed language, it has a relatively simple programming model and type system. Furthermore, the discipline imposed by $S4$ could be advantageous because it simplifies the runtime support for marshalling and distributed garbage collection. It also encourages the programmer to work locally (as noted by Jagannathan [10]).

In this instance, we treated stores H as the fundamental distinguishing property of locations, but the problem of local resources is more general. Store addresses serve as canonical example localized entities, but the type system is independent of this choice. Besides mutable references, file handles, or other pointers to OS data structures, it is not so clear what other classes of localized value there might be. Certainly mobility (by-copying) is not tenable in situations where identity of an object must be preserved. But one might choose to fix certain resources to locations for reasons of efficiency, privacy, or security.

In future work, we plan to continue this abstract investigation of distributed computation. Various second-order extensions of the type theory are under investigation. Hopefully this will shed new light on how abstract datatypes should behave in a distributed computation, and the meaning of abstraction-safety in that context. A prototype implementation is also planned, to determine where and to what degree the execution model of $S4$-based programs leads to savings in cost and complexity.

Acknowledgements. Frank Pfenning for feedback on a draft of this paper. This material is based upon work supported under a National Science Foundation Graduate Research Fellowship.

References

1. Tijn Borghuis and Loe Feijs. A constructive logic for services and information flow in computer networks. *The Computer Journal*, 43(4), 2000.

2. Luís Caires and Luca Cardelli. A spatial logic for concurrency (part I). In *Theoretical Aspects of Computer Software (TACS)*, volume 2215 of *LNCS*, pages 1–37. Springer, October 2001.
3. Luís Caires and Luca Cardelli. A spatial logic for concurrency (part II). In *CONCUR*, volume 2421 of *LNCS*, pages 209–225. Springer, August 2002.
4. Luca Cardelli, Giorgio Ghelli, and Andrew D. Gordon. Mobility types for mobile ambients. In Jiri Wiedermann, Peter van Emde Boas, and Mogens Nielsen, editors, *Automata, Languagese and Programming, 26th International Colloquium (ICALP)*, volume 1644 of *LNCS*, pages 230–239. Springer, 1999.
5. Luca Cardelli, Giorgio Ghelli, and Andrew D. Gordon. Mobility types for mobile ambients. Technical Report MSR-TR-99-32, Microsoft, June 1999.
6. Luca Cardelli and Andrew D. Gordon. Mobile ambients. In *Foundations of Software Science and Computation Structures (FOSSACS)*, volume 1378 of *LNCS*, pages 140–155. Springer-Verlag, 1998.
7. Luca Cardelli and Andrew D. Gordon. Logical properties of name restriction. In Samson Abramsky, editor, *Typed Lambda Calculi and Applications*, volume 46-60 of *LNCS*, pages 46–60. Springer, May 2001.
8. Luca Cardelli and Andrew D. Gordon. Ambient logic. Technical report, Microsoft, 2002.
9. Matthew Hennessy and James Riely. Resource access control in systems of mobile agents. *Information and Computation*, 173:82–120, 2002.
10. Suresh Jagannathan. Continuation-based transformations for coordination languages. *Theoretical Computer Science*, 240(1):117–146, 2000.
11. Limin Jia and David Walker. Modal proofs as distributed programs. Technical Report TR-671-03, Princeton University, August 2003.
12. Limin Jia and David Walker. Modal proofs as distributed programs. In *European Symposium on Programming Languages*, April 2004.
13. D. A. Kranz, R. H. Halstead, Jr., and E. Mohr. Mul-T: a high-performance parallel lisp. In *Proceedings of the ACM SIGPLAN 1989 Conference on Programming language design and implementation*, pages 81–90. ACM Press, 1989.
14. Robin Milner, Joachim Parrow, and David Walker. A calculus of mobile processes (I & II). *Information and Computation*, 100(1):1–40 & 41–77, 1992.
15. Jonathan Moody. Modal logic as a basis for distributed computation. Technical Report CMU-CS-03-194, Carnegie Mellon University, October 2003.
16. Jonathan Moody. Logical mobility and locality types (extended report). Technical Report CMU-CS-05-128, CMU, 2005.
17. R. De Nicola, G. Ferrari, R. Pugliese, and B. Venneri. Types for access control. *Theoretical Computer Science*, 240(1):215–254, 2000. Klaim and tuple-spaces.
18. Frank Pfenning and Rowan Davies. A judgmental reconstruction of modal logic. *Mathematical Structures in Computer Science*, 11(4):511–540, August 2001.
19. António Ravara, Ana G. Matos, Vasco T. Vasconcelos, and Luís Lopes. Lexically scoped distribution: what you see is what you get. In *Foundations of Global Computing*. Elsevier, 2003.
20. Alex K. Simpson. *Proof Theory and Semantics of Intuitionistic Modal Logic*. PhD thesis, University of Edinburgh, 1994.
21. Tom Murphy VII, Karl Crary, Robert Harper, and Frank Pfenning. A symmetric modal lambda calculus for distributed computing. In *LICS (to appear)*, 2004.
22. Tom Murphy VII, Karl Crary, Robert Harper, and Frank Pfenning. A symmetric modal lambda calculus for distributed computing. Technical Report CMU-CS-04-105, Carnegie Mellon University, 2004.

Unwinding Conditions for Security
in Imperative Languages[*]

Annalisa Bossi[1], Carla Piazza[1,2], and Sabina Rossi[1]

[1] Dipartimento di Informatica, Università Ca' Foscari di Venezia,
via Torino 155, 30172 Venezia, Italy
[2] Dipartimento di Matematica ed Informatica, Università degli Studi di Udine,
via Le Scienze 206, 33100 Udine, Italy
{bossi, piazza, srossi}@dsi.unive.it

Abstract. We study unwinding conditions for the definition of non-interference properties of a simple imperative language, admitting parallel executions on a shared memory. We present different classes of programs obtained by instantiating a general unwinding framework and show that all the programs in these classes satisfy the non-interference principle. Moreover, we introduce a subclass of secure programs which is compositional with respect to the language constructors and we discuss verification techniques.

1 Introduction

The problem of ensuring that a given program respects the security level of its variables has been deeply investigated for a variety of programming languages and by many authors. We refer the reader to [16] for a clear and wide overview of the various proposals. All of these proposals accomplish the non-interference principle introduced by Goguen and Meseguer [8] which asserts that secret input data cannot be inferred through the observation of non confidential outputs. Beside the approaches based on formal methods for controlling information flow we find formalizations of non-interference in terms of behavioural equivalences, e.g., [6, 14], type-systems, e.g., [16, 19], and logical formulations, e.g., [2, 3].

In the context of process algebra, security properties are often expressed in terms of *unwinding conditions* [9] which demand properties of individual actions and are easier to handle with respect to global conditions. Intuitively, an unwinding condition requires that each high level transition is simulated in such a way that a low level observer cannot infer whether a high level action has been performed or not. Thus the low level observation of the process is not influenced in any way by its high behaviour.

In our previous works (see [4] for an overview) we studied many information flow security properties for the *Security Process Algebra* (SPA) [6] and char-

---

[*] This work has been partially supported by the EU Contract IST-2001-32617 and the FIRB project RBAU018RCZ.

acterized them in terms of unwinding conditions. In particular, we introduced a generalized unwinding condition which can be instantiated to define security properties and we identified classes of secure processes which can be constructed in a compositional way.

In this paper we show how our framework can be used also to define non-interference security properties for a simple imperative language, admitting parallel executions on a shared memory. We extend the language **IMP** defined in [20] by partitioning the locations (variables) into two levels: a public level and a confidential one and by adding a parallel composition operator.

We present a generalized unwinding condition for our language and study three different classes of programs obtained by instantiating the unwinding framework. These three instances are based on a notion of low level bisimulation and allow us to express timing-sensitive security properties for imperative languages. In particular, we show that all the programs in these classes satisfy the non-interference principle. Moreover, we introduce a subclass of secure programs which is compositional with respect to the language constructors. This class is useful to define proof systems which allow one both to verify and to build programs which are secure by construction.

The paper is organized as follows. In Section 2 we introduce the language together with its syntax and semantics. In Section 3 we define a general unwinding schema for our imperative language and study three different instantiations of it. We also prove a soundness theorem with respect to the standard non-interference property. In Section 4 we define a compositional class of secure programs and discuss its verification. Finally, in Section 5 we draw some conclusions.

2   The Language: Syntax and Semantics

The language we consider is an extension of the **IMP** language defined in [20] where parallel executions are admitted and the locations (variables) are partitioned into two levels: a public level and a confidential one. Intuitively, the values contained in the confidential locations are accessible only to authorized users (high level users), while the values in the public locations are available to all the users. We present an operational semantics and a notion of behavioral equivalence for our language which will be at the basis of our security properties. The aim of our properties is to detect any flow of information from high level to low level locations, i.e., at any point of the execution the values in the low level locations have not to depend on high level inputs. In our operational semantics programs are associated to *labelled transition systems*, i.e., graphs with labels on the edges and on the nodes. The labels on the nodes correspond to the states of the locations and are used in the definition of the behavioral equivalence. The labels on the edges denote the level (high or low) of transitions, i.e., they individuate the transitions which depend on the values of high level locations.

Let $\mathbb{R}$ be the set of real numbers, $\mathbb{T} = \{\text{true}, \text{false}\}$ be the set of boolean values, $\mathbb{L}$ be a set of low level locations and $\mathbb{H}$ be a set of high level locations, with $\mathbb{L} \cap \mathbb{H} = \emptyset$. The set **Aexp** of arithmetic expressions is defined by:

$$a ::= r \mid X \mid a_0 + a_1 \mid a_0 - a_1 \mid a_0 * a_1$$

where $r \in \mathbb{R}$ and $X \in \mathbb{L} \cup \mathbb{H}$. The set **Bexp** of boolean expressions is defined by:

$$b ::= \texttt{true} \mid \texttt{false} \mid (a_0 = a_1) \mid (a_0 \leq a_1) \mid \neg b \mid b_0 \wedge b_1 \mid b_0 \vee b_1$$

where $a_0, a_1 \in \textbf{Aexp}$.

We say that an arithmetic expression a is *confidential*, denoted by $a \in \texttt{high}$, if there is a high level location which occurs in it. Otherwise we say that a is *public*, denoted by $a \in \texttt{low}$. Similarly, we say that a boolean expression b is *confidential*, denoted by $b \in \texttt{high}$, if there is a confidential arithmetic expression which occurs in it. Otherwise we say that b is *public*, denoted by $b \in \texttt{low}$. This notion of confidentiality, both for arithmetic and boolean expressions, is purely syntactic. Notice that a high level expression can contain low level locations, i.e., its value can depend on the values of low level locations. This reflects the idea that a high level user can read both high and low level data.

The set **Prog** of programs of our language is defined as follows:

$$P ::= \texttt{skip} \mid X := a \mid P_0; P_1 \mid \texttt{if } b \texttt{ then } P_0 \texttt{ else } P_1 \mid \texttt{while } b \texttt{ do } P \mid P_0 \| P_1$$

where $a \in \textbf{Aexp}$, $X \in \mathbb{L} \cup \mathbb{H}$, and $b \in \textbf{Bexp}$.

A *high program* is a program which only uses high level locations (i.e., it syntactically contains only high level variables). We denote by **Prog$_H$** the set of all high programs.

Example 1. Consider the program $P \equiv L := H$, where H is a high level location and L is a low level location. P consists of a unique assignment instruction. Its effect is to assign to the low level location L the value contained in the high level location H. Hence, after the execution of P the low level user can read the high level data contained in H by reading L. $\square$

The operational semantics of our language is based on the notion of *state*. A state σ is a function which assigns to each location a real, i.e., $\sigma : \mathbb{L} \cup \mathbb{H} \longrightarrow \mathbb{R}$. Given a state σ, we denote by $\sigma[X/r]$ the state σ' such that $\sigma'(X) = r$ and $\sigma'(Y) = \sigma(Y)$ for all $Y \neq X$. Moreover, we denote by σ_L the restriction of σ to the low level locations and we write $\sigma =_L \theta$ for $\sigma_L = \theta_L$.

Given an arithmetic expression $a \in \textbf{Aexp}$ and a state σ, the evaluation of a in σ, denoted by $\langle a, \sigma \rangle \rightarrow r$ with $r \in \mathbb{R}$, is defined as in [20]. Similarly, $\langle b, \sigma \rangle \rightarrow v$ with $b \in \textbf{Bexp}$ and $v \in \{\texttt{true}, \texttt{false}\}$, denotes the evaluation of a boolean expression b in a state σ and is defined as in [20].

The operational semantics of our programs is expressed in terms of state transitions. A transition from a program P and a state σ has the form $\langle P, \sigma \rangle \xrightarrow{\epsilon} \langle P', \sigma' \rangle$ where P' is either a program or end (termination) and $\epsilon \in \{\texttt{high}, \texttt{low}\}$ stating that the transition is either confidential or public. Let $\mathbb{P} = \textbf{Prog} \cup \{\texttt{end}\}$ and Σ be the set of all the possible states. In Fig. 1 we define the operational semantics of $\langle P, \sigma \rangle \in \mathbb{P} \times \Sigma$ by structural induction on P.

For each pair $\langle P, \sigma \rangle$, where P is a program and σ is a state, the semantic rules define a *labelled transition system* (LTS) whose nodes are elements of $\mathbb{P} \times \Sigma$ and

$$\frac{}{\langle\text{skip},\sigma\rangle \xrightarrow{\text{low}} \langle\text{end},\sigma\rangle}$$

$$\frac{\langle a,\sigma\rangle \to r}{\langle X := a,\sigma\rangle \xrightarrow{\epsilon} \langle\text{end},\sigma[X/r]\rangle} \quad a \in \epsilon$$

$$\frac{\langle P_0,\sigma\rangle \xrightarrow{\epsilon} \langle P_0',\sigma'\rangle}{\langle P_0; P_1,\sigma\rangle \xrightarrow{\epsilon} \langle P_0'; P_1,\sigma'\rangle} \quad P_0' \not\equiv \text{end}$$

$$\frac{\langle P_0,\sigma\rangle \xrightarrow{\epsilon} \langle\text{end},\sigma'\rangle}{\langle P_0; P_1,\sigma\rangle \xrightarrow{\epsilon} \langle P_1,\sigma'\rangle}$$

$$\frac{\langle b,\sigma\rangle \to \text{true}}{\langle\text{if } b \text{ then } P_0 \text{ else } P_1,\sigma\rangle \xrightarrow{\epsilon} \langle P_0,\sigma\rangle} \quad b \in \epsilon$$

$$\frac{\langle b,\sigma\rangle \to \text{false}}{\langle\text{if } b \text{ then } P_0 \text{ else } P_1,\sigma\rangle \xrightarrow{\epsilon} \langle P_1,\sigma\rangle} \quad b \in \epsilon$$

$$\frac{\langle b,\sigma\rangle \to \text{false}}{\langle\text{while } b \text{ do } P,\sigma\rangle \xrightarrow{\epsilon} \langle\text{end},\sigma\rangle} \quad b \in \epsilon$$

$$\frac{\langle b,\sigma\rangle \to \text{true}}{\langle\text{while } b \text{ do } P,\sigma\rangle \xrightarrow{\epsilon} \langle P;\text{while } b \text{ do } P,\sigma\rangle} \quad b \in \epsilon$$

$$\frac{\langle P_0,\sigma\rangle \xrightarrow{\epsilon} \langle P_0',\sigma'\rangle}{\langle P_0\|P_1,\sigma\rangle \xrightarrow{\epsilon} \langle P_0'\|P_1,\sigma'\rangle} \quad P_0' \not\equiv \text{end}$$

$$\frac{\langle P_0,\sigma\rangle \xrightarrow{\epsilon} \langle\text{end},\sigma'\rangle}{\langle P_0\|P_1,\sigma\rangle \xrightarrow{\epsilon} \langle P_1,\sigma'\rangle}$$

$$\frac{\langle P_1,\sigma\rangle \xrightarrow{\epsilon} \langle P_1',\sigma'\rangle}{\langle P_0\|P_1,\sigma\rangle \xrightarrow{\epsilon} \langle P_0\|P_1',\sigma'\rangle} \quad P_1' \not\equiv \text{end}$$

$$\frac{\langle P_1,\sigma\rangle \xrightarrow{\epsilon} \langle\text{end},\sigma'\rangle}{\langle P_0\|P_1,\sigma\rangle \xrightarrow{\epsilon} \langle P_0,\sigma'\rangle}$$

Fig. 1. The operational semantics

whose edges are labelled with high or low. The notion of reachability does not depend on the labels of the edges. We use $\langle P,\sigma\rangle \to \langle P',\sigma'\rangle$ to denote $\langle P,\sigma\rangle \xrightarrow{\epsilon} \langle P',\sigma'\rangle$ with $\epsilon \in \{\text{low},\text{high}\}$. We write $\langle P_0,\sigma_0\rangle \to^n \langle P_n,\sigma_n\rangle$ for $\langle P_0,\sigma_0\rangle \to \langle P_1,\sigma_1\rangle \to \cdots \to \langle P_{n-1},\sigma_{n-1}\rangle \to \langle P_n,\sigma_n\rangle$. Given $\langle P,\sigma\rangle \in \textbf{Prog} \times \Sigma$, we denote by $Reach(\langle P,\sigma\rangle)$ the set of pairs $\langle P',\sigma'\rangle$ such that there exists $n \geq 0$ and $\langle P,\sigma\rangle \to^n \langle P',\sigma'\rangle$. Moreover we denote by $Reach(P)$ the set of programs P' such that $\langle P',\sigma'\rangle \in Reach(\langle P,\sigma\rangle)$ for some states σ and σ'.

Example 2. Assume L is a low level location and σ is a state such that $\sigma(L) = 1$. Consider the program $P_1 \equiv$ while $(L \leq 1)$ do $L := L + 1$; we obtain the following LTS

$$\langle P_1, \sigma \rangle$$

$$\text{low}\downarrow$$

$$\langle L := L+1; \ \text{while} \ (L \leq 1) \ \text{do} \ L := L+1, \sigma \rangle$$

$$\text{low}\downarrow$$

$$\langle \text{while} \ (L \leq 1) \ \text{do} \ L := L+1, \sigma[L/2] \rangle$$

$$\text{low}\downarrow$$

$$\langle \text{end}, \sigma[L/2] \rangle$$

Consider now the program $P_2 \equiv$ if $(H \leq 3)$ then $L := L+1$ else $L := L+2$ where H is a high level location. Let σ_1, σ_2 be states such that $\sigma_1(H) \leq 3$ and $\sigma_2(H) > 3$. The LTS's associated to the pairs $\langle P_2, \sigma_1 \rangle$ and $\langle P_2, \sigma_2 \rangle$ are

$$\langle P_2, \sigma_1 \rangle \qquad\qquad \langle P_2, \sigma_2 \rangle$$

$$\text{high}\downarrow \qquad\qquad\qquad \text{high}\downarrow$$

$$\langle L := L+1, \sigma_1 \rangle \qquad\qquad \langle L := L+2, \sigma_2 \rangle$$

$$\text{low}\downarrow \qquad\qquad\qquad\qquad \text{low}\downarrow$$

$$\langle \text{end}, \sigma_1[L/\sigma_1(L)+1] \rangle \qquad\qquad \langle \text{end}, \sigma_2[L/\sigma_2(L)+2] \rangle$$

In this case the final value of the low level location depends on the initial value of the high level one. Hence a low level user can infer whether H is less or equal than 3 or not just by observing the initial and final values of L. $\square$

We are interested in a notion of behavioural equivalence which equates two programs if they are indistinguishable for a low level observer.

Example 3. Consider the programs $H := 1; L := 1$ and $H := 2; L := 1$, where H is a high level location while L is a low level location. Given a state σ the LTS's associated to the two programs are respectively

$$\langle H := 1; L := 1, \sigma \rangle \qquad \langle H := 2; L := 1, \sigma \rangle$$

$$\text{low} \downarrow \qquad\qquad\qquad \text{low} \downarrow$$

$$\langle L := 1, \sigma[H/1] \rangle \qquad \langle L := 1, \sigma[H/2] \rangle$$

$$\text{low} \downarrow \qquad\qquad\qquad \text{low} \downarrow$$

$$\langle \text{end}, \sigma[H/1, L/1] \rangle \qquad \langle \text{end}, \sigma[H/2, L/1] \rangle$$

We would like to consider this two programs equivalent for a low level observer which can only read the values in the low level locations. $\square$

We consider two programs equivalent from the low level point of view if they are *low level bisimilar* as defined below.

Definition 1 (Low Level Bisimulation). *A binary symmetric relation* $\mathcal{B}$ *over* $\mathbb{P} \times \Sigma$ *is a* low level bisimulation *if for each* $(\langle P, \sigma \rangle, \langle Q, \theta \rangle) \in \mathcal{B}$ *it holds that:*

- $\sigma =_L \theta$, *i.e., the states coincide on low level locations;*
- *if* $\langle P, \sigma \rangle \rightarrow \langle P', \sigma' \rangle$ *then there exists* $\langle Q', \theta' \rangle$ *such that* $\langle Q, \theta \rangle \rightarrow \langle Q', \theta' \rangle$ *and* $(\langle P', \sigma' \rangle, \langle Q', \theta' \rangle) \in \mathcal{B}$.

Two pairs $\langle P, \sigma \rangle$ and $\langle Q, \theta \rangle \in \mathbb{P} \times \Sigma$ are low level bisimilar, denoted by $\langle P, \sigma \rangle \sim_l$ $\langle Q, \theta \rangle$ if there exists a low level bisimulation $\mathcal{B}$ such that $(\langle P, \sigma \rangle, \langle Q, \theta \rangle) \in \mathcal{B}$. Two programs P and Q are said to be low level bisimilar, denoted by $P \simeq_l Q$, if for each $\sigma, \theta \in \Sigma$ it holds that if $\sigma =_L \theta$ then $\langle P, \sigma \rangle \sim_l \langle Q, \theta \rangle$.

A *partial equivalence relation (per)* [17] is a symmetric and transitive relation.

Lemma 1. *The relation $\sim_l \subseteq (\mathbb{P} \times \Sigma)^2$ is the largest low level bisimulation and it is an equivalence relation. The relation $\simeq_l \subseteq \mathbb{P}^2$ is a partial equivalence relation.*

Proof. If $\langle P, \sigma \rangle \sim_l \langle Q, \theta \rangle$, then there exists a low level bisimulation $\mathcal{B}$ such that it holds $(\langle P, \sigma \rangle, \langle Q, \theta \rangle) \in \mathcal{B}$. Hence if $\langle P, \sigma \rangle \to \langle P', \sigma' \rangle$ we have that $\langle Q, \theta \rangle \to \langle Q', \theta' \rangle$ with $(\langle P', \sigma' \rangle, \langle Q', \theta' \rangle) \in \mathcal{B}$, i.e., $\langle P', \sigma' \rangle \sim_l \langle Q', \theta' \rangle$. So we have that $\sim_l$ is a low level bisimulation. It is the largest since by definition all the other low level bisimulations are included in it.

It is easy to prove that $\sim_l$ is reflexive and symmetric. Transitivity follows from the fact that if $\mathcal{B}_1, \mathcal{B}_2$ are low level bisimulations then the relation $\mathcal{B}_1 \circ \mathcal{B}_2$, where $\circ$ is the composition of relations, is still a low level bisimulation.

The relation $\simeq_l \subseteq \mathbb{P}^2$ is symmetric and transitive since $\sim_l$ is symmetric and transitive. $\qquad \square$

The relation $\simeq_l$ is not reflexive. For example, the program $L := H$ is not low level bisimilar to itself, as the low equality of states can be broken by a computation step.

Example 4. Consider the programs $P \equiv H := H + 1; L := L + 1$ and $Q \equiv H := H + 2; L := L + 1$, where H is a high level location and L is a low level location. It is easy to prove that $P \simeq_l Q$. In fact, a low level user which can only observe the low level location L cannot distinguish the two programs. $\qquad \square$

The notion of bisimulation as observation equivalence assumes that during each computation step a user can read the values in the locations. If we are working with a pure imperative language this assumption could seem too strong, since usually the values are read only at the end of the computation. However, if we consider parallel executions, during each step of the computation one of the parallel components could store the partial results of the other components.

Example 5. Let $P \equiv L := H; L := 1$ and $Q \equiv H := H; L := 1$, where H is a high level location and L is a low level location. The programs P and Q could be considered equivalent if one assumes that the low level user can observe the low level locations only at the end of the computation. However, they are not low level bisimilar. Indeed, if $R \equiv L_1 := L$ with L_1 being a low level location, then the programs $P \| R$ and $Q \| R$ are not equivalent from the low level point view. In fact, there is one execution of $P \| R$ in which the low level user can discover the high level value of H by reading L_1. This is never possible in $Q \| R$. $\qquad \square$

The relation $\sim_l$ equates programs which simulate each other step by step. This is stated in the following lemma. In the next section we will exploit such relation to define security properties which imply the timing-sensitive (lockstep) non-interference principle studied in, e.g., [15, 18].

Lemma 2. *Let P and Q be two programs and σ and θ be two states such that $\langle P, \sigma \rangle \sim_l \langle Q, \theta \rangle$. If $\langle P, \sigma \rangle \to^n \langle P', \sigma' \rangle$ then there exists Q' and θ' such that $\langle Q, \theta \rangle \to^n \langle Q', \theta' \rangle$ and $\langle P', \sigma' \rangle \sim_l \langle Q', \theta' \rangle$, and viceversa.*

Proof. By induction on n.

- Base: $n = 1$. We immediately have the thesis by definition of $\sim_l$.
- Step: $n = m + 1$ and we proved the thesis for m. We have that $\langle P, \sigma \rangle \to^m \langle P'', \sigma'' \rangle \to \langle P', \sigma' \rangle$. By inductive hypothesis we get $\langle Q, \theta \rangle \to^m \langle Q'', \theta'' \rangle$ with $\langle P'', \sigma'' \rangle \sim_l \langle Q'', \theta'' \rangle$. By definition of bisimulation we get the thesis. $\square$

Example 6. Consider the programs $P \equiv$ if $(L = 0)$ then $L := L+1$ else $L := 2$ and $Q \equiv$ if $(L = 0)$ then $\{L := L + 1; \text{skip}\}$ else $L := 2$. Although, for all σ and θ such that $\sigma =_L \theta$, P and Q execute exactly the same assignment commands, $P \not\sim_l Q$. In fact the two programs exhibit different timing behaviours due to the presence of the skip command in the first branch of Q. $\square$

3   Unwinding Conditions for Security of IMP

In [4] we introduced a general framework to define classes of secure processes written in the SPA language, an extension of Milner's CCS [12]. The framework is based on a generalized unwinding condition which is a local persistent property parametric with respect to a low behavioral equivalence, a transition relation independent from the high level behavior and a reachability relation. We proved that many non-interference properties can be seen as instances of this framework. In all the considered cases, the three relations are defined on the processes LTS's and thus the corresponding unwinding classes depend only on the operational semantics of processes. Following a similar approach, we introduce a generalized unwinding condition to define classes of programs which is parametric with respect to

- an observation equivalence relation $\doteq$ which equates two pairs $\langle P, \sigma \rangle$ and $\langle Q, \theta \rangle$ if they are indistinguishable for a low level observer,
- a binary relation $\hookrightarrow$ which, from the low level point of view, is independent from the values of high locations, and
- a reachability function $\mathcal{R}$ associating to each pair $\langle P, \sigma \rangle$ the set of pairs $\langle F, \psi \rangle$ which, in some sense, are reachable from $\langle P, \sigma \rangle$.

Definition 2 (Generalized Unwinding). *Let $\doteq$ be a binary equivalence relation over $\mathbf{Prog} \times \Sigma$, $\hookrightarrow$ be a binary relation over $\mathbf{Prog} \times \Sigma$ and $\mathcal{R}$ be a function from $\mathbf{Prog} \times \Sigma$ to $\wp(\mathbf{Prog} \times \Sigma)$. We define the unwinding class $\mathcal{W}(\doteq, \hookrightarrow, \mathcal{R})$ as follows:*

$$\mathcal{W}(\doteq, \hookrightarrow, \mathcal{R}) \stackrel{\text{def}}{=} \{\langle P, \sigma \rangle \in \mathbf{Prog} \times \Sigma \mid \forall \langle F, \psi \rangle \in \mathcal{R}(\langle P, \sigma \rangle)$$
$$\text{if } \langle F, \psi \rangle \stackrel{\text{high}}{\to} \langle G, \varphi \rangle \text{ then } \exists \langle M, \mu \rangle \text{ such that } \langle F, \psi \rangle \hookrightarrow \langle M, \mu \rangle \text{ and}$$
$$\langle G, \varphi \rangle \doteq \langle M, \mu \rangle\}.$$

The intuition behind the unwinding condition is that any high level transition should be simulated by a high independent transition guaranteeing that the high level transitions have no influence on the low level observation.

We say that the function $\mathcal{R}$ is *transitive* if $\langle F'', \psi'' \rangle \in \mathcal{R}(\langle F', \psi' \rangle)$ and $\langle F', \psi' \rangle \in \mathcal{R}(\langle F, \psi \rangle)$ imply $\langle F'', \psi'' \rangle \in \mathcal{R}(\langle F, \psi \rangle)$, i.e., it is a transitive relation. If $\mathcal{R}$ is transitive, the generalized unwinding condition defined above allows us to specify properties which are closed under $\mathcal{R}$. In this sense we say that our properties are *persistent*. The next lemma follows immediately by Definition 2.

Lemma 3. *Let $\mathcal{R}$ be a transitive reachability function and $\langle P, \sigma \rangle \in \mathbf{Prog} \times \Sigma$. If $\langle P, \sigma \rangle \in \mathcal{W}(\doteq, \hookrightarrow, \mathcal{R})$ then $\langle F, \psi \rangle \in \mathcal{W}(\doteq, \hookrightarrow, \mathcal{R})$ for all $\langle F, \psi \rangle \in \mathcal{R}(\langle P, \sigma \rangle)$.*

Proof. Let $\mathcal{R}$ be transitive, $\langle P, \sigma \rangle \in \mathcal{W}(\doteq, \hookrightarrow, \mathcal{R})$, and $\langle F, \psi \rangle \in \mathcal{R}(\langle P, \sigma \rangle)$. If $\langle F', \psi' \rangle \in \mathcal{R}(\langle F, \psi \rangle)$, then by transitivity we have that $\langle F', \psi' \rangle \in \mathcal{R}(\langle P, \sigma \rangle)$. Hence we get that if $\langle F', \psi' \rangle \overset{\text{high}}{\to} \langle G', \varphi' \rangle$ then $\langle F', \psi' \rangle \hookrightarrow \langle M', \mu' \rangle$ with $\langle G', \varphi' \rangle \doteq \langle M', \mu' \rangle$, i.e., the thesis. ☐

Below we instantiate our generalized unwinding condition by exploiting the notion of low level bisimulation $\sim_l$ as behavioral equivalence and by introducing a suitable high independent transition relation $\dashrightarrow$.

Definition 3 ($\dashrightarrow$). *The relation $\dashrightarrow$ on $\mathbf{Prog} \times \Sigma$ is defined as follows: $\langle F, \psi \rangle \dashrightarrow \langle M, \mu \rangle$ if for each π such that $\pi =_L \psi$ there exist R and ρ such that $\langle F, \pi \rangle \to \langle R, \rho \rangle$ and $\langle R, \rho \rangle \sim_l \langle M, \mu \rangle$.*

Example 7. Let $F \equiv \text{if } (H > 1) \text{ then } M \text{ else } R$ where $M \equiv H := 1; L := L + 1$ and $R \equiv H := 2; L := L + 1$, and ψ be such that $\psi(H) > 1$. In this case $\langle F, \psi \rangle \dashrightarrow \langle M, \psi \rangle$. Indeed, for each π such that $\pi =_L \psi$ either $\langle F, \pi \rangle \to \langle M, \pi \rangle$ or $\langle F, \pi \rangle \to \langle R, \pi \rangle$ and both $\langle M, \pi \rangle \sim_l \langle M, \psi \rangle$ and $\langle R, \pi \rangle \sim_l \langle M, \psi \rangle$.

Consider now the program $F \equiv L := 2; R$ and $R \equiv \text{if } (H > 1) \text{ then } \{H := 1; L := 2\} \text{ else } \{H := 2; L := 1\}$. In this case does not exist any $\langle M, \mu \rangle$ such that $\langle F, \psi \rangle \dashrightarrow \langle M, \mu \rangle$. Indeed, if ψ and π are two states such that $\psi =_L \pi$, $\psi(H) > 1$ and $\pi(H) \leq 1$, then $\langle F, \psi \rangle \to \langle R, \psi[L/2] \rangle$ and $\langle F, \pi \rangle \to \langle R, \pi[L/2] \rangle$ but $\langle R, \psi[L/2] \rangle \not\sim_l \langle R, \pi[L/2] \rangle$. ☐

By Definition 3 and by transitivity of $\sim_l$ we get the following characterization of our unwinding condition.

Proposition 1. *Let $\mathcal{R}$ be a reachability function, P be a program, and σ be a state. $\langle P, \sigma \rangle \in \mathcal{W}(\sim_l, \dashrightarrow, \mathcal{R})$ if and only if for each $\langle F, \psi \rangle \in \mathcal{R}(\langle P, \sigma \rangle)$ it holds that if $\langle F, \psi \rangle \overset{\text{high}}{\to} \langle G, \varphi \rangle$ then for each π such that $\pi =_L \psi$ there exist R and ρ such that $\langle F, \pi \rangle \to \langle R, \rho \rangle$ and $\langle R, \rho \rangle \sim_l \langle G, \varphi \rangle$.*

As far as the function $\mathcal{R}$ is concerned, we consider three different instantiations: $\mathcal{R}_{lts}$ which coincides with the rechability relation *Reach* in the LTS, $\mathcal{R}_{hpar}$ which intuitively represents reachability under the parallel composition with any high level program, and $\mathcal{R}_{par}$ which denotes reachability under the parallel composition with any program.

The class of secure imperative programs $\mathbf{SIMP}_{lts}$ is based on function $\mathcal{R}_{lts}$.

Definition 4 (SIMP$_{lts}$). *Let $\mathcal{R}_{lts}$ be the function Reach. A program P is in* **SIMP$_{lts}$** *if for each state σ, $\langle P, \sigma \rangle \in \mathcal{W}(\sim_l, \dashrightarrow, \mathcal{R}_{lts})$.*

Example 8. Consider the program $Q \equiv H := L$, where H is a high level location and L is a low level location. The program Q is in **SIMP$_{lts}$**. In fact, the low level execution is not influenced by the values in the high level location.

Consider again the program $P \equiv L := H; L := 1$ of Example 5, where H is a high level location and L is a low level location. It is easy to prove that for any $\sigma \in \Sigma$, $\langle P, \sigma \rangle \notin \mathcal{W}(\sim_l, \dashrightarrow, \mathcal{R}_{lts})$. In fact, let for instance $\sigma(H) = 1$, $\sigma(L) = 0$, $\theta(H) = 2$, $\theta(L) = 0$. It holds that $\sigma =_L \theta$, but after the execution of the first high level transition we reach the states σ' and θ', where $\sigma'(L) = 1 \neq \theta'(L) = 2$.

Consider now $R \equiv H := 4; L := 1;$ if $(L = 1)$ then skip else $L := H$. The program R belongs to **SIMP$_{lts}$**. In fact, the first branch of the conditional is always executed independently of the value in the high level location.   □

Since $\mathcal{R}_{lts}$ is transitive, by Lemma 3 we get that $\mathcal{W}(\sim_l, \dashrightarrow, \mathcal{R}_{lts})$ is persistent, i.e., if a program P starting in a state σ is secure then also each pair $\langle P', \sigma' \rangle$ reachable from $\langle P, \sigma \rangle$ does. However, in general it does not hold that if a program P is in **SIMP$_{lts}$** then also each program P' reachable from P is in **SIMP$_{lts}$**. This is illustrated in the following example.

Example 9. Let $P \equiv L := 0;$ if $L := 1$ then $L := H$ else skip. It holds that $P \in$ **SIMP$_{lts}$** since, for each state σ, $\langle P, \sigma \rangle$ will never perform any high transition. Moreover, the program $P' \equiv$ if $L := 1$ then $L := H$ else skip is reachable from P but it does not belong to **SIMP$_{lts}$**.   □

We now introduce a more restrictive class of secure imperative programs, namely **SIMP$_{hpar}$**, which is based on the reachability function $\mathcal{R}_{hpar}$ below.

Definition 5. *The function $\mathcal{R}_{hpar}$ from* **Prog** $\times \Sigma$ *to $\wp(\mathbf{Prog} \times \Sigma)$ is defined by:*
$\mathcal{R}_{hpar}(\langle P_0, \sigma_0 \rangle) = \{ \langle P_n, \theta_n \rangle \mid n \geq 0, \exists P_1, \ldots, P_{n-1}, \exists \sigma_1, \ldots, \sigma_n, \exists \theta_0, \ldots, \theta_{n-1}$
such that $\sigma_i =_L \theta_i$ and $\langle P_i, \theta_i \rangle \rightarrow \langle P_{i+1}, \sigma_{i+1} \rangle$ for $i \in [0 .. n-1]$ and $\sigma_n =_L \theta_n \}$.

Intuitively, $\langle F, \psi \rangle \in \mathcal{R}_{hpar}(\langle P, \sigma \rangle)$ if $\langle F, \psi \rangle$ is reachable from $\langle P \| P_H, \sigma \rangle$ where P_H is a high level program.

Lemma 4. *Let P be a program and σ be a state. $\langle F, \psi \rangle \in \mathcal{R}_{hpar}(\langle P, \sigma \rangle)$ if and only if F is a subprogram of P and $\langle F, \psi \rangle \in Reach(\langle P \| P_H, \sigma \rangle)$ for some high program P_H.*

Proof. (sketch) $\Leftarrow$) The parallel composition of two programs performs the interleaving of the actions of the two components. Hence, when executing $\langle P \| P_H, \sigma \rangle$, since P_H can only modify high level variables, each time an action $\langle P_H^i, \sigma_i \rangle \rightarrow \langle P_H^{i+1}, \theta_i \rangle$ of P_H is performed, we have that $\theta_i =_L \sigma_i$. On the other hand, when an action $\langle P_i, \sigma_i \rangle \rightarrow \langle P_{i+1}, \sigma_{i+1} \rangle$ of P is performed then we can define $\theta_i = \sigma_i$. Hence, $\exists \sigma_1, \ldots, \sigma_n, \theta_0, \ldots, \theta_{n-1}$ such that $\sigma_i =_L \theta_i$ and $\langle P_i, \theta_i \rangle \rightarrow \langle P_{i+1}, \sigma_{i+1} \rangle$ for $i \in [0 .. n-1]$ where $\langle P_0, \sigma_0 \rangle \equiv \langle P, \sigma \rangle$ and $\langle P_n, \theta_n \rangle \equiv \langle F, \psi \rangle$.

$\Rightarrow$) In each step of the computation P_H can only change the value of high level variables, hence we immediately get the thesis.   □

Definition 6 (SIMP$_{hpar}$). *A program P is in* **SIMP**$_{hpar}$ *if for each state σ,* $\langle P, \sigma \rangle \in \mathcal{W}(\sim_l, \dashrightarrow, \mathcal{R}_{hpar})$.

It is clear that the class **SIMP**$_{hpar}$ is more restrictive than **SIMP**$_{lts}$.

Lemma 5. SIMP$_{hpar} \subseteq$ **SIMP**$_{lts}$

Example 10. Consider the program $P \equiv H := 1; \text{if } (H = 1) \text{ then } \{\text{skip}; L := 1\} \text{ else } \{H := 1; L := H\}$, where H is a high level location and L is a low level location. The program P belongs to the class **SIMP**$_{lts}$ but it does not belong to the class **SIMP**$_{hpar}$. In fact, given an initial state σ there exists a state ψ such that the pair $\langle L := H, \psi \rangle$ belongs to $\mathcal{R}_{hpar}(\langle P, \sigma \rangle)$. Moreover $\langle L := H, \psi \rangle \stackrel{\text{high}}{\rightarrow} \langle \text{end}, \varphi \rangle$ but clearly it does not hold that for each π such that $\pi =_L \psi$ there exist R and ρ such that $\langle L := H, \pi \rangle \rightarrow \langle R, \rho \rangle$ and $\langle R, \rho \rangle \sim_l \langle \text{end}, \varphi \rangle$.

Notice that if we consider the program $Q \equiv H := 3$ then $P \| Q$ is not in **SIMP**$_{lts}$ although both P and Q are in **SIMP**$_{lts}$. $\qquad\square$

It is easy to prove that the reachability function $\mathcal{R}_{hpar}$ is transitive. Hence by Lemma 3 the class $\mathcal{W}(\sim_l, \dashrightarrow, \mathcal{R}_{hpar})$ is persistent. Indeed, we have that if a program P starting in a state σ is in $\mathcal{W}(\sim_l, \dashrightarrow, \mathcal{R}_{hpar})$ then also each pair $\langle P', \sigma' \rangle \in \mathcal{R}_{hpar}(\langle P, \sigma \rangle)$ is in $\mathcal{W}(\sim_l, \dashrightarrow, \mathcal{R}_{hpar})$. However, as for **SIMP**$_{lts}$, in general it does not hold that if a program P is in **SIMP**$_{hpar}$ then also each program P' reachable from P is in **SIMP**$_{hpar}$. In order to see this, it is sufficient to consider again the program of Example 9.

Finally, we introduce the class of secure imperative programs **SIMP**$_{par}$ by using the reachability function $\mathcal{R}_{par}$ defined below.

Definition 7. *The function $\mathcal{R}_{par}$ from* **Prog** $\times \Sigma$ *to* $\wp(\textbf{Prog} \times \Sigma)$ *is defined as follows:* $\mathcal{R}_{par}(\langle P_0, \sigma_0 \rangle) = \{\langle P_n, \theta_n \rangle \mid n \geq 0, \ \theta_n \in \Sigma, \ \exists P_1, \ldots, P_{n-1}, \ \exists \sigma_1, \ldots, \sigma_n, \ \exists \theta_0, \ldots, \theta_{n-1} \text{ such that } \langle P_i, \theta_i \rangle \rightarrow \langle P_{i+1}, \sigma_{i+1} \rangle \text{ for } i \in [0 .. n - 1]\}$.

Intuitively, a pair $\langle F, \psi \rangle$ is in $\mathcal{R}_{par}(\langle P, \sigma \rangle)$ if $\langle F, \psi \rangle$ is reachable from $\langle P \| Q, \sigma \rangle$ for some program Q. The following lemma is similar to Lemma 4.

Lemma 6. *Let P be a program and σ be a state. $\langle F, \psi \rangle \in \mathcal{R}_{par}(\langle P, \sigma \rangle)$ if and only if F is a subprogram of P and $\langle F, \psi \rangle \in Reach(\langle P \| Q, \sigma \rangle)$ for a program Q.*

Definition 8 (SIMP$_{par}$). *A program P is in* **SIMP**$_{par}$ *if for each state σ,* $\langle P, \sigma \rangle \in \mathcal{W}(\sim_l, \dashrightarrow, \mathcal{R}_{par})$.

The class **SIMP**$_{par}$ is more restrictive than **SIMP**$_{hpar}$.

Lemma 7. SIMP$_{par} \subseteq$ **SIMP**$_{hpar} \subseteq$ **SIMP**$_{lts}$.

Example 11. Consider the program $P \equiv H := 4; L := 1; \text{if } (L = 1) \text{ then skip}$ $\text{else } L := H$. It belongs to **SIMP**$_{lts}$ and **SIMP**$_{hpar}$ but it does not belong to **SIMP**$_{par}$. In fact given an initial state σ there exists a state ψ such that the pair $\langle L := H, \psi \rangle$ belongs to $\mathcal{R}_{par}(\langle P, \sigma \rangle)$. Moreover $\langle L := H, \psi \rangle \stackrel{\text{high}}{\rightarrow} \langle \text{end}, \varphi \rangle$ but clearly it does not hold that for each π such that $\pi =_L \psi$ there exist R and ρ such that $\langle L := H, \pi \rangle \rightarrow \langle R, \rho \rangle$ and $\langle R, \rho \rangle \sim_l \langle \text{end}, \varphi \rangle$. $\qquad\square$

The reachability function $\mathcal{R}_{par}$ is transitive and then, by Lemma 3, the class $\mathcal{W}(\sim_l, \dashrightarrow, \mathcal{R}_{par})$ is persistent in the sense that if $\langle P, \sigma \rangle$ is in $\mathcal{W}(\sim_l, \dashrightarrow, \mathcal{R}_{par})$ then also each pair $\langle P', \sigma' \rangle \in \mathcal{R}_{par}(\langle P, \sigma \rangle)$ is in $\mathcal{W}(\sim_l, \dashrightarrow, \mathcal{R}_{par})$. Moreover, differently from $\mathbf{SIMP}_{lts}$ and $\mathbf{SIMP}_{hpar}$, if a program P is in $\mathbf{SIMP}_{par}$ then also each program P' reachable from P is in $\mathbf{SIMP}_{par}$.

Lemma 8. *Let P be a program. If $P \in \mathbf{SIMP}_{par}$ then for all $P' \in Reach(P)$, $P' \in \mathbf{SIMP}_{par}$.*

Proof. Let $P' \in Reach(P)$, i.e., $\langle P', \sigma' \rangle \in Reach(\langle P, \sigma \rangle)$ for some σ and σ'. By definition of $\mathcal{R}_{par}$, $\langle P', \theta \rangle \in \mathcal{R}_{par}(\langle P, \sigma \rangle)$ for all state θ. Hence, by persistence of $\mathcal{W}(\sim_l, \dashrightarrow, \mathcal{R}_{par})$, $\langle P', \theta \rangle \in \mathcal{W}(\sim_l, \dashrightarrow, \mathcal{R}_{par})$, i.e., $P' \in \mathbf{SIMP}_{par}$. □

The three instances of our generalized unwinding condition introduced above allow us to express timing-sensitive notions of secuirity for imperative programs. This is a consequence of the fact that $\sim_l$ equates programs which exhibit the same timing behavior (see Lemma 2).

Example 12. Let $P \equiv \text{if } (H = 0) \text{ then } \{H := H + 1; \text{skip}\} \text{ else } H := 2$. The program P does not belong to any class $\mathbf{SIMP}_*$ with $* \in \{lts, hpar, par\}$. This is due to the fact that if $\langle P, \sigma \rangle \overset{high}{\twoheadrightarrow} \langle \{H := H+1; \text{skip}\}, \sigma \rangle$ for some state σ then it does not hold that for each θ such that $\sigma =_L \theta$ there exist R and θ' such that $\langle P, \theta \rangle \rightarrow \langle R, \theta' \rangle$ and $\langle \{H := H + 1; \text{skip}\}, \sigma \rangle \sim_l \langle R, \theta' \rangle$. In fact, if $\theta(H) \neq 0$, $\langle P, \theta \rangle \rightarrow \langle H := 2, \theta \rangle$ but $\langle \{H := H + 1; \text{skip}\}, \sigma \rangle \not\sim_l \langle H := 2, \theta \rangle$ because of their different timing behaviour. □

In the previous section we observed that the relation $\simeq_l$ is not reflexive. However, $\simeq_l$ is reflexive over the set of programs belonging to $\mathbf{SIMP}_{lts}$ (and then, by Lemma 7, to $\mathbf{SIMP}_{hpar}$ and $\mathbf{SIMP}_{par}$).

Lemma 9. *Let P be a program. If $P \in \mathbf{SIMP}_{lts}$ then $P \simeq_l P$.*

Proof. First, the following claim follows by structural induction on programs.

Claim. For each ψ and π such that $\psi_L = \pi_L$, if $\langle F, \psi \rangle \overset{low}{\twoheadrightarrow} \langle F', \psi' \rangle$ then $\langle F, \pi \rangle \overset{low}{\twoheadrightarrow} \langle F', \pi' \rangle$ with $\pi'_L = \psi'_L$.

Now assume that $P \in \mathbf{SIMP}_{lts}$. Then for all states σ and θ, $\langle P, \sigma \rangle, \langle P, \theta \rangle \in \mathcal{W}(\sim_l, \dashrightarrow, \mathcal{R}_{lts})$. Hence, in order to prove that $P \simeq_l P$, it is sufficient to show that for all σ and θ such that $\langle P, \sigma \rangle, \langle P, \theta \rangle \in \mathcal{W}(\sim_l, \dashrightarrow, \mathcal{R}_{lts})$ and $\sigma_L = \theta_L$, it holds $\langle P, \sigma \rangle \sim_l \langle P, \theta \rangle$. Consider the binary relation

$$\mathcal{S} = \{(\langle P, \sigma \rangle, \langle P, \theta \rangle) \mid \langle P, \sigma \rangle, \langle P, \theta \rangle \in \mathcal{W}(\sim_l, \dashrightarrow, \mathcal{R}_{lts}), \ \sigma_L = \theta_L\}$$

$$\cup \ \{(\langle P, \sigma \rangle, \langle Q, \theta \rangle) \mid \langle P, \sigma \rangle \sim_l \langle Q, \theta \rangle\}.$$

We show that $\mathcal{S}$ is a low level bisimulation.

If $\langle P, \sigma \rangle \overset{high}{\twoheadrightarrow} \langle P', \sigma' \rangle$, then since $\langle P, \sigma \rangle \in \mathcal{W}(\sim_l, \dashrightarrow, \mathcal{R}_{lts})$, by Proposition 1, we have that $\langle P, \theta \rangle \rightarrow \langle P'', \theta' \rangle$ with $\langle P', \sigma' \rangle \sim_l \langle P'', \theta' \rangle$. Hence, by definition of $\mathcal{S}$, $(\langle P', \sigma' \rangle, \langle P'', \theta' \rangle) \in \mathcal{S}$.

If $\langle P,\sigma\rangle \xrightarrow{\text{low}} \langle P',\sigma'\rangle$, then by Claim 3 we have that $\langle P,\theta\rangle \xrightarrow{\text{low}} \langle P',\theta'\rangle$ with $\sigma'_L = \theta'_L$. By Lemma 3, since $\mathcal{R}_{lts}$ is transitive, we have that $\mathcal{W}(\sim_l, \dashrightarrow, \mathcal{R}_{lts})$ is persistent, i.e., both $\langle P',\sigma'\rangle \in \mathcal{W}(\sim_l, \dashrightarrow, \mathcal{R}_{lts})$ and $\langle P',\theta'\rangle \in \mathcal{W}(\sim_l, \dashrightarrow, \mathcal{R}_{lts})$. Hence we have that $(\langle P',\sigma'\rangle, \langle P',\theta'\rangle) \in \mathcal{S}$, i.e., the thesis. □

The converse of Lemma 9 does not hold as illustrated below.

Example 13. Consider the program $P \equiv$ if $(H = 1)$ then P_0 else P_1 where $P_0 \equiv$ while $(H > 1)$ do skip and $P_1 \equiv$ skip. In this case $P \simeq_l P$, i.e., for all states σ and θ such that $\sigma =_L \theta$, $\langle P,\sigma\rangle \sim_l \langle P,\theta\rangle$. Indeed, if σ and θ are such that both $\sigma(H) = 1$ and $\theta(H) = 1$, the LTS's of $\langle P,\sigma\rangle$ and $\langle P,\theta\rangle$ have the form

$$
\begin{array}{cc}
\langle P,\sigma\rangle & \langle P,\theta\rangle \\
\downarrow & \downarrow \\
\langle P_0,\sigma\rangle & \langle P_0,\theta\rangle \\
\downarrow & \downarrow \\
\langle \text{end},\sigma\rangle & \langle \text{end},\theta\rangle
\end{array}
$$

and thus $\langle P,\sigma\rangle \sim_l \langle P,\theta\rangle$. The case in which both $\sigma(H) \neq 1$ and $\theta(H) \neq 1$ is analogous. On the other hand, if $\sigma(H) = 1$ and $\theta(H) \neq 1$ the LTS's of $\langle P,\sigma\rangle$ and $\langle P,\theta\rangle$ have the form

$$
\begin{array}{cc}
\langle P,\sigma\rangle & \langle P,\theta\rangle \\
\downarrow & \downarrow \\
\langle P_0,\sigma\rangle & \langle P_1,\theta\rangle \\
\downarrow & \downarrow \\
\langle \text{end},\sigma\rangle & \langle \text{end},\theta\rangle
\end{array}
$$

and again $\langle P,\sigma\rangle \sim_l \langle P,\theta\rangle$.

However, the program $P \notin \textbf{SIMP}_{lts}$. In fact $\langle P_0,\sigma\rangle \in Reach(\langle P,\sigma\rangle)$ and $\langle P_0,\sigma\rangle \xrightarrow{\text{high}} \langle \text{end},\sigma\rangle$ but it does not hold that for all ρ such that $\sigma =_L \rho$ there exist R and ρ' such that $\langle P_0,\rho\rangle \rightarrow \langle R,\rho'\rangle$ and $\langle \text{end},\sigma\rangle \sim_l \langle R,\rho'\rangle$. Indeed, if $\rho(H) > 1$, $\langle P_0,\rho\rangle \rightarrow \langle \text{skip}; P_0,\rho\rangle$ and $\langle \text{end},\sigma\rangle \not\sim_l \langle \text{skip}; P_0,\rho\rangle$. This is due to the fact that the subprogram P_0 of P is not in $\textbf{SIMP}_{lts}$. □

Finally, we show that our security properties expressed in terms of unwinding conditions imply the standard non-interference principle which requires that high level values do not affect the low level observation.

Theorem 1 (Soundness). *Let P be a program such that $P \in \textbf{SIMP}_*$ with $* \in \{lts, hpar, par\}$. For each state σ and θ such that $\sigma =_L \theta$,*

– $\langle P,\sigma\rangle \rightarrow^n \langle \text{end},\sigma'\rangle$ *if and only if* $\langle P,\theta\rangle \rightarrow^n \langle \text{end},\theta'\rangle$ *with* $\sigma'_L = \theta'_L$.

Proof. By Lemma 9, since $\sigma =_L \theta$, we have that $\langle P,\sigma\rangle \sim_l \langle P,\theta\rangle$. Then, by Lemma 2, we get that $\langle P,\theta\rangle$ reaches a pair $\langle P',\theta'\rangle$ with $\langle P',\theta'\rangle \sim_l \langle \text{end},\sigma'\rangle$. Hence we immediately have $\sigma' =_L \theta'$. Moreover, since end is not bisimilar to any program, it must be $P' \equiv \text{end}$. □

4   Compositionality

The classes $\mathbf{SIMP}_{lts}$, $\mathbf{SIMP}_{hpar}$ and $\mathbf{SIMP}_{par}$ introduced above are, in general, not compositional with respect to the language constructors. In particular, they are not compositional with respect to the parallel composition constructor as illustrated by the following example.

Example 14. Consider the program $P \equiv$ if $(H = 1 \wedge L = 1)$ then P_0 else P_1 where $P_0 \equiv$ if $(L = 1)$ then skip else $L := 2$ while $P_1 \equiv$ if $(L \neq 1)$ then $L := 3$ else skip. The program P belongs to the class $\mathbf{SIMP}_{par}$ (and then also to the classes $\mathbf{SIMP}_{lts}$ and $\mathbf{SIMP}_{hpar}$). In fact, given an initial state σ, $\langle P, \sigma \rangle \overset{\text{high}}{\to} \langle P_i, \sigma \rangle$ for some $i \in \{0,1\}$ and for each π such that $\pi =_L \sigma$ there always exist R and ρ such that $\langle P, \pi \rangle \to \langle R, \rho \rangle$ and $\langle R, \rho \rangle \sim_l \langle P_i, \sigma \rangle$. Now consider the program $Q \equiv L := 4$ which clearly belongs to $\mathbf{SIMP}_{par}$. We show that the program $P \| Q$ does not belong to $\mathbf{SIMP}_{lts}$ (and thus neither to $\mathbf{SIMP}_{hpar}$ and $\mathbf{SIMP}_{par}$). Indeed, let σ be a state such that $\sigma(H) = \sigma(L) = 1$. Then $\langle P \| Q, \sigma \rangle \overset{\text{high}}{\to} \langle P_0 \| Q, \sigma \rangle$. Now let π be a state such that $\pi =_L \sigma$ and in particular $\pi(L) = 1$ but $\pi(H) \neq 1$. Hence $\langle P \| Q, \pi \rangle \overset{\text{high}}{\to} \langle P_1 \| Q, \pi \rangle$. However, $\langle P_0 \| Q, \sigma \rangle \not\sim_L \langle P_1 \| Q, \pi \rangle$: in fact if the assigment $L := 4$ of Q is performed at the first step, then $\langle P_0 \| Q, \sigma \rangle$ ends in a state σ' such that $\sigma'(L) = 2$ while $\langle P_1 \| Q, \pi \rangle$ ends in a state π' such that $\pi'(L) = 3$.   □

Compositionality is useful both for verification and synthesis: if a property is preserved when programs are composed, then the analysis may be performed on subprograms and, in case of success, the program as a whole will satisfy the desired property by construction. In the next definition we introduce a class $\mathcal{C}$ of programs which is closed under composition and it is a subclass of $\mathbf{SIMP}_{par}$ (and then also of $\mathbf{SIMP}_{lts}$ and $\mathbf{SIMP}_{hpar}$).

Definition 9. *Let H be a high level location, L be a low level location, a_h and b_h be high level expressions, and a_l and b_l be low level expressions. The class of programs $\mathcal{C}$ is recursively defined as follows.*

1. skip *is in $\mathcal{C}$;*
2. $L := a_l$ *is in $\mathcal{C}$;*
3. $H := a_h$ *is in $\mathcal{C}$;*
4. $H := a_l$ *is in $\mathcal{C}$;*
5. $P_0; P_1$ *is in $\mathcal{C}$ if P_0, P_1 are in $\mathcal{C}$;*
6. if b_l then P_0 else P_1 *is in $\mathcal{C}$, if P_0, P_1 are in $\mathcal{C}$;*
7. if b_h then P_0 else P_1 *is in $\mathcal{C}$ if P_0, P_1 are in $\mathcal{C}$ and $P_0 \simeq_l P_1$;*
8. while b_l do P_0 *is in $\mathcal{C}$, if P_0 is in $\mathcal{C}$;*
9. $P_0 \| P_1$ *is in $\mathcal{C}$, if P_0, P_1 are in $\mathcal{C}$.*

Theorem 2. *The class of programs $\mathcal{C}$ of Definition 9 is included in $\mathbf{SIMP}_{par}$.*

Proof. We first prove the following claim.

Claim. Let $G, F, R \in \mathcal{C}$. If $\varphi =_L \rho$ then $\langle F, \varphi \rangle \sim_l \langle F, \rho \rangle$. Moreover, if $\langle G, \varphi \rangle \sim_l$ $\langle R, \rho \rangle$, then $\langle G; F, \varphi \rangle \sim_l \langle R; F, \rho \rangle$ and $\langle G \| F, \varphi \rangle \sim_l \langle R \| F, \rho \rangle$.

Proof. It is sufficient to show that

$$\mathcal{S} = \{(\langle G; F, \varphi \rangle, \langle R; F, \rho \rangle), (\langle G \| F, \varphi \rangle, \langle R \| F, \rho \rangle), \mid G, F, R \in \mathcal{C}, \langle G, \varphi \rangle \sim_l \langle R, \rho \rangle\}$$
$$\cup \{(\langle F, \varphi \rangle, \langle F, \rho \rangle) \mid F \in \mathcal{C}, \varphi =_L \rho\}$$
$$\cup \{\langle F_0, \varphi \rangle, \langle F_1, \rho \rangle \mid F_0, F_1 \in \mathcal{C}, \varphi =_L \rho, F_0 \sim_l F_1\}$$
$$\cup \{(\langle F_0, \varphi \rangle, \langle F_1, \rho \rangle) \mid \langle F_0, \varphi \rangle \sim_l \langle F_1, \rho \rangle\}$$

is a low level bisimulation.

In order to prove Theorem 2 we show that if $P \in \mathcal{C}$, then for each $F \in Reach(P)$ and for each ψ it holds that if $\langle F, \psi \rangle \xrightarrow{h} \langle G, \varphi \rangle$, then for each π such that $\pi =_L \psi$ we have $\langle F, \pi \rangle \to \langle R, \rho \rangle$ with $\langle R, \rho \rangle \sim_l \langle G, \varphi \rangle$. Indeed, from the fact that $P \in \mathcal{C}$ and $F \in Reach(P)$ we get that $F \in \mathcal{C}$. We prove the thesis for a generic $F \in \mathcal{C}$ and a generic state ψ. We proceed by structural induction on F.

The only interesting cases are $F \equiv F_0; F_1$ and $F \equiv F_0 \| F_1$. We consider the case $F \equiv F_0; F_1$ since the other one is similar. If $\langle F, \psi \rangle \xrightarrow{h} \langle F_0'; F_1, \varphi \rangle$, then we have $\langle F_0, \psi \rangle \xrightarrow{h} \langle F_0', \varphi \rangle$. Hence by inductive hypothesis on F_0 we have $\langle F_0, \pi \rangle \xrightarrow{h} \langle F_0'', \rho \rangle$ with $\langle F_0', \varphi \rangle \sim_l \langle F_0'', \rho \rangle$. Then we get that $\langle F, \pi \rangle \xrightarrow{h} \langle F_0''; F_1, \rho \rangle$ and by Claim 4 $\langle F_0''; F_1, \rho \rangle \sim_l \langle F_0'; F_1, \varphi \rangle$. If $\langle F, \psi \rangle \xrightarrow{h} \langle F_1, \varphi \rangle$, then $\langle F_1, \psi \rangle \xrightarrow{h}$ $\langle end, \varphi \rangle$. Hence by Claim 4 we get that $\langle F_1, \pi \rangle \xrightarrow{h} \langle end, \rho \rangle$ with $\rho =_L \varphi$. So, $\langle F, \pi \rangle \xrightarrow{h} \langle F_1, \rho \rangle$, and again by Claim 4 we have $\langle F_1, \rho \rangle \sim_l \langle F_1, \varphi \rangle$. $\square$

We conclude this section by observing that membership to the class $\mathcal{C}$ is not decidable due to the presence of the low level observation equivalence $\simeq_l$ in point 7 of Definition 9. However, a sound but incomplete method could be find to compute $\simeq_l$ by applying a suitable abstraction which guarantees equivalence up to high level locations as discussed, e.g., in [1].

5   Conclusion and Related Work

In this paper we introduced a generalized unwinding schema for the definition of non-interference properties of programs of a simple imperative language, admitting parallel executions on a shared memory. We studied three different instances of our unwinding condition and defined a subclass of programs which is compositional with respect to the language constructors.

There is a widespread literature on secure information flow in imperative languages (see [16] for a recent survey). A common approach is based on types in such a way that well-typed programs do not leak secrets (see, e.g., [17, 19]). Other approaches consider logical formulations of non-interference, e.g., [2, 3, 10], and abstract interpretation-based formalizations, e.g., [5, 7].

As far as we know, this is the first attempt of defining security properties of imperative languages through unwinding conditions. As observed by many authors (e.g., [11, 13]) such conditions are easier to handle and more amenable to automated proof with respect to global conditions. Similarly to what we already did in [4] for systems written in a process algebra, we plan to exploit unwinding conditions for defining proof systems both to verify whether a program is secure and to build programs which are secure by construction in an incremental way.

Finally, we observe that the properties we have defined in terms of unwinding conditions characterize the security of programs againts so-called *passive attacks*, i.e., low level users which try to infer the values of the high level variables just by observing the values of the low level ones. On the contrary, in defining non-interference one usually explicitly characterize the class of *active attacks*, i.e., malicious users or programs which try to directly transmit confidential information to the low level observer. Some authors have proved that there is a connection between properties characterizing passive attacks and properties involving active attacks [21]. In our approach an active attacker can be seen as a high program which intentionally manipulates high level variables. We can prove that if P is a secure program belonging to the class $\mathbf{SIMP}_{hpar}$ (and hence to $\mathbf{SIMP}_{par}$) then a low level user cannot distiguish P running in parallel with different (malicious) high programs P_H and P_K exhibiting the same timing behaviour (i.e., $P_H \simeq_l P_K$).

Theorem 3. *If* $P \in \mathbf{SIMP}_{hpar}$ *then* $P\|P_H \simeq_l P\|P_K$ *for all* $P_H, P_K \in \mathbf{Prog_H}$ *such that* $P_H \simeq_l P_K$.

Proof. It follows from the fact that

$$
\mathcal{S} = \{(\langle P\|P_H, \sigma\rangle, \langle Q\|P_K, \theta\rangle)| \ \langle P, \sigma\rangle \sim_l \langle Q, \theta\rangle, \ P_H \sim_l P_K, \ P_H, P_K \in \mathbf{Prog_H}
$$
$$
\langle P, \sigma\rangle, \langle Q, \theta\rangle \in \mathcal{W}(\sim_l, \dashrightarrow, \mathcal{R}_{hpar})\} \ \cup \ \{(\langle P, \sigma\rangle, \langle Q, \theta\rangle)| \ \langle P, \sigma\rangle \sim_l \langle Q, \theta\rangle\}
$$

is a low level bisimulation $\sim_l$. $\qquad\square$

Intuitively, this theorem states that if a program P belongs to $\mathbf{SIMP}_{hpar}$ then even if the values of the high level variables are changed during the computation, a low level user will never observe any difference on the values of low variables.

References

1. J. Agat. Transforming out Timing Leaks. In *Proc. of ACM Symposium on Principles of Programming Languages (POPL'00)*, pages 40–53. ACM Press, 2000.
2. T. Amtoft and A. Banerjee. Information Flow Analysis in Logical Form. In *Proceedings of the 11th Static Analysis Symposium (SAS'04)*, volume 3148 of *LNCS*, pages 100–115. Springer-Verlag, 2004.
3. G. Barthe, P. D'Argenio, and T. Rezk. Secure Information Flow by Self Composition. In *Proc. of the 17th IEEE Computer Security Foundations Workshop (CSFW'04)*, pages 100–114. IEEE Computer Society Press, 2004.
4. A. Bossi, R. Focardi, C. Piazza, and S. Rossi. Verifying Persistent Security Properties. *Computer Languages, Systems and Structures*, 30(3-4):231–258, 2004.
5. A. Di Pierro, C. Hankin, and H.Wiklicky. Approximate Non-Interference. In *Proc. of the IEEE Computer Security Foundations Workshop (CSFW'02)*, pages 3–17. IEEE Computer Society Press, 2002.

6. R. Focardi and R. Gorrieri. Classification of Security Properties (Part I: Information Flow). In R. Focardi and R. Gorrieri, editors, *Proc. of Foundations of Security Analysis and Design (FOSAD'01)*, volume 2171 of *LNCS*, pages 331–396. Springer-Verlag, 2001.
7. R. Giacobazzi and I. Mastroeni. Abstract Non-Interference: Parameterizing Non-Interference by Abstract Interpretation. In *Proc. of ACM Symposium on Principles of Programming Languages (POPL'04)*, pages 186–197. ACM Press, 2004.
8. J. A. Goguen and J. Meseguer. Security Policies and Security Models. In *Proc. of the IEEE Symposium on Security and Privacy (SSP'82)*, pages 11–20. IEEE Computer Society Press, 1982.
9. J. A. Goguen and J. Meseguer. Unwinding and Inference Control. In *Proc. of the IEEE Symposium on Security and Privacy (SSP'84)*, pages 75–86. IEEE Computer Society Press, 1984.
10. R. Joshi and K. R. M. Leino. A Semantic Approach to Secure Information Flow. *Science of Computer Programming*, 37(1–3):113–138, 2000.
11. H. Mantel. Unwinding Possibilistic Security Properties. In *Proc. of the European Symposium on Research in Computer Security (ESoRiCS'00)*, volume 2895 of *LNCS*, pages 238–254. Springer-Verlag, 2000.
12. R. Milner. *Communication and Concurrency*. Prentice-Hall, 1989.
13. P. Y. A. Ryan. A CSP Formulation of Non-Interference and Unwinding. *Cipher*, pages 19–27, 1991.
14. P.Y.A. Ryan and S. Schneider. Process Algebra and Non-Interference. *Journal of Computer Security*, 9(1/2):75–103, 2001.
15. A. Sabelfeld and H. Mantel. Static Confidentiality Enforcement for Distributed Programs. In M. V. Hermenegildo and G. Puebla, editors, *Proc. of Int. Static Analysis Symposium (SAS'02)*, volume 2477 of *LNCS*, pages 376–394. Springer-Verlag, 2002.
16. A. Sabelfeld and A. C. Myers. Language-Based Information-Flow Security. *IEEE Journal on Selected Areas in Communication*, 21(1):5–19, 2003.
17. A. Sabelfeld and D. Sands. A Per Model of Secure Information Flow in Sequential Programs. *Higher-Order and Symbolic Computation*, 14(1):59–91, 2001.
18. G. Smith and D. M. Volpano. Secure Information Flow in a Multi-threaded Imperative Language. In *Proc. of ACM SIGPLAN-SIGACT Symposium on Principles of Programming Languages (POPL'98)*, pages 355–364. ACM Press, 1998.
19. D. M. Volpano and G. Smith. A Type-Based Approach to Program Security. In *TAPSOFT*, pages 607–621, 1997.
20. G. Winskel. *The formal semantics of programming languages*. The MIT Press, 1993.
21. S. Zdancewic and A. C. Myers. Robust Declassification. In *Proc. of the IEEE Computer Security Foundations Workshop (CSFW'01)*, pages 15–23. IEEE Computer Society Press, 2001.

Natural Rewriting for
General Term Rewriting Systems

Santiago Escobar[1], José Meseguer[2], and Prasanna Thati[3]

[1] Universidad Politécnica de Valencia, Spain
sescobar@dsic.upv.es
[2] University of Illinois at Urbana-Champaign, USA
meseguer@cs.uiuc.edu
[3] Carnegie Mellon University, USA
thati@cs.cmu.edu

Abstract. We address the problem of an efficient rewriting strategy for general term rewriting systems. Several strategies have been proposed over the last two decades for rewriting, the most efficient of all being the natural rewriting strategy [9]. All the strategies so far, including natural rewriting, assume that the given term rewriting system is a left-linear constructor system. Although these restrictions are reasonable for some functional programming languages, they limit the expressive power of equational languages, and they preclude certain applications of rewriting to equational theorem proving and to languages combining equational and logic programming. In this paper, we propose a conservative generalization of natural rewriting that does not require the rules to be left-linear and constructor-based. We also establish the soundness and completeness of this generalization.

1 Introduction

A challenging problem in modern programming languages is the discovery of sound and complete evaluation strategies which are: (i) optimal w.r.t. some efficiency criterion (typically the number of rewrite steps), (ii) easily implementable, and (iii) applicable for a large class of programs. In this paper, we focus on (iii).

The evaluation strategies for programming languages so far can be classified into two classical families: *eager strategies* (also known as *innermost* or *call-by-value*) and *lazy strategies* (also known as *outermost* or *call-by-need*). The choice of the strategy can have a big impact on performance and semantics of programming languages: for instance, lazy rewriting typically needs more resources than eager rewriting [22], but the former improves termination of the program w.r.t. the latter. To define a lazy rewriting strategy, we have to define what a *needed computation* is and also have to provide an efficient procedure to determine whether some computation is needed. These two problems were first addressed for rewriting in a seminal paper by Huet and Levy [18], where the *strongly needed reduction* strategy was proposed. Several refinements of this

S. Etalle(Ed.): LOPSTR 2004, LNCS 3573, pp. 101–116, 2005.
© Springer-Verlag Berlin Heidelberg 2005

strategy have been proposed over the last two decades, the most significant ones being Sekar and Ramakrishnan's *parallel needed reduction* [24], and Antoy, Echahed and Hanus' *(weakly) outermost-needed rewriting* [1, 3, 4]. Recently, (weakly) outermost-needed rewriting has been improved by Escobar by means of the *natural rewriting strategy* [9, 10]. Natural rewriting is based on a suitable extension of the demandedness notion associated to (weakly) outermost-needed rewriting. Moreover, the strategy enjoys good computational properties such as soundness and completeness w.r.t. head-normal forms, and it preserves optimality w.r.t. the number of reduction steps for sequential parts of the program.

A typical assumption of previous strategies [14, 19, 16, 24, 1, 3, 4, 2, 9, 10] is that the rewrite rules are *left-linear* and *constructor*. These restrictions are reasonable for some functional programming languages, but they limit the expressive power of equational languages such as OBJ [15], CafeOBJ [13], ASF+SDF [8], and Maude [7], where non-linear left-hand sides are perfectly acceptable. This extra generality is also necessary for applications of rewriting to equational theorem proving, and to languages combining equational and logic programming, since in both cases assuming left-linearity is too restrictive. Furthermore, for rewrite systems whose semantics is not equational but is instead rewriting logic based, such as rewrite rules in ELAN [6], or Maude system modules, the constructor assumption is unreasonable and almost never holds.

In summary, generalizing the natural rewriting strategy to *general* rewriting systems, without left-linearity and constructor conditions, will extend the scope of applicability of the strategy to more expressive equational languages and to rewriting logic based languages, and will open up a much wider range of applications. In the following, we give the reader a first intuitive example of how that generalization will work.

Example 1. Consider the following TRS for proving equality ($\approx$) of arithmetic expressions built using division ($\div$), modulus or remainder ($\%$), and subtraction ($-$) operations on natural numbers.

(1) $0 \div s(N) \to 0$

(2) $s(M) \div s(N) \to s((M-N) \div s(N))$

(3) $M \% s(N) \to (M-s(N)) \% s(N)$

(4) $(0 - s(M)) \% s(N) \to N - M$

(5) $M - 0 \to M$

(6) $s(M) - s(N) \to M-N$

(7) $X \approx X \to True$

Note that this TRS is not left-linear because of rule (7) and it is not constructor because of rule (4). Therefore, it is outside the scope of all the strategies mentioned above. Furthermore, note that the TRS is neither terminating nor confluent due to rule (3).

Consider the term[1] $t_1 = 10! \div 0$. If we only had rules (1), (2), (5) and (6), the natural rewriting strategy [9] would be applicable and no reductions on t_1 would be performed, since t_1 is a head-normal form. In contrast, the other strate-

---

[1] The subterm $10!$ represents factorial of $s^{10}(0)$ but we do not include the rules for ! because we are only interested in the fact that it has a remarkable computational cost, and therefore we would like to avoid its reduction in the examples whenever possible.

gies mentioned above, for example, outermost-needed rewriting, would force[2] the evaluation of the computationally expensive subterm 10!. Hence, we would like to generalize natural rewriting to a version that enjoys this optimality (w.r.t. the number of rewrite steps) and that can also handle non-left-linear and non-constructor rules such as (7) and (4).

Consider the term $t_2 = $ 10! % (s(0)−s(0)) ≈ 10! % 0. We would like the generalization of the natural rewriting strategy to perform only the optimal computation:

10! % (s(0)−s(0)) ≈ 10! % 0
    → 10! % (0−0) ≈ 10! % 0 → 10! % 0 ≈ 10! % 0 → True

that avoids unnecessary reduction of the subterm 10! % 0 at the final rewrite step, and also avoids reductions on the computationally expensive term 10! during the whole rewrite sequence.

Since natural rewriting [9] uses a more refined demandedness notion for re-dexes in comparison with other strategies such as outermost needed rewriting [1, 4], it leads to a very efficient lazy evaluation strategy. In this paper, we propose a conservative generalization of this demandedness notion that drops the assumptions that the rewrite rules are left-linear and constructor, while retaining soundness and completeness w.r.t. head-normal forms.

It is worthy to mention that an exception in the previous strategies about the left-linearity requirement is [2]. In [2], a non-left-linear rule "$l \to r$" is transformed into a left-linear conditional rule "$l' \to r$ if $\ldots, X \downarrow X_1, \ldots, X \downarrow X_n, \ldots$" by renaming, in the linear term l', extra occurrences of a variable X to $X_1, \ldots, X_n$. However, $t \downarrow s$ succeeds only if there exists a constructor term w such that $t \to^* w$ and $s \to^* w$ and this is an unreasonable condition for the kind of rewrite systems with a non-equational semantics, like rewriting logic, consid-ered in this paper. Anyway, the strategy of [2] is not applicable to Example 1, since imposes the constructor condition.

The reader might wonder if a suitable program transformation that converts a term rewriting system into a left-linear constructor system whose semantics is equivalent to the original is possible. However, existing techniques for lineariza-tion of term rewriting systems, such as [17], or for transformation of a term rewriting system into a constructor system, such as [23], are not applicable in

---

[2] Note that this behavior is independent of the fact that two possible definitional trees, a data structure guiding the outermost-needed rewriting strategy [1], exist for symbol ÷; see [9–Example 21]. The idea is that for any of the two definitional trees available, there will exist terms for which the previous problem still persists. Note that this problem becomes unavoidable, since a definitional tree is fixed for a program, not for a source term. Specifically, if we consider that the set of constructor symbols is {0, s, pred} (instead of simply {0, s}), then the subterm 10! in the term $s_1 = $ 10! ÷ pred(0) is uselessly reduced for one of the definitional trees, whereas subterm 10! in the term $s_2 = $ pred(0) ÷ 10! is uselessly reduced for the other definitional tree. However, both terms are detected as head-normal forms by natural rewriting [9], like the previous term 10! ÷ 0.

general to term rewriting systems; for instance, these two techniques do not apply to Example 1, since they require the TRS to be terminating, confluent and forward-branching (see [23] for further details).

After some preliminaries in Section 2, we present our generalization of natural rewriting strategy in Section 3, and formally define its properties. We show soundness and completeness of the generalized rewrite strategy w.r.t. head-normal forms. In Section 4, we further refine the strategy to obtain a more optimal one, without losing the soundness and completeness properties. Finally, we conclude in Section 5. Missing proofs can be found in [11].

2   Preliminaries

We assume a finite alphabet (function symbols) $\mathcal{F} = \{f, g, \ldots\}$, and a countable set of variables $\mathcal{X} = \{X, Y, \ldots\}$. We denote the set of terms built from $\mathcal{F}$ and $\mathcal{X}$ by $\mathcal{T}(\mathcal{F}, \mathcal{X})$ and write $\mathcal{T}(\mathcal{F})$ for ground terms built only from $\mathcal{F}$. We write $Var(t)$ for the set of variables occurring in t. A term is said to be linear if it has no multiple occurrences of a single variable. We use finite sequences of integers to denote a position in a term. Given a set $S \subseteq \mathcal{F} \cup \mathcal{X}$, $\mathcal{P}os_S(t)$ denotes positions in t where symbols or variables in S occur. We write $\mathcal{P}os_f(t)$ and $\mathcal{P}os(t)$ as a shorthand for $\mathcal{P}os_{\{f\}}(t)$ and $\mathcal{P}os_{\mathcal{F} \cup \mathcal{X}}(t)$, respectively. We denote the *root position* by Λ. Given positions p, q, we denote its concatenation as $p.q$ and define $p/q = p'$ if $p = q.p'$. Positions are ordered by the standard prefix ordering $\leq$. We say p and q are *disjoint positions* and write $p \parallel q$, if $p \not\leq q$ and $q \not\leq p$. For sets of positions P, Q we define $P.Q = \{p.q \mid p \in P \wedge q \in Q\}$. We write $P.q$ as a shorthand for $P.\{q\}$ and similarly for $p.Q$. The subterm of t at position p is denoted as $t|_p$, and $t[s]_p$ is the term t with the subterm at position p replaced by s. We define $t|_P = \{t|_p \mid p \in P\}$. The symbol labeling the root of t is denoted as $root(t)$. Given a set of positions P, we call $p \in P$ an *outermost position* in P if there is no $q \in P$ such that $q < p$.

A *substitution* is a function $\sigma : \mathcal{X} \to \mathcal{T}(\mathcal{F}, \mathcal{X})$ which maps variables to terms, and which is different from the identity only for a finite subset $\mathcal{D}om(\sigma)$ of $\mathcal{X}$. We denote the homomorphic extension of σ to $\mathcal{T}(\mathcal{F}, \mathcal{X})$ also by σ, and its application to a term t by $\sigma(t)$. The set of variables introduced by σ is $\mathcal{R}an(\sigma) = \cup_{x \in \mathcal{D}om(\sigma)} Var(\sigma(x))$. We denote by id the identity substitution: $id(x) = x$ for all $x \in \mathcal{X}$. Terms are ordered by the preorder $\leq$ of "relative generality", i.e., $s \leq t$ if there exists σ s.t. $\sigma(s) = t$. We write $\sigma^{-1}(x) = \{y \in \mathcal{D}om(\sigma) \mid \sigma(y) = x\}$.

A rewrite rule is an ordered pair (l, r) of terms, also written $l \to r$, with $l \notin \mathcal{X}$. The left-hand side (*lhs*) of the rule is l, and r is the right-hand side (*rhs*). A TRS is a pair $\mathcal{R} = (\mathcal{F}, R)$ where R is a set of rewrite rules. $L(\mathcal{R})$ denotes the set of *lhs*'s of $\mathcal{R}$. A TRS $\mathcal{R}$ is left-linear if for all $l \in L(\mathcal{R})$, l is a linear term. Given $\mathcal{R} = (\mathcal{F}, R)$, we assume that $\mathcal{F}$ is defined as the disjoint union $\mathcal{F} = \mathcal{C} \uplus \mathcal{D}$ of symbols $c \in \mathcal{C}$, called *constructors*, and symbols $f \in \mathcal{D}$, called *defined symbols*, where $\mathcal{D} = \{root(l) \mid l \to r \in R\}$ and $\mathcal{C} = \mathcal{F} - \mathcal{D}$. A pattern is a term $f(l_1, \ldots, l_k)$ where $f \in \mathcal{D}$ and $l_i \in \mathcal{T}(\mathcal{C}, \mathcal{X})$, for $1 \leq i \leq k$. A TRS $\mathcal{R} = (\mathcal{C} \uplus \mathcal{D}, R)$ is a constructor system (CS) if every $l \in L(\mathcal{R})$ is a pattern.

A term t rewrites to s at position $p \in \mathcal{P}os(t)$ using the rule $l \to r \in R$, called a *rewrite step* and written $t \to_{\langle p,l\to r\rangle} s$ ($t \xrightarrow{p} s$ or simply $t \to s$), if $t|_p = \sigma(l)$ and $s = t[\sigma(r)]_p$. The pair $\langle p, l \to r \rangle$ is called a redex and we also refer to the subterm $t|_p$ in a rewrite step from t at position p as a redex. We often underline the redex in a rewrite step for readability. We denote the reflexive and transitive closure of the rewrite relation $\to$ by $\to^*$. We call t *the source* and s *the target* of a rewrite sequence $t \to^* s$. A term t is a $\to$-*normal form* (or normal form) if it contains no redex, i.e., there is no s such that $t \to s$. A term t is a $\to$-*head-normal form* (or head-normal form) if it cannot be reduced to a redex, i.e., there are no s, s' such that $t \to^* s \xrightarrow{\Lambda} s'$. We denote by $\xrightarrow{>\Lambda}$ a rewrite step at a position $p > \Lambda$.

A *(sequential) rewrite strategy* $\mathcal{S}$ for a TRS $\mathcal{R}$ is a subrelation $\xrightarrow{\mathcal{S}} \subseteq \to$ [21]. A rewrite strategy is *head normalizing* [21] if it provides a head-normal form for every source term, if such head-normal form exists. In this paper, we are only interested in *head-normalizing* rewrite strategies, since they are the basis for lazy rewriting strategies, and the following correctness and completeness criteria:

1. (Correctness) If a term t is a $\xrightarrow{\mathcal{S}}_{\mathcal{R}}$-normal form, then t is a head-normal form.
2. (Completeness) If $t \to^* s$, then $\exists s'$ s.t. $t \xrightarrow{\mathcal{S}}^* s'$, $root(s') = root(s)$ and $s' \xrightarrow{>\Lambda}^* s$.

3   Generalizing Natural Rewriting

As mentioned earlier, we are interested in a lazy strategy that, to the extent possible, performs only those reductions that are essential for reaching head-normal forms. Now, if a term t is not a head-normal form; then we know that after a (possibly empty) sequence of rewrites at positions other than the root, a rule $l \to r$ can be applied at the root. Accordingly, we adopt the approach of computing a *demanded* set of redexes in t such that *at least* one of the redexes in the demanded set has to be reduced before *any* rule can be applied at the root position in t. This idea of demandedness for reductions at the root is common in lazy evaluation strategies for programming languages, such as outermost needed rewriting [4]; see [5] for a survey on demandedness in programming languages.

Definition 1. *For a term s and a set of terms $T = \{t_1, \ldots, t_n\}$ we say that s is a* context *of the terms in T if $s \leq t_i$ for all $1 \leq i \leq n$. There is always a* least general context s *of T, i.e., one such that for any other context s' we have $s' \leq s$; furthermore s is unique up to renaming of variables. For $1 \leq i \leq n$, let the substitution σ_i be such that $\sigma_i(s) = t_i$ and $\mathcal{D}om(\sigma_i) \subseteq \mathcal{V}ar(s)$. We define the set $\mathcal{P}os_{\neq}(T)$ of disagreeing positions between the terms in T as those $p \in \mathcal{P}os_{\mathcal{X}}(s)$ such that there is an i with $\sigma_i(s|_p) \neq s|_p$.*

Example 2. Consider the set of terms $T = \{10! \ \% \ (s(0)-s(0)), \ 10! \ \% \ 0\}$ borrowed from Example 1. The least general context of T is the term $s = 10! \ \% \ Z$ and the set of disagreeing positions between terms in T is $\mathcal{P}os_{\neq}(T) = \{2\}$.

Definition 2 (Demanded positions). *For terms l and t, let s be the least general context of l and t, and let σ be the substitution such that $\sigma(s) = l$. We define the set of demanded positions in t w.r.t. l as*

$$DP_l(t) = \bigcup_{x \in Var(s)} \begin{array}{l} \text{if } \sigma(x) \notin \mathcal{X} \text{ then } \mathcal{P}os_x(s) \text{ else } Q.\mathcal{P}os_{\neq}(t|_Q) \\ \text{where } Q = \mathcal{P}os_{\sigma^{-1}(\sigma(x))}(s) \end{array}$$

Let us unpack the definition above. Intuitively, the set $DP_l(t)$ returns a set of positions in t at which t necessarily has to be "changed" before applying the rule $l \rightarrow r$ at the root position, i.e., for l to be able to match the term under consideration. Suppose, s is the least general context of l and t, and σ is such that $\sigma(s) = l$. Note that for every non-variable position p in s, it is the case that t and l have the same symbol at p. Now, if σ maps a variable $x \in Var(s)$ to a non-variable term, then t and l disagree (have a different symbol) at every position $p \in \mathcal{P}os_x(s)$; this is a consequence of the fact that s is the least general context of l and t. The other case is where a variable $x \in Var(s)$ is mapped to a possibly non-linear variable of l. In this case, consider the positions of all the variables in s that are mapped to the same variable as x, namely $Q = \mathcal{P}os_{\sigma^{-1}(\sigma(x))}(s)$. Now, l matches t only if all the subterms of t at positions in Q are identical. Thus, we compute the disagreeing positions $\mathcal{P}os_{\neq}(t|_Q)$, and add $Q.\mathcal{P}os_{\neq}(t|_Q)$ to the set $DP_l(t)$. Finally, note that when $l \leq t$, it is the case that l is the least general context of l and t, and $DP_l(t) = \varnothing$.

Example 3. Consider the left-hand side $l_7 = X \approx X$ and the term $t_2 = 10! \ \% \ (s(0)-s(0)) \approx 10! \ \% \ 0$ of Example 1. The least general context of l_7 and t_2 is $s = W \approx Y$. Now, for $\sigma = \{W \mapsto X, Y \mapsto X\}$, we have $\sigma(s) = l_7$. While computing $DP_{l_7}(t_2)$, we obtain the set of disagreeing positions between the subterms in t_2 corresponding to the non-linear variable X in l_7, i.e., the set $\mathcal{P}os_{\neq}(10! \ \% \ (s(0)-s(0)), 10! \ \% \ 0) = \{2\}$. Thus, $DP_{l_7}(t_2) = \{1, 2\}.\{2\} = \{1.2, 2.2\}$.

Note that the symbol at a position $p \in DP_l(t)$ in t can be changed by not only a rewrite at p, but also by a rewrite at a position $q < p$. Thus, besides considering the positions in $DP_l(t)$ as candidates for rewrites, we also need to consider the positions q in t that are above some position in $DP_l(t)$. Thus, for a position q in a term t, we define $D_t^{\uparrow}(q) = \{p \mid p \leq q \ \wedge \ p \in \mathcal{P}os_D(t)\}$. We lift this to sets of positions as $D_t^{\uparrow}(Q) = \cup_{q \in Q} D_t^{\uparrow}(q)$.

Example 4. Consider the TRS in Example 1, the left-hand side $l_7 = X \approx X$, and the new term $t = 0 \div s(10!) \approx 0 \div s(s(10!))$. We have $DP_{l_7}(t) = \{1.2.1, 2.2.1\}$, and the subterms at positions 1.2.1 and 2.2.1 should be identical for the above rule to be applied at the root position. Now, reductions in only the subterm 10! at position 1.2.1 would never result in s(10!), which is the subterm at position 2.2.1, and vice versa. The right reduction sequence leading to constant True is the one reducing the symbols $\div$ above the demanded positions 1.2.1 and 2.2.1:

$$\frac{0 \div \text{s(10!)} \approx 0 \div \text{s(s(10!))}}{\rightarrow 0 \approx \underline{0 \div \text{s(s(10!))}} \rightarrow \underline{0 \approx 0} \rightarrow \text{True}}$$

We are now ready to compute the demanded set of redexes of a given term t.

Definition 3 (Demanded redexes). *We define the* sufficient *set of positions of a term t as*

$$SP(t) = \bigcup_{l \in L(\mathcal{R}) \wedge l \leq t} D_l^\uparrow(\mathcal{P}os_\mathcal{X}(l)) \ \cup \ D_t^\uparrow(FP(t))$$

where $FP(t) = \bigcup_{l \in L(\mathcal{R})} DP_l(t)$. Then, we define the demanded set of redexes of *a term t as*

$$DR(t) = \{\langle \Lambda, l \rightarrow r \rangle \mid l \in L(\mathcal{R}) \wedge l \leq t\} \ \cup \ \bigcup_{q \in SP(t) \setminus \{\Lambda\}} q.DR(t|_q)$$

where for a set of redexes S, we define $q.S = \{\langle q.p, l \rightarrow r \rangle \mid \langle p, l \rightarrow r \rangle \in S\}$.

The set $DR(t)$ is recursively computed as follows. Whenever $l \leq t$ for a rule $l \rightarrow r$, the redex $\langle \Lambda, l \rightarrow r \rangle$ is included in $DR(t)$. When $l \not\leq t$, we recursively compute $DR(t|_q)$ for each position $q \in D_t^\uparrow(DP_l(t))$. The case $l \leq t$ has an additional subtlety; specifically, in this case, we also have to recursively compute $DR(t|_q)$ for the positions q in t that have a defined symbol and that are above a variable position in l. This is necessary for the strategy to be complete, as illustrated by the following example.

Example 5. Consider the TRS

(i) first(pair(X,Y)) $\rightarrow$ X   (ii) pair(X,Y) $\rightarrow$ pair(Y,X)

and the term $t = $ first(pair(a,b)). If we simply define $SP(t) = D_t^\uparrow(FP(t))$, then $DR(t) = \{\langle \Lambda, (i) \rangle\}$, and the only rewrite sequence starting from t and beginning with a redex in $DR(t)$ would be

first(pair(a,b)) $\rightarrow$ a

But the term t can also be reduced to the head-normal form b as follows

first(<u>pair(a,b)</u>) $\rightarrow$ <u>first(pair(b,a))</u> $\rightarrow$ b (*)

Hence, although the left-hand side of rule (i) matches t, for the strategy to be complete, we also have to consider the subterm pair(a,b) of t at position 1 (which is above variable positions 1.1 and 1.2 in the left-hand side of rule (i)), and recursively compute $DR($pair(a,b)$)$. Then we will have $DR(t) = \{\langle \Lambda, (i) \rangle, \langle 1, (ii) \rangle\}$, which enables us to account for the rewrite sequence (*) above.

From now on, while displaying the sets $DR(t)$ in examples, we will omit the rule $l \rightarrow r$ in a redex $\langle p, l \rightarrow r \rangle$ and simply write $\langle p \rangle$, whenever there is no scope for ambiguity about the rule.

Example 6. Consider again the term $t_2 = 10! \% (s(0)-s(0)) \approx 10! \% 0$ from Example 1, and the computation of $DR(t_2)$. Since t_2 is not a redex, we have that

$$DR(t_2) = \cup_{q \in SP(t_2) \setminus \{\Lambda\}} q.DR(t_2|_q).$$

But, since t_2 is not a redex, we have $SP(t_2) = D^{\uparrow}_{t_2}(FP(t_2)) = D^{\uparrow}_{t_2}(\cup_{l \in L(\mathcal{R})} DP_l(t_2))$. Now, from Example 3, we have that $DP_{l_7}(t_2) = \{1.2, 2.2\}$ for the rule $l_7 = X \approx X$ and $DP_l(t_2) = \{\Lambda\}$ for any other rule l in $\mathcal{R}$. So then, $D^{\uparrow}_{t_2}(\cup_{l \in L(\mathcal{R})} DP_l(t_2)) = \{\Lambda, 1, 2, 1.2\}$, where the position 2.2 has been removed since it is not rooted by a defined symbol. Hence, we have

$$DR(t_2) = 1.DR(t_2|_1) \cup 2.DR(t_2|_2) \cup 1.2.DR(t_2|_{1.2}).$$

Now, we consider $DR(t_2|_{1.2})$. Subterm $s(0)-s(0)$ at position 1.2 is a redex and thus $\langle \Lambda \rangle \in DR(t_2|_{1.2})$. Furthermore, $SP(t_2|_{1.2}) \setminus \{\Lambda\} = \varnothing$, because all symbols under root position in $s(0)-s(0)$ are constructor symbols. Thus, we have $DR(t_2|_{1.2}) = \{ \langle \Lambda \rangle \}$.

Next, we consider $DR(t_2|_1)$. The subterm $10! \% (s(0)-s(0))$ is not a redex, and thus

$$DR(t_2|_1) = \cup_{q \in SP(t_2|_1) \setminus \{\Lambda\}} q.DR(t_2|_{1.q}).$$

Now consider $SP(t_2|_1)$. Since $10! \% (s(0)-s(0))$ is not a redex, we have $SP(t_2|_1) = D^{\uparrow}_{t_2|_1}(FP(t_2|_1)) = D^{\uparrow}_{t_2|_1}(\cup_{l \in L(\mathcal{R})} DP_l(t_2|_1))$. Consider $DP_{l_3}(t_2|_1)$ and $DP_{l_4}(t_2|_1)$ for left-hand sides $l_3 = M \% s(N)$ and $l_4 = (0 - s(M)) \% s(N)$; note that $DP_l(t_2|_1) = \{\Lambda\}$ for any other rule l in $\mathcal{R}$. Then, we have $DP_{l_3}(t_2|_1) = \{2\}$ and $DP_{l_4}(t_2|_1) = \{1, 2\}$ and therefore we have

$$DR(t_2|_1) = 1.DR(t_2|_{1.1}) \cup 2.DR(t_2|_{1.2}).$$

Now, this implies that we have to compute recursively $DR(t_2|_{1.1})$ and $DR(t_2|_{1.2})$. Now, $DR(t_2|_{1.2})$ was already computed before, and the reader can check that $DR(t_2|_{1.1}) = \{\langle \Lambda \rangle\}$. So, we can conclude $DR(t_2|_1) = \{ \langle 1 \rangle, \langle 2 \rangle \}$.

Finally, consider $DR(t_2|_2)$. The subterm $10! \% 0$ is not a redex, thus

$$DR(t_2|_2) = \cup_{q \in SP(t_2|_2) \setminus \{\Lambda\}} q.DR(t_2|_{2.q}).$$

But using a similar reasoning that in the previous term $t_2|_1$, we can conclude $DR(t_2|_2) = \{ \langle 1 \rangle \}$. Finally, we have that $DR(t_2) = \{\langle 1.1 \rangle, \langle 1.2 \rangle, \langle 2.1 \rangle\}$.

We are now ready to formally define the natural rewriting strategy.

Definition 4 (Natural rewriting). *We say that term t reduces by* natural rewriting *to term s, denoted by $t \xrightarrow{m}_{\langle p, l \to r \rangle} s$ (or simply $t \xrightarrow{m} s$) if $t \to_{\langle p, l \to r \rangle} s$ and $\langle p, l \to r \rangle \in DR(t)$.*

Example 7. Continuing Example 6, we have three possible natural rewriting steps from the term t_2: (i) a rewriting step reducing the subterm $s(0)-s(0)$ at position 1.2, (ii) a rewriting step reducing the subterm $10!$ at position 1.1, and (iii) a rewriting step reducing the subterm 10! at position 2.1. The last two rewriting steps are undesirable and unnecessary for obtaining the normal form True, as shown in Example 1. Using the further refinements to the natural rewriting strategy presented in the next section, we will be able to avoid reducing these unnecessary redexes.

It is worthy to note that although some refinements are still necessary to obtain the efficient rewrite strategy we desire, we are already able to avoid some unnecessary rewrite steps while computing head-normal forms, as shown in the following example.

Example 8. Consider Example 1 and the term $t = 0 \div s(10!)$. The term is a redex, so we have $DR(t) = \{ \langle \Lambda \rangle \} \cup \bigcup_{q \in SP(t) \setminus \{\Lambda\}} q.DR(t|_q)$. Now we have $SP(t) = \{\Lambda\} \cup D_t^\uparrow (\bigcup_{l \in L(\mathcal{R})} DP_l(t))$. Now, $DP_{l_1}(t) = \varnothing$ for $l_1 = 0 \div s(M)$, $DP_{l_2}(t) = \{1\}$ for $l_2 = s(M) \div s(N)$, and $DP_l(t) = \{\Lambda\}$ for any other rule l in $\mathcal{R}$. Then, $SP(t) = \{\Lambda\}$, since position 1 corresponds to a constructor, and therefore $DR(t) = \{ \langle \Lambda \rangle \}$. So, our natural rewriting strategy performs only the sequence: $\underline{0 \div s(10!)} \to 0$, and avoids any reduction on the computational expensive term 10!.

In the remaining part of this section, we show that the natural rewriting strategy defined above satisfies the correctness and completeness criteria w.r.t. head-normal forms, that are described in Section 2.

The following is a property of $DR(t)$ that is easy to check, and that will be useful.

Remark 1. If $\langle q, l \to r \rangle \in DR(t)$ and $p < q.q'$ for $q' \in Pos_{\mathcal{X}}(l)$, then $p.DR(t|_p) \subseteq DR(t)$.

In order to prove completeness of the generalized natural rewriting strategy, we introduce some auxiliary notation. Given two rewrite sequences $\pi = t \to^* s$ and $\pi' = s \to^* w$, we write $\pi; \pi'$ for the sequence $t \to^* s \to^* w$. Given a rewrite sequence $\pi = t_0 \xrightarrow{p_1} t_1; \pi'$ with $\pi' = t_1 \xrightarrow{p_2} t_2 \cdots \xrightarrow{p_n} t_n$ and given an outermost position p_k amongst $p_1, \ldots, p_n$, we define the projection $\pi|_{p_k}$ as follows:

$$
\pi|_{p_k} = \begin{cases} \pi & \text{if } n = 0 \\ \pi'|_{p_k} & \text{if } p_1 \parallel p_k \\ t_0|_{p_k} \xrightarrow{p_1/p_k} t_1|_{p_k}; \pi'|_{p_k} & \text{otherwise} \end{cases}
$$

We now establish a key property of the set $DR(t)$ that will be useful in proving the correctness and completeness results.

Lemma 1. *Consider a rewrite sequence* $t \to_{\langle p_1, l_1 \to r_1 \rangle} t_1 \cdots \to_{\langle p_n, l_n \to r_n \rangle} t_n$ *such that* $p_n = \Lambda$. *Then, there is a k s.t. $1 \leq k \leq n$ and $\langle p_k, l_k \to r_k \rangle \in DR(t)$.*

Now, we prove correctness of our generalized rewrite strategy w.r.t. head-normal forms.

Theorem 1 (Correctness). *If a term t is a $\xrightarrow{m}$ -normal form, then t is a head-normal form.*

Proof. We prove the contrapositive. Specifically, if t is not a head-normal form, then, by Lemma 1, we have $t \xrightarrow{m}_{\langle p,l \to r \rangle} s$ for some s and t is not a $\xrightarrow{m}$ -normal form. $\qquad\square$

In the following, we give some useful definitions and results that will be useful in proving completeness.

Lemma 2. *Consider a rewrite sequence $t \to_{\langle p_1, l_1 \to r_1 \rangle} t_1 \cdots \to_{\langle p_n, l_n \to r_n \rangle} t_n$ such that $\langle p_i, l_i \to r_i \rangle \notin DR(t)$ for all i s.t. $1 \le i \le n$. Then, there is no i and $\langle q, l \to r \rangle \in DR(t)$ such that $p_i < q.q'$ for $q' \in \mathcal{P}os_{\mathcal{X}}(l)$.*

To prove completeness, we will show that whenever there is a rewrite sequence $\pi = t \to^* t'$, then there is also a rewrite sequence $t \to_{\langle q, l \to r \rangle} s \to^* t'$ that begins with a redex $\langle q, l \to r \rangle \in DR(t)$. Furthermore, the rewrite sequence $\pi' = s \to^* t'$ is "smaller" in an appropriate sense in comparison to π. Specifically, we will define a well-founded metric on rewrite sequences, and show that the metric of π' is strictly smaller than that of π. The completeness result will then follow by noetherian induction on this metric.

Definition 5. *Given a rewrite sequence $\pi = t_0 \xrightarrow{p_1} t_1 \cdots \xrightarrow{p_n} t_n$, we define a metric $\mu(\pi)$ returning a sequence of natural numbers as follows.*

- *Let k be the smallest integer such that $p_k = \Lambda$, if any. Then,*

$$\mu(\pi) = \mu(\pi_1).1.\mu(\pi_2)$$

  where $\pi_1 = t_0 \to^* t_{k-1}$ and $\pi_2 = t_k \to^* t_n$.
- *If $p_i \ne \Lambda$ for all i, then let $q_1, \ldots, q_k$ be the outermost positions in $p_1, \ldots, p_n$. We define*

$$\mu(\pi) = \sum_{i=1}^{k} \mu(\pi|_{q_i})$$

  where $+$ is inductively defined as: $n_1.v_1 + n_2.v_2 = (n_1+n_2).(v_1+v_2)$, $\epsilon + v = v$, and $v + \epsilon = v$.

We define the ordering $<$ on metrics as follows $v_1 < v_2$ if (i) $|v_1| < |v_2|$, or (ii) $|v_1| = |v_2|$, $v_1 = v_1'.n_1.v$, $v_2 = v_2'.n_2.v$, and $n_1 < n_2$; where $|\cdot|$ denotes the length of a sequence of natural numbers. Note that $<$ is a well-ordering.

The metric $\mu(\pi)$ essentially represents the parallelism that is implicit in the rewrite sequence π. Specifically, consider the rewrite sequence in Definition 5. If $p_k = \Lambda$, then the first $k - 1$ rewrites in π have to be performed before the kth rewrite, and similarly the kth rewrite has to be performed before any of the remaining $n - k$ rewrites. On the other hand, if p_i and p_j are two different outermost positions in $p_1, \ldots, p_n$ then all the rewrites in $\pi|_{p_i}$ and $\pi|_{p_j}$ can be performed in parallel. Thus, $|\mu(\pi)|$ is the number of sequential steps that would remain when π is parallelized to the extent possible, and further, if the ith number in the sequence $\mu(\pi)$ is n_i then the ith step in the parallelized version of π would contain n_i parallel reductions.

Example 9. Consider the TRS of Example 1 and the following sequence π:

$$s((\underline{0-0}) - 0) - s(0-0)$$
$$\rightarrow s(\underline{0-0}) - s(0-0) \quad \rightarrow \quad s(0) - s(\underline{0-0}) \quad \rightarrow \quad \underline{s(0)-s(0)} \quad \rightarrow \quad \underline{0-0} \rightarrow 0$$

The metric for this sequence is $\mu(\pi) = \mu(\pi').1.\mu(\pi'')$, where π' is the sequence containing the first three steps of π and π'' is the sequence containing the last step of π. Further, $\mu(\pi'') = 1$, since there is only one step at root position. Now, the outermost positions of π' are namely 1.1 and 2.1, and hence we have $\mu(\pi') = \mu(\pi'|_{1.1}) + \mu(\pi'|_{2.1})$. Further, $\pi'|_{1.1} = (\underline{0-0})-0 \rightarrow \underline{0-0} \rightarrow 0$, and $\pi'|_{2.1} = \underline{0-0} \rightarrow 0$. Now, $\mu(\pi'|_{2.1}) = 1$, and the reader can check that $\mu(\pi'|_{1.1}) = 1.1$. So finally, $\mu(\pi) = \mu(\pi').1.\mu(\pi'') = \mu(\pi').1.1 = (\mu(\pi'|_{1.1}) + \mu(\pi'|_{2.1})).1.1 = (1.1 + 1).1.1 = 2.1.1.1$, that indicates that there are two steps at the beginning that can be performed in parallel, followed by three other steps that cannot be performed in parallel.

The following are some useful properties of the metric.

Lemma 3. $|\mu(\pi_1 ; \pi_2)| \leq |\mu(\pi_1)| + |\mu(\pi_2)|$.

Lemma 4. *Let $\pi = t_1 \rightarrow^* t_2 \xrightarrow{q} t_3 \rightarrow^* t_4$ and $\rho = t_1' \rightarrow^* t_3 \rightarrow^* t_4$ be rewrite sequences such that $|\mu(t_1' \rightarrow^* t_3)| \leq |\mu(t_1 \rightarrow^* t_2)|$, and all the reductions in both $t_1 \rightarrow^* t_2$ and $t_1' \rightarrow^* t_3$ happen under the position q. Then $\mu(\rho) < \mu(\pi)$.*

Lemma 5. *Let $\pi = t_1 \rightarrow^* t_2 \rightarrow_{\langle q,l \rightarrow r \rangle} t_3 \rightarrow^* t_4$ where $\langle q, l \rightarrow r \rangle \in DR(t_1)$ and none of the redexes in $t_1 \rightarrow^* t_2$ is in $DR(t_1)$. Then, there is a rewrite sequence $t_1 \rightarrow_{\langle q,l \rightarrow r \rangle} s \rightarrow^* t_4$ such that $\mu(s \rightarrow^* t_4) < \mu(\pi)$.*

Theorem 2 (Completeness). *If $t \rightarrow^* s$, then there is an s' such that $t \xrightarrow{m}^* s'$, $root(s') = root(s)$ and $s' \xrightarrow{>\Lambda}^* s$.*

Proof. Let $\pi = t \rightarrow_{\langle p_1, l_1 \rightarrow r_1 \rangle} t_1 \cdots \rightarrow_{\langle p_n, l_n \rightarrow r_n \rangle} s$. We prove the theorem by noetherian induction on $\mu(\pi)$. The base case $\mu(\pi) = \epsilon$ is obvious, since $|\pi| = 0$. For the induction step there are two cases:

- Suppose there is no i such that $1 \leq i \leq n$ and $\langle p_i, l_i \rightarrow r_i \rangle \in DR(t)$. Then, by Lemma 1, $p_i > \Lambda$ for all i, and thus the statement holds by taking $s' = t$.
- Now, we consider the least k such that $\langle p_k, l_k \rightarrow r_k \rangle \in DR(t)$. Then, by Lemma 5, we have $\pi' = t \rightarrow_{\langle p_k, l_k \rightarrow r_k \rangle} t_1' ; \delta$ for some t_1' and a rewrite sequence δ with target s. Furthermore, $\mu(\delta) < \mu(\pi)$. By induction hypothesis, we have $t_1' \xrightarrow{m}^* s'$ for some s' such that $root(s') = root(s)$ and $s' \xrightarrow{>\Lambda}^* s$. Then, the statement follows from the observation that $t \xrightarrow{m}^* s'$. $\qquad \square$

4   Refinements of the Strategy

In this section, we further refine the natural rewriting strategy, using the notions of *failing terms* and *most frequently demanded positions*, both of which were originally introduced in [9], although not in an explicit way and for left-linear constructor systems.

4.1   Failing Terms

For a position p and a term t, we define the set $R_t(p)$ of *reflections* of p w.r.t. t as follows: if p is under a variable position in t, i.e., $p = q.q'$ for some q such that $t|_q = x$, then $R_t(p) = \mathcal{P}os_x(t).q'$, else $R_t(p) = \{p\}$. We say that the path to p in t is *stable* (or simply p is stable) if $D_t^\uparrow(p) \setminus \{\Lambda\} = \varnothing$.

Definition 6 (Failing term). *Given terms l, t, we say t fails w.r.t. l, denoted by $l \blacktriangleleft t$, if there is $p \in DP_l(t)$ such that p is stable, and one of the following holds: (i) $R_l(p) \cap DP_l(t) = \{p\}$; or (ii) there is $q \in R_l(p) \cap DP_l(t)$ with $root(t|_p) \neq root(t|_q)$, and q is also stable. We denote by $l \blacktriangleleft\!\!\!\!\! \triangleleft\, t$ that t is not failing w.r.t. l.*

The idea behind the definition above is that if $l \blacktriangleleft t$, then no sequence of reductions in t will help produce a term to which the rule $l \to r$ can be applied at the root. We can thus safely ignore the positions demanded by l while computing the set $DR(t)$.

Example 10. Consider the terms $t = 10! \ \% \ 0$ and $l_3 = \mathtt{M} \ \% \ \mathtt{s(N)}$ from Example 1. We have that $l_3 \blacktriangleleft t$, because position $2 \in DP_{l_3}(t)$ is stable and $R_{l_3}(2) = \{2\}$. Now, consider the terms $t' = \mathtt{s(Z)} \approx 0$ and $l_7 = \mathtt{X} \approx \mathtt{X}$, again from Example 1. We have $l_7 \blacktriangleleft t'$, since position $1 \in DP_{l_7}(t')$ is stable, $R_{l_7}(1) = \{1, 2\}$, $root(t'|_1) = \mathtt{s} \neq 0 = root(t'|_2)$, and position 2 is also stable.

Definition 7 (Demanded redexes). *We improve the set $DR(t)$ in Definition 3 and replace the former set $FP(t)$ by $FP(t) = \bigcup_{l \in L(\mathcal{R}) \wedge l \blacktriangleleft\!\!\!\!\! \triangleleft\, t} DP_l(t)$.*

With trivial modifications to the proofs, the correctness and completeness properties of natural rewriting hold with this refined Definition 7 instead of Definition 3.

Example 11. Consider again the term $t_2 = 10! \ \% \ (\mathtt{s(0)} - \mathtt{s(0)}) \approx 10! \ \% \ 0$ from Example 7. With the refined Definition 7 we have $DR(t_2) = \{\langle 1.1 \rangle, \langle 1.2 \rangle\}$ and the redex at position 2.1 is not considered anymore. The reason is that from Example 10, it follows that the subterm $10! \ \% \ 0$ is failing w.r.t. rules l_3 and l_4, and hence $SP(t_2|_2) \setminus \{\Lambda\} = \varnothing$. Therefore, we have only two possible rewriting steps from the term t_2: (i) a rewriting step reducing the subterm $\mathtt{s(0)} - \mathtt{s(0)}$ at position 1.2, and (ii) a rewriting step reducing the subterm $10!$ at position 1.1. The second rewrite step is still undesirable and its removal motivates the next refinement.

4.2   Most Frequently Demanded Positions

Suppose $l \not\leq t$, $l \blacktriangleleft t$, and that we have a rewrite sequence $t \xrightarrow{p_1} \ldots t_{n-1} \rightarrow_{\langle p_n, l \rightarrow r \rangle}$ t_n where $p_n = \Lambda$. Then, observe that for *every* $q \in DP_l(t)$, there is a reduction above a position in $R_l(q)$, i.e., there is $q' \in R_l(q)$ and k such that $p_k \in D_t^{\uparrow}(q')$; clearly, only then it is possible that $l \leq t_{n-1}$. Now, recall that we are only interested in computing a demanded set of redexes in t such that before any rule can be applied at the root position in t, *at least* one of the redexes in the demanded set has to be reduced. Therefore, while computing the set $SP(t)$ in Definition 7, for each $l \in L(\mathcal{R})$ such that $l \blacktriangleleft t$, instead of considering (the defined symbols above) every position in $DP_l(t)$, it is sufficient to consider only the positions $R_l(q)$ for at least one $q \in DP_l(t)$. This motivates the following refinement of Definition 7.

Definition 8 (Set cover). *For a set of positions P, a sequence of lhs's $l_1, \ldots, l_n$, and a sequence of sets of positions $Q_1, \ldots, Q_n$, we say that P covers $l_1, \ldots, l_n$ and $Q_1, \ldots, Q_n$ if for all $1 \leq i \leq n$, there is a position $p \in P \cap Q_i$ such that $R_{l_i}(p) \subseteq P$.*

Definition 9 (Demanded redexes). *We improve the set $DR(t)$ in Definition 7 and replace the former set $FP(t)$ by the set $FP(t)$ returning one of the minimal sets of positions that cover $l_1, \ldots, l_n$ and $DP_{l_1}(t), \ldots, DP_{l_n}(t)$, where $\{l_1, \ldots, l_n\} = \{l \in L(\mathcal{R}) \mid l \blacktriangleleft t\}$.*

The set $FP(t)$ above is a minimal set cover that is closed under reflection. Roughly, minimality amounts to giving priority to those positions in t that are demanded by the maximum number of rules, i.e., what we call the *most frequently demanded positions*. This idea of giving priority to 'popular' demanded positions is familiar from other lazy evaluation strategies such as outermost needed rewriting [4], and was first formalized in a similar fashion as above in [9]. With trivial modifications to the proofs, the correctness and completeness properties of natural rewriting hold also with the above refinement.

Example 12. Consider the subterm $t = $ 10! % (s(0)−s(0)) of the term t_2 in Example 1. Consider also the left-hand sides of the rules (3) and (4): $l_3 = $ M % s(N) and $l_4 = $ (0 − s(M)) % s(N). We have that $DP_{l_3}(t) = \{2\}$, $DP_{l_4}(t) = \{1, 2\}$, and $DP_{l'}(t) = \{\Lambda\}$ for any other lhs l'. Then, the set $P = \{2, \Lambda\}$ covers all lhs's. Now, let us continue with term $t_2 = $ 10! % (s(0)−s(0)) $\approx$ 10! % 0 from Example 11. With Definition 9, the redexes computed by the natural rewriting strategy become even more refined. Specifically, we have $DR(t_2) = \{\langle 1.2 \rangle\}$ and the redex at position 1.1 is not considered anymore. The reason is that since position 2 in 10! % (s(0)−s(0)) is enough to obtain a set cover of all the positions demanded by rules (3) and (4), position 1 in the subterm $t_2|_1$ is not considered as demanded, i.e., $SP(t_2|_1) = FP(t_2|_1) = \{2, \Lambda\}$. Finally, we have only the optimal rewriting step for position 1.2 from the term t_2 and the optimal rewrite sequence:

10! % (s(0)−s(0)) $\approx$ 10! % 0

$\rightarrow$ 10! % (0−0) $\approx$ 10! % 0 $\rightarrow$ 10! % 0 $\approx$ 10! % 0 $\rightarrow$ True

Note that we have $DR(t_3) = \{\langle 1.2 \rangle\}$ and $DR(t_4) = \{\langle \Lambda \rangle\}$ for the terms $t_3 =$ 10! % (0−0)) $\approx$ 10! % 0 and $t_4 =$ 10! % 0 $\approx$ 10! % 0 above.

5   Conclusion

We have extended natural rewriting to general rewriting systems while preserving correctness and completeness w.r.t. head-normal forms. A noteworthy feature of this generalization is that it is conservative, i.e., the generalized strategy coincides with the original one for the class of left-linear constructor systems. This makes the strategy available for both expressive equational languages and for rewriting logic languages. Since our generalization is conservative, we inherit all the optimality results presented in [9] for left-linear constructor systems. An important problem for future research is to identify optimality results for this new generalized natural rewriting strategy. We believe that the notion of *inductively sequential terms* introduced in [9] can provide significant insights for the more general optimality results, since this notion identifies specific terms, rather than classes of rewrite systems, that can be optimally evaluated. Another observation is that our generalized natural rewriting is easily implementable, since the demanded set of redexes is computed using simple recursive procedures. Indeed in [10], we have proposed a technique for the efficient implementation of the natural rewriting strategy of [9] for left-linear constructor systems, which moves the computation of the demanded set of redexes to compilation phase instead of execution phase. Extending this implementation technique to the generalized rewriting strategy would be considered as future work. However, a complexity analysis of the generalized natural rewriting strategy is also planned.

This work provides a basis for a subsequent generalization of natural rewriting first to narrowing, already achieved in [12], and second to even more expressive rewrite theories suited for concurrent system specifications [20] and supporting: (i) sorts and subsorts; (ii) rewriting *modulo* axioms such as associativity, commutativity, identity, and so on; and (iii) conditional rewriting.

Acknowledgements. S. Escobar has been partially supported by projects MEC TIN 2004-07943-C04-02, EU ALA/95/23/2003/077-054, GV Grupos03/025 and grant 2667 of *Universidad Politécnica de Valencia* during a stay at Urbana-Champaign, USA.

References

1. S. Antoy. Definitional trees. In *Proc. of the 3rd International Conference on Algebraic and Logic Programming ALP'92*, volume 632 of *Lecture Notes in Computer Science*, pages 143–157. Springer-Verlag, Berlin, 1992.
2. S. Antoy. Constructor-based conditional narrowing. In *Proc. of 3rd International ACM SIGPLAN Conference on Principles and Practice of Declarative Programming, PPDP'01*, pages 199–206, Florence, Italy, Sept. 2001. ACM.

3. S. Antoy, R. Echahed, and M. Hanus. Parallel evaluation strategies for functional logic languages. In *Proc. of the Fourteenth International Conference on Logic Programming (ICLP'97)*, pages 138–152. MIT Press, 1997.

4. S. Antoy, R. Echahed, and M. Hanus. A needed narrowing strategy. In *Journal of the ACM*, volume 47(4), pages 776–822, 2000.

5. S. Antoy and S. Lucas. Demandness in rewriting and narrowing. In M. Comini and M. Falaschi, editors, *Proc. of the 11th Int'l Workshop on Functional and (Constraint) Logic Programming WFLP'02*, volume 76 of *Electronic Notes in Theoretical Computer Science*. Elsevier Sciences Publisher, 2002.

6. P. Borovanský, C. Kirchner, H. Kirchner, and P.-E. Moreau. ELAN from a rewriting logic point of view. *Theoretical Computer Science*, 285:155–185, 2002.

7. M. Clavel, F. Durán, S. Eker, P. Lincoln, N. Martí-Oliet, J. Meseguer, and J. Quesada. Maude: specification and programming in rewriting logic. *Theoretical Computer Science*, 285:187–243, 2002.

8. A. Deursen, J. Heering, and P. Klint. *Language Prototyping: An Algebraic Specification Approach*. World Scientific, 1996.

9. S. Escobar. Refining weakly outermost-needed rewriting and narrowing. In D. Miller, editor, *Proc. of 5th International ACM SIGPLAN Conference on Principles and Practice of Declarative Programming, PPDP'03*, pages 113–123. ACM Press, New York, 2003.

10. S. Escobar. Implementing natural rewriting and narrowing efficiently. In Y. Kameyama and P. J. Stuckey, editors, *7th International Symposium on Functional and Logic Programming (FLOPS 2004)*, volume 2998 of *Lecture Notes in Computer Science*, pages 147–162. Springer-Verlag, Berlin, 2004.

11. S. Escobar, J. Meseguer, and P. Thati. Natural narrowing as a general unified mechanism for programming and proving. Technical Report DSIC-II/16/04, DSIC, Universidad Politécnica de Valencia, 2004. Available at http://www.dsic.upv.es/users/elp/papers.html.

12. S. Escobar, J. Meseguer, and P. Thati. Natural narrowing for general term rewriting systems. In J. Giesl, editor, *Proc. of 16th International Conference on Rewriting Techniques and Applications, RTA'05*, Lecture Notes in Computer Science. Springer-Verlag, Berlin, 2005.

13. K. Futatsugi and R. Diaconescu. *CafeOBJ Report*. World Scientific, AMAST Series, 1998.

14. E. Giovannetti, G. Levi, C. Moiso, and C. Palamidessi. Kernel Leaf: A Logic plus Functional Language. *Journal of Computer and System Sciences*, 42(2):139–185, 1991.

15. J. Goguen, T. Winkler, J. Meseguer, K. Futatsugi, and J.-P. Jouannaud. Introducing OBJ. In *Software Engineering with OBJ: Algebraic Specification in Action*, pages 3–167. Kluwer, 2000.

16. J. C. González-Moreno, M. T. Hortalá-González, F. J. López-Fraguas, and M. Rodríguez-Artalejo. An approach to declarative programming based on a rewriting logic. *Journal of Logic Programming*, 40(1):47–87, 1999.

17. D. Hofbauer and M. Huber. Linearizing term rewriting systems using test sets. *Journal of Symbolic Computation*, 17:91–129, 1994.

18. G. Huet and J.-J. Lévy. Computations in Orthogonal Term Rewriting Systems, Part I + II. In *Computational logic: Essays in honour of J. Alan Robinson*, pages 395–414 and 415–443. The MIT Press, Cambridge, MA, 1992.

19. R. Loogen, F. López-Fraguas, and M. Rodríguez-Artalejo. A Demand Driven Computation Strategy for Lazy Narrowing. In *Proc. of PLILP'93*, volume 714 of *Lecture Notes in Computer Science*, pages 184–200. Springer-Verlag, Berlin, 1993.

20. J. Meseguer. Conditional rewriting logic as a unified model of concurrency. *Theoretical Computer Science*, 96(1):73–155, 1992.
21. A. Middeldorp. Call by need computations to root-stable form. In *Proceedings of the 24th Annual ACM SIGPLAN-SIGACT Symposium on Principles of Programming Languages*, pages 94–105. ACM Press, New York, 1997.
22. S. Peyton-Jones. *The Implementation of Functional Programming Languages*. Prentice Hall International, London, 1987.
23. B. Salinier and R. Strandh. Efficient simulation of forward-branching systems with constructor systems. *Journal of Symbolic Computation*, 22:381–399, 1996.
24. R. Sekar and I. Ramakrishnan. Programming in equational logic: Beyond strong sequentiality. *Information and Computation*, 104(1):78–109, 1993.

Negation Elimination for Finite PCFGs

Taisuke Sato and Yoshitaka Kameya

Tokyo Institute of Technology,
2-12-1 Ookayama, Meguro, Tokyo, Japan, CREST/JST
{sato, kameya}@mi.cs.titech.ac.jp
http://sato-www.cs.titech.ac.jp

Abstract. We introduce negation to a symbolic-statistical modeling language PRISM and propose to eliminate negation by program transformation called negation technique which is applicable to probabilistic logic programs. We also introduce finite PCFGs (probabilistic context free grammars) as PCFGs with finite constraints as part of generative modeling of stochastic HPSGs (head-driven phrase structure grammars). They are a subclass of log-linear models and allow exact computation of normalizing constants. We apply the negation technique to a PDCG (probabilistic definite clause grammar) program written in PRISM that describes a finite PCFG with a height constraint. The resulting program computes a normalizing constant for the finite PCFG in time linear in the given height. We also report on an experiment of parameter learning for a real grammar (ATR grammar) with the height constraint. We have discovered that the height constraint does not necessarily lead to a significant decrease in parsing accuracy.

1 Introduction

1.1 Background

Symbolic-statistical modeling is a discipline where symbolic reasoning and statistical inference cooperate to identify the underlying structure of our observations of interest such as genome sequences, disease pedigrees and documents in a natural language that consist of structured symbols with various types of uncertainty. There are several formalisms already developed. HMMs (hidden Markov models) are a kind of stochastic automata used to identify for instance genes in genome sequences (and in many other areas) [1]. PCFGs (probabilistic context free grammars) are CFGs such that rule selection in a string derivation is probabilistic and they are applied to parsing and scene analysis [2, 3]. The most popular one is BNs (Bayesian networks) that can represent finite distributions of any type [4]. Recently they were applied to linkage analysis and beat competitors [5].

However, while HMMs, PCFGs and BNs can express uncertainty in terms of probabilities, they are all at propositional level and their logical power is limited. They do not have logical variables or quantifiers. There is no explicit treatment of negation either. Naturally there have been efforts for upgrading these formalisms to the first-order level in various communities including the LP (logic

S. Etalle(Ed.): LOPSTR 2004, LNCS 3573, pp. 117–132, 2005.

programming) community, the ILP (inductive logic programming) community and the BN community among which is PRISM, a symbolic-statistical modeling language, we have been developing.

PRISM[1] is a probabilistic extension of Prolog augmented with a built-in EM learning routine[2] for statistical inference of parameters embedded in PRISM programs [7]. It is intended for modeling complex systems governed by rules and probability. Theoretically PRISM is a probabilistic Turing machine with a parameter learning mechanism which subsumes HMMs, PCFGs and discrete BNs in terms of expressive power, probability computation and parameter learning [8]. But what is genuinely innovative about it is that it opens a way to use programs as statistical models (programs are statistical models themselves in PRISM) and frees the user of having to derive a new EM algorithm for parameter learning for a new statistical model everytime he/she invents it.

Unfortunately the current PRISM lacks negation, which narrows the class of definable distributions and also causes inconveniences in modeling. To overcome this limitation, we propose to deal with negation by program transformation. The point is that we allow negated PRISM programs but eliminate negation by program transformation, thus recover negation-free PRISM programs.

There are two deterministic algorithms available for negation elimination of source programs. A general one is FOC (first order compiler), a deterministic program transformation algorithm originally developed for non-probabilistic logic programs containing universally quantified implications[3] [9]. It uses continuation[4] to compile universally quantified implications into executable form. FOC is general and can deal with large programs but tends to generate complicated and less efficient programs from the viewpoint of the PRISM's tabled search[5] [10, 11]. In this paper, we alternatively propose to use the negation technique [12]. It is a deterministic transformation algorithm to synthesize a logic program that traces failed computation paths of the original program. While the

---

[1] URL = http://sato-www.cs.titech.ac.jp/prism/

[2] EM learning here means parameter learning by the EM algorithm which is an iterative algorithm for maximum likelihood estimation of parameters associated with a probabilistic model with hidden variables [6]. Hidden variables are those that are not directly observable like a disease in contrast to symptoms thereof.

[3] Universally quantified implications are formulas of the form $\forall x\,(\phi \Rightarrow \varphi)$ and negation is a special case ($\neg\phi$ is equal to $\phi \Rightarrow$ false).

[4] Continuation is a data to represent the *rest* of computation. Usually it is a higher order object in functional programming but here we just use a first order term called continuation term, representing the next goal to be executed with the help of auxiliary clauses.

[5] Tabling is a search technique to record calling patterns of goals and their solutions for later use not to repeat the same search. It can avoid exponential explosion in the search space by sharing computation paths and brings about the same effect as dynamic programming in top-down search. Compilation by FOC introduces continuation terms that can be an obstacle to tabled search as they differentiate similar goals syntactically.

negation technique is only applicable to the negation of definite clause programs, synthesized programs do not carry continuation terms and hence are more preferable in view of the tabled search in PRISM. The original negation technique was intended for non-probabilistic programs but we use here an extended version the use of which is justified by the *distribution semantics* [13], the formal semantics of PRISM programs.

1.2   Generative Modeling and Failure

Negation significantly expands the applicability of PRISM modeling, far beyond HMMs and PCFGs. We here detail our statistical motivation behind the introduction of negation. In the following we do not make a distinction between negation (logical notion) and failure (procedural notion) for brevity as we deal only with cases where they coincide.

Statistical models defined by PRISM are basically *generative*. By generative we mean PRISM programs describe a sequential stochastic process of generating observations such as one for the left-most derivation of sentences by a PCFG, where rules are probabilistically chosen to expand non-terminals. The implicit assumption is that the generation process never fails regardless of whether it is finite or infinite. Popular probabilistic models such as HMMs, PCFGs and BNs are considered generative and belong to the failure-free class.

We now allow a generative process to fail. So PRISM programs may fail. If failure occurs after a probabilistic choice is made, we lose probability mass placed on the choice and the sum of probabilities of all successful computation paths will be less than one. Statistically this implies that we have to renormalize probabilities by computing a normalizing constant $P(\mathsf{success})$ where $\mathsf{success}$ denotes an event of occurrence of successful computation. Also we have to assume that what is observed is conditional probabilities $P(x \mid \mathsf{success})$ where x is an observation. In other words, by introducing failure, we shift to a class of log-linear models in general[6] [14]. They are quite flexible but the computational burden, especially computing a normalizing constant, is sometimes so high as to make their use prohibitive.

Despite such difficulty, we allow failure in our modeling because it enables us to use complex constraints for precise modeling. We impose constraints on each computation path that possibly generates an observation and filter out those paths that fail to satisfy the constraints. The probability mass is distributed over the remaining successful paths. The mathematical correctness of this modeling, i.e. probabilities sum to unity, is guaranteed by renormalizing success probabilities. This approach looks naive but in reality unavoidable when constraints are too complex for human beings to check their consistency.

In our case, we are aiming to model generative stochastic HPSGs (head-driven phrase structure grammars) [15] as one of the PRISM targets. Stochastic

---

[6]   A distribution has the form $p(x) = Z^{-1} \exp(\sum_i \nu_i f_i(x))$ where ν_i is a coefficient, $f_i(x)$ a *feature* and Z a normalizing constant. HMMs and PCFGs correspond to the special case where $Z = 1$.

HPSGs are a class of highly sophisticated unification grammars where lexical constraints and a few linguistic principles interact to specify a distribution of sentences. There was an attempt to formalize generative stochastic HPSGs by Brew [16] but faced with theoretical difficulties due to failure caused by conflicting constraints. As a result researchers in the area turned to non-generative log-linear models and their parameter learning [17, 18, 19]. Notwithstanding we, appreciating the simplicity and understandability of generative models, decided to pursue a generate-and-test approach using failure to generative stochastic HPSGs. As a concrete step toward this end, we introduce finite PCFGs which we explain next.

1.3   Finite PCFGs

Finite PCFGs are PCFGs with finite constraints that make them generate only a finite number of sentences. We for example impose an upper bound of the height of parse trees as a finite constraint. As long as the tree being derived is within the limit, we allow free derivation but once a constraint is violated we force the derivation to fail. Other types of finite constraint are possible such as the number of rule applications but we use the height constraint as a canonical one in this paper.

As a result of the height constraint, the number of sentences licensed by a PCFG becomes finite and we can, at least in theory, exactly compute a normalizing constant $P(\text{success})$. Once this is done, it is possible to statistically infer parameters associated with the PCFG from data by applying a new EM algorithm proposed for generative models with failure [11]. The new EM algorithm requires a failure program which simulates failed computations of the finite PCFG program. We synthesize it by applying the negation technique [12] to a PDCG (probabilistic definite clause grammar) program describing the PCFG.

Our contributions are as follows. We allow negation of probabilistic logic programs and propose negation elimination by the negation technique at compile time. We then apply it to a specific case of finite PCFGs which play an important role in our approach to generative stochastic HPSG modeling and show that computations concerning finite PCFGs with a height constraint can be done in polynomial time, not in exponential time. We also show by a learning experiment that the difference in parsing tasks between a finite PCFG with a height constraint and the corresponding non-finite PCFG is small.

In what follows, we first give an overview of PRISM [7]. We then review the negation technique by an example and show how we should modify it to accommodate probabilistic primitives in PRISM while keeping its semantics. We then apply the negation technique to finite PCFGs. Finally we report an experiment of parameter learning with a finite PCFG applied to a real corpus.

Our work lies at the borders of probabilistic semantics, negation, tabling and statistical natural language processing. Due to space limitation however, an in-depth treatment of each topic is difficult and our explanations will be example-based to save space for formal definitions. The formal description of the semantics of PRISM and the analysis of its statistical learning are detailed in [8]. Most of the related work concerning first-order probabilistic modeling is omitted. The reader is referred to [7, 20, 14, 21, 22, 23, 24, 8, 25, 26, 27, 28]. He/she is assumed to be familiar with basics of statistical language models [2] as well as logic programming [29].

2   Preliminaries

Hereafter we use logic programs and follow Prolog conventions. A logic program DB is a set of definite clauses A :- $B_1, \ldots, B_n$ $(n \geq 0)$ where A is a head and B_i $(1 \leq i \leq n)$, an atom, is a subgoal. Unit clauses are those with $n = 0$ and goal clauses are those without a head. Variables in a clause are assumed to be universally quantified at the clause head. They are expressed by a string beginning with an upper case letter such as X1 or just by underscore '_' in case of anonymous variables. Expressions (clauses, atoms, terms) without variables are said to be ground.

PRISM is a symbolic-statistical modeling language which is a probabilistic extension of Prolog such that unit clauses have a parameterized distribution. So unit clauses are probabilistically true. PRISM has been used to describe (and perform parameter learning of) a variety of probabilistic models including naive Bayes classifiers, Bayesian networks, HMMs, PCFGs, probabilistic left corner parsing models, probabilistic graph grammars, linkage analysis programs etc. Now we show in this paper that PRISM can also describe finite PCFGs and learn their parameters. Before proceeding we have a quick review of PRISM for self-containedness.

A PRISM program DB' is the union of a set of definite clauses and a set of ground atoms $F = \{\texttt{msw}_1, \texttt{msw}_2, \ldots\}$. Each $\texttt{msw} = \texttt{msw}(id, v)$ represents a probabilistic choice v by a trial of random switch id. A value declaration $\texttt{value}(id, [v_1, \ldots, v_k])$ attached to DB' specifies that v is one of $v_1, \ldots, v_k$. (The Herbrand interpretations of) F has a parameterized probability measure $P_{\texttt{msw}}$ (basic distribution)[7]. PRISM has a formal semantics called distribution semantics in light of which DB' denotes a probability measure extending $P_{\texttt{msw}}$ over the set of possible Herbrand interpretations of the program. The execution of a PRISM program is just an SLD derivation except that a PRISM primitive $\texttt{msw}(id, \texttt{V})$ returns a probabilistically chosen value v for V. Because PRISM semantics is a generalization of the standard logic programming semantics, in an extreme case of assigning probabilities 0 or 1 to $\texttt{msw}$ atoms, PRISM is reduced to Prolog.

We write a PRISM program to define a distribution such as the distribution of sentences. Statistical inference of parameters associated with the basic distribution $P_{\texttt{msw}}$ is carried out by special EM algorithms developed for PRISM programs. The gEM (graphical EM) algorithm incorporates the idea of dynamic programming and is applicable to non-failing PRISM programs [30]. Also there

---

[7] We interchangeably use a probability measure and a probability distribution for the sake of familiarity. $P_{\texttt{msw}}$ is a direct product of infinitely many Bernoulli trials of finitely many types specified by the user.

is an enhanced version [11] which amalgamates the gEM algorithm and the FAM algorithm [24] to efficiently deal with PRISM programs that may fail.

Here is an example of PRISM program reproduced from [11]. This program simulates a sequence of Bernoulli trials and gives a distribution over ground atoms of the form $ber(n,l)$ such that l is a list of outcomes of n coin tosses.

```
target(ber,2).
values(coin,[heads,tails]).
:- set_sw(coin,0.6+0.4).

ber(N,[R|Y]):-
    N>0,
    msw(coin,R),    % probabilistic choice
    N1 is N-1,
    ber(N1,Y).      % recursion
ber(0,[]).
```

Fig. 1. Bernoulli program

We use target(ber,2) to declare that we are interested in the distribution of ber/2 atoms[8]. To define a Bernoulli trial we declare values(coin,[heads,tails]) which introduces a discrete binary random variable named coin whose range is {heads, tails} in the disguise of exclusively true atoms msw(coin,v) where v is either heads or tails. In PRISM a program is executed like Prolog, i.e. in a top-down left-to-right manner in the sampling mode (there are two other execution modes) and a call to msw(coin,R) returns a sampled value in R. msw atoms are primitives to make a probabilistic choice and their probabilities are called *parameters*.

:- set_sw(coin,0.6+0.4) is a directive on loading this program. It sets parameters of msw(coin,$\cdot$), i.e. the probability of msw(coin,heads) to 0.6 and that of msw(coin,tails) to 0.4, respectively. Next two clauses about ber/2 should be self-explanatory. Clauses behave just like Prolog clauses except that R works as a random variable such that $P(\text{R} = \text{heads}) = 0.6$ and $P(\text{R} = \text{tails}) = 0.4$. The query :- ber(3,L) will return for instance L = [heads,heads,tails].

3   Finite PDCG Program and the Success Probability

We here closely examine a PRISM program defining a finite PCFG. The PRISM program in Figure 2 is a probabilistic DCG (definite clause grammar) program written as a meta interpreter.

---

[8] p/n means that a predicate p has n arguments. We call an atom A p atom if the predicate symbol of A is p.

```
pdcg(L):-
    start_symbol(A), max_height(N), pdcg2(A,L,N).

pdcg2(A,[A],N):-
    N>=0, terminal(A).
pdcg2(A,L,N):-
    N>=0, \+terminal(A), msw(A,RHS), N1 is N-1, pdcg3(RHS,L,N1).

pdcg3([],[],_).
pdcg3([X|R],L3,N):-
    pdcg2(X,L1,N), pdcg3(R,L2,N), app(L1,L2,L3).

app([],A,A).
app([A|B],C,[A|D]):- app(B,C,D).
```

Fig. 2. A PDCG program with a height constraint

This program succinctly specifies a finite PCFG with a height constraint and simulates the leftmost derivation of sentences. CFG rules are supplied in the form of
PRISM's value declarations. We for example declare value(np,[[n],[s,np]])
to say that np has two rules np -> n and np -> s np[9]. max_height(N) says that
the height of a parse tree must be at most N. msw(A,RHS) represents a probabilistic choice in the derivation. When msw(A,RHS) is executed with $A = np$, one
of [n] or [s,np] is probabilistically chosen as RHS. start_symbol(A) returns in
A a start symbol such as 's' corresponding to the category of sentence.

The counter N holds the allowed height of the parse trees and is decremented
by one whenever a production rule is applied. When N becomes less than 0, the
derivation fails. So the program never generates a sentence whose height is more
than N asserted by max_height(N).

EM Learning from observed sentences of parameters associated with this
finite PCFG is performed by a new EM algorithm for generative models with
failure proposed in [11]. Unlike the Inside-Outside algorithm[10] however, it needs
a program that traces failed computation paths of the PDCG program, which
is a challenging task. As an intermediate step, we derive a program specialized
to computing the success probability. We transform the PDCG program to the

---

[9]   We also accept left recursive rules such as s -> s s. An infinite loop caused by
      them in top-down parsing is detected and properly handled by the PRISM's tabling
      mechanism.
[10] The Inside-Outside algorithm is a standard EM algorithm for PCFGs [31]. It takes
      $O(n^3)$ time for each iteration where n is a sentence length. Compared to the gEM
      (graphical EM) algorithm employed by PRISM however, it is experimentally con-
      firmed that it runs much slower, sometimes hundred times slower than the gEM
      algorithm depending on grammars [32].

```
success:-          % success:- pdcg(_).
    start_symbol(A),
    max_height(N),
    success2(A,N).

success2(A,N):-
    N>=0,
    ( terminal(A)
    ; \+terminal(A),
        msw(A,RHS),
        N1 is N-1,
        success3(RHS,N1) ).

success3([],_).
success3([A|R],N):-
    success2(A,N),
    success3(R,N).
```

Fig. 3. success program

success program shown in Figure 3 by dropping the arguments holding a partial sentence as a list.

This program is obtained by applying unfold/fold transformation to success:- pdcg(L) [33]. In the transformation we used a special property (law) of the append predicate such that $\forall L1, L2 \exists L3$ app$(L1, L2, L3)$ holds for lists L1, L2 and L3. The correctness of unfold/fold transformation, i.e. the source program and the transformed program define the same probability measure, is proved from the fact that the distribution semantics is an extension of the least model semantics. We here present a sketch of the proof.

Let R_{success} be the clauses in Figure 3. Theoretically the success program DB_{success} is the union of R_{success} and the set of probabilistic ground atoms $F = \{\mathrm{msw}_1, \mathrm{msw}_2, \ldots\}$ with a basic distribution P_{msw}. To prove that the transformation preserves the distribution semantics, it is enough to prove that for any true atoms $F' = \{\mathrm{msw}'_1, \mathrm{msw}'_2, \ldots\}(\subseteq F)$ sampled from P_{msw}, the transformation preserves the least model of $R \cup F'$. However this is apparent because our transformation is unfold/fold transformation (using a 'law' about the append predicate) that preserves the least model semantics.

Since the computation by the query :- success w.r.t. the success program faithfully traces all successful paths generated by :- pdcg(_) and vice versa, we have

$$\sum_{x:\mathrm{sentence}} P(x) = P(\mathrm{pdcg}(\_)) = P(\mathrm{success}).$$

Note that the success program runs in time linear in the maximum height N thanks to the PRISM's tabling mechanism [10] as is shown in Figure 7 (left).

The graph is plotted using the ATR grammar, a CFG grammar for the ATR corpus[11] [34]. In the probability computation, we employed a uniform distribution, i.e. every rule is chosen with the same probability for each nonterminal. The success program is further transformed to derive a special program necessary for maximum likelihood estimation.

4   Negation Technique

In order to perform EM learning of parameters associated with the PDCG program in the previous section, we have to know not only the probability of derivation failure, but have to know how production rules are used in the failed derivation [11]. To obtain such information is not a trivial task. We have to record each occurrence of msw atoms in every computation path regardless of whether it leads to success or not, which, naively done, would take exponential time.

Fortunately we can suppress the exponential explosion by sharing partial computation paths even for failed computations. As far as successful computations are concerned, it has been proved to be possible by the tabled search mechanism of PRISM [8]. Hence we have only to synthesize an ordinary PRISM program whose successful computation corresponds to the failed computation of the original program and apply the tabled search to the synthesized program. We here employ the *negation technique* [12] to synthesize such a negated program. We give a short synthesis example in Figure 4 in place of the formal description.

```
mem(V,[V|W]).
mem(V,[U|W]):- mem(V,W).
%-------------------------------------------
mem(X,Y) :-
 ( exists([V,W],[X,Y]=[V,[V|W]])
 ; exists([V,U,W],[X,Y]=[V,[U|W]], mem(V,W)) )
%-------------------------------------------
not_mem(X,Y) :-
  \+([X,Y]=[V,[V|W]]),
  ( \+([X,Y]=[V,[U|W]])
 ; [X,Y]=[V,[U|W]],not_mem(V,W) ).
```

Fig. 4. Negation example

We negate a familiar logic program mem/2 program by the negation technique. The source program is placed on the top layer in Figure 4. First we take

---

[11]   The ATR corpus is a collection of 10,995 Japanese conversational sentences and their parses. The ATR grammar is a manually developed CFG grammar for the ATR corpus. It contains 861 CFG rules.

the iff form of the source program (middle layer). The iff form is a canonical representation of the source program and `exists([V,W],[X,Y]=[V,[V|W]])` is a Prolog representation of $\exists V,W([X,Y]=[V,[V|W]])$. We then negate both sides of the iff form. The left hand side `mem(X,Y)` is negated to `not(mem(X,Y))`. On the right hand side, the first disjunct `exists([V,W],[X,Y]=[V,[V|W]])` is negated to `all([V,W],not([X,Y]=[V,[V|W]]))`, a Prolog term representing $\forall V,W\neg([X,Y]=[V,[V|W]])$.

Likewise the second disjunct `exists([V,U,W],([X,Y]=[V,[U|W]], mem(V, W)))` is negated to `all([V,U,W],([X,Y]=[V,[U|W]]` $\Rightarrow$ `not(mem(V,W))))`.This is further transformed to `all([V,U,W],not([X,Y]=[V,[U|W]]);` `exists([V,U, W], ([X,Y]=[V,[U|W]],not(mem(V,W))))` by using the property of '=' predicate such that $\forall X(Y = t[X] \Rightarrow \phi) \Leftrightarrow \forall X(Y \neq t[X]) \vee \exists X(Y = t[X] \wedge \neg\phi)$ holds for any ϕ in the Herbrand universe[12]. Finally we replace `not(mem(·,·))` with a new predicate `not_mem(·,·)` and `not(s = t)` with `\+(s = t)` to be executable. The bottom program computes exactly the complement of `mem` relation defined by the top layer `mem` program.

Let DB be the source program and DB^c the negated program. A logic program is said to be *terminating* if an SLD derivation using a fair selection rule for `:-A` w.r.t. the program terminates successfully or finitely fails for every ground atom A. A relation $q(x)$ is said to be complementary to $r(x)$ if $q(x) \vee r(x)$ is true for every x and there is no x such that $q(x) \wedge r(x)$.

Theorem 1. *[12] Suppose DB^c is terminating. Relations over the Herbrand universe defined by DB^c through its least model are complementary to those defined by DB.*

Proof: The least model of DB defines relations over the Herbrand universe for an interpretation of each predicate $q(x)$. They satisfy the if-and-only-if definition $q(x) \Leftrightarrow W[x]$. Hence the complementary relations satisfy the negated if-and-only-if definition $\neg q(x) \Leftrightarrow \neg W[x]$. Since operations on $\neg W[x]$ used in the negation technique are *substitution of equals for equals* in the Herbrand universe, these complementary relations satisfy iff(DB^c), i.e. the collection of the if-and-only-if definition for each predicate, thereby giving a fixed point of iff(DB^c) which must coincide with the least model of DB^c because iff(DB^c) is terminating, and hence has only one fixed point of the immediate consequence operator.   □

5   Negating 'Success' Program

We apply an extended negation technique to the `success` program in Figure 3 and obtain the PRISM program for failure shown in Figure 5 after simplifications. We extend the original negation technique in two points. First noticing that

---

[12]   The reason is that for the given `Y`, the equation $Y = t[X]$ determines at most one `X` occurring in t.

```
failure:-           % failure:- not(success).
   start_symbol(A),
   max_height(N),
   failure2(A,N).

failure2(A,N):-  % failure2(A,N):- not(success2(A,N)).
   N>=0,
   \+terminal(A),
   msw(A,RHS),
   N1 is N-1,
   failure3(RHS,N1).
failure2(_,N):- N<0.

failure3([A|R],N):-
   ( failure2(A,N)
   ; success2(A,N), failure3(R,N) ).
```

Fig. 5. `failure` program

$\forall y(q(x,y) \Rightarrow \psi)$ is equivalent to $\forall y \, \neg q(x,y) \vee \exists y(q(x,y) \wedge \psi)$ provided there exists at most one y satisfying $q(x,y)$ for given x, we use this equivalence to rewrite the program in the negation process. The use of this equivalence does not invalidate the proof of Theorem 1 as long as the definition of $q(x,y)$ remains intact. Second we apply the negation technique to programs containing `msw` atoms which are a basic probabilistic primitive in PRISM. $\neg(\exists \text{RHS}(\text{msw}(A, \text{RHS}) \wedge \psi))$ is transformed to $\forall \text{RHS}(\text{msw}(A, \text{RHS}) \Rightarrow \neg\psi)$, and further transformed to $\exists \text{RHS}(\text{msw}(A, \text{RHS}) \wedge \neg\psi)$. This transformation is justified by the PRISM's distribution semantics according to which `msw(A,RHS)` should be treated as a normal user-defined predicated defined by a single ground atom. So we may assume in the transformation there exists at most one RHS for a given A. We also use the fact that during the computation of `:- failure`, when `msw(A,RHS)` is called with A ground, it never fails.

The `failure` program in Figure 5 is terminating. We prove using Theorem 1 and the definition of the formal semantics of PRISM programs that the probability of `failure` is exactly $1 - P(\text{success})$[13].

Proposition 1. $P(\text{success}) + P(\text{failure}) = 1$.

Proof: Suppose $F' = \{\text{msw}'_1, \text{msw}'_2, \ldots\}$ is an arbitrary set of `msw` atoms. Let DB_{success} (resp. DB_{failure}) be a program consisting of F' and the clauses in

---

[13] The generalization of Proposition 1 for negated programs which are terminating is easy.

Figure 3 (resp. the clauses in Figure 5) respectively. Since $DB_{\texttt{failure}}$ is terminating, it follows from Theorem 1 that relations defined by $DB_{\texttt{success}}$ and those by $DB_{\texttt{failure}}$ are complementary, in particular success and failure are complementary. As F' is arbitrary, it follows from the definition of the distribution semantics [8] that $1 = P(\texttt{success} \vee \texttt{failure}) = P(\texttt{success}) + P(\texttt{failure})$.   □

To confirm Proposition 1, we let each program compute the success probability and the failure probability respectively, using a real grammar, the ATR grammar. We use a uniform distribution for rule selection probabilities for this test. The maximum height is set to 20. As the snapshot in Figure 6 testifies, probabilities for success and failure exactly sum to one[14].

```
?- prob(success,Ps),prob(failure,Pf),X is Ps+Pf.
X = 1.0
Pf = 0.295491045124576
Ps = 0.704508954875424
```

Fig. 6. Probabilities sum to one

The failure program runs in time linear in the maximum height N though we do not prove it (see Figure 7). We thus have reached an efficient PRISM program for computing failure required by EM learning.

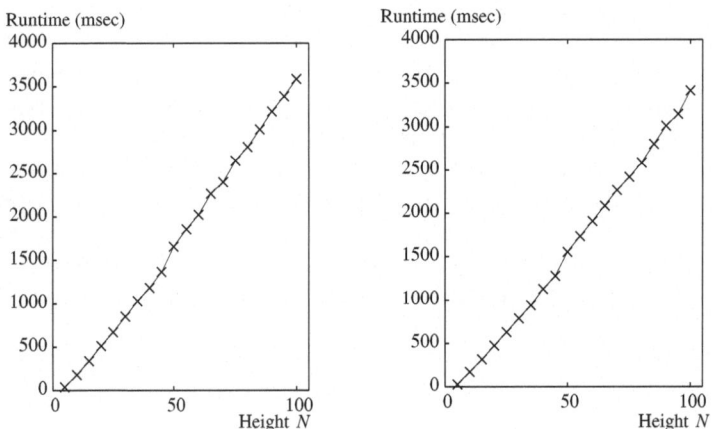

Fig. 7. Time for computing $P(\texttt{success})$ (left) and $P(\texttt{failure})$ (right) for the ATR grammar

---

[14] prob/2 is a PRISM built-in to compute the probability of a given atom under the current parameter values.

6   Learning Example: The ATR Grammar

To gauge the effect of the height constraint in finite PCFGs, we conducted a small learning experiment with real data, the ATR corpus and the ATR grammar [34]. In the experiment, as a training corpus and a test corpus, we first randomly picked up 2,500 and 1,000 sentences from the original corpus, respectively. For the maximum height N, the sentences which have only parse trees higher than N are excluded from the training and test corpora[15]. For each test sentence, we compared the height of the Viterbi parse, i.e. most likely parse based on the pure PCFG (whose parameters are learned by the Inside-Outside algorithm) and that based on the finite PCFG using a learning algorithm for finite PCFGs is described in [11].

The results are shown in Table 1. In the headers, h_1 (resp. h_2) indicates the height of the Viterbi parse based on the pure PCFG (resp. the finite PCFG). The column headed by '$h_1 > h_2$' shows the percentages of test sentences which hold $h_1 > h_2$, and so on. Table 1 shows that the finite PCFG model prefers shorter parse trees compared to the pure PCFG, hence we may say that we can add a height preference for parses by finite PCFGs, which is not easily realizable solely by pure PCFGs.

Table 1. Comparison on the height on Viterbi parses

N	$h_1 > h_2$	$h_1 < h_2$	$h_1 = h_2$
15	11.2%	2.1%	86.7%
18	14.2%	1.8%	84.0%
20	6.5%	3.6%	89.9%

Furthermore we evaluate the parsing accuracy with the finite PCFG based on the traditional criteria[16] [2]. The measured accuracy is given in Table 2. As the size of learning corpus is not large enough compared to the grammar size, we cannot make a definite comment on the performance differences between the pure PCFG and and the finite PCFG. However we may say that the parameters learned only from the parse trees with finite size does not necessarily lead to a significant decrease in parsing accuracy.

---

[15] The sizes of the training and test corpus are as follows:

height N	#training	#test
15	2,252	913
18	2,465	990
20	2,492	996

[16] The criterion LT (labeled tree) is the ratio of test sentences in which the Viterbi parse completely matches the answer, i.e. the parse annotated by human. BT (bracketed tree) is the ratio of test sentences in which the Viterbi parse matches the answer ignoring nonterminal labels in non-leaf nodes. 0-CB (zero crossing brackets) is the ratio of test sentences in which the Viterbi parse does not conflict in bracketing with the answer.

Table 2. Parsing accuracy with the pure PCFG and the finite PCFG

	LT		BT		0-CB	
N	Pure	Finite	Pure	Finite	Pure	Finite
15	73.9%	73.7%	75.1%	75.3%	85.2%	84.2%
18	73.4%	72.5%	75.2%	74.5%	85.6%	83.5%
20	73.6%	73.2%	75.8%	75.2%	86.2%	85.3%

7   Conclusion

We have introduced negation to a symbolic-statistical modeling language PRISM and proposed to synthesize positive PRISM programs from negated ones by using the negation technique. The synthesized programs are used for PRISM to perform statistical parameter learning of generative models with failure.

The negation technique in this paper is more general than the original one presented in [12]. It allows us to use clauses that have internal variables[17] as long as they are uniquely determined by the (left-to-right) execution of the body[18]. We have shown in Section 5 that the synthesized PRISM program can exactly compute the probabilities of complementary relations, in particular the failure probability.

We also introduced finite PCFGs as PCFGs with finite constraints as part of generative modeling of stochastic HPSGs. They are a subclass of log-linear models and allow exact computation of normalizing constants. We have applied the negation technique to a PDCG program written in PRISM that describes a finite PCFG with a height constraint. The resulting program can compute a normalizing constant for the finite PCFG in time linear in the given height. Although we have shown only one example of finite PCFG, we have tested two other types of finite PCFG and found that their normalizing constants are computable in polynomial time.

Finally we conducted an EM learning experiment using the ATR corpus and the ATR grammar with a height constraint. We discovered that the height constraint does not heavily affect the performance of parsing tasks. Such comparison of finite and non-finite grammars is unprecedented in statistical natural language processing to our knowledge, though to what extent this result is generalized remains a future research topic.

References

1. Rabiner, L.R., Juang, B.: Foundations of Speech Recognition. Prentice-Hall (1993)
2. Manning, C.D., Schütze, H.: Foundations of Statistical Natural Language Processing. The MIT Press (1999)

---

[17] Internal variables are those occurring only in a clause body.

[18] For example the negation technique is applicable to a clause such as `p(X):-length(X,Y),q(X,Y)` where Y is the length of a list X.

3. Ivanov, Y., Bobick, A.: Recoginition of visual activities and interactions by stochastic parsing. IEEE Trans. Pattern Aanl. and Mach. Intell. **22** (2000) 852–872

4. Pearl, J.: Probabilistic Reasoning in Intelligent Systems. Morgan Kaufmann (1988)

5. Fishelson, M., Geiger, D.: Exact genetic linkage computations for general pedigrees. Bioinformatics **18 Suppl. 1** (2002) S189–S198

6. McLachlan, G.J., Krishnan, T.: The EM Algorithm and Extensions. Wiley Interscience (1997)

7. Sato, T., Kameya, Y.: PRISM: a language for symbolic-statistical modeling. In: Proceedings of the 15th International Joint Conference on Artificial Intelligence (IJCAI'97). (1997) 1330–1335

8. Sato, T., Kameya, Y.: Parameter learning of logic programs for symbolic-statistical modeling. Journal of Artificial Intelligence Research **15** (2001) 391–454

9. Sato, T.: First order compiler: A deterministic logic program synthesis algorithm. Journal of Symbolic Computation **8** (1989) 605–627

10. Zhou, N.F., Sato, T.: Efficient Fixpoint Computation in Linear Tabling. In: Proceedings of the Fifth ACM-SIGPLAN International Conference on Principles and Practice of Declarative Programming (PPDP2003). (2003) 275–283

11. Sato, T., Kameya, Y.: A dynamic programming approach to parameter learning of generative models with failure. to be presented at ICML 2004 workshop SRL2004 (2004)

12. Sato, T., Tamaki, H.: Tansformational logic program synthesis. In: Proceedings of the International Conferenece on Fifth Generation Computer Systems FGCS84. (1984) 195–201

13. Sato, T.: A statistical learning method for logic programs with distribution semantics. In: Proceedings of the 12th International Conference on Logic Programming (ICLP'95). (1995) 715–729

14. Cussens, J.: Loglinear models for first-order probabilistic reasoning. In: Proceedings of the 15th Conference on Uncertainty in Artificial Intelligence (UAI'99). (1999) 126–133

15. Sag, I., Wasow, T.: Syntactic Theory: A Formal Introduction. Stanford: CSLI Publications (1999)

16. Brew, C.: Stochastic HPSG. In: Proceedings of the 7th Conference of European Chapter of the Association for Computational Linguistics (EACL'95). (1995) 83–89

17. Abney, S.: Stochastic attribute-value grammars. Computational Linguistics **23** (1997) 597–618

18. Riezler, S.: Probabilistic Constraint Logic Programming. PhD thesis, Universität Tübingen (1998)

19. Johnson, M., Geman, S., Canon, S., Chi, Z., Riezler, S.: Estimators for stochastic unification-based grammars. In: Proceedings of the 37th Annual Meeting of the Association for Computational Linguistics (ACL'99). (1999) 535–541

20. Koller, D., Pfeffer, A.: Learning probabilities for noisy first-order rules. In: Proceedings of the 15th International Joint Conference on Artificial Intelligence (IJCAI'97). (1997) 1316–1321

21. Friedman, N., Getoor, L., Koller, D., Pfeffer, A.: Learning probabilistic relational models. In: Proceedings of the 16th International Joint Conference on Artificial Intelligence (IJCAI'99). (1999) 1300–1309

22. Muggleton, S.: Learning stochastic logic programs. In Getoor, L., Jensen, D., eds.: Proceedings of the AAAI-2000 Workshop on Learning Statistical Models from Relational Data. (2000)

23. Getoor, L., Friedman, N., Koller, D.: Learning probabilistic models of relational structure. In: Proceedings of the Eighteenth International Conference on Machine Learning (ICML 01). (2001) 170–177
24. Cussens, J.: Parameter estimation in stochastic logic programs. Machine Learning **44** (2001) 245–271
25. Kersting, K., De Raedt, L.: Basic principles of learning bayesian logic programs. Technical Report Technical Report No. 174, Institute for Computer Science, University of Freiburg (2002)
26. De Raedt, L., Kersting, K.: Probabilistic logic learning. ACM-SIGKDD Explorations, special issue on Multi-Relational Data Mining **5** (2003) 31–48
27. Marthi, B., Milch, B., Russell, S.: First-order probabilistic models for information extraction. In: Proceedigs of IJCAI 2003 Workshop on Learning Statistical Models from Relational Data (SRL03). (2003)
28. Jaeger, J.: Complex probabilistic modeling with recursive relational bayesian networks. Annals of Mathematics and Artificial Intelligence **32** (2001) 179–220
29. Doets, K.: From Logic to Logic Programming. The MIT Press (1994)
30. Kameya, Y., Sato, T.: Efficient EM learning for parameterized logic programs. In: Proceedings of the 1st Conference on Computational Logic (CL2000). Volume 1861 of Lecture Notes in Artificial Intelligence., Springer (2000) 269–294
31. Baker, J.K.: Trainable grammars for speech recognition. In: Proceedings of Spring Conference of the Acoustical Society of America. (1979) 547–550
32. Sato, T., Abe, S., Kameya, Y., Shirai, K.: A separate-and-learn approach to EM learning of PCFGs. In: Proceedings of the 6th Natural Language Processing Pacific Rim Symposium (NLRPS2001). (2001) 255–262
33. Tamaki, H., Sato, T.: Unfold/fold transformation of logic programs. In: Proceedings of the 2nd International Conference on Logic Programming (ICLP'84). Lecture Notes in Computer Science, Springer (1984) 127–138
34. Uratani, N., Takezawa, T., Matsuo, H., Morita, C.: ATR integrated speech and language database. Technical Report TR-IT-0056, ATR Interpreting Telecommunications Research Laboratories (1994) In Japanese.

Specialization of Concurrent Guarded Multi-set Transformation Rules

Thom Frühwirth

Faculty of Computer Science, University of Ulm, Germany
`www.informatik.uni-ulm.de/pm/mitarbeiter/fruehwirth/`

Abstract. Program transformation and in particular partial evaluation are appealing techniques for declarative programs to improve not only their performance. This paper presents the first step towards developing program transformation techniques for a concurrent constraint programming language where guarded rules rewrite and augment multi-sets of atomic formulae, called Constraint Handling Rules (CHR).

We study the specialization of rules with regard to a given goal (query). We show the correctness of this program transformation: Adding and removing specialized rules in a program does not change the program's operational semantics. Furthermore termination and confluence of the program are shown to be preserved.

1 Introduction

Program transformation [PP96] is understood as a sequence of program text transformations that preserves semantic equivalence but at the same time improves the run-time, space-consumption or other aspects of the given program. *Partial evaluation* [MS97] is a popular instance of program transformation and of *program specialization*, which optimizes a given program for known values of the input.

Program transformation goes especially well with declarative (functional, logic, constraint) programming languages due to their clean semantics (avoidance of side-effects).

In the rule-based CHR language, we are interested in program specialization with regard to a given goal (query). We consider the rules that are applicable to the goal in any possible context (state of computation). We would like to *specialize these rules for the given goal.*

Our work is motivated by a renewed (and as we think, increasing) interest in program transformation and by the unique combination of features that the CHR language offers, in particular the multi-set programming style and the so-called propagation rules that add information without removing any. On one hand, these features mean that we have to adopt existing program transformation techniques for them or even come up with new ones, and on the other hand, there is hope that they make certain program transformations more straightforward.

We now discuss the appeal of program transformation and the special features of the CHR language in more detail.

S. Etalle(Ed.): LOPSTR 2004, LNCS 3573, pp. 133–148, 2005.

Appeal of Program Transformation. Program transformation, and in particular rule specialization, have potential applications in the following areas:

- Using the specialized rules at run-time should *increase time and space efficiency*.
- In concurrent languages like CHR, we also can *eliminate communication channels, synchronization points and don't care nondeterminism* [EGM01].
- *Verification and model checking* can be done by program transformation [DP99, FPP01, RKRR04].
- *Agent can be specialized* to a specific context (Example in [EGM01]).
- *Constraint solving can be improved*, since particular classes of optimization problems like scheduling typically have a certain structure [Wal03].
- A complete set of specialized rules can be regarded as *conditional or qualified answer* for the user.
- *Agent communication can be improved* by exchanging conditional answers [PGGS98].

Constraint Handling Rules (CHR). In *constraint solving*, efficient special-purpose algorithms are employed to solve sub-problems involving distinguished relations referred to as constraints. CHR [Frü98] is a concurrent committed-choice constraint logic programming language consisting of guarded rules that transform multi-sets of constraints into simpler ones until they are solved.

In CHR, one distinguishes two kinds of rules: Simplification rules replace constraints by simpler constraints while preserving logical equivalence, e.g. $X \geq Y \wedge Y \geq X \Leftrightarrow X = Y$. Propagation rules add new constraints, which are logically redundant, but may cause further simplification, e.g. $X \geq Y \wedge Y \geq Z \Rightarrow X \geq Z$. The combination of propagation and multi-set transformation of logical formulae in a rule-based language that is concurrent, guarded and constraint-based make CHR a rather unique declarative programming language.

Typically, CHR programs are *well-behaved*, i.e. terminating and confluent. *Confluence* means that the result of a computation is independent from the order in which rules are applied to the constraints. Once termination has been established [Frü02], there is a decidable, sufficient and necessary test for confluence [Abd97, AFM99].

Related Work. Since CHR can be seen as an extension of concurrent constraint programming (CCP) [SR90] by multiple heads (multi-sets) and propagation rules, literature on program transformation for concurrent constraint and logic-based programming languages is relevant: [EGM01] deals with transformations of concurrent constraint logic programs, [FPP04] deals with constraint logic programs (CLP), and [UF88] deals with a guarded concurrent logic programming language called GHC.

Due to propagation rules and the multi-set character of CHR, the above results are not directly applicable. For example, multiple heads mean that unlike CCP, constraints are usually defined by several rules, and that unlike CCP and GHC, different constraints can be defined in one rule by their interaction. GHC lacks built-in constraints and thus does not feature guard checking by logical implication. CLP among other things lacks concurrency. Moreover, these related works are not concerned directly with rule specialization, but with unfold/fold transformations.

Outline of the Paper. In Section 2, we define the CHR programming language. Section 3 introduces rule specialization. The next section shows correctness by considering specialized rules as redundant rules. The section also shows preservation of well-behavedness. Before we conclude, Section 5 gives some more examples.

2   The CHR Language

In this section we give an overview of syntax and semantics for constraint handling rules (CHR) [Frü98, FA03]. Readers familiar with CHR can skip this section (except for the introduction of the running example max maybe).

2.1   Syntax of CHR

We use two disjoint sets of predicate symbols for two different kinds of constraints: built-in constraint symbols and CHR constraint symbols (user-defined symbols).

Built-in constraints are handled by a given, predefined constraint solver. We assume that these solvers are well-behaved (terminating and confluent). Built-in constraints include $=$, *true*, and *false*. The semantics of the built-in constraints is defined by a consistent first-order *constraint theory CT*. In particular, *CT* defines $=$ as the syntactic equality over finite terms.

CHR (user-defined) constraints are defined by a CHR program.

Definition 1. A *CHR program* is a finite set of rules. There are two kinds of rules:

A *simplification rule* is of the form

$$Name @ H \Leftrightarrow C \mid B.$$

A *propagation rule* is of the form

$$Name @ H \Rightarrow C \mid B,$$

where *Name* is an optional, unique identifier of a rule, the *head H* is a non-empty conjunction of CHR constraints, the *guard C* is a conjunction of built-in constraints, and the *body B* is a goal. A *goal* is a conjunction of built-in and CHR constraints. A trivial guard "*true*" can be omitted together with "⌐".

A CHR symbol is *defined* in a CHR program if it occurs in the head of a rule in the program.

Example 1. Let $\leq$ and $<$ be built-in constraint symbols with the usual meaning. We define a CHR symbol max, where max(X,Y,Z) means that Z is the maximum of X and Y:

max(X,Y,Z) $\Leftrightarrow$ X$\leq$Y | Z=Y.
max(X,Y,Z) $\Leftrightarrow$ Y$\leq$X | Z=X.
max(X,Y,Z) $\Rightarrow$ X$\leq$Z $\wedge$ Y$\leq$Z.

The first rule states that max(X,Y,Z) is logically equivalent Z=Y if X$\leq$Y. Analogously for the second rule. The third rule states that max(X,Y,Z) unconditionally implies X$\leq$Z $\wedge$ Y$\leq$Z.

Note that max *will be our running example throughout this text.*

2.2   Operational Semantics of CHR

The operational semantics of CHR is given by a transition system.

Let P be a CHR program. We define the transition relation $\mapsto_P$ by introducing two computation steps (transitions), one for each kind of CHR rule (cf. Figure 1). Since the two computation steps (transitions) are structurally very similar, we first describe their common behavior and then explain the difference.

In the figure, all meta-variables stand for (possibly empty) conjunctions of constraints. C and D stand for built-in constraints only, H and H' for CHR constraints only.

Simplify

If $(H \Leftrightarrow C \,|\, B)$ is a fresh variant of a rule in P with variables $\bar{x}$
and $CT \models \forall\, (D \rightarrow \exists \bar{x}(H=H' \wedge C))$
then $(H' \wedge G \wedge D) \mapsto_P^{\textbf{Simplify}} (G \wedge D \wedge B \wedge C \wedge H=H')$

Propagate

If $(H \Rightarrow C \,|\, B)$ is a fresh variant of a rule in P with variables $\bar{x}$
and $CT \models \forall\, (D \rightarrow \exists \bar{x}(H=H' \wedge C))$
then $(H' \wedge G \wedge D) \mapsto_P^{\textbf{Propagate}} (H' \wedge G \wedge D \wedge B \wedge C \wedge H=H')$

Fig. 1. Computation Steps of Constraint Handling Rules

A state is simply a goal, i.e. a conjunction of built-in and CHR constraints. Conjunctions are considered as multi-sets of conjuncts (conjuncts can be permuted). We will usually partition a state into subconjunctions of specific kinds of constraints. For example, any state can be written as $(H' \wedge G \wedge D)$, where H' contains only CHR constraints, D only built-in constraints, and G arbitrary constraints. Each of the subconjunctions may be empty (equivalent to *true*).

A (fresh variant of a) rule is *applicable to a state* $(H' \wedge G \wedge D)$ if H' matches its head H and its guard C hold when the built-in constraints D of the state hold. A *fresh variant* of a rule is obtained by renaming its variables to fresh variables, $\bar{x}$.

Matching (one-sided unification) succeeds if H' is an instance of H, i.e. it is only allowed to instantiate (bind) variables of H but not variables of H'. Matching is logically expressed by equating H' and H but existentially quantifying all variables from the rule, $\bar{x}$. This equation $H'=H$ is shorthand for pairwise equating the arguments of the constraints in H' and H, provided their constraint symbols are equal.

If an *applicable rule is applied*, the equation $H=H'$, its guard C and its body B are added to the resulting state. Any of the applicable rule can be applied (don't care non-determinism). A rule application cannot be undone (CHR is a committed-choice language without backtracking).

When a simplification rule is applied in the transition **Simplify**, the matching CHR constraints H' are removed from the state.

The **Propagate** transition is like the **Simplify** transition, except that it keeps the constraints H' in the resulting state. Trivial non-termination caused by applying the same propagation rule again and again is avoided by applying it at most once to the same constraints [Abd97].

A *computation* of a goal G in a program P is a sequence $S_0, S_1, \ldots$ of states with $S_i \mapsto_P S_{i+1}$ beginning with the initial state $S_0 = G$ and ending in a final state or diverging. $\mapsto_P^*$ denotes the reflexive and transitive closure of $\mapsto_P$. A *final state* is one where either no computation step is possible anymore or where the built-in constraints are inconsistent (unsatisfiable). When it is clear from the context, we will drop the reference to the program P.

Example 2. Recall the program for `max` from Example 1. The first two rules are simplification rules, that replace `max(X,Y,Z)` by simpler constraints provided a guard holds. The third rule propagates constraints. Operationally, we add the body of the rule as redundant constraints, the `max` constraint is kept.

To the goal `max(1,2,M)` the first rule is applicable:

$$\mathtt{max}(1, 2, \mathtt{M}) \mapsto^{\textbf{Simplify}} \mathtt{M}{=}2.$$

To the goal `max(A,B,M)` $\wedge$ `A<B` the first rule is applicable:

$$\mathtt{max(A,B,M)} \wedge \mathtt{A{<}B} \mapsto^{\textbf{Simplify}} \mathtt{M{=}B} \wedge \mathtt{A{<}B}.$$

To the goal `max(A,A,M)` both simplification rules are applicable. In both cases the result is `M=A`.

$$\mathtt{max}(\mathtt{A}, \mathtt{A}, \mathtt{M}) \mapsto^{\textbf{Simplify}} \mathtt{M{=}A}.$$

Redundancy from the propagation rule is useful, as the goal `max(A,3,3)` shows. Only the propagation rule is applicable, and then the first rule:

$$\mathtt{max}(\mathtt{A}, 3, 3) \mapsto^{\textbf{Propagate}} \mathtt{max(A,3,3)} \wedge \mathtt{A}{\leq}3 \mapsto^{\textbf{Simplify}} \mathtt{A}{\leq}3.$$

(The constraint $3{=}3$ is simplified away by the built-in constraint solver.)

2.3   Well-Behavedness: Termination and Confluence

A CHR program is *well-behaved* if it is terminating and confluent.

Definition 2. A CHR program is called *terminating*, if there are no infinite computations.

For many existing CHR programs simple well-founded orderings are sufficient to prove termination [Frü02]. Problems arise with non-trivial interactions between simplification and propagation rules.

The confluence property of a program guarantees that any computation for a goal results in the same final state no matter which of the applicable rules are applied.

Definition 3. A CHR program is *confluent* if for all states S, S_1, S_2: If $S \mapsto^* S_1$ and $S \mapsto^* S_2$ then there exist states T_1 and T_2 such that $S_1 \mapsto^* T_1$ and $S_2 \mapsto^* T_2$ and T_1 and T_2 are identical up to renaming of local variables and logical equivalence of built-in constraints.

The papers [Abd97, AFM99] give a decidable, sufficient and necessary condition for confluence for terminating CHR programs.

Example 3. The program for `max` from Example 1 is well-behaved. It is trivially terminating, since the bodies of the rules do not contain any CHR constraints. Thus confluence is decidable and can be shown to hold.

For example, to the state `max(X,Y,Z)` $\land$ `X=Y` all three rules are applicable, but in all cases, the final state is a built-in constraint logically equivalent to $X = Y \land Y = Z$.

3   Rule Specialization

We are interested in any rule whose head could match (a part of) the given goal, taking into account any possible context. Therefore we consider all rules that have an overlap with the given goal. For an *overlap*, the head of the rule and the goal must have at least one CHR constraint in common. This is achieved by equating one or more constraints of the head and the goal.

We assume without loss of generality that rules (and goals) have disjoint sets of variables (if necessary, their variables have been renamed apart), unless otherwise noted.

In the following, meta-variables stand for (possibly empty) conjunctions of constraints. Unless otherwise noted, the letters C and D stand for built-in constraints, H for CHR constraints of the head of a rule, B for arbitrary constraints of the body of a rule, G for constraints in general.

We first specialize simplification rules.

Definition 4. Let G be a goal. Without loss of generality (w.l.o.g.), G can be written as

$$G_1 \land G_2 \land D,$$

where G_1 and G_2 are CHR constraints and D are built-in constraints.

Let R be a simplification rule

$$H_1 \wedge H_2 \Leftrightarrow C \,|\, B.$$

Then a *specialization of the simplification rule R with regard to the goal G* is the simplification rule

$$H_1 \wedge H_2 \wedge G_2 \Leftrightarrow H_1 {=} G_1 \wedge C \wedge D \,|\, B \wedge G_2,$$

provided G_1 and H_1 are non-empty conjunctions and $CT \models \exists (H_1 {=} G_1 \wedge C \wedge D)$.

$H_1 {=} G_1$ defines the overlap of the goal with the head of the rule. (G_1 and H_1 are non-empty conjunctions, so that trivial overlaps are avoided.) G_2, the remainder of the goal G, occurs in both head and body of the specialized rule, since it will not be changed by the rule. The condition $CT \models \exists (H_1 {=} G_1 \wedge C \wedge D)$ ensures that the specialized rule is not trivial. (With an unsatisfiable guard a rule is never applicable).

Example 4. Let G be the goal

$\max(\mathsf{A}, \mathsf{B}, \mathsf{C}) \wedge \mathsf{A} \geq \mathsf{B}$

Of course, this goal can be unfolded with the second rule of the program defining $\max$ (from Example 1), but for the sake of a simple example, let us specialize the first rule with it. Let R be the rule

$\max(\mathsf{X}, \mathsf{Y}, \mathsf{Z}) \Leftrightarrow \mathsf{X} \leq \mathsf{Y} \,|\, \mathsf{Z}{=}\mathsf{Y}$

We have a complete overlap with $\max$, i.e.

$G_1 = \max(\mathsf{A}, \mathsf{B}, \mathsf{C}), G_2 = true, D = (\mathsf{A} \geq \mathsf{B}),$
$H_1 = \max(\mathsf{X}, \mathsf{Y}, \mathsf{Z}), H_2 = true, C = (\mathsf{X} \leq \mathsf{Y}), B = (\mathsf{Z}{=}\mathsf{Y}).$

The resulting specialized rule is:

$\max(\mathsf{X}, \mathsf{Y}, \mathsf{Z}) \wedge true \wedge true \Leftrightarrow \max(\mathsf{X}, \mathsf{Y}, \mathsf{Z}){=}\max(\mathsf{A}, \mathsf{B}, \mathsf{C}) \wedge \mathsf{X} \leq \mathsf{Y} \wedge \mathsf{A} \geq \mathsf{B} \,|\, \mathsf{Z}{=}\mathsf{Y} \wedge$
$true$

After removal of redundant $true$ constraints and after propagation and simplification of variable equalities and other built-in constraints, the above rule can be written as:

$\max(\mathsf{X}, \mathsf{Y}, \mathsf{Z}) \Leftrightarrow \mathsf{X}{=}\mathsf{Y} \,|\, \mathsf{Z}{=}\mathsf{Y}.$

The conditional answer that we get from this rule reads as:

Given G, if $\mathsf{A}{=}\mathsf{B}$ *then* $\mathsf{C}{=}\mathsf{B}$.

We now specialize propagation rules.

Definition 5. Let G be a goal of the form

$$G_1 \wedge G_2 \wedge D,$$

where G_1 and G_2 are CHR constraints and D are built-in constraints.

Let R be a propagation rule

$$H_1 \wedge H_2 \Rightarrow C \mid B.$$

Then a *specialization of the propagation rule R with regard to the goal G* is the propagation rule

$$H_1 \wedge H_2 \wedge G_2 \Rightarrow H_1{=}G_1 \wedge C \wedge D \mid B,$$

provided G_1 and H_1 are non-empty conjunctions and $CT \models \exists(H_1{=}G_1 \wedge C \wedge D)$.

In the propagation rule, we do not have to add the remainder G_2 of the goal to the body as in the case of a simplification rule, since it will not be removed from the head.

Example 5. Let G be the goal

$$\max(\mathsf{A}, \mathsf{B}, \mathsf{C}) \wedge \mathsf{A} \geq \mathsf{B}.$$

Let R be the propagation rule

$$\max(\mathsf{X}, \mathsf{Y}, \mathsf{Z}) \Rightarrow \mathsf{X} \leq \mathsf{Z} \wedge \mathsf{Y} \leq \mathsf{Z}.$$

The complete overlap with `max` is

$$G_1 = \max(\mathsf{A}, \mathsf{B}, \mathsf{C}), G_2 = \mathit{true}, D = (\mathsf{A} \geq \mathsf{B}),$$
$$H_1 = \max(\mathsf{X}, \mathsf{Y}, \mathsf{Z}), H_2 = \mathit{true}, C = \mathit{true}, B = (\mathsf{X} \leq \mathsf{Z} \wedge \mathsf{Y} \leq \mathsf{Z}).$$

The specialized rule is

$$\max(\mathsf{X}, \mathsf{Y}, \mathsf{Z}) \wedge \mathit{true} \wedge \mathit{true} \Rightarrow \max(\mathsf{X}, \mathsf{Y}, \mathsf{Z}){=}\max(\mathsf{A}, \mathsf{B}, \mathsf{C}) \wedge \mathit{true} \wedge \mathsf{A} \geq \mathsf{B} \mid$$
$$\mathsf{X} \leq \mathsf{Z} \wedge \mathsf{Y} \leq \mathsf{Z} \wedge \mathit{true}$$

After simplification of built-in constraints, the rule can be written as

$$\max(\mathsf{X}, \mathsf{Y}, \mathsf{Z}) \Rightarrow \mathsf{Y} \leq \mathsf{X} \mid \mathsf{X} \leq \mathsf{Z}.$$

In practice, we may introduce a new definition for the goal G, say `gmax`, and thus write the above rule as

$$\mathtt{gmax}(\mathsf{A}, \mathsf{B}, \mathsf{C}) \Rightarrow \mathsf{A} \leq \mathsf{C}.$$

More examples can be found in Section 5.

Remarks. If a goal is not specializable with any rule of the program, a programming error is likely. (The CHR constraints of the goal are either not defined or too specific.)

There are some interesting special cases of the above transformation: If we know that at run-time, the goal will not occur in any context with additional (CHR) constraints, we let H_2 be the empty conjunction. If in addition, G_2 is empty, we only specialize with rules whose heads overlap completely with the given goal.

A most general goal $G = c(X_1, \ldots, X_n)$, where X_i $(0 \leq i \leq n)$ are pairwise distinct variables, will return all rules that contain the constraint symbol c with arity n in their heads as a result of specialization.

4   Redundant Rules for Correctness

We show that the transformed rules are redundant in the program from which they derive. Hence they cannot change the operational semantics of the program. This result will establish correctness of the rule specialization transformation. We use a strict notion of correctness, where the observables are complete states (not only built-in constraints as usual in CC languages). We also show that specialized rules preserve termination and confluence (well-behavedness).

In this paper, we do not address the question whether original rules can be removed from the program once specialized rules are added. At the current state of research, we would like to refer to the papers [AF04] in which techniques to detect redundant rules in a program is described.

We start with a slightly more general definition of specialized rules than the ones derived in the previous section. Then we define redundant rules.

Definition 6. A rule R' is *special(ized)* in a CHR program P iff P contains another rule of the form

$$H \odot C \mid B \text{ where } \odot \in \{ \Leftrightarrow, \Rightarrow \}.$$

and R' is of the form

$$H \wedge G \odot C \wedge D \mid B \wedge G \text{ if } \odot = \Leftrightarrow,$$

$$H \wedge G \odot C \wedge D \mid B \text{ if } \odot = \Rightarrow,$$

provided the variables in the added goals G and D are either new or occur in H.

In [AF04] rule redundancy is defined in terms of finite computations.

Definition 7. A rule R is *redundant* in a CHR program P iff for all states S:

$$\text{If } S \mapsto_P^* S_1 \text{ then } S \mapsto_{P \setminus \{R\}}^* S_2,$$

where S_1 and S_2 are final states and S_1 and S_2 are identical up to renaming of local variables and logical equivalence of built-in constraints.

We need some statements about preservation of well-behavedness under addition and removal of redundant rules.

The addition of rules to a CHR program cannot inhibit computations.

Lemma 1. Given a CHR program P and a rule R. For all states S and S': If $S \mapsto_P^* S'$ then $S \mapsto_{P \cup \{R\}}^* S'$.

Proof. This is a direct consequence of the operational semantics of CHR. In a computation step, one may apply any of the applicable rules. So it suffices to ignore the newly added rule R to reproduce all computations of the original program without R.

The lemma also means that the removal of rules from a CHR program cannot introduce new computations.

From the above Lemma 1 the following two corollaries are immediate consequences.

Corollary 1. Removal of a redundant rule preserves termination and confluence of the program.

Proof. The claim holds since all computations are finite in a terminating program and since removal of a rule cannot introduce more computations.

Removal preserves confluence by definition of redundant rules, because a redundant rule could have only introduced computations that are also possible without it.   □

Corollary 2. Addition of a redundant rule preserves confluence, but may destroy termination.

Proof. Addition of a redundant rule preserves confluence by definition, because a redundant rule only has finite computations that are also possible without it.

For termination, a counterexample suffices. Consider adding p(X) ⇔ p(X) to a program that defines p. Every finite computation with the new rule will be redundant, but there are obviously also infinite computations possible with the new rule.   □

In order to arrive at our desired correctness result, we show that special rules are redundant rules. For the proof, we need the following three lemmata from [AF99].

Lemma 2. A computation can be repeated in any larger context, i.e. with states in which built-in and CHR constraints have been added.

$$\text{If } G \mapsto^* G' \text{ then } (G \wedge H) \mapsto^* (G' \wedge H).$$

Lemma 3. A computation can be repeated in a state where redundant built-in constraints have been removed. Let $CT \models \forall (D \rightarrow C)$.

$$\text{If } (H \wedge C \wedge D \wedge G) \mapsto^* S \text{ then } (H \wedge D \wedge G) \mapsto^* S.$$

Lemma 4. A computation can be repeated in a state where variables have been instantiated. Let H' and H be CHR constraints without common variables.

$$\text{If } (H \wedge H=H' \wedge C) \mapsto^*_P S \text{ then } (H' \wedge C[H=H']) \mapsto^*_P S,$$

where $C[H=H']$ denotes the substitution of the variables in C which also occur in H as prescribed by the syntactic equality $H=H'$.

We are now ready to prove that special rules are special redundant rules.

Theorem 1. Special rules are redundant rules.

Proof. By contradiction. We try to find a computation in a given CHR program P that is possible with the special rule R' but not possible without it (the program P still contains R). W.l.o.g. we consider single computation steps $S' \mapsto_{\{R'\}} S'_1$. We got to show that then $S' \mapsto_{\{R\}} S_1$ is always possible and S'_1 and S_1 are equivalent.

Consider the case where R' and R are simplification rules. Let R of the form

$$\mathbf{H} \Leftrightarrow \mathbf{C} \mid \mathbf{B}$$

Let R' be a special rule of R of the form

$$\mathbf{H} \wedge G \Leftrightarrow \mathbf{C} \wedge D \mid \mathbf{B} \wedge G$$

(Note that $\mathbf{H}$, $\mathbf{C}$ and $\mathbf{B}$ are identical in both rules.)

Consider any state S' with $S' \mapsto_{\{R'\}} S'_1$. Since R' is applicable, S' must be of the form

$$H' \wedge G' \wedge G'' \wedge D',$$

where $CT \models \forall(D' \to \mathbf{H}=H' \wedge G=G' \wedge \mathbf{C} \wedge D)$, and S'_1 must be of the form

$$\mathbf{B} \wedge G \wedge G'' \wedge \mathbf{H}=H' \wedge G=G' \wedge \mathbf{C} \wedge D \wedge D'.$$

But then a very similar computation step is possible with R, since $CT \models \forall(\mathbf{H}=H' \wedge G=G' \wedge \mathbf{C} \wedge D) \to \mathbf{H}=H' \wedge \mathbf{C})$, the applicability condition $CT \models \forall(D' \to \mathbf{H}=H' \wedge \mathbf{C})$ is fulfilled, and consequently S_1 is of the form

$$\mathbf{B} \wedge G' \wedge G'' \wedge \mathbf{H}=H' \wedge \mathbf{C} \wedge D'.$$

We now show that the two states S'_1 and S_1 are the equivalent up to renaming of local variables and equivalence of built-in constraints. More precisely, we are interested in operational equivalence of states: Given the program P, all computations with S'_1 as initial state are also possible with S_1 as initial state and vice versa.

Since S'_1 strictly contains S_1, we know by Lemma 2 that all computations with S_1 are also possible with S'_1.

We still have to show that S'_1 does not admit more computations than S_1. We transform S'_1 into S_1 while preserving logical and operational equivalence of states.

Since $CT \models \forall(D' \to D)$ as a consequence of the fulfilled rule applicability condition, we can remove D from state S'_1 according to Lemma 3.

Finally, we apply Lemma 4 and compute $S'_1[G=G']$. The substitution affects the variables in G and their occurences in other subconjunctions of the state S'_1 that stem from the rule. Clearly, $G[G=G'] = G'$. Also, H', G'' and D' remain unaffected, since they are subconjunctions from the goal that cannot have any variables in common with the rule from which G stems. Finally, $(\mathbf{H}=H')[G=G']$ can be left as $(\mathbf{H}=H')$ since the fulfilled applicability condition of R', $CT \models \forall(D' \to \mathbf{H}=H' \wedge G=G' \wedge \mathbf{C} \wedge D)$, implies that a variable common to H and G must be equated to the same term in both equations $\mathbf{H}=H'$ and $G=G'$. Since by definition of special rules, if G contains variables from the rule, they must also occur in $\mathbf{H}$, the subconjunction $\mathbf{C}$ is not affected either. So the overall result is the state:

$$\mathbf{B} \wedge G' \wedge G'' \wedge \mathbf{H}=H' \wedge \mathbf{C} \wedge D'.$$

We have successfully transformed S'_1 into S_1. Hence there cannot exist a computation with R' that is not possible with R, i.e. the special rule R' is redundant in the program P that contains the rule R.

The proof for propagation rules is analogous.   □

Corollary 3. The addition and removal of special rules to a program preserves its confluence.

Proof. Obvious, since special rules are redundant rules by Theorem 1 and Corollaries 1 and 2 for redundant rules.   □

Theorem 2. The addition and removal of special rules to a program preserves its termination.

Proof. Since special rules are redundant rules by Theorem 1, their removal preserves termination by Corollary 1.

We show that the addition of special rules preserves termination by contradiction. In an infinite computation, the special rule must be applied infinitely often, since any sub-computation between the applications of the special rule must be finite, since the program without addition of the special rule is terminating.

The proof of Theorem 1 showed, that each computation step, where the special rules is applied, can be mimicked by exactly one computation steps without the special rule. But then the complete computation can be mimicked by applications of rules of the original program. Since the program was terminating, this computation cannot be infinite.   □

5   More Examples

In this section, we use the concrete syntax of CHR implementations in Prolog instead of the abstract syntax presented so far. The reason for this is that we have transformed the following programs in that setting with a first implementation of rule specialization.

Recall the program for `max(X,Y,Z)` from Example 1.

```
max(X,Y,Z) <=> X=<Y | Z=Y.
max(X,Y,Z) <=> Y=<X | Z=X.
max(X,Y,Z) ==> X=<Z, Y=<Z.
```

Even though we did not adress unfolding of rules and simplification of built-in constraints in rules in this paper for space reasons, we will use these program manipulations in the following examples in a mild way in order to illustrate the usefulness of rule specialization.

Unfolding basically means to replace the body of a rule by the result of a computation starting with the guard and body of the rule. Note that in the case of propagation rules, we also add the head of the rule to the initial state of the computation (here the technical term "unfolding" turns into a misnomer). Since we assume well-behaved programs, unfolding will terminate and it suffices to consider any one computation because of confluence. *Built-in constraint simplification* basically replaces built-in constraints of the guard and body by simpler ones.

In the examples, we will derive all specialized rules for a given goal. However, we will not bother to derive specialized rules that are equivalent (up to reordering of head constraints and variable renaming) to other already derived specialized rules.

Example 6. Let the goal for specialization be:

`max(X,Y,Z), max(Y,X,Z)`

Specialization with the first conjunct of the goal, `max(X,Y,Z)` results in the specialized rules:

```
max(X,Y,Z), max(Y,X,Z) <=> X=<Y | Z=Y, max(Y,X,Z).
max(X,Y,Z), max(Y,X,Z) <=> Y=<X | Z=X, max(Y,X,Z).
max(X,Y,Z), max(Y,X,Z) ==> X=<Z, Y=<Z.
```

Unfolding of `max(Y,X,Z)` in each of the specialized rules:

```
max(X,Y,Z), max(Y,X,Z) <=> X=<Y | Z=Y, Z=Y.
max(X,Y,Z), max(Y,X,Z) <=> Y=<X | Z=X, Z=X.
max(X,Y,Z), max(Y,X,Z) ==> X=<Z, Y=<Z, Y=<Z, X=<Z.
```

Trivial simplification of built-in constraint in the rule bodies:

```
max(X,Y,Z), max(Y,X,Z) <=> X=<Y | Z=Y.
max(X,Y,Z), max(Y,X,Z) <=> Y=<X | Z=X.
max(X,Y,Z), max(Y,X,Z) ==> X=<Z, Y=<Z.
```

When specializing with the second conjunct `max(Y,X,Z)`, the same rules are derived (up to permutation of head constraints). These rules are obviously redundant.

Comparing the original and the specialized rules, we see that one of the `max` constraints in the goal is redundant, and, more generally, that `max` is commutative in its first two arguments. So an appropriate folding program transformation would allow us to derive the rule:

```
max(X,Y,Z), max(Y,X,Z) <=> max(X,Y,Z).
```

Example 7. The goal to specialize is now:

```
max(X,Y,Z), max(X,Y,U)
```

Specialization with first conjunct `max(X,Y,Z)` of the goal:

```
max(X,Y,Z), max(X,Y,U) <=> X=<Y | Z=Y, max(X,Y,U).
max(X,Y,Z), max(X,Y,U) <=> Y=<X | Z=X, max(X,Y,U).
max(X,Y,Z), max(X,Y,U) ==> X=<Z, Y=<Z.
```

Specialization with the other conjunct of the goal leads to the same rules (up to variable renaming). Unfolding of `max(X,Y,U)` in specialized rules:

```
max(X,Y,Z), max(X,Y,U) <=> X=<Y | Z=Y, U=Y.
max(X,Y,Z), max(X,Y,U) <=> Y=<X | Z=X, U=X.
max(X,Y,Z), max(X,Y,U) ==> X=<Z, Y=<Z, X=<U, Y=<U.
```

The built-in constraints in each simplification rules imply that `Z=U`. This reminds us that the third argument of `max` is functionally dependent on the first two arguments.

In the next example, we add a rule for functional dependency and specialize it with regard to the goal of Example 6. Because the goal and the head of the rule each have two constraints, there will be a more interesting overlap.

Example 8. The goal is:

```
max(X,Y,Z), max(Y,X,Z).
```

The functional dependency rule for `max` is:

```
max(X,Y,Z), max(X,Y,U) <=> max(X,Y,Z), Z=U.
```

Specialization with the functional dependency rule (again deriving the minimal number of rules):

```
max(A,B,C), max(A,B,D), max(B,A,C) <=> max(A,B,C), C=D,max(B,A,C).
max(A,A,C), max(A,A,C) <=> max(A,A,C), C=C.
```

If the folded rule of Example 6 is available, we can also unfold and simplify the first rule:

```
max(A,B,C), max(A,B,D), max(B,A,C) <=> C=D, max(A,B,C).
max(A,A,C), max(A,A,C) <=> A=C.
```

6 Conclusions

The current work is a first, small step into considering program transformation for the constraint handling rule (CHR) language. This line of research is motivated by two working hypothesis (as explained in the introduction):

- New applications of program transformation to problems such as verification, constraint solver optimization and agent specialization.
- The suitability of CHR as a declarative, concurrent constraint-based programming language with multi-headed rules for powerful program transformation techniques.

Here we have studied the specialization of rules with regard to a given goal. We have shown that the correctness of this program transformation: Adding and removing such specialized rules in a program does not change the program's operational semantics. Furthermore well-behavedness, i.e. termination and confluence, is preserved by these operations.

The additional examples in the previous section give some hints of what should be next:

- Unfolding and folding as well as rule simplifying program transformations for CHR.
- A methodology (strategies) how to employ these transformations to improve the performance of a program. In general, these strategies depend on the intended application of the programn transformation. A particular and basic question is to clarify which derived rules one should add and which original rules one should remove.

Finally, and not surprisingly, future work also concerns the practical aspects of improving the current preliminary ad-hoc implementation for rule specialization and applying it to larger examples.

References

[Abd97]   Slim Abdennadher. Operational semantics and confluence of constraint propagation rules. In *Third International Conference on Principles and Practice of Constraint Programming, CP97*, LNCS 1330. Springer, 1997.

[AF99]   Slim Abdennadher and Thom Frühwirth. Operational equivalence of CHR programs and constraints. In *Fifth International Conference on Principles and Practice of Constraint Programming, CP99*, LNCS 1713, pages 43–57. Springer, 1999.

[AF04]   Slim Abdennadher and Thom Frühwirth. Integration and optimization of rule-based constraint solvers. In Maurice Bruynooghe, editor, *Logic Based Program Synthesis and Transformation - LOPSTR 2003, Revised Selected Papers*, LNCS. Springer, 2004.

[AFM99]   Slim Abdennadher, Thom Frühwirth, and Holger Meuss. Confluence and semantics of constraint simplification rules. *Constraints Journal*, 4(2), 1999.

[DP99]   Giorgio Delzanno and Andreas Podelski. Model checking in CLP. *Lecture Notes in Computer Science*, 1579:223–239, 1999.

[EGM01]   Sandro Etalle, Maurizio Gabbrielli, and Maria Chiara Meo. Transformations of CCP programs. *ACM Trans. Program. Lang. Syst.*, 23(3):304–395, 2001.

[FA03]   Thom Frühwirth and Slim Abdennadher. *Essentials of Constraint Programming*. Springer, 2003.

[FPP01]   Fabio Fioravanti, Alberto Pettorossi, and Maurizio Proietti. Verifying CTL properties of infinite state systems by specializing constraint logic programs. In M. Leuschel, A. Podelski, C.R. Ramakrishnan, and U. Ultes-Nitsche, editors, *ACM SIGPLAN International Workshop on Verification and Computational Logic*, pages 85–96, 2001.

[FPP04]   Fabio Fioravanti, Alberto Pettorossi, and Maurizio Proietti. Transformation rules for locally stratified constraint logic programs. 2004.

[Frü98]   Thom Frühwirth. Theory and practice of constraint handling rules. *Journal of Logic Programming*, 37(1-3):95–138, 1998.

[Frü02]   Thom Frühwirth. As time goes by: Automatic complexity analysis of simplification rules. In *8th International Conference on Principles of Knowledge Representation and Reasoning*, Toulouse, France, 2002.

[MS97]   Torben Mogensen and Peter Sestoft. Partial evaluation. In Allen Kent and James G. Williams, editors, *Encyclopedia of Computer Science and Technology*, volume 37, pages 247–279. 1997.

[PGGS98]   Josep Puyol-Gruart, Llus Godo, and Carles Sierra. Specialisation calculus and communication. *International Journal of Approximate Reasoning*, 18(1/2):107–130, 1998.

[PP96]   Alberto Pettorossi and Maurizio Proietti. Rules and strategies for transforming functional and logic programs. *ACM Comput. Surv.*, 28(2):360–414, 1996.

[RKRR04]   Abhik Roychoudhury, K. Narayan Kumar, C. R. Ramakrishnan, and I. V. Ramakrishnan. An unfold/fold transformation framework for definite logic programs. *ACM Trans. Program. Lang. Syst.*, 26(3):464–509, 2004.

[SR90]   Vijay A. Saraswat and Martin Rinard. Concurrent constraint programming. In *Proceedings of the 17th ACM SIGPLAN-SIGACT symposium on Principles of programming languages*, pages 232–245. ACM Press, 1990.

[UF88]   Kazunori Ueda and Koichi Furukawa. Transformation rules for GHC programs. In *Proc. Int. Conf. on Fifth Generation Computer Systems 1988 (FGCS'88)*, pages 582–591, 1988.

[Wal03]   Toby Walsh. Constraint patterns. In F. Rossi, editor, *9th International Conference on Principles and Practices of Constraint Programming (CP-2003)*, volume 2833, pages 53–64. Springer LNCS, 2003.

Efficient Local Unfolding with Ancestor Stacks for Full Prolog

G. Puebla[1], E. Albert[2], and M. Hermenegildo[1,3]

[1] School of Computer Science, Technical U. of Madrid
{german, herme}@fi.upm.es
[2] School of Computer Science, Complutense U. of Madrid
elvira@sip.ucm.es
[3] Depts. of Comp. Sci. and El. and Comp. Eng., U. of New Mexico
herme@unm.edu

Abstract. The integration of powerful partial evaluation methods into practical compilers for logic programs is still far from reality. This is related both to 1) efficiency issues and to 2) the complications of dealing with practical programs. Regarding efficiency, the most successful unfolding rules used nowadays are based on structural orders applied over (covering) *ancestors*, i.e., a subsequence of the atoms selected during a derivation. Unfortunately, maintaining the structure of the ancestor relation during unfolding introduces significant overhead. We propose an efficient, practical *local* unfolding rule based on the notion of covering ancestors which can be used in combination with any structural order and allows a stack-based implementation without losing any opportunities for specialization. Regarding the second issue, we propose assertion-based techniques which allow our approach to deal with real programs that include (Prolog) built-ins and external predicates in a very extensible manner. Finally, we report on our implementation of these techniques in a practical partial evaluator, embedded in a state of the art compiler which uses global analysis extensively (the Ciao compiler and, specifically, its preprocessor CiaoPP). The performance analysis of the resulting system shows that our techniques, in addition to dealing with practical programs, are also significantly more efficient in time and somewhat more efficient in memory than traditional tree-based implementations.

1 Introduction

In spite of the important research efforts in the area, the integration of *Partial Deduction* (PD) [16, 8] methods into compilers seems to be still far from reality. We believe that the general uptake of PD methods is being hindered by two factors: the relative inefficiency of the PD method, and the complications brought about by the treatment of real programs. Indeed, the integration of powerful strategies to the unfolding rule –like the use of structural orders combined with the ancestor relation– can introduce a significant cost both in time and memory consumption of the specialization process. Regarding the treatment of real programs which include external predicates, non-declarative features, etc, the

S. Etalle(Ed.): LOPSTR 2004, LNCS 3573, pp. 149–165, 2005.

complications range from how to identify which predicates include these non-declarative features (ad-hoc but difficult to maintain tables are often used in practice for this purpose) to how to deal with such predicates during PD. A main objective of this paper is to contribute to the uptake of PE techniques by addressing some of these issues.

State-of-the-art partial evaluators integrate terminating unfolding rules for local control based on *structural* orders, like homeomorphic embedding [14] which can obtain very powerful optimizations. Moreover, they allow performing the ordering comparisons over *subsequences* of the full sequence of the selected atoms. In particular, the use of *ancestors* for refining sequences of visited atoms, originally proposed in [4], greatly improves the specialization power of unfolding while still guaranteeing termination and also reduces the length of the sequences for which admissibility of new atoms has to be checked. Unfortunately, having to maintain dependency information for the individual atoms in each derivation during the generation of SLD trees has turned out to introduce overheads which seem to cancel out the theoretical efficiency gains expected. In order to address this issue, we introduce a novel unfolding rule based on the notion of covering ancestors which allows a very efficient implementation technique based on stacks. Our technique can significantly reduce the overhead incurred by the use of covering ancestors without losing any opportunities for specialization. We outline as well a generalization that allows certain non-leftmost unfoldings with the same assurances.

In order to deal with real programs that include (Prolog) built-ins and external predicates, we rely on assertion-based techniques [20]. The use of assertions provides *extensibility* in the sense that users and developers of partial evaluators can deal with new external predicates during PE by just adding the proper assertions to these predicates –without having to maintain ad-hoc tables or modifying the partial evaluator itself. We report on our implementation of our technique in a practical, state-of-the-art partial evaluator, embedded in a production compiler which uses assertions and global analysis extensively (the Ciao compiler [5] and, specifically, its preprocessor CiaoPP[9]).

2   Background

We assume some basic knowledge on the terminology of logic programming. See for example [17] for details.

2.1   Basics of Partial Deduction

Very briefly, an *atom* A is a syntactic construction of the form $p(t_1, \ldots, t_n)$, where p/n, with $n \geq 0$, is a predicate symbol and $t_1, \ldots, t_n$ are terms. The function *pred* applied to atom A, i.e., $pred(A)$, returns the predicate symbol p/n for A. A *clause* is of the form $H \leftarrow B$ where its head H is an atom and its body B is a conjunction of atoms. A *definite program* is a finite set of clauses. A *goal* (or query) is a conjunction of atoms. The concept of *computation rule* is used to select an atom within a goal for its evaluation.

Definition 1 (computation rule). *A computation rule is a function $\mathcal{R}$ from goals to atoms. Let G be a goal of the form $\leftarrow A_1, \ldots, A_R, \ldots, A_k$, $k \geq 1$. If $\mathcal{R}(G) = A_R$ we say that A_R is the selected atom in G.*

The operational semantics of definite programs is based on derivations.

Definition 2 (derivation step). *Let G be $\leftarrow A_1, \ldots, A_R, \ldots, A_k$. Let $\mathcal{R}$ be a computation rule and let $\mathcal{R}(G) = A_R$. Let $C = H \leftarrow B_1, \ldots, B_m$ be a renamed apart clause in P. Then G' is* derived *from G and C via $\mathcal{R}$ if the following conditions hold:*

$$\theta = mgu(A_R, H)$$
$$G' \text{ is the goal } \leftarrow \theta(B_1, \ldots, B_m, A_1, \ldots, A_{R-1}, A_{R+1}, \ldots, A_k)$$

The definition above differs from standard formulations (such as that in [17]) in that the atoms newly introduced in G' are not placed in the same position where the selected atom A_R used to be, but rather they are placed to the left of any atom in G. For definite programs, this is correct since goals are conjunctions, which enjoy the commutative property.

As customary, given a program P and a goal G, an *SLD derivation* for $P \cup \{G\}$ consists of a possibly infinite sequence $G = G_0, G_1, G_2, \ldots$ of goals, a sequence $C_1, C_2, \ldots$ of properly renamed apart clauses of P, and a sequence $\theta_1, \theta_2, \ldots$ of mgus such that each G_{i+1} is derived from G_i and C_{i+1} using θ_{i+1}. A derivation step can be non-deterministic when A_R unifies with several clauses in P, giving rise to several possible SLD derivations for a given goal. Such SLD derivations can be organized in *SLD trees*. A finite derivation $G = G_0, G_1, G_2, \ldots, G_n$ is called *successful* if G_n is empty. In that case $\theta = \theta_1 \theta_2 \ldots \theta_n$ is called the computed answer for goal G. Such a derivation is called *failed* if it is not possible to perform a derivation step with G_n.

In order to compute a *partial deduction* (PD) [16], given an input program and a set of atoms (goal), the first step consists in applying an *unfolding rule* to compute finite (possibly incomplete) SLD trees for these atoms. Given an atom A, an unfolding rule computes a set of finite SLD derivations $D_1, \ldots, D_n$ (i.e., a possibly incomplete SLD tree) of the form $D_i = A, \ldots, G_i$ with computer answer substitution θ_i for $i = 1, \ldots, n$ whose associated resultants are $\theta_i(A) \leftarrow G_i$. Therefore, this step returns the set of resultants, i.e., a program, associated to the root-to-leaf derivations of these trees. We refer to [14] for details. In order to ensure the local termination of the PD algorithm while producing useful specializations, the unfolding rule must incorporate some non-trivial mechanism to stop the construction of SLD trees. Nowadays, well-founded orderings (wfo) [4, 18] and well-quasi orderings (wqo) [22, 13] are broadly used in the context of on-line PE techniques (see, e.g., [8, 15, 22]). Formally, let $\leq_S$ be a wqo, we denote by $Admissible(A, (A_1, \ldots, A_n), \leq_S)$, with $n \geq 0$, the truth value of the expression $\forall A_i, i \in \{1, \ldots, n\} : A \leq_S A_i$. In wfo, it is sufficient to verify that the selected atom is strictly smaller than the previous comparable one (if one exists). Let $<$ be a wfo, by $Admissible(A, (A_1, \ldots, A_n), <)$, with $n \geq 0$, we denote the truth value of the expression $A < A_n$ if $n \geq 1$ and *true* if $n = 0$. We will denote by *structural order* a wfo or a wqo (written as $\lhd$ to represent any of them). Among the structural orders, well-quasi orderings (and *homeomorphic embedding* [10] in particular) have proved to be very powerful in practice.

State-of-the-art unfolding rules allow performing ordering comparisons over *subsequences* of the full sequence of the selected atoms of a derivation by organizing atoms in a *proof tree* [3], achieving further specialization in many cases while still guaranteeing termination. The essence of the most advanced techniques is based on the notion of *covering ancestors* [4].

Definition 3 (ancestor relation). *Given a derivation step and A_R, B_i, $i = 1, \ldots, m$ as in Def. 2, we say that A_R is the* parent *of the instance of B_i, $i = 1, \ldots, m$, in the resolvent and in each subsequent goal where the instance originating from B_i appears. The* ancestor *relation is the transitive closure of the parent relation.*

Usually, the ancestor test is only applied on *comparable* atoms, i.e., ancestor atoms with the same predicate symbol. This corresponds to the original notion of covering ancestors [4]. Given an atom A and a derivation D, we denote by $Ancestors(A, D)$ the sequence of ancestors of A in D as defined in Def. 3. It captures the dependency relation implicit within a *proof tree*.

It has been proved [4] that any infinite derivation must have at least one inadmissible *covering ancestor* sequence, i.e., a subsequence of the atoms selected during a derivation. Therefore, it is sufficient to check the selected ordering relation ⊲ over the covering ancestor subsequences in order to detect inadmissible derivations. An SLD derivation is *safe* with respect to an order (wfo or wqo) if all covering ancestor sequences of the selected atoms are admissible with respect to that order.

3   The Usefulness of Ancestors

We now illustrate some of the ideas discussed so far and, specially, the relevance of ancestor tracking, through an example. Our running example is the program in Figure 1, which implements the well known quick-sort algorithm, "qsort", using difference lists. Given an initial query of the form ←*qsort(List,Result,Cont)*, where *List* is a list of numbers, the algorithm returns in *Result* a sorted difference list which is a permutation of *List* and such that its continuation is *Cont*. For example, for the query ← $qsort([1, 1, 1], L, [])$, the program should compute L=[1,1,1], constructing a finite SLD tree.

Consider now Fig. 2, which presents an incomplete SLD derivation for our quick-sort program and the query ← $qsort([1, 1, 1], R, [])$ using a leftmost unfolding rule. For conciseness, predicates qsort and partition are abbreviated as qs

```
qsort([],R,R).                    partition([],_,[],[]).
qsort([X|L],R,R2) :-              partition([E|R],C,[E|Left1],Right) :-
   partition(L,X,L1,L2),             E =< C, partition(R,C,Left1,Right).
   qsort(L2,R1,R2),              partition([E|R],C,Left,[E|Right1]) :-
   qsort(L1,R,[X|R1]).              E > C,  partition(R,C,Left,Right1).
```

Fig. 1. A quick-sort program

$$\mathbf{1}.\underline{\mathtt{qs}}([1,1,1],\mathtt{R},[])^{\{\}}$$

$$\downarrow$$

$$\mathbf{2}.\underline{\mathtt{p}}([1,1],1,\mathtt{L1},\mathtt{L2})^{\{1\}}, \mathbf{3}.\mathtt{qs}(\mathtt{L2},\mathtt{R1},[])^{\{1\}}, \mathbf{4}.\mathtt{qs}(\mathtt{L1},\mathtt{R},[1|\mathtt{R1}])^{\{1\}}$$

$$\downarrow \{\mathtt{L1}\mapsto[1|\mathtt{L}]\}$$

$$\mathbf{5}.\underline{1 =< 1}^{\{1,2\}}, \mathbf{6}.\mathtt{p}([1],1,\mathtt{L},\mathtt{L2})^{\{1,2\}}, \mathbf{3}.\mathtt{qs}(\mathtt{L2},\mathtt{R1},[])^{\{1\}}, \mathbf{4}.\mathtt{qs}([1|\mathtt{L}],\mathtt{R},[1|\mathtt{R1}])^{\{1\}}$$

$$\downarrow$$

$$\mathbf{6}.\boxed{\mathtt{p}([1],1,\mathtt{L},\mathtt{L2})}^{\{1,2\}}, \mathbf{3}.\mathtt{qs}(\mathtt{L2},\mathtt{R1},[])^{\{1\}}, \mathbf{4}.\mathtt{qs}([1|\mathtt{L}],\mathtt{R},[1|\mathtt{R1}])^{\{1\}}$$

$$\downarrow \{\mathtt{L}\mapsto[1|\mathtt{L}']\}$$

$$\mathbf{7}.\underline{1 =< 1}^{\{1,2,6\}}, \mathbf{8}.\mathtt{p}([],1,\mathtt{L}',\mathtt{L2})^{\{1,2,6\}}, \mathbf{3}.\mathtt{qs}(\mathtt{L2},\mathtt{R1},[])^{\{1\}}, \mathbf{4}.\mathtt{qs}([1,1|\mathtt{L}'],\mathtt{R},[1|\mathtt{R1}])^{\{1\}}$$

$$\downarrow$$

$$\mathbf{8}.\underline{\mathtt{p}}([],1,\mathtt{L}',\mathtt{L2})^{\{1,2,6\}}, \mathbf{3}.\mathtt{qs}(\mathtt{L2},\mathtt{R1},[])^{\{1\}}, \mathbf{4}.\mathtt{qs}([1,1|\mathtt{L}'],\mathtt{R},[1|\mathtt{R1}])^{\{1\}}$$

$$\downarrow \{\mathtt{L}'\mapsto[],\mathtt{L2}\mapsto[]\}$$

$$\mathbf{3}.\underline{\mathtt{qs}}([],\mathtt{R1},[])^{\{1\}}, \mathbf{4}.\mathtt{qs}([1,1],\mathtt{R},[1|\mathtt{R1}])^{\{1\}}$$

$$\downarrow \{\mathtt{R1}'\mapsto[]\}$$

$$\mathbf{4}.\underline{\mathtt{qs}}([1,1],\mathtt{R},[1])^{\{1\}}$$

$$\downarrow$$

$$\mathbf{9}.\boxed{\mathtt{p}([1],1,\mathtt{L1'},\mathtt{L2'})}^{\{1,4\}}, \mathbf{10}.\mathtt{qs}(\mathtt{L2'},\mathtt{R1'},[1])^{\{1,4\}}, \mathbf{11}.\mathtt{qs}(\mathtt{L1'},\mathtt{R},[1|\mathtt{R1'}])^{\{1,4\}}$$

Fig. 2. Derivation with Ancestor Annotations

and p, respectively in the figure. Note that each atom is labeled with a number (an identifier) for future reference[1] and a superscript which contains the list of ancestors of that atom. Let us assume that we use the *homeomorphic embedding* order [13] as structural order. If we check admissibility w.r.t. the full sequence of atoms, i.e., we do not use the ancestor relation, the derivation will stop when atom number **9**, i.e., $\mathtt{p}([1],1,\mathtt{L}',\mathtt{L2}')$, is found for the second time. The reason is that this atom is not strictly smaller than atom number **6** which was selected in the third step, indeed, they are equal modulo renaming.[2]

This unfolding rule is too conservative, since the process can proceed further without risking termination. The crucial point is that the execution of atom number **9** does not depend on atom number **6** (and, actually, the unfolding of **6** has been already *completed* when atom number **9** is being considered for unfolding). Figure 3 shows the proof tree associated to this derivation where nodes are labeled with the numbers assigned to each atom, instead of the atoms

---

[1] By abuse of notation, we keep the same number for each atom throughout the derivation although it may be further instantiated (and thus modified) in subsequent steps. This will become useful for continuing the example later.

[2] Let us note that the two calls to the builtin predicate =< which appear in the derivation can be executed since the arguments are properly instantiated. However, they have not been considered in the admissibility test since these calls do not endanger the termination of the derivation, as we will discuss in Sect. 5.

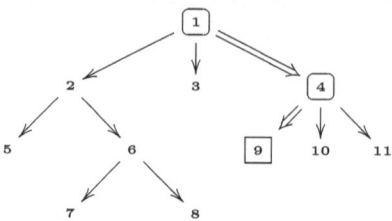

Fig. 3. Proof tree for the example

themselves. Note that, in order to decide whether or not to evaluate atom number **9**, it is only necessary to check that it is strictly smaller than atoms **4** and **1**, i.e., than those which are its *ancestors* in the proof tree. On the other hand, and as we saw before, if the full derivation is considered instead, as in Fig. 2, atom **9** will be compared also with atom **6** concluding imprecisely that the derivation may not be safe.

Despite their obvious relevance, unfortunately the practical applicability of unfolding rules based on the notion of covering ancestor is threatened by the overhead introduced by the implementation of this notion. A naive implementation of the notion of ancestor keeps –for each atom– the list of its ancestors, as it is depicted in Fig. 2. This implementation is relatively efficient in time but presents a high overhead in memory consumption. Our experiments show that the partial evaluator can run out of memory even for simple examples. A more reasonable implementation maintains the proof tree as a global structure. This greatly reduces memory consumption but the cost of traversing the tree for retrieving the ancestors of each atom introduces a significant slowdown in the PE process. We argue that our implementation technique is efficient in time and space, overcoming the above limitations.

4   An Efficient Implementation for Local Unfolding

Our definition of *local unfolding* is based on the notion of *ancestor depth*.

Definition 4 (ancestor depth). *Given an SLD derivation $D = G_0, \ldots, G_m$ with $G_m =\leftarrow A_1, \ldots, A_k$, $k \geq 1$, the ancestor depth of A_i for $i = 1, \ldots, k$, denoted $depth(A_i, D)$ is the cardinality of the ancestor relation for A_i in D.*

Intuitively, the ancestor depth of an atom in a goal is the depth at which this atom is located in the proof tree associated to the derivation.

Definition 5 (local computation rule). *A computation rule $\mathcal{R}$ is local if $\forall D = G_0, \ldots, G_n$ such that $G_i =\leftarrow A_{i1}, \ldots, A_{im_i}$ for $i = 0, .., n$, it holds that:*
$$depth(\mathcal{R}(G_i), D) \geq depth(A_{ij}, D) \quad \forall j = 1, \ldots, m_i$$

Intuitively, a computation rule is local if it always selects one of the atoms which is deepest in the proof tree for the derivation. As a result, local computation rules traverse proof trees in a depth-first fashion, though not necessarily left to right nor in any other fixed order. Thus, in principle, in order to implement a local computation rule we need to record (part of) the derivation history (its proof tree). Note that the computation rule used in most implementations of logic programming languages, such as Prolog, always selects the leftmost atom. This computation rule, often referred to as left-to-right computation rule, is clearly a local computation rule. Selecting the leftmost atom in all goals guarantees that the selected atom is of maximal depth within the proof tree as it is traversed in a depth-first fashion –without the need of storing any history about the derivation.

An instrumental observation in our approach is that if the proof tree which is used in order to capture the ancestor relation is traversed depth-first, left-to-right, it can be interpreted as an *activation tree* [1]. In fact, the ancestor subsequence in any point in time corresponds to the current *control word* [21] by simply regarding selected atoms as procedure calls. The control word for each execution state can be seen as the set of procedures whose execution has started and is not yet completed, bearing a strong relation with the stack of activation records which most compilers use as a run-time data structure. This data structure takes normally the form of a stack, and this suggests one of the central ideas of our approach: using stacks for storing ancestors. Another important observation is that the control word idea does not need to be restricted to leftmost computation and it works equally well as long as the computation rule is local. Indeed, sibling atoms have the same ancestor depth, they can be selected in any order and the notion of control word still applies. The advantages of computing the control word instead of the proof tree are clear: the control word corresponds to a single branch in the proof tree from the current selected atom to all its ancestors in the proof tree. Thus, the control word offers advantages both from memory and time consumption. The main difficulty for computing control words is to determine exactly when each item in the control word should be removed. To do this, we need to know when the computation of each predicate is finished. In logic programming terminology this corresponds to determining the success states for all predicates in the derivation. In principle, success states are not observable in SLD resolution other than for the top-level query.

We now propose an easy-to-implement modification to SLD resolution as presented in Section 2 in which success states for all internal calls are observable –and where the control word is available at each state. We will refer to this resolution as SLD resolution with ancestor stacks, or *ASLD* for short. The proposed modification involves 1) augmenting goals with an *ancestor stack*, which at each stage of the computation contains the control word of the derivation, which corresponds to *the ancestors of the next atom which will be selected for resolution*, and 2) adding pseudo-atoms to the goals used during resolution which mark a scope whose purpose is twofold: 2.1) when a mark is leftmost in a goal, it indicates that the current state corresponds to the success state for the call which is now on top of the ancestor stack, i.e., the call is completed, and the atom on top of the ancestor stack should be popped; 2.2) the atoms within the scope of the leftmost mark have maximal ancestor depth and thus a local unfolding strategy can be easily defined in the presence of these pseudo-atoms. We use the pseudo-atom $\uparrow$ (read as "pop") to indicate the end of a depth scope, i.e., after it we move up in the proof tree. It is guaranteed not to clash with any existing predicate name.

The following two definitions present the derivation rules in our ASLD semantics. Now, a state S is a tuple of the form $\langle G \mid AS \rangle$ where G is a goal and AS is an ancestor stack (or *stack* for short). To handle such stacks, we will use the usual stack operations: empty, which returns an empty stack, push($AS, Item$), which pushes *Item* onto the stack AS, and pop(AS), which pops an element from AS. In addition, we will use the operation contents(AS), which returns the sequence of atoms contained in AS in the order in which they would be popped from the stack AS and leaves AS unmodified.

Definition 6 (derive). *Let* $G = \leftarrow A_1, \ldots, A_R, \ldots, A_k$ *be a goal with* $A_1 \neq \uparrow$. *Let* $S = \langle G \mid AS \rangle$ *be a state and* AS *be a stack. Let* $\lhd$ *be a structural order. Let* $\mathcal{R}$ *be a computation rule and let* $\mathcal{R}(G) = A_R$ *with* $A_R \neq \uparrow$. *Let* $C = H \leftarrow B_1, \ldots, B_m$ *be a renamed apart clause. Then* $S' = \langle G' \mid AS' \rangle$ *is derived from* S *and* C *via* $\mathcal{R}$ *if the following conditions hold:*

$$Admissible(A_R, \mathsf{contents}(AS), \lhd)$$
$$\theta = mgu(A_R, H)$$
$$G' \text{ is the goal } \leftarrow \theta(B_1, \ldots, B_m, \uparrow, A_1, \ldots, A_{R-1}, A_{R+1}, \ldots, A_k)$$
$$AS' = \mathsf{push}(AS, ren((A_R)))$$

The **derive** rule behaves as the one in Definition 2 but in addition: i) the mark $\uparrow$ ("pop") is added to the goal, and ii) a renamed apart copy of A_R, denoted $ren(A_R)$, is pushed onto the ancestor stack. As before, the **derive** rule is nondeterministic if several clauses in P unify with the atom A_R. However, in contrast to Definition 2, this rule can only be applied if 1) the leftmost atom in the goal is not a $\uparrow$ mark, and 2) the current selected atom A_R together with its ancestors does constitute an admissible sequence. If 1) holds but 2) does not, this derivation is stopped and we refer to such a derivation as *inadmissible*.

Definition 7 (pop-derive). *Let* $G = \leftarrow A_1, \ldots, A_k$ *be a goal with* $A_1 = \uparrow$. *Let* $S = \langle G \mid AS \rangle$ *be a state and* AS *be a stack. Then* $S' = \langle G' \mid AS' \rangle$ *with* $G' = \leftarrow A_2, \ldots, A_k$ *and* $AS' = \mathsf{pop}(AS)$ *is pop-derived from* S.

The **pop-derive** rule is used when the leftmost atom in the resolvent is a $\uparrow$ mark. Its effect is to eliminate from the ancestor stack the topmost atom, which is guaranteed not to belong to the ancestors of any selected atom in any possible continuation of this derivation.

Computation for a query G starts from the state $S_0 = \langle G \mid \mathsf{empty} \rangle$. Given a non-empty derivation D, we denote by *curr_goal(D)* and *curr_ancestors(D)* the goal and the stack in the last state in D, respectively. At each step of a derivation D at most one rule, either **derive** or **pop-derive**, can be applied depending on whether the first atom in *curr_goal(D)* is a mark $\uparrow$ or not.

Example 1. Fig. 4 illustrates the ASLD derivation corresponding to the derivation with explicit ancestor annotations of Fig. 2. Sometimes, rather than writing

$$\langle \{\underline{qs([1,1,1],R,[])}\} \ \mathbf{I} \ [] \rangle$$

$$\downarrow derive$$

$$\langle \{\mathbf{2,3,4}, \uparrow \} \ \mathbf{I} \ [qsort([1,1,1],R,[])] \rangle$$

$$\downarrow derive$$

$$\langle \{\mathbf{5,6}, \uparrow, \mathbf{3,4}, \uparrow \} \ \mathbf{I} \ [part([1,1],1,L1,L2), qs([1,1,1],R,[])] \rangle$$

$$\downarrow external-derive$$

$$\langle \{\mathbf{6}, \uparrow, \mathbf{3,4}, \uparrow \} \ \mathbf{I} \ [part([1,1],1,L1,L2), qs([1,1,1],R,[])] \rangle$$

$$\downarrow derive$$

$$\langle \{\mathbf{7,8}, \uparrow, \uparrow, \mathbf{3,4}, \uparrow \} \ \mathbf{I} \ [part([1],1,L,L2), part([1,1],1,L1,L2), qs([1,1,1],R,[])] \rangle$$

$$\downarrow external-derive$$

$$\langle \{\mathbf{8}, \uparrow, \uparrow, \mathbf{3,4}, \uparrow \} \ \mathbf{I} \ [part([1],1,L,L2), part([1,1],1,L1,L2), qs([1,1,1],R,[])] \rangle$$

$$\downarrow derive, pop-derive$$

$$\langle \{ \uparrow, \uparrow, \mathbf{3,4}, \uparrow \} \ \mathbf{I} \ [part([1],1,L,L2), part([1,1],1,L1,L2), qs([1,1,1],R,[])] \rangle$$

$$\downarrow pop-derive$$

$$\langle \{ \uparrow, \mathbf{3,4}, \uparrow \} \ \mathbf{I} \ [part([1,1],1,L1,L2), qs([1,1,1],R,[])] \rangle$$

$$\downarrow pop-derive$$

$$\langle \{\mathbf{3,4}, \uparrow \} \ \mathbf{I} \ [qsort([1,1,1],R,[])] \rangle$$

$$\downarrow derive, pop-derive$$

$$\langle \{\mathbf{4}, \uparrow \} \ \mathbf{I} \ [qsort([1,1,1],R,[])] \rangle$$

$$\downarrow derive$$

$$\langle \{part([1],1,L1',L2'), \mathbf{10,11}, \uparrow, \uparrow \} \ \mathbf{I} \ [qsort([1,1],R,[1]), qsort([1,1,1],R,[])] \rangle$$

Fig. 4. ASLD Derivation for the example

the atoms themselves, we use the same numbers assigned to the corresponding atoms in Fig. 2. Each step has been appropriately labeled with the applied derivation rule. Although rule *external-derive* has not been presented yet, we can just assume that the code for the external predicate =< is available and has the expected behavior.

It should be noted that, in the last state, the stack contains exactly the ancestors of partition([1],1,L1',L2'), i.e., the atoms **4** and **1**, since the previous calls to partition have already finished and thus their corresponding atoms have been popped off the stack. Thus, the admissibility test for partition([1],1,L1',L2') succeeds, and unfolding can proceed further without risking termination. Note that *derive* steps w.r.t. a clause which is a fact are always followed by a *pop-derive* and thus they are optimized in the figure (and in the implementation, described in Section 6) by not pushing the selected atom A_R onto the stack and not including a $\uparrow$ mark into the goal which would immediately pop A_R from the stack.

Finally, since the goals obtained by ASLD resolution may contain atoms of the form $\uparrow$, resultants are cleaned up before being transferred to the global control level or during the code generation phase by simply eliminating all atoms of the form $\uparrow$.

It is easy to see that for each ASLD derivation D_S there is a corresponding SLD derivation D with the same computed answer substitution and the same goal without the $\uparrow$ atoms. Such SLD derivation is the one obtained by performing the same *derive* steps (with exactly the same clauses) using the same computation rule and by ignoring the *pop-derive* steps since goals in SLD resolution do not contain $\uparrow$ atoms. We will use $simplify(D_S) = D$ to denote that D is the SLD derivation which corresponds to D_S.

We would now like to impose a condition on the computation rule which allows ensuring that the contents of the stack are precisely the ancestors of the atom to be selected.

Definition 8 (depth-preserving). *A computation rule $\mathcal{R}$ is depth-preserving if for each non-empty goal $G = \leftarrow A_1, \ldots, A_k$ with $A_1 \neq \uparrow$, $\mathcal{R}(G) = A_R$ and $\uparrow \notin \{A_1, \ldots, A_R\}$.*

Intuitively, a depth-preserving computation rule always returns an atom which is strictly to the left of the first (leftmost) $\uparrow$ mark. Note that $\uparrow$ is used to separate groups of atoms which are at different depth in the proof tree. Thus, the notion of depth-preserving computation rules in ASLD resolution is *equivalent* to that of local computation rules in SLD resolution.

Proposition 1 (ancestor stack). *Let D_S be an ASLD derivation for initial query G in program P via a depth-preserving computation rule. Let D be an SLD derivation such that $simplify(D_S) = D$. Let $curr\_goal(D_S) = A_1, \ldots, A_n, \uparrow$,... with $A_i \neq \uparrow$ for $i = 1, \ldots, n$. Let $curr\_ancestors(D_S) = AS$. Then,* contents$(AS) = Ancestors(A_i, D)$ *for $i = 1, \ldots, n$.*

The next theorem guarantees that we do not lose any specialization opportunities by using our stack-based implementation for ancestors instead of the more complex tree-based implementation, i.e., our proposed semantics will not stop "too early". It is a consequence of the above proposition and the results in [4].

Theorem 1 (accuracy). *Let D be an SLD derivation for query G in a program P via a local computation rule. Let $\triangleleft$ be a structural order. If the derivation D is safe w.r.t $\triangleleft$ then there exists an ASLD derivation D_S for G and P via a depth-preserving computation rule such that $simplify(D_S) = D$.*

Note that since our semantics disables performing any further steps as soon as inadmissible sequences are detected, not all local SLD derivations have a corresponding ASLD derivation. However, if a local SLD derivation is safe, then its corresponding D_S derivation can be found.

It is interesting to note that we can allow more flexible computation rules which are not necessarily depth-preserving while still ensuring termination. For instance, consider state $\langle A_1, \ldots, A_n, \uparrow, A_R, \ldots \mid [P_1 | P] \rangle$ with $\uparrow \notin \{A_1, \ldots, A_n\}$ and a non depth-preserving computation rule which selects the atom A_R to the right of the $\uparrow$ mark. Then, rule *derive* will check admissibility of A_R w.r.t. all atoms in the stack $[P_1 | P]$. However, the topmost atom P_1 is an ancestor only of the atoms A_i to the left of A_R but it is not an ancestor of A_R. The more ↑ marks the computation rule jumps over to select an atom, the more atoms which do not belong to the ancestors of the selected atom will be in the stack, thus, the more accuracy and efficiency we lose. In any case, the stack will always be an over-approximation of the actual set of ancestors of A_R.

In principle, our local unfolding rule based on ancestor stacks can be used within any PD framework, including Conjunctive Partial Deduction (CPD). It should be noted that some CPD examples may require the use of an unfolding rule which is not depth-preserving to obtain the optimal specialization. As we discuss above, we cannot ensure accuracy results in these cases but in turn the use of local unfolding will clearly improve the efficiency of the PD process.

5   Assertion-Based Unfolding for External Predicates

Most of real-life Prolog programs use predicates which are not defined in the program (module) being developed. We will refer to such predicates as *external*. Examples of external predicates are the traditional "built-in" predicates such as arithmetic operations (e.g., is/2, <, =<, etc.) or basic input/output facilities. We will also consider as external predicates those defined in a different module, predicates written in another language, etc. This section deals with the difficulties which such *external* predicates pose during PD.

When an atom A, such that $pred(A) = p/n$ is an external predicate, is selected during PD, it is not possible to apply the *derive* rule in Definition 2 due to several reasons. First, we may not have the code defining p/n and, even if we have it, the derivation step may introduce in the residual program calls to predicates which are private to the module M where p/n is defined. In spite of this, if the executable code for the external predicate p/n is available, and under certain conditions, it can be possible to fully evaluate calls to external predicates at specialization time. We use $\mathsf{Exec}(Sys, M, A)$ to denote the execution of atom A on a logic programming system Sys (e.g., Ciao or Sicstus) in which the module M where the external predicate p/n is defined has been loaded. In the case of logic programs, $\mathsf{Exec}(Sys, M, A)$ can return zero, one, or several computed answers for $M \cup A$ and then execution can either terminate or loop. We will use substitution sequences [6] to represent the outcome of the execution of external predicates. A *substitution sequence* is either a finite sequence of the form $\langle \theta_1, \ldots, \theta_n \rangle$, $n \geq 0$, or an incomplete sequence of the form $\langle \theta_1, \ldots, \theta_n, \perp \rangle$, $n \geq 0$, or an infinite sequence $\langle \theta_1, \ldots, \theta_i, \ldots \rangle$, $i \in I\!N^*$, where $I\!N^*$ is the set of positive natural numbers and $\perp$ indicates that the execution loops. We say that an execution *universally terminates* if $\mathsf{Exec}(Sys, M, A) = \langle \theta_1, \ldots, \theta_n \rangle$, $n \geq 0$.

In addition to producing substitution sequences, it can be the case that the execution of atoms for (external) predicates produces other outcomes such as side-effects, errors, and exceptions. Note that this precludes the evaluation of such atoms to be performed at PE time, since those effects need to be performed at run-time. We say that an expression is *evaluable* when its execution 1) universally terminates, 2) it does not produce side-effects, 3) it is sufficiently instantiated to be executed, 4) it does not issue errors and 5) it does not generate exceptions. Clearly, some of the above properties are not computable (e.g., termination is undecidable in the general case). However, it is often possible to determine some *sufficient conditions* (*SC*) which are *decidable* and ensure that, if an atom A satisfies such conditions, then A is evaluable. Intuitively, *SC* can be thought of as a traditional precondition which ensures a certain behaviour of the execution of a procedure provided they are satisfied. To formalize this, we propose to use the "*computational* assertions" which are part of the assertion language [20] of CiaoPP in order to express that a certain predicate is evaluable under certain conditions. The following definition introduces the notion of an eval *annotation* as (part of) a computational assertion. We use id to denote the empty substitution, i.e., $\forall t$, $\text{id}(t) = t$.

Definition 9 (eval annotations). *Let p/n be an external predicate defined in module M. The assertion* :- trust comp p(X1,...,Xn) : *SC* + eval. *in the code for M is a correct eval annotation for predicate p/n in a logic programming system Sys if, $\forall \theta$, the expression $\theta(SC)$ is evaluable, and*
if $\text{Exec}(Sys, M, \theta(SC)) = \langle \text{id} \rangle$ *then* $\theta(p(X1, ..., Xn))$ *is evaluable*

One of the advantages of using this kind of assertion is that it makes it possible to deal with new external predicates (e.g., written in other languages) in user programs or in the system libraries without having to modify the partial evaluator itself. Also, the fact that the assertions are co-located with the actual code defining the external predicate, i.e., in the module M (as opposed to being in a large table inside the PD system) makes it more difficult for the assertion to be left out of sync when a modification is made to the external predicate. We believe this to be very important to the maintainability of a real application or system library.

Example 2. The computational assertions in CiaoPP for the builtin predicate $\leq$ include, among others, the following one:

```
:- trust comp A =< B : (arithexpr(A), arithexpr(B)) + eval.
```

which states that if predicate =</2 is called with both arguments instantiated to a term of type arithexpr, then the call is evaluable. The type arithexpr corresponds to arithmetic expressions which, as expected, are built out of numbers and the usual arithmetic operators. The type arithexpr is expressed in Ciao as a unary regular logic program. This allows using the underlying Ciao system in order to effectively decide whether a term is an arithexpr or not.

The following definition extends our ASLD semantics by providing a new rule, **external-derive**, for evaluating calls to external predicates. Given a sequence of substitutions $\langle \theta_1, \ldots, \theta_n \rangle$, we define $Subst(\langle \theta_1, \ldots, \theta_n \rangle) = \{\theta_1, \ldots, \theta_n\}$.

Definition 10 (external-derive). *Let Sys be a logic programming system. Let $G = \leftarrow A_1, \ldots, A_R, \ldots, A_k$ be a goal. Let $S = \langle G \mid AS \rangle$ be a state and AS a stack. Let $\mathcal{R}$ be a computation rule such that $\mathcal{R}(G) =A_R$ with $pred(A_R) = p/n$ an external predicate from module M. Let C be a renamed apart assertion* :- trust comp p(X1,...,Xn) : *SC* + eval. *Then, $S' = \langle G' \mid AS' \rangle$ is external-derived from S and C via $\mathcal{R}$ in Sys if: 1) $\sigma = mgu(A_R, p(X1, ..., Xn))$,*

2) $\mathsf{Exec}(Sys, M, \sigma(SC)) = \langle id \rangle$, 3) $\theta \in Subst(\mathsf{Exec}(Sys, M, A_R))$, 4) G' is the goal $\theta(A_1, \ldots, A_{R-1}, A_{R+1}, \ldots, A_k)$, 5)$AS' = AS$.

Notice that, since after computing $\mathsf{Exec}(Sys, M, A_R)$ the computation of A_R is finished, there is no need to push (a copy of) A_R into AS and the ancestor stack is not modified by the **external-derive** rule. This rule can be nondeterministic if the substitution sequence for the selected atom A_R contains more than one element, i.e., the execution of external predicates is not restricted to atoms which are deterministic. The fact that A_R is evaluable implies universal termination. This in turn guarantees that in any ASLD tree, given a node S in which an external atom has been selected for further resolution, only a finite number of descendants exist for S and they can be obtained in finite time.

Example 3. Consider the assertion in Example 2 and the atoms **5** and **7**, which are of the form 1=<1, in the ASLD derivation of Fig. 2. Both atoms can be evaluated because $\mathsf{Exec}(ciao, arithmetic, (arithexpr(1), arithexpr(1))) = \langle id \rangle$. This is a sufficient condition for $\mathsf{Exec}(ciao, arithmetic, (1 =< 1))$ to be evaluable. Its execution returns $\mathsf{Exec}(ciao, arithmetic, (1 =< 1)) = \langle id \rangle$.

6   Experimental Results

We have implemented in our PD system the unfolding rule we propose, together with other variations in order to evaluate the efficiency of our proposal. Our PD system has been integrated in a practical state of the art compiler which uses global analysis extensively: the CiaoPP preprocessor [9]. For the tests, the whole system has been compiled using Ciao 1.11#275 [5], with the bytecode generation option. All of our experiments have been performed on a Pentium 4 at 2.4GHz and 512MB RAM running GNU Linux RH9.0. The Linux kernel used is 2.4.25.

The results in terms of execution time are presented in Table 1. The programs used as benchmarks are indicated in the **Bench** column. We have chosen

Table 1. Comparison of Proof Trees Vs.Ancestor Stacks (Execution Time)

Bench	Execution Times				Relative Speed Up		
	Relation	Trees	Stacks	MEcce	Relation	Trees	MEcce
advisor3	144	192	106	1240	1.36	1.81	11.70
nrev_80	mem	106490	15040	64970	∞	7.08	4.32
nrev_38	998	2804	806	4370	1.24	3.48	5.42
permute_7	mem	5226	2800	34680	∞	1.87	12.39
permute_6	476	614	336	3530	1.42	1.83	10.51
query	166	214	116	1290	1.43	1.84	11.12
qsort_80	mem	98514	8970	71870	∞	10.98	8.01
qsort_33	686	2432	454	4580	1.51	5.36	10.09
rev_80	984	1102	960	1400	1.02	1.15	1.46
zebra	1562	2276	994	186620	1.57	2.29	187.75
Overall					mem	7.19	12.25

a number of classical programs for the analysis and PD of logic programs as benchmarks. In order to factor out the cost of global control, we have used in our experiments initial queries which can be fully unfolded using homeomorphic embedding with ancestors. The program `advisor3` is a variation of the advisor program in the DPPD [12] library. The programs `query` and `zebra` are classical benchmarks for program analysis. Programs `qsort_80` and `qsort_33` correspond to the quick-sort program shown in the paper with pseudo-random lists of natural numbers of length 80 and 33 respectively. `nrev_80` and `nrev_38` correspond to the well-known naive reverse with lists of 80 and 38 natural numbers. `rev_80` is a reverse program with linear complexity which uses an accumulator. The initial query is, as before, a list of 80 natural numbers. Finally, `permute` is a permutation program which uses a nondeterministic deletion predicate. It is partially evaluated w.r.t. a list of 6 and 7 elements respectively. None of `advisor3`, `query`, nor `zebra` can be fully unfolded using homeomorphic embedding over the full sequence of selected atoms. Also, `nrev` and, as seen in the running example, `qsort` are potentially not fully unfolded if the input lists contain repetitions unless ancestors are considered. In the table, the following group of columns show execution time of the unfolding process with the different implementations of unfolding:

Relation. We refer to an implementation where each atom in the resolvent is annotated with the list of atoms which are in its ancestor relation, as done in the example in Figure 2.

Trees. This column refers to the implementation where the ancestor relations of the different atoms are organized in a proof tree.

Stacks. The column **Stacks** refers to our proposed implementation based on ancestor stacks.

MEcce. We have also measured the time that it takes to process the same benchmarks using Leuschel's M-Ecce (modular Ecce [12]) system, compiled with the same version of Ciao and in the same machine.

The last set of columns compare the relative measures of the different approaches w.r.t. the **Stacks** algorithm. Finally, in the last row, labeled **Overall**, we summarize the results for the different benchmarks using a weighted mean, which places more importance on those benchmarks with relatively larger unfolding figures. We use as weight for each program its actual unfolding time. We believe that this weighted mean is more informative than the arithmetic mean, as, for example, doubling the speed in which a large unfolding tree is computed is more relevant than achieving this for small trees.

Let us explain the results in Table 1. Times are in milliseconds, measuring *runtime*, and are computed as the arithmetic mean of five runs. Three entries in the **Relation** column contain the value "mem", instead of a number, to indicate that the PD system has run out of memory. For each of these three cases, we have repeated the experiment with the largest possible initial query that **Relation** can handle in our system before running out of memory. This explains that the three benchmarks are specialized w.r.t. two different initial queries. As it can be seen in the column for relative speedups, **Relation** is quite efficient in time for those benchmarks it can handle, though a bit slower than the one based on stacks. However, its memory consumption is extremely high, which makes this implementation inadmissible in practice. Regarding column **Trees**, the implementation based on proof trees has a good memory consumption but is slower than **Relation** due to the overhead of traversing the tree for retrieving the ancestors of each atom. In comparison to M-ecce, the results provide evidence that our proof tree-based implementation is indeed comparable to state of the art systems, since the execution times are similar in some cases or even better in others. The last set of columns compares the relative execution times of the different approaches w.r.t. the **Stacks** algorithm which is the fastest in all cases. Indeed, **Stacks** is even faster than the implementation based on explicitly storing all ancestors of all atoms (**Relation**) while having a memory consumption comparable to (and in fact, slightly better than) the implementation based on proof trees. The actual speedup ranges from 1.15 in the case of rev_80 to 10.98 in the case of qsort_80. This variation is due to the different shapes which the proof trees can have for the (derivations in the) SLD tree. In the case of rev, the speedup is low since the SLD tree consists of a single derivation whose proof tree has a single branch. Thus, in this case considering the ancestor sequence is indeed equivalent to considering the whole sequence of selected atoms. But note that this only happens for binary clauses. It is also worth noticing that the speedup achieved by the **Stacks** implementation increases with the size of the SLD tree, as can be seen in the three benchmarks which have been specialized w.r.t. different queries. The overall resulting speedup of our proposed unfolding rule over other existing ones is significant: over 7 times faster than our tree-based implementation.

We have also studied the memory required by the unfolding process (for lack of space details are in [19]). As for the case of execution time, the **Stacks** algorithm presents lower consumption than any other algorithm for all programs studied. The memory required by the **Relation** algorithm precludes it from its practical usage. Regarding the **Stacks** algorithm, not only it is significantly faster than the implementation based on trees. Also it provides a relatively important reduction (1.18 overall, computed again using a weighted mean) in memory consumption over **Trees**, which already has a good memory usage.

Altogether, when the results of Table 1 and the memory figures are combined, they provide evidence that our proposed techniques allow significant speedups while at the same time requiring somewhat less memory than tree based implementations and much better memory consumptions than implementations where the ancestor relation is directly computed. This suggests that our techniques are indeed effective and can contribute to making PD a practical tool.

As for future work, we plan to provide additional solutions for the problems involved in non-leftmost unfolding for programs with extra logical predicates beyond those presented in the literature [11, 7, 2, 14]. In particular, the intensive use of static analysis techniques in this context seems particularly promising. In our case we plan to take advantage of the fact that our PD system is integrated in `CiaoPP` which includes extensive program analysis facilities.

Acknowledgments

The authors would like to thank the anonymous referees and the participants of LOPSTR'04 for their useful comments. This work was funded in part by the Information Society Technologies programme of the European Commission, Future and Emerging Technologies under the IST-2001-38059 *ASAP* project and by the Spanish Ministry of Science and Education under the MCYT TIC 2002-0055 *CUBICO* project. Part of this work was performed during a research stay of Elvira Albert and Germán Puebla at University of Roskilde supported by respective grants from the Secretaría de Estado de Educación y Universidades, Spanish Ministry of Science and Education. Manuel Hermenegildo is also supported by the Prince of Asturias Chair in Information Science and Technology at UNM.

References

1. A. V. Aho, R. Sethi, and J. D. Ullman. *Compilers – Principles, Techniques and Tools.* Addison-Wesley, 1986.
2. E. Albert, M. Hanus, and G. Vidal. A practical partial evaluation scheme for multi-paradigm declarative languages. *Journal of Functional and Logic Programming*, 2002(1), 2002.
3. M. Bruynooghe. A Practical Framework for the Abstract Interpretation of Logic Programs. *Journal of Logic Programming*, 10:91–124, 1991.
4. M. Bruynooghe, D. De Schreye, and B. Martens. A General Criterion for Avoiding Infinite Unfolding during Partial Deduction. *New Generation Computing*, 1(11):47–79, 1992.
5. F. Bueno, D. Cabeza, M. Carro, M. Hermenegildo, P. López-García, and G. Puebla (Eds.). The Ciao System. Reference Manual (v1.10). Technical Report CLIP3/97.1.10(04), School of Computer Science (UPM), August 2004. Available at `http://clip.dia.fi.upm.es/Software/Ciao/`.
6. B. Le Charlier, S. Rossi, and P. Van Hentenryck. Sequence Based Abstract Interpretation of Prolog. *Theory and Practice of Logic Programming*, 2(1):25–84, 2002.
7. S. Etalle, M. Gabbrielli, and E. Marchiori. A Transformation System for CLP with Dynamic Scheduling and CCP. In *Proc. of the ACM Sigplan PEPM'97*, pages 137–150. ACM Press, New York, 1997.
8. J.P. Gallagher. Tutorial on specialisation of logic programs. In *Proceedings of PEPM'93, the ACM Sigplan Symposium on Partial Evaluation and Semantics-Based Program Manipulation*, pages 88–98. ACM Press, 1993.
9. M. Hermenegildo, G. Puebla, F. Bueno, and P. López-García. Program Development Using Abstract Interpretation (and The Ciao System Preprocessor). In *Proc. of SAS'03*, pages 127–152. Springer LNCS 2694, 2003.
10. J.B. Kruskal. Well-quasi-ordering, the tree theorem, and Vazsonyi's conjecture. *Transactions of the American Mathematical Society*, 95:210–225, 1960.

11. Michael Leuschel. Partial evaluation of the "real thing". *Proceedings of LOP-STR'94 and META'94*, Lecture Notes in Computer Science 883, pages 122–137. Springer-Verlag.
12. Michael Leuschel. The ECCE partial deduction system and the DPPD library of benchmarks. Obtainable via `http://www.ecs.soton.ac.uk/~mal`, 1996-2002.
13. Michael Leuschel. On the power of homeomorphic embedding for online termination. In Giorgio Levi, editor, Static Analysis. *Proceedings of SAS'98*, LNCS 1503, pages 230–245, Pisa, Italy, September 1998. Springer-Verlag.
14. Michael Leuschel and Maurice Bruynooghe. Logic program specialisation through partial deduction: Control issues. *Theory and Practice of Logic Programming*, 2(4 & 5):461–515, July & September 2002.
15. Michael Leuschel, Bern Martens, and Danny De Schreye. Controlling generalisation and polyvariance in partial deduction of normal logic programs. *ACM Transactions on Programming Languages and Systems*, 20(1):208–258, January 1998.
16. J. W. Lloyd and J. C. Shepherdson. Partial evaluation in logic programming. *The Journal of Logic Programming*, 11:217–242, 1991.
17. J.W. Lloyd. *Foundations of Logic Programming*. Springer, second, extended edition, 1987.
18. B. Martens and D. De Schreye. Automatic finite unfolding using well-founded measures. *The Journal of Logic Programming*, 28(2):89–146, August 1996.
19. G. Puebla, E. Albert, and M. Hermenegildo. Efficient Local Unfolding with Ancestor Stacks for Full Prolog. Technical Report CLIP2/2005.0, Technical University of Madrid, February 2005.
20. G. Puebla, F. Bueno, and M. Hermenegildo. An Assertion Language for Constraint Logic Programs. In *Analysis and Visualization Tools for Constraint Programming*, pages 23–61. Springer LNCS 1870, 2000.
21. G. Rozenberg and A. Salomaa, editors. *Handbook of Formal Languages: Word Language Grammar*, volume 1. Springer-Verlag, 1997.
22. M.H. Sørensen and R. Glück. An Algorithm of Generalization in Positive Supercompilation. In *Proc. of ILPS'95*, pages 465–479. The MIT Press, 1995.

Schema-Guided Synthesis of Imperative Programs by Constraint Solving

Michael A. Colón*

Center for High Assurance Computer Systems,
Naval Research Laboratory,
Washington, D.C.
colon@itd.nrl.navy.mil

Abstract. We present a method for schema-guided synthesis of imperative programs computing polynomial functions and their inverses. The schemas of our approach contain parameters representing both fragments of code and fragments of invariants, and they generate programs annotated with loop invariants establishing partial correctness. Schema application entails simultaneously instantiating the code parameters to polynomials and the invariant parameters to systems of polynomial equalities. By bounding the degrees of these polynomials and their number, our method reduces schema instantiation to non-linear constraint solving, based on the theory of polynomial ideals. Although non-linear constraint solving is NP-hard, a solution can be generated automatically when the resulting system contains few constraints. A specialization of our method yields linear constraints by further restricting the form of the invariants. This restriction improves the efficiency of constraint solving, but may fail to synthesize programs derivable by the general method.

1 Introduction

Program synthesis is the process of generating a concrete implementation of a program from an abstract specification of its behavior [8, 2]. Program synthesis is also known as *automatic programming* and is a form of *program transformation*, i.e., the translation of programs written in one formalism to another. The conventional wisdom is that a program transformation entails *synthesis* when it introduces iterative or recursive constructs not manifest in the specification [9]. *Deductive* program synthesis is the synthesis of programs based on sound logical reasoning, while *inductive* synthesis extrapolates program behavior from a set of examples [8]. Deductive program synthesis comes in three forms: transformational, constructive, and schema-guided.

In *transformational synthesis*, a program is derived by applying a sequence of transformations to an initial declarative specification, resulting in a final executable implementation [18]. The principal difficulty with automating transformational synthesis is the enormous search space that results from a large number

---

* Supported by the Office of Naval Research.

S. Etalle(Ed.): LOPSTR 2004, LNCS 3573, pp. 166–181, 2005.
© Springer-Verlag Berlin Heidelberg 2005

in x : **rational**;	in x : **rational**;
out y : **integer**;	out y : **integer**;
local z : **rational**;	local z : **rational**;
$\ell_1 : \langle y, z \rangle := \langle 0, 0 \rangle;$	$\ell_1 : \langle y, z \rangle := \langle 0, \alpha \rangle;$
$\ell_2 : \{z = y^2\}$	$\ell_2 : \{\mathcal{I}\}$
while $2y + z + 1 \leq x$ **do**	**while** $\gamma \leq x$ **do**
$\ell_3 : \langle y, z \rangle := \langle y + 1, 2y + z + 1 \rangle;$	$\ell_3 : \langle y, z \rangle := \langle y + 1, \beta \rangle;$
$\ell_4 : $ **halt**	$\ell_4 : $ **halt**
(a) Program	(b) Template

Fig. 1. Square root by linear search

of transformation rules, which are usually of fine granularity. Thus, transformational synthesis tools often require human guidance. In *constructive synthesis*, the problem is reduced to one of proving an existentially quantified formula in a sufficiently constructive fragment of logic [14]. The program is then extracted from the proof. Constructive synthesis trades the enormous space of potential transformation rule applications for a seemingly larger space of inference rule applications [8], and the principal difficulty with automating constructive synthesis is the need to find proofs of the resulting formulas, which normally require induction. For this reason, tools for automatic constructive synthesis wisely limit themselves to generating loop-free programs [23].

A third approach to automatic programming is *schema-guided synthesis* [10]. A schema is a parameterized program capturing the commonalities among the solutions to a family of related problems. Schema-guided synthesis involves selecting one of a collection of available schemas and instantiating its parameters to produce an implementation conforming to the specification. The principal advantage of schema-guided synthesis is that a well-chosen collection of domain-specific schemas can quickly guide the tool to a solution by pruning away large portions of the space of potential implementations – portions normally explored by constructive and transformational methods. Its principal disadvantage is its incompleteness. The only synthesizable programs are those which are instances of schemas appearing in the collection. This incompleteness notwithstanding, the schema-guided approach is the basis of several synthesis tools [21, 2].

Consider the program shown in Fig. 1(a), which computes the integer square root y of a non-negative rational x, i.e., the largest integer whose square is less than or equal to x. This program initializes y to zero, then repeatedly increments y, provided the square of $y + 1$ does not exceed x. Note that all expressions evaluated at run time are linear. As a result, this program can run on a machine without a hardware multiplier, and it runs faster than the obvious approach of computing y^2 with each iteration on machines for which shifts and additions are faster than multiplications. The correctness of the program depends crucially on the invariant $z = y^2$, which implies the equivalence of $2y + z + 1$ and $(y + 1)^2$.

Fig. 1(b) presents a parameterized program for function inversion by linear search, with the invariant parameter $\mathcal{I}$ and the expression parameters α, β and γ. The program of Fig. 1(a) can be derived from this template by instantiating $\mathcal{I}$ to $z = y^2$, α to 0 and instantiating both β and γ to $2y + z + 1$. However, not all instances of the template compute the integer square root of x. A correct instance must ensure that γ is equivalent to $(y+1)^2$ whenever the loop condition is evaluated. This constraint can be met by instantiating $\mathcal{I}$ to an assertion which entails the equivalence and is invariant at ℓ_2.

A *program schema* is a parameterized program together with constraints on its instances guaranteeing correctness. The problem of finding expressions for the parameters which satisfy the correctness constraints is known as *schema instantiation*. We present a method for schema instantiation for imperative programs computing polynomial functions and their inverses. Our method simultaneously finds polynomials for the expression parameters and a system of polynomial equalities to serve as the loop invariant. By placing a heuristic bound on the degrees of the polynomials, as well as the number of equations appearing in the invariant, our method reduces schema instantiation to non-linear constraint solving over the rationals, based on the theory of *polynomial ideals*. These constraints are then solved using a constraint solver.

Although the constraints produced by our method are decidable, the high complexity of non-linear constraint solving limits its applicability to schemas with relatively few parameters. Hence, we present a specialization of our method which restricts the form of the equalities appearing in generated invariants, in addition to their degrees, thereby reducing instantiation to linear constraint solving. While our specialized method is fast enough for practical application, it may fail to synthesize programs which are derivable by our general method. We have implemented both of these methods in Java and applied them to the synthesis of several imperative programs.

2   Preliminaries

Let $X = \{x_1, \ldots, x_n\}$ be a finite set of *variables*. A *state* σ maps each variable to a rational, and Σ denotes the set of all states. A *state formula* φ is a first-order expression whose free variables belong to X. A state σ *satisfies* φ, denoted by $\sigma \models \varphi$, precisely when φ holds in the model which interprets the variables of X as in σ. A state formula is also known as an *assertion* or a *condition*.

A *(binary) relation* on Σ is a subset of $\Sigma \times \Sigma$. Each pair $\langle \sigma, \sigma' \rangle$ of a relation consists of a *prestate* σ and a *poststate* σ'. A *relation formula* ρ is a first-order expression whose free variables belong to $X \cup X'$, where the variables in X denote the values in the prestate, and those in $X' = \{x'_1, \ldots, x'_n\}$ denote values in the poststate. A pair $\langle \sigma, \sigma' \rangle$ *satisfies* ρ, denoted by $\langle \sigma, \sigma' \rangle \models \rho$, if ρ holds in the model which interprets X as in the prestate σ and X' as in the poststate σ'. If every pair which satisfies ρ_1 also satisfies ρ_2, then ρ_1 *entails* ρ_2, written $\rho_1 \models \rho_2$. The *primed version* φ' of a state formula is $\varphi[X \mapsto X']$, where $\Psi[X \mapsto W]$ denotes the safe replacement in Ψ of the variables in X by the corresponding expressions in W. The *composition* $\rho_1 \circ \rho_2$ of two relations is the set of all pairs $\langle \sigma, \sigma' \rangle$ such that $\langle \sigma, \bar{\sigma} \rangle \in \rho_1$ and $\langle \bar{\sigma}, \sigma' \rangle \in \rho_2$ for some *intermediate state* $\bar{\sigma}$.

Although the programs we consider are written in a structured language containing assignments, conditionals, and iteration, we define the semantics of programs in terms of transition systems. A *program* $P = \langle L, \mathcal{T}, L_i, L_f \rangle$ consists of a finite set of *locations* L; a finite set of *transitions* $\mathcal{T}$, where each $\tau \in \mathcal{T}$ is a tuple $\langle \ell, \ell', \rho \rangle$ consisting of a *prelocation* ℓ, a *postlocation* ℓ', and a relation ρ, called the *transition relation*; a subset $L_i \subseteq L$ of *initial* locations, and a subset $L_f \subseteq L$ of *final* locations. A *configuration* $\langle \ell, \sigma \rangle$ is a location paired with a state, and a *computation* is a potentially infinite sequence $\langle \ell_0, \sigma_0 \rangle \xrightarrow{\tau_1} \langle \ell_1, \sigma_1 \rangle \xrightarrow{\tau_2} \dots \xrightarrow{\tau_n} \langle \ell_n, \sigma_n \rangle \xrightarrow{\tau_{n+1}} \dots$ of configurations and transitions such that for each $i \geq 1$, $\tau_i = \langle \ell_{i-1}, \ell_i, \rho \rangle$ with $\langle \sigma_{i-1}, \sigma_i \rangle \models \rho$. A finite computation $\langle \ell_0, \sigma_0 \rangle \xrightarrow{\tau_1} \dots \xrightarrow{\tau_n} \langle \ell_n, \sigma_n \rangle$ is *proper* if $\ell_0 \in L_i$ and $\ell_n \in L_f$. A *specification* $\langle \varphi, \psi \rangle$ consists of a *precondition* φ and a *postcondition* ψ. A program P *satisfies* the specification $\langle \varphi, \psi \rangle$ iff for every proper computation $\langle \ell_0, \sigma_0 \rangle \xrightarrow{\tau_1} \dots \xrightarrow{\tau_n} \langle \ell_n, \sigma_n \rangle$, if $\sigma_0 \models \varphi$ then $\sigma_n \models \psi$.

Inductive Assertions

A *path* $\pi = \ell_0 \xrightarrow{\tau_1} \ell_1 \dots \ell_{n-1} \xrightarrow{\tau_n} \ell_n \xrightarrow{\tau_{n+1}} \dots$ of a program P is a potentially infinite sequence of interleaved locations and transitions such that, for each $i \geq 1$, ℓ_{i-1} is the prelocation of τ_i, and ℓ_i is its postlocation. The *path relation* ρ_π of a finite path π is the composition of the transition relations along π. A *cycle* is a finite path $\ell_0 \xrightarrow{\tau_1} \dots \xrightarrow{\tau_n} \ell_0$ of P which begins and ends at the same location. A *cut set* C is a subset of L containing at least one location from each cycle. A path is ℓ-*free* if it does not contain ℓ or contains ℓ only as its initial or final location, and C-*free* if ℓ-free for all $\ell \in C$.

An assertion $\mathcal{I}$ is *invariant* at location ℓ given precondition φ, if $\mathcal{I}$ holds whenever ℓ is reached in every computation whose initial state satisfies φ. An *annotation* A of program P is a partial function from locations to assertions. An annotation is *inductive* given precondition φ if its domain is a cut set C such that for all $c_1, c_2 \in C$, we have i) $\varphi \wedge \rho_\pi \models A(c_1)'$ for every C-free path π from an initial location to c_1 and ii) $A(c_1) \wedge \rho_\pi \models A(c_2)'$ for every C-free path π from c_1 to c_2. The first condition is known as *initiation*, while the second is called *preservation*. If, in addition, for some assertion ψ we have i) $\varphi \wedge \rho_\pi \models \psi'$ for every C-free path π from an initial to a final location and ii) $A(c) \wedge \rho_\pi \models \psi'$ for every C-free path π from a location $c \in C$ to a final location, then A *certifies* that P satisfies the specification $\langle \varphi, \psi \rangle$. The *inductive assertions* method of program verification is due to Floyd [11, 13].

Polynomial Constraints

A *monomial* in $x_1, \dots, x_n$ is a product of powers $\boldsymbol{x}^{\boldsymbol{e}} \stackrel{\text{def}}{=} x_1^{d_1} \cdots x_n^{d_n}$. A *polynomial* p is a linear combination $c_1 \boldsymbol{x}^{\boldsymbol{e}_1} + \cdots + c_m \boldsymbol{x}^{\boldsymbol{e}_m}$ of monomials with rational coefficients $c_1, \dots, c_m$. The *polynomial ring* $\mathbb{Q}[X, X']$ is the set of all polynomials in X and X'. The *degree* $\deg(x_1^{d_1} \cdots x_n^{d_n})$ of a monomial is the sum $d_1 + \cdots + d_n$.

The degree $\deg(p)$ of a polynomial p is the maximal degree of its (non-zero) monomials. A polynomial is *linear* if its degree is one; *quadratic* if two.

A nonempty set of polynomials I forms a *polynomial ideal* iff i) $p_1 + p_2 \in I$ for all $p_1, p_2 \in I$ and ii) $qp \in I$ for all $p \in I$ and $q \in \mathbb{Q}[X, X']$. The ideal $\mathcal{I}d(P)$ *generated* by a set of polynomials P is the set of linear combinations $q_1 p_1 + \cdots + q_m p_m$, with $p_1, \ldots, p_m \in P$ and $q_1, \ldots, q_m \in \mathbb{Q}[X, X']$. A set P is a *basis* of an ideal I iff $I = \mathcal{I}d(P)$. The membership problem for polynomial ideals is decidable, but requires exponential space [15].

A *polynomial constraint* is either an *equality* $p = 0$ or an *inequality* $p \geq 0$, and a set of constraints is known as a *system*. The satisfiability of a system of polynomial constraints can be decided by quantifier elimination [24], while systems consisting solely of equalities can be solved using Gröbner bases [3], resultants [4], or interval methods [17]. However, the problem is NP-hard [4]. Linear equalities can be solved in polynomial time by Gaussian elimination, while linear inequalities can be solved efficiently using interior point methods [20].

A system S *entails* the constraint c, denoted by $S \models c$, when every solution of S is a solution of c. In such a case, the members of S are the *antecedents* of the entailment, and c is the *consequent*. Entailment can be approximated by polynomial ideal membership when the constraints are all equalities:

Lemma 1. *A system of polynomial equalities $p_1 = 0, \ldots, p_m = 0$ entails the equality $p = 0$ if $p \in \mathcal{I}d(p_1, \ldots, p_m)$.*

In other words, $p_1 = 0, \ldots, p_m = 0 \models p = 0$ if $p = q_1 p_1 + \cdots + q_m p_m$, for some polynomial coefficients $q_1, \ldots, q_m$. Given a system $S : p_1 = 0, \ldots, p_m = 0$ and a constraint $c : p = 0$, the polynomials $q_1, \ldots, q_m$ establishing $S \models c$ can be found by heuristically bounding the degrees of terms appearing in the linear combination $q_1 p_1 + \cdots + q_m p_m$ and solving the system of linear equalities characterizing the coefficients of $q_1, \ldots, q_m$.

3   Schema-Guided Synthesis

Central to our method is the notion of a program schema. A *program schema* $S = \langle P, T, \langle \varphi, \psi \rangle, A, C \rangle$ consists of a finite set of *parameters* P, a function T from parameters to programs known as the *template*, a pair of functions $\langle \varphi, \psi \rangle$ from parameters to assertions, a function A from parameters to annotations, and a set of schema *constraints* C. An *instance* of a schema is a triple $\langle T(\theta), \langle \varphi(\theta), \psi(\theta) \rangle, A(\theta) \rangle$, where θ is an assignment of expressions to parameters which satisfies the constraints. A schema is *sound* if, for every satisfying assignment θ, $A(\theta)$ is inductive and certifies that $T(\theta)$ satisfies $\langle \varphi(\theta), \psi(\theta) \rangle$.

Figure 2 presents a schema to invert a function $f(w) = \kappa$, where κ is a polynomial in w. Note that the precondition, postcondition and annotation have been incorporated into the template. Given a rational $x \geq f(0)$, the schema computes the largest integer y for which $f(y) \leq x$ by linear search. While the polynomial κ defining f can be of arbitrary degree, as can the polynomials of the invariant $\mathcal{I}$,

Parameters:
- κ: polynomial in w,
- $\mathcal{I}$: system of polynomial equalities in $x, y, z_1, \ldots, z_n$,
- $\alpha_1, \ldots, \alpha_n$: linear polynomials in x, and
- $\beta_1, \ldots, \beta_n, \gamma$: linear polynomials in $x, y, z_1, \ldots, z_n$.

Template:
    in x : **rational**;

    out y : **integer**;

    local $z_1, \ldots, z_n$: **rational**;

        $\{\varphi : x \geq \kappa[w \mapsto 0]\}$

    $\ell_1 : \langle y, z_1, \ldots, z_n \rangle := \langle 0, \alpha_1, \ldots, \alpha_n \rangle;$

    $\ell_2 : \{A : \kappa[w \mapsto y] \leq x \wedge \mathcal{I}\}$

        while $\gamma \leq x$ **do**

            $\ell_3 : \langle y, z_1, \ldots, z_n \rangle := \langle y + 1, \beta_1, \ldots, \beta_n \rangle;$

    $\ell_4 :$ **halt**

        $\{\psi : \kappa[w \mapsto y] \leq x < \kappa[w \mapsto y + 1]\}$

Constraints:
1. $\exists \Delta > 0. \forall y \geq 0. \kappa[w \mapsto y + 1] \geq \kappa[w \mapsto y] + \Delta,$
2. $x' = x, y' = 0, z_1' = \alpha_1, \ldots, z_n' = \alpha_n \models \mathcal{I}',$
3. $\mathcal{I}, x' = x, y' = y + 1, z_1' = \beta_1, \ldots, z_n' = \beta_n \models \mathcal{I}'$, and
4. $\mathcal{I} \models \gamma = \kappa[w \mapsto y + 1].$

Fig. 2. Schema for function inversion by linear search

the schema restricts the polynomials appearing in the code to linear polynomials. Since this restriction on degrees would otherwise limit the functions that can be inverted, the schema provides an arbitrary number of *scratch variables* $z_1, \ldots, z_n$ for use as temporary storage.

In addition to the restriction to linear polynomials in the program body, the schema limits its instances to those satisfying the four given constraints. The first mandates that κ define a function which increases discretely. This requirement ensures that the loop terminates since $f(0), f(1), \ldots$ increases without bound. The second and third constraints guarantee that $\mathcal{I}$ is inductive at ℓ_2. The fourth ensures that the loop condition is equivalent to $f(y + 1) \leq x$.

To instantiate the schema, we must find a polynomial κ, a system of polynomial equalities $\mathcal{I}$, and linear polynomials $\alpha_1, \ldots, \alpha_n, \beta_1, \ldots, \beta_n$, and γ satisfying the given constraints. Along the way, we must also determine the number of scratch variables needed. Normally, the polynomial κ is provided by the specification of the program to be synthesized, and the satisfaction of the first constraint can be established using quantifier elimination. Thus, we focus on the remaining constraints.

Instantiation by Non-linear Constraint Solving

Our method for schema instantiation reduces the problem to non-linear constraint solving and instantiates the schema based on a solution generated by a constraint solver. Notice that the second, third, and fourth constraints of the schema are entailments between systems of polynomial equalities. By Lemma 1, the parameters appearing in these constraints can be instantiated by solving systems of non-linear equalities characterizing the coefficients of the unknown polynomials for which entailment is guaranteed. The non-linearity of these equalities is due to the parameters. However, to apply this reduction, we must first guess the number of linear polynomials $\alpha_1, \ldots, \alpha_n, \beta_1, \ldots, \beta_n$, and both the number and the degrees of the polynomials appearing in the invariant $\mathcal{I}$. Our method combines heuristics with backtracking to determine the appropriate settings.

The method is best explained by example: Suppose our goal is to instantiate the schema of Fig. 2 to invert $f(w) = w^2$, i.e., to compute integer square roots. We will assume that the first constraint has already been established for $\kappa : w^2$. Since we have no basis for determining the number of scratch variables $z_1, \ldots, z_n$ needed for a correct solution, we simply enumerate positive values of n until a solution is found. Thus, suppose $n = 1$. We must find a system of polynomial equalities $\mathcal{I}$ in x, y, and z_1, a linear polynomial α_1 in x, and linear polynomials β_1, γ in x, y, and z_1 satisfying the remaining schema constraints. Our reduction requires us to bound the number and degrees of the polynomials comprising $\mathcal{I}$. As the purpose of $\mathcal{I}$ is to express relationships between the scratch variables $z_1, \ldots, z_n$ and the remaining variables, a reasonable choice for the number of equalities in $\mathcal{I}$ is n. Thus, we suppose $\mathcal{I}$ consists of a single equality. As for the degree of $\mathcal{I}$, we limit the search to a quadratic equality, based on the fact that κ is quadratic. These choices, while well-motivated, are nonetheless heuristic. It may be necessary to backtrack and entertain less restrictive bounds.

Having bounded the number of scratch variables and the number and degree of the equalities in $\mathcal{I}$, we now construct a system of polynomial constraints on the coefficients of the invariant $\mathcal{I}$ and the polynomials α_1, β_1, and γ:

$$\mathcal{I} : \underbrace{d_1 x^2 + d_2 xy + d_3 xz_1 + d_4 y^2 + d_5 yz_1 + d_6 z_1^2 + d_7 x + d_8 y + d_9 z_1 + d_{10}}_{p} = 0,$$

$$\alpha_1 : a_1 x + a_2, \quad \beta_1 : b_1 x + b_2 y + b_3 z_1 + b_4, \quad \text{and} \quad \gamma : c_1 x + c_2 y + c_3 z_1 + c_4$$

These constraints are crafted to ensure that any solution corresponds to a correct instance of the schema, based on Lemma 1. For example, the second constraint of the schema is satisfied provided

$$p' = q_1 p_1 + q_2 p_2 + q_3 p_3, \tag{1}$$

where

$$p_1 : x - x', \quad p_2 : y', \quad \text{and} \quad p_3 : a_1 x + a_2 - z_1'$$

and q_1, q_2, and q_3 are arbitrary. The final step of the reduction requires a bound on the degree of each term in (1). Since the polynomial p' is quadratic, a

in x : **rational**;

out y : **integer**;

local z_1 : **rational**;

$\quad \{x \geq 0\}$

$\ell_1 : \langle y, z_1 \rangle := \langle 0, \boxed{-x - 1} \rangle;$

$\ell_2 : \{y^2 \leq x \wedge \boxed{z_1 = y^2 + y - x - 1}\}$

$\quad$ **while** $\boxed{x + y + z_1 + 2} \leq x$ **do**

$\quad\quad \ell_3 : \langle y, z_1 \rangle := \langle y + 1, \boxed{2y + z_1 + 2} \rangle;$

ℓ_4 : **halt**

$\quad \{y^2 \leq x < (y + 1)^2\}$

Fig. 3. Integer square root by linear search

reasonable bound is two. Since p_1, p_2, and p_3 are each linear, a quadratic bound on the terms implies that q_1, q_2 and q_3 must also be linear:

$$q_1 : r_1 x + r_2 y + r_3 z_1 + r_4 x' + r_5 y' + r_6 z_1' + r_7$$
$$q_2 : s_1 x + s_2 y + s_3 z_1 + s_4 x' + s_5 y' + s_6 z_1' + s_7$$
$$q_3 : t_1 x + t_2 y + t_3 z_1 + t_4 x' + t_5 y' + t_6 z_1' + t_7$$

Expressing (1) as constraints on the coefficients of p', p_1, p_2, p_3 and those of q_1, q_2, q_3 yields the following system of polynomial equalities:

$$r_1 + a_1 t_1 = r_2 + a_1 t_2 = r_3 + a_1 t_3 = r_1 - r_4 - a_1 t_4 = r_5 - s_1 + a_1 t_5 = 0,$$
$$r_6 - t_1 + a_1 t_6 = r_2 = s_2 = t_2 = r_3 = s_3 = t_3 = r_4 + d_1 = r_5 + s_4 + d_2 = 0,$$
$$r_6 + t_4 + d_3 = s_5 + d_4 = s_6 + t_5 + d_5 = t_6 + d_6 = r_7 + a_2 t_1 + a_1 t_7 = a_2 t_2 = 0,$$
$$a_2 t_3 = r_7 - a_2 t_4 + d_7 = s_7 - a_2 t_5 + d_8 = a_2 t_6 - t_7 - d_9 = a_2 t_7 - d_{10} = 0$$

Continuing in this fashion, the third and fourth constraints of the schema are reduced to systems of polynomial equalities.

Combining all of the constraints produced by this reduction yields a system of 64 equations in as many variables. This system is generated by our implementation in 63 ms.[1] Applying the interval solver RealPaver [12] yields the following solution in 1.6 s:

$$\mathcal{I} \; : \; z_1 = y^2 + y - x - 1 \quad\quad \alpha_1 : \; -x - 1,$$
$$\beta_1 : \; 2y + z_1 + 2 \quad\quad\quad\quad \gamma \; : \; x + y + z_1 + 2$$

The program corresponding to this solution, shown in Fig. 3, is somewhat unnatural, but nonetheless correct, and can be proven so using the generated

---

[1] Reported times are for a 2.5GHz Pentium 4 with 1GB RAM running NetBeans 3.5.1.

Parameters:

- κ: polynomial in w,
- $\mathcal{I}$: system of polynomial equalities in $x, y_1, y_2, z_1, \ldots, z_n$,
- $\alpha_1, \ldots, \alpha_n$: linear polynomials in x,
- $\beta_1, \ldots, \beta_n, \gamma$: linear polynomials in $x, y_1, y_2, z_1, \ldots, z_n$, and
- $\delta_1, \ldots, \delta_n, \epsilon_1, \ldots, \epsilon_n, \zeta$: linear polynomials $x, y_1, y_2, z_1, \ldots, z_n$.

Template:

in x : **rational;**

out y_1 : **integer;**

local y_2 : **integer,** $z_1, \ldots, z_n$: **rational;**

$$\{x \geq \kappa[w \mapsto 0]\}$$

ℓ_1 : $\langle y_1, y_2, z_1, \ldots, z_n \rangle := \langle 0, 1, \alpha_1, \ldots, \alpha_n \rangle;$

ℓ_2 : $\{\kappa[w \mapsto 0] \leq x \ \wedge \ y_1 = 0 \ \wedge \ (\exists k \in \mathbb{N}.y_2 = 2^k) \ \wedge \ \mathcal{I}\}$

    while $\gamma \leq x$ **do**

        ℓ_3 : $\langle y_2, z_1, \ldots, z_n \rangle := \langle 2y_2, \beta_1, \ldots, \beta_n \rangle;$

ℓ_4 : $\{\kappa[w \mapsto y_1] \leq x < \kappa[w \mapsto y_1 + y_2] \ \wedge \ (\exists k \in \mathbb{N}.y_2 = 2^k) \ \wedge \ \mathcal{I}\}$

    while $y_2 \neq 1$ **do**

$$\left[\begin{array}{l} \ell_5 : \langle y_2, z_1, \ldots, z_n \rangle := \langle \frac{1}{2}y_2, \delta_1, \ldots, \delta_n \rangle; \\ \ell_6 : \textbf{if } \zeta \leq x \textbf{ then} \\ \qquad \ell_7 : \langle y_1, z_1, \ldots, z_n \rangle := \langle y_1 + y_2, \epsilon_1, \ldots, \epsilon_n \rangle \end{array} \right]$$

ℓ_8 : **halt**

$$\{\kappa[w \mapsto y_1] \leq x < \kappa[w \mapsto y_1 + 1]\}$$

Constraints:

1. $\forall w \geq 0.f(w + 1) > f(w)$,
2. $x' = x, y_1' = 0, y_2' = 1, z_1' = \alpha_1, \ldots, z_n' = \alpha_n \models \mathcal{I}'$,
3. $\mathcal{I}, x' = x, y_1' = y_1, y_2' = 2y_2, z_1' = \beta_1, \ldots, z_n' = \beta_n \models \mathcal{I}'$,
4. $\mathcal{I} \models \gamma = \kappa[w \mapsto y_2]$,
5. $\mathcal{I}, x' = x, y_1' = y_1, y_2' = \frac{1}{2}y_2, z_1' = \delta_1, \ldots, z_n' = \delta_n \models \mathcal{I}'$,
6. $\mathcal{I}, x' = x, y_1' = y_1 + y_2, y_2' = y_2, z_1' = \epsilon_1, \ldots, z_n' = \epsilon_n \models \mathcal{I}'$, and
7. $\mathcal{I} \models \zeta = \kappa[w \mapsto y_1 + y_2]$.

Fig. 4. Schema for function inversion by binary search

invariant. The program is slow, however. The number of iterations of the while loop is linear in x and thus exponential in the size of the representation of x. Since $f(w) = w^2$ is monotone when $w \geq 0$, the integer square root of x can be computed much more efficiently by binary search.

Figure 4 presents a schema for inversion of a monotone function $f(w) = \kappa$. The schema operates in two phases. During the first phase, an upper bound on the inverse image of x under f is found and stored in variable y_2. This bound is guaranteed to be a power of two. During the second phase, the inverse image of x is found by binary search. With each iteration, the interval $[y_1, y_1 + y_2]$ is divided in two, and the program chooses between the lower- and upper-half based on the comparison at ℓ_6, while maintaining the invariant $f(y_1) \leq x < f(y_1 + y_2)$. The loop terminates when $y_2 = 1$, with $f(y_1) \leq x < f(y_1 + 1)$.

Searching first for an instance of the schema with one scratch variable, i.e., $n = 1$, and considering only quadratic invariants and quadratic entailment proofs, our method produces, in 94 ms, a system of 204 equations in 191 variables. In 26.6 s, RealPaver determines that this system is unsatisfiable – at least when the coefficients are restricted to small intervals around zero. While not conclusive, we take this finding as evidence that there is no correct instance of the schema making use of only one scratch variable, and we increase n to two. Our method then produces a system of 379 constraints in 361 variables in 140 ms. Unfortunately, RealPaver can neither find a solution to the resulting system nor determine its unsatisfiability within a reasonable amount of time – measured in days. The inability of existing non-linear constraint solvers to handle the larger systems generated by our method is the principal motivation for specializing our method to produce linear constraints.

Instantiation by linear constraint solving

Our specialized method for schema instantiation is based on the observation that the non-linearity of the generated constraints is largely attributable to the unknown coefficients of the invariant $\mathcal{I}$ and the potential non-linearity of the scratch variables $z_1, \ldots, z_n$ appearing in $\mathcal{I}$. By fixing $\mathcal{I}$ to a system of equalities before applying the reduction, we can ensure that the resulting constraints are linear, provided each scratch variable appears only linearly in the chosen system. Consider again the schema for binary search shown in Fig. 4, and suppose we have chosen a system of polynomial equalities for $\mathcal{I}$ in which scratch variables appear at most linearly. The parameters appearing in the antecedents of the second, third, fifth, and sixth constraints are potential sources of non-linearity. However, these parameters can be moved to the consequents simply by replacing each scratch variable in $\mathcal{I}'$ by its corresponding parameter. As each scratch variable appears at most linearly in $\mathcal{I}$, each parameter will appear at most linearly after substitution. Once all parameters are eliminated from the antecedents, our reduction is guaranteed to produce only linear equalities.

The method we present is an iterative one which repeatedly chooses an invariant $\mathcal{I}$ and then attempts to instantiate the remaining parameters by constraint solving. If no solution can be found, the invariant is weakened and another attempt is made until the schema is instantiated correctly or the process fails. The initial invariant is chosen by computing the set of non-linear monomials in the schema variables with degree no greater than some bound and assigning each monomial to a unique scratch variable. With each chosen invariant, our method first focuses on instantiating the schema parameters which determine inductiveness: For each initiation or preservation constraint and for each scratch variable, we produce a system of linear equalities characterizing the correct instantiations of the schema parameter assigned to that variable. We then solve the resulting system to extract the coefficients of the polynomial. Should the resulting system have no solution, we weaken the invariant by dropping the equality corresponding to the offending scratch variable and repeat the process, searching for polynomials that establish the inductiveness of the new invariant. Since the initial invariant contains only finitely many equalities, this process terminates with an inductive invariant, perhaps the empty system. This invariant is then used to solve for the remaining parameters of the schema, if possible.

Again, an example serves to clarify the approach: Suppose our goal is to synthesize a program for computing integer square roots by instantiating the schema of Fig. 4 with $\kappa : w^2$. As the initial invariant, we take the following system of equalities:

$$\mathcal{I}_0 : z_1 = x^2, \quad z_2 = xy_1, \quad z_3 = xy_2, \quad z_4 = y_1^2, \quad z_5 = y_1y_2, \quad z_6 = y_2^2$$

Notice how our method for selecting the initial invariant dispenses with the need to guess the number of scratch variables. Next, we attempt to instantiate the parameters $\alpha_1, \ldots, \alpha_6$ to linear polynomials in x satisfying the second schema constraint. Replacing $z_1', \ldots, z_6'$ in $\mathcal{I}'$ with $\alpha_1, \ldots, \alpha_6$ yields the equivalent constraint

$$x' = x, y_1' = 0, y_2' = 1 \models \left(\begin{array}{l} \alpha_1 = (x')^2, \alpha_2 = x'y_1', \alpha_3 = x'y_2', \\ \alpha_4 = (y_1')^2, \alpha_5 = y_1'y_2', \alpha_6 = (y_2')^2 \end{array} \right).$$

We then consider each consequent in turn and instantiate its parameter by solving linear equalities. For α_1, the resulting system is unsatisfiable, i.e., there is no linear polynomial in x equal to x^2 for all x, while α_2 can be instantiated to 0. Continuing in this fashion yields the following solutions:

$$\alpha_2 : 0, \quad \alpha_3 : x, \quad \alpha_4 : 0, \quad \alpha_5 : 0, \quad \alpha_6 : 1$$

Since we are unable to instantiate α_1, we weaken the invariant by dropping the first equality:

$$\mathcal{I}_1 : z_2 = xy_1, \quad z_3 = xy_2, \quad z_4 = y_1^2, \quad z_5 = y_1y_2, \quad z_6 = y_2^2$$

Turning to the three preservation constraints of the schema, our method instantiates their parameters to linear polynomials which preserve $\mathcal{I}_1$:

$$\begin{array}{lllll} \beta_2 : z_2, & \beta_3 : 2z_3, & \beta_4 : z_4, & \beta_5 : 2z_5, & \beta_6 : 4z_6 \\ \delta_2 : z_2, & \delta_3 : \frac{1}{2}z_3, & \delta_4 : z_4, & \delta_5 : \frac{1}{2}z_5, & \delta_6 : \frac{1}{4}z_6 \\ \epsilon_2 : z_2 + z_3, & \epsilon_3 : z_3, & \epsilon_4 : z_4 + 2z_5 + z_6, & \epsilon_5 : z_5 + z_6, & \epsilon_6 : z_6 \end{array}$$

As these solutions guarantee the inductiveness of $\mathcal{I}_1$, we take the invariant $\mathcal{I}$ to be $\mathcal{I}_1$. Finally, we use $\mathcal{I}$ to instantiate the remaining parameters:

$$\gamma : z_6 \quad \zeta : z_4 + 2z_5 + z_6$$

An implementation of our specialized method discovers this solution in 187 ms.

The resulting program, shown in Fig. 5, is somewhat inefficient due to the scratch variables z_2 and z_3, which are updated with each iteration of the loop,

in x : **rational**;

out y_1 : **integer**;

local y_2 : **integer**, z_2, z_3, z_4, z_5, z_6 : **rational**;

$\{x \geq 0\}$

$\ell_1 : \langle y_1, y_2, z_2, z_3, z_4, z_5, z_6 \rangle := \langle 0, 1, \boxed{0, x, 0, 0, 1} \rangle$;

$\ell_2 :$
$$\left\{ \begin{array}{c} 0 \leq x \;\wedge\; y_1 = 0 \;\wedge\; (\exists k \in \mathbb{N}. y_2 = 2^k) \;\wedge \\ \boxed{z_2 = xy_1 \;\wedge\; z_3 = xy_2 \;\wedge\; z_4 = y_1^2 \;\wedge\; z_5 = y_1 y_2 \;\wedge\; z_6 = y_2^2} \end{array} \right\}$$

while $\boxed{z_6} \leq x$ **do**

$\ell_3 : \langle y_2, z_2, z_3, z_4, z_5, z_6 \rangle := \langle 2y_2, \boxed{z_2, 2z_3, z_4, 2z_5, 4z_6} \rangle$;

$\ell_4 :$
$$\left\{ \begin{array}{c} y_1^2 \leq x < (y_1 + y_2)^2 \;\wedge\; (\exists k \in \mathbb{N}. y_2 = 2^k) \;\wedge \\ \boxed{z_2 = xy_1 \;\wedge\; z_3 = xy_2 \;\wedge\; z_4 = y_1^2 \;\wedge\; z_5 = y_1 y_2 \;\wedge\; z_6 = y_2^2} \end{array} \right\}$$

while $y_2 \neq 1$ **do**

$\qquad \left[\begin{array}{l} \ell_5 : \langle y_2, z_2, z_3, z_4, z_5, z_6 \rangle := \langle \frac{1}{2}y_2, \boxed{z_2, \frac{1}{2}z_3, z_4, \frac{1}{2}z_5, \frac{1}{4}z_6} \rangle; \\[2mm] \ell_6 : \textbf{if } \boxed{z_4 + 2z_5 + z_6} \leq x \textbf{ then} \\[2mm] \qquad \ell_7 : \langle y_1, z_2, z_3, z_4, z_5, z_6 \rangle := \\[2mm] \qquad\qquad \langle y_1 + y_2, \boxed{z_2 + z_3, z_3, z_4 + 2z_5 + z_6, z_5 + z_6, z_6} \rangle \end{array} \right]$

$\ell_8 :$ **halt**

$\{y_1^2 \leq x < (y_1 + 1)^2\}$

Fig. 5. Integer square root by binary search

but are never used in computing the integer square root. These variables can be identified using live variable analysis and eliminated by a post processing phase, which we have not yet implemented in our prototype. Applying the transformation manually results in a program reminiscent of Dijkstra's well-known algorithm for integer square roots [7]. This similarity is not surprising given the fact that the process Dijkstra uses to derive his algorithm – introducing three variables to hold the values of three non-linear polynomials and maintaining these values using only linear assignments in the loop body – is analogous to the strategy incorporated into our specialized method for schema instantiation.

4   Applications

We have applied our methods to synthesize a handful of programs computing polynomial functions and their inverses, two of which we present. For the sake of readability, we have manually eliminated the superfluous scratch variables from the generated programs.

in x : **integer**;

out y_3 : **rational**;

local y_1, y_2 : **integer**, z_8 : **rational**;

$\quad \{x \geq 0\}$

$\ell_1 : \langle y_1, y_2, y_3, z_8 \rangle := \langle 1, 0, \boxed{0, 0} \rangle;$

$\ell_2 : \{x \geq 0 \wedge (\exists k \in \mathbb{N}.y_1 = 2^k) \wedge y_2 = 0 \wedge y_3 = y_2^3 \wedge \boxed{z_8 = y_2^2} \}$

$\quad$ **while** $y_1 \leq x$ **do**

$\qquad \ell_3 : \langle y_1, z_8 \rangle := \langle 2y_1, \boxed{z_8} \rangle;$

$\ell_4 : \{x \geq 0 \wedge (\exists k \in \mathbb{N}.y_1 = 2^k) \wedge y_2 = \lfloor x/y_1 \rfloor \wedge y_3 = y_2^3 \wedge \boxed{z_8 = y_2^2} \}$

$\quad$ **while** $y_1 \neq 1$ **do**

$$\left[\begin{array}{l} \ell_5 : y_1 := \tfrac{1}{2}y_1; \\ \ell_6 : \textbf{if } \text{even}(\lfloor x/y_1 \rfloor) \textbf{ then} \\ \qquad \ell_7 : \langle y_2, y_3, z_8 \rangle := \langle 2y_2, \boxed{8y_3, 4z_8} \rangle \\ \quad \textbf{else} \\ \qquad \ell_8 : \langle y_2, y_3, z_8 \rangle := \langle 2y_2 + 1, \boxed{6y_2 + 8y_3 + 12z_8 + 1, 4y_2 + 4z_8 + 1} \rangle \end{array} \right]$$

$\ell_9 : $ **halt**

$\quad \{y_3 = x^3\}$

Fig. 6. Cube by binary decomposition

Cube by Binary Decomposition

Our first example, shown in Fig. 6, is a program which computes the cube of an integer x by binary decomposition. It uses the binary representation of x to compute x^3 in time polynomial in the size of the representation of x, using only addition and multiplication by constants. Like the program of Fig. 5, this program works in two phases: During the first phase, an upper bound on x is computed in y_1. This bound is guaranteed to be the smallest power of two which exceeds x. During the second phase, y_1 is used as a mask to extract the bits of x from most- to least-significant and copy them into y_2, while maintaining the invariant $y_3 = y_2^3$.

This program was synthesized in 281 ms by instantiating a schema for function computation by binary decomposition, which we omit for lack of space. However, it should be noted that one of the virtues of our approach to schema-guided synthesis is that the correctness of the generated program can be judged without reference to the schema from which it was derived. We need not certify the entire process, but only the result.

Quotient by Binary Search

Our last example illustrates the applicability of our method to functions defined by multivariate polynomials. The program presented in Fig. 7 computes the

in x_1, x_2 : **rational**;

out y_1 : **integer**;

local y_2 : **integer**, z_6, z_7 : **rational**;

$\quad\{x_1 \geq 0 \,\wedge\, x_2 > 0\}$

$\ell_1 : \langle y_1, y_2, z_6, z_7 \rangle := \langle 0, 1, \boxed{0, x_2} \rangle;$

$\ell_2 : \{0 \leq x_1 \,\wedge\, y_1 = 0 \,\wedge\, (\exists k \in \mathbb{N}.y_2 = 2^k) \,\wedge\, \boxed{z_6 = x_2 y_1 \,\wedge\, z_7 = x_2 y_2}\}$

$\quad$ **while** $\boxed{z_7} \leq x_1$ **do**

$\qquad \ell_3 : \langle y_2, z_6, z_7 \rangle := \langle 2y_2, \boxed{z_6, 2z_7} \rangle;$

$\ell_4 : \{x_2 y_1 \leq x_1 < x_2(y_1 + y_2) \,\wedge\, (\exists k \in \mathbb{N}.y_2 = 2^k) \,\wedge\, \boxed{z_6 = x_2 y_1 \,\wedge\, z_7 = x_2 y_2}\}$

$\quad$ **while** $y_2 \neq 1$ **do**

$\qquad \left[\begin{array}{l} \ell_5 : \langle y_2, z_6, z_7 \rangle := \langle \tfrac{1}{2}y_2, \boxed{z_6, \tfrac{1}{2}z_7} \rangle; \\[2mm] \ell_6 : \textbf{if } \boxed{z_6 + z_7} \leq x_1 \textbf{ then} \\[2mm] \qquad \ell_7 : \langle y_1, z_6, z_7 \rangle := \langle y_1 + y_2, \boxed{z_6 + z_7, z_7} \rangle \end{array}\right]$

$\ell_8 :$ **halt**

$\quad\{x_2 y_1 \leq x_1 < x_2(y_1 + 1)\}$

Fig. 7. Quotient by binary search

quotient of integers x_1 and x_2 by searching for the inverse image of x_1 under $f(w) = x_2 w$, and our implementation synthesizes this program in 266 ms by instantiating the schema of Fig. 4. It should be noted that the first constraint of the schema requires f to be a monotone, but f is monotone only for positive values of x_2. To discharge this constraint, the inequality $x_2 > 0$ has been added to the precondition.

5   Conclusion

We have presented an approach to schema-guided synthesis of imperative programs computing polynomial functions and their inverses. Following Flener et al. [10], the schemas of our approach contain not only parameterized programs, but also parameterized specifications and instantiation constraints. The constraints serve to limit schema application to produce only correct programs, while the specifications characterize the behavior of the resulting code. In addition, our schemas contain parameterized inductive assertions, and schema instantiation produces programs annotated with loop invariants establishing partial correctness, i.e., *proof-carrying code* [16]. As a result, the programs we generate can be proved correct without appealing to the correctness of the process by which they are derived. In this respect, our approach is similar to that of Stark and Ireland, who generate annotated imperative programs in a constructive setting [22].

The constraints of our schemas not only prevent incorrect schema application, but also guide the search for correct instances. Our method for schema instantiation, which we have implemented in a Java prototype, translates the schema constraints to systems of non-linear equalities, based on an approximation of entailment provided by polynomial ideals. It then uses a constraint solver to explore the space of solutions. This deductively-motivated constraint-based approach has been applied previously to synthesize linear ranking functions [6], invariant linear inequalities [5], and invariant non-linear equalities [19] of imperative programs.

Another perspective on our schemas is that they represent derived rules of inference in a Hoare logic [1]. This view blurs the distinction between constructive and schema-guided synthesis, but serves to clarify the role played by schemas. A purely constructive derivation of integer square root by binary search requires reasoning with inequalities, exponentiation, divisibility, etc. A schema-guided derivation only requires reasoning with polynomial equalities. Automated schema-guided synthesis appears more plausible than constructive synthesis because the deductive machinery needed to instantiate a schema need not be as powerful as the machinery needed to derive the resulting program from first principles.

Acknowledgments

Many thanks are due to Myla Archer, Constance Heitmeyer, Ralph Jeffords, and Elizabeth Leonard for their helpful suggestions.

References

1. P. Anderson and D. Basin. Program development schemata as derived rules. *Journal of Symbolic Computation*, 30(1):5–36, 2000.
2. D. Basin, Y. Deville, P Flener, A. Hamfelt, and J. F. Nilsson. Synthesis of programs in computational logic. In M. Bruynooghe and K.-K. Lau, editors, *Program Development in Computational Logic*, pages 30–65. Springer-Verlag, 2004.
3. T. Becker and V. Weispfenning. *Gröbner Bases: A Computational Approach to Commutative Algebra*. Springer-Verlag, New York, 1993.
4. J. F. Canny, E. Kaltofen, and L. Yagati. Solving systems of non-linear polynomial equations faster. In G. H. Gonnet, editor, *International Symposium on Symbolic and Algebraic Computation*, pages 121–128. ACM Press, 1989.
5. M. Colón, S. Sankaranarayanan, and H. Sipma. Linear invariant generation using non-linear constraint solving. In F. Somenzi and W. Hunt Jr, editors, *15th International Conference on Computer Aided Verification*, pages 420–432. Springer-Verlag, 2003.
6. M. A. Colón and H. B. Sipma. Synthesis of linear ranking functions. In T. Margaria and W. Yi, editors, *7th International Conference on Tools and Algorithms for the Construction and Analysis of Systems*, pages 67–81. Springer-Verlag, 2001.
7. E. W. Dijkstra. *A Discipline of Programming*. Prentice-Hall, Inc., Englewood Cliffs, New Jersey, 1976.

8. P. Flener. Achievements and prospects of program synthesis. In A. C. Kakas and F. Sadri, editors, *Computational Logic: Logic Programming and Beyond, Essays in Honour of Robert A. Kowalski*, pages 310–346. Springer-Verlag, 2002.

9. P. Flener and Y. Deville. Towards stepwise, schema-guided synthesis of logic programs. In T. P. Clement and K.-K. Lau, editors, *International Workshop on Logic Program Synthesis and Transformation*, pages 46–64. Springer-Verlag, 1992.

10. P. Flener, K.-K. Lau, M. Ornaghi, and J. Richardson. An abstract formalization of correct schemas for program synthesis. *Journal of Symbolic Computation*, 30(1):93–127, 2000.

11. R. W. Floyd. Assigning meanings to programs. In *Proceedings of the Symposium on Applied Mathematics*, volume 19 (Mathematical Aspects of Computer Science), pages 19–32. 1967.

12. L. Granvilliers. *RealPaver User's Manual*. Institut de Recherche en Informatique de Nantes, 0.3 edition, July 2003.

13. Z. Manna. *Mathematical Theory of Computation*. McGraw-Hill, New York, 1974.

14. Z. Manna and R. J. Waldinger. Fundamentals of deductive program synthesis. *IEEE Transactions on Software Engineering*, 18(8):674–704, 1992.

15. E. Mayr and A. Meyer. The complexity of the word problems for commutative semigroups and polynomial ideals. *Advances in Mathematics*, 46(3):305–329, 1982.

16. G. C. Necula. Proof-carrying code. In *24th ACM Symposium on Principles of Programming Languages*, pages 106–119. ACM, 1997.

17. A. Neumaier. *Interval Methods for Systems of Equations*. Cambridge University Press, Cambridge, 1990.

18. C. Rich and R. C. Waters. Approaches to automatic programming. *Advances in Computers*, 37:1–57, 1993.

19. S. Sankaranarayanan, H. B. Sipma, and Z. Manna. Non-linear loop invariant generation using Gröbner bases. In N. D. Jones and X. Leroy, editors, *31st ACM Symposium on Principles of Programming Languages*, pages 318–329. ACM, 2004.

20. A. Schrijver. *Theory of Linear and Integer Programming*. John Wiley & Sons, Chichester, 1986.

21. D. R. Smith. KIDS: A semiautomatic program development system. *IEEE Transactions on Software Engineering*, 16(9):1024–1043, 1990.

22. J. Stark and A. Ireland. Towards automatic imperative program synthesis through proof planning. In *14th IEEE International Conference on Automated Software Engineering*, pages 44–51. IEEE Computer Society, 1999.

23. M. E. Stickel, R. J. Waldinger, M. R. Lowry, T. Pressburger, and I. Underwood. Deductive composition of astronomical software from subroutine libraries. In A. Bundy, editor, *12th International Conference on Automated Deduction*, pages 341–355. Springer-Verlag, 1994.

24. A. Tarski. *A Decision Method for Elementary Algebra and Geometry*. University of California Press, 1951.

Run-Time Profiling of Functional Logic Programs[*]

B. Brassel[1], M. Hanus[1], F. Huch[1], J. Silva[2], and G. Vidal[2]

[1] Institut für Informatik, CAU Kiel,
Olshausenstr. 40, D-24098 Kiel, Germany
{bbr, mh, fhu}@informatik.uni-kiel.de
[2] DSIC, Tech. University of Valencia,
Camino de Vera s/n, E-46022 Valencia, Spain
{jsilva, gvidal}@dsic.upv.es

Abstract. In this work, we introduce a profiling scheme for modern functional logic languages covering notions like laziness, sharing, and non-determinism. Firstly, we instrument a natural (big-step) semantics in order to associate a symbolic cost to each basic operation (e.g., variable updates, function unfoldings, case evaluations). While this *cost semantics* provides a formal basis to analyze the cost of a computation, the implementation of a cost-augmented interpreter based on it would introduce a huge overhead. Therefore, we also introduce a sound transformation that instruments a program such that its execution—under the standard semantics—yields not only the corresponding results but also the associated costs. Finally, we describe a prototype implementation of a profiler based on the developments in this paper.

1 Introduction

The importance of profiling in improving the performance of programs is widely recognized. Profiling tools are essential for the programmer to analyze the effects of different source-to-source program manipulations (e.g., partial evaluation, specialization, optimization, etc). Despite this, one can find very few profiling tools for modern declarative languages. This situation is mainly explained by the difficulty to correctly map execution costs to source code, which is much less obvious than for imperative languages. In this work, we tackle the definition of a profiling scheme for modern functional logic languages covering notions like laziness, sharing, and non-determinism (like Curry [6] and Toy [13]); currently, there is no profiling tool practically applicable to such languages.

When profiling the run time of a given program, the results highly depend on the considered language implementation. However, computing actual

[*] This work was partially supported by the Spanish *Ministerio de Educación y Ciencia* under grant TIN2004-00231, by Generalitat Valenciana GRUPOS03/025, by the ICT for EU-India Cross-Cultural Dissemination Project ALA/95/23/2003/077-054, and by the German Research Council (DFG) under grant Ha 2457/5-1.

S. Etalle(Ed.): LOPSTR 2004, LNCS 3573, pp. 182–197, 2005.

run times is not always the most useful information for the programmer. Run times may help to detect that some function is expensive but they do not explain *why* it is expensive (e.g., is it called many times? Is it heavily non-deterministic?).

In order to overcome these drawbacks, we introduce a *symbolic* profiler which outputs the number of basic operations performed in a computation. For this purpose, we start from a natural semantics for functional logic programs [1] and instrument it with the computation of symbolic costs associated to the basic operations of the semantics: variable lookups, function unfoldings, case evaluations, etc. These operations are performed, in one form or another, by likely implementations of modern functional logic languages. Our *cost semantics* constitutes a formal model of the attribution of costs in our setting. Therefore, it is useful not only as a basis to develop profiling tools but also to analyze the costs of a program computation (e.g., to formally prove the effectiveness of some program transformation).

Trivially, one can develop a profiler by implementing an instrumented interpreter which follows the previous cost semantics. However, this approach is not useful in practice as it demands a huge overhead, making the profiling of realistic programs impossible. Thus, in a second step, we design a source-to-source transformation that instruments a program such that its execution—under the standard semantics—outputs not only the corresponding results but also the associated costs. We formally state the correctness of our transformation (i.e., the costs computed in a source program w.r.t. the cost semantics are equivalent to the costs computed in the transformed program w.r.t. the standard semantics). Finally, we describe a prototype implementation of a profiler for Curry programs based on the developments in this paper.

The main contributions of this work are the following. Firstly, we introduce a cost semantics for functional logic programs which covers laziness, sharing and non-determinism. This contrasts with [14], where logical features are not considered, and [2], where sharing is not covered (which drastically reduces its applicability). Secondly, we introduce a program transformation for instrumenting a program—so that its execution returns also the cost of the computation—and prove its correctness. We are not aware of any other transformation for lazy functional (logic) programs that is proved correct w.r.t. an associated cost semantics.

The paper is organized as follows. In the next section, we recall some foundations for understanding the subsequent developments. Section 3 informally introduces our model for profiling functional logic computations. Section 4 formalizes an instrumented semantics which also computes cost information. Section 5 introduces a transformation instrumenting programs to compute symbolic costs. Section 6 describes an implementation of a profiler for Curry programs and Section 7 illustrates its use by means of an example. Finally, Section 8 includes a comparison to related work and concludes. An extended version of this paper (including the proof of Theorem 1) can be found in [5].

2 Flat Programs

In this work we consider *flat* programs [9], a convenient standard representation of functional logic programs which makes explicit the pattern matching strategy by case expressions. This flat representation constitutes the kernel of modern functional logic languages like Curry [8, 6] or Toy [13]. We assume that flat programs are *normalized*, i.e., *let* constructs are used to ensure that the arguments of function and constructor calls are always variables (not necessarily pairwise different). As in [12], this is essential to express sharing without the use of complex graph structures. A normalization algorithm can be found in [1]. Basically, normalization introduces one new let construct for each non-variable argument, e.g., $f(e)$ is transformed into "*let* $x = e$ *in* $f(x)$".

The syntax for normalized flat programs is shown in Figure 1, where we write $\overline{o_n}$ for the *sequence of objects* $o_1, \ldots, o_n$. A program consists of a sequence of function definitions such that the left-hand side has pairwise different variable arguments. The right-hand side is an expression composed by variables, data constructors, function calls, let bindings (where the local variable x is only visible in e_1, e_2), disjunctions (e.g., to represent non-deterministic operations), and case expressions of the following form (we write $(f)case$ for either *fcase* or *case*):

$$(f)case \ x \ of \ \{c_1(\overline{x_{n_1}}) \rightarrow e_1; \ldots; c_k(\overline{x_{n_k}}) \rightarrow e_k\}$$

where x is a variable, $c_1, \ldots, c_k$ are different constructors, and $e_1, \ldots, e_k$ are expressions. The *pattern variables* $\overline{x_{n_i}}$ are locally introduced and bind the corresponding variables of the subexpression e_i. The difference between *case* and *fcase* only shows up when the argument x evaluates (at run time) to a free variable: *case* suspends whereas *fcase* non-deterministically binds this variable to the pattern in a branch of the case expression.

Laziness of computations will show up in the description of the behavior of function calls and case expressions. In a function call, parameters are not evaluated but directly passed to the body of the function. In a case expression, only the outermost symbol of the case argument is required. Therefore, the case argument should be evaluated to *head normal form* [4] (i.e., a variable or

$P ::= D_1 \ldots D_m$	(program)	*Domains*	
$D ::= f(x_1, \ldots, x_n) = e$	(function definition)		
$e ::= x$	(variable)	$P_1, P_2, \ldots \in Prog$	(Programs)
$\quad \mid \ c(x_1, \ldots, x_n)$	(constructor call)	$x, y, z, \ldots \in Var$	(Variables)
$\quad \mid \ f(x_1, \ldots, x_n)$	(function call)	$a, b, c, \ldots \in \mathcal{C}$	(Constructors)
$\quad \mid \ let \ x = e_1 \ in \ e_2$	(let binding)	$f, g, h, \ldots \in \mathcal{F}$	(Functions)
$\quad \mid \ e_1 \ or \ e_2$	(disjunction)	$p_1, p_2, \ldots \in Pat$	(Patterns)
$\quad \mid \ case \ x \ of \ \{\overline{p_k \rightarrow e_k}\}$	(rigid case)		
$\quad \mid \ fcase \ x \ of \ \{\overline{p_k \rightarrow e_k}\}$	(flexible case)		
$p ::= c(x_1, \ldots, x_n)$	(pattern)		

Fig. 1. Syntax for normalized flat programs

an expression with a constructor at the outermost position). Consequently, our operational semantics will describe the evaluation of expressions only to head normal form. This is not a restriction since the evaluation to normal form or the solving of equations can be reduced to head normal form computations (see, e.g., [9]).

Extra variables are those variables in a rule which do not occur in the left-hand side. Such extra variables are intended to be instantiated by flexible case expressions. In the following, we assume that all extra variables x are explicitly introduced in flat programs by a direct circular let binding of the form "*let $x = x$ in e*". We call such variables which are bound to themselves *logical variables*.

In the remainder of this paper, we assume that computations always start from the distinguished function main which has no arguments.

3   A Run-Time Profiling Scheme

Traditionally, profiling tools attribute execution costs to the functions or procedures of the considered program. Following [2, 14], in this work we take a more flexible approach which allows us to associate a *cost center* with any expression of interest. This allows the programmer to choose an appropriate granularity for profiling, ranging from whole program phases to single subexpressions in a function. Nevertheless, our approach can easily be adapted to work with automatically instrumented cost centers; for instance, if one wants to use the traditional approach in which all functions are profiled, each function can be automatically annotated by introducing a cost center for the entire right-hand side. Cost centers are marked with the (built-in) function scc (for set cost center).

Intuitively speaking, given an expression "scc(cc, e)", the costs attributed to cost center cc are the entire costs of evaluating e as far as the enclosing context demands it, including the cost of

– evaluating any function called by the evaluation of the expression e,

but excluding the cost of

– evaluating the *free* variables of e (i.e., those variables which are not introduced by a let binding in e) and
– evaluating any scc-expressions within e or within any function which is called from e.

The following program contains two versions of a function to compute the length of a list (for readability, we show the non-normalized version of function main):

Table 1. Basic costs

Cost criteria	Symbol	Cost criteria	Symbol	Cost criteria	Symbol
Function unfolding	F	Allocating a heap object	H	Case evaluation	C
Variable update	U	Non-deterministic choice	N	Variable lookup	V
Entering an scc	E	Binding a logical variable	B		

```
len(x) = fcase x of { []        → 0
                    ; (y:ys) → let z = 1, w = len(ys) in z + w }
len2s(x) = fcase x of { []       → 0
                     ; (y:ys) → fcase ys of
                                  { []       → 1
                                  ; (z:zs) → let w = 2,
                                                 v = len2s(zs)
                                             in w + v        } }
main = let list = scc("list",[1..5000])
         in scc("len",len(list)) + scc("len2s",len2s(list))
```

Here, main computes twice the length of the list [1..5000], which is a standard predefined way to define the list [1,2,3,...,4999,5000]. Each computation of the length uses a different function, len and len2s, respectively. In principle, len2s could seem more efficient than len because it performs half the number of function calls (indeed, len2s has been obtained by unfolding function len). This is difficult to check with traditional profilers because the overhead introduced to build the list hides the differences between len and len2s. For instance, the computed run times in the PAKCS environment [10] for Curry are 9980 ms and 9990 ms for len([1..5000]) and len2s([1..5000]), respectively.[1]

From these figures, should one conclude that len and len2s are equally efficient? In order to answer this question, a profiler based on *cost centers* can be very useful. In particular, by including the three cost centers shown in the program above (function main), the costs of len, len2s, and the construction of the input list can be clearly distinguished. With our execution profiler which distributes the execution time to different cost centers (its implementation is discussed in Section 6.1), we have measured the following run times:

cost center	main	list	len	len2s
run times	17710	7668966	1110	790

Here, run times are expressed in a number of "ticks" (an artificial time unit provided by the SICStus Prolog profiling facilities [7]). Thanks to the use of cost centers, we can easily check that len2s is slightly more efficient than len. However, what is the reason for these different run times? We introduce *symbolic* costs—associated with the basic operations of the language semantics—so that a deeper analysis can be made. The considered kinds of costs are shown in Table 1. For the example above, our symbolic profiler returns the following cost attributions (only the most relevant costs for this example are shown):

---

[1] The slow execution is due to the fact that experiments were performed with a version of the above program where a symbolic (Peano) representation of natural numbers is used.

	main	list	len	len2s
H	5000	61700	5100	5100
V	5100	280400	5100	5100
C	5100	280400	5100	5100
F	5300	168100	5100	2600

From this information, we observe that only function unfoldings (F) are halved, while the remaining costs are equal for both len and len2s. Therefore, we can conclude that, in this example, unfolding function len with no input data only improves cost F (which has a small impact on current compilers, as has been shown before).

4   Cost Semantics

In this section, we instrument a natural (big-step) semantics for functional logic languages (defined in [1]) with the computation of symbolic costs. Figure 2 shows

---

(VarCons) $cc, \Gamma[x \overset{cc_c}{\longmapsto} c(\overline{x_n})] : x \Downarrow_{\{cc \leftarrow V\}} \Gamma[x \overset{cc_c}{\longmapsto} c(\overline{x_n})] : c(\overline{x_n}), cc_c$

(VarExp) $\dfrac{cc_e, \Gamma : e \Downarrow_\theta \Delta : v, cc_v}{cc, \Gamma[x \overset{cc_e}{\longmapsto} e] : x \Downarrow_{\{cc \leftarrow V\}+\theta+\{cc_v \leftarrow U\}} \Delta[x \overset{cc_v}{\longmapsto} v] : v, cc_v}$ (where e is not a value)

(Val) $cc, \Gamma : v \Downarrow_{\{\}} \Gamma : v, cc$ (where v is a value)

(Fun) $\dfrac{cc, \Gamma : \rho(e) \Downarrow_\theta \Delta : v, cc_v}{cc, \Gamma : f(\overline{x_n}) \Downarrow_{\{cc \leftarrow F\}+\theta} \Delta : v, cc_v}$ (where $f(\overline{y_n}) = e \in P$ and $\rho = \{\overline{y_n \mapsto x_n}\}$)

(Let) $\dfrac{cc, \Gamma[y \overset{cc}{\longmapsto} \rho(e')] : \rho(e) \Downarrow_\theta \Delta : v, cc_v}{cc, \Gamma : \text{let } x = e' \text{ in } e \Downarrow_{\{cc \leftarrow H\}+\theta} \Delta : v, cc_v}$ (where $\rho = \{x \mapsto y\}$ and y is fresh)

(Or) $\dfrac{cc, \Gamma : e_i \Downarrow_\theta \Delta : v, cc_v}{cc, \Gamma : e_1 \text{ or } e_2 \Downarrow_{\{cc \leftarrow N\}+\theta} \Delta : v, cc_v}$ (where $i \in \{1,2\}$)

(Select) $\dfrac{cc, \Gamma : x \Downarrow_{\theta_1} \Delta : c(\overline{y_n}), cc_c \quad cc, \Delta : \rho(e_i) \Downarrow_{\theta_2} \Theta : v, cc_v}{cc, \Gamma : (f)\text{case } x \text{ of } \{\overline{p_k \to e_k}\} \Downarrow_{\theta_1 + \{cc \leftarrow C\} + \theta_2} \Theta : v, cc_v}$.

(where $p_i = c(\overline{x_n})$ and $\rho = \{\overline{x_n \mapsto y_n}\}$)

(Guess) $\dfrac{cc, \Gamma : x \Downarrow_{\theta_1} \Delta : y, cc_y \quad cc, \Delta[y \overset{cc}{\mapsto} \rho(p_i), \overline{y_n} \overset{cc}{\mapsto} \overline{y_n}] : \rho(e_i) \Downarrow_{\theta_2} \Theta : v, cc_v}{cc, \Gamma : \text{fcase } x \text{ of } \{\overline{p_k \to e_k}\} \Downarrow_{\theta_1 + \{cc \leftarrow V, cc \leftarrow U, cc \leftarrow B, cc \leftarrow n*H\} + \theta_N + \theta_2} \Theta : v, cc_v}$

(where $p_i = c(\overline{x_n})$, $\rho = \{\overline{x_n \mapsto y_n}\}$, $\overline{y_n}$ are fresh variables, and $\theta_N = \{cc \leftarrow N\}$ if $k > 1$ and $\theta_N = \{\}$ if $k = 1$)

(SCC) $\dfrac{cc', \Gamma : e \Downarrow_\theta \Delta : v, cc_v}{cc, \Gamma : scc(cc', e) \Downarrow_{\theta + \{cc' \leftarrow E\}} \Delta : v, cc_v}$

Fig. 2. Rules of the cost semantics

the cost-augmented semantics. A *heap*, denoted by Γ, Δ, or Θ, is a partial mapping from variables to expressions (the *empty heap* is denoted by $[\,]$). The value associated to variable x in heap Γ is denoted by $\Gamma[x]$. $\Gamma[x \overset{cc}{\mapsto} e]$ denotes a heap with $\Gamma[x] = e$ and associated cost center cc; we use this notation either as a condition on a heap Γ or as a modification of Γ. A logical variable x is represented by a circular binding of the form $\Gamma[x] = x$. A *value* v is a constructor-rooted term $c(\overline{e_n})$ (i.e., a term whose outermost function symbol is a constructor symbol) or a logical variable (w.r.t. the associated heap). We use judgements of the form "$cc, \Gamma : e \Downarrow_\theta \Delta : v, cc_v$" which are interpreted as "in the context of heap Γ and cost center cc, the expression e evaluates to value v with associated cost θ, producing a new heap Δ and cost center cc_v".

In order to evaluate a variable which is bound to a constructor-rooted term in the heap, rule VarCons reduces the variable to this term. Here, cost V is attributed to the current cost center cc to account for the variable lookup (this attribution is denoted by $\{cc \leftarrow V\}$ and similarly for the other cost symbols).

Rule VarExp achieves the effect of *sharing*. If the variable to be evaluated is bound to some expression in the heap, then the expression is evaluated and the heap is updated with the computed value; finally, we return this value as the result. In addition to counting the cost θ of evaluating expression e, both V and U are attributed to cost centers cc and cc_v, respectively.

For the evaluation of a value, rule Val returns it without modifying the heap. No costs are attributed in this rule since actual implementations have no counterpart for this action.

Rule Fun corresponds to the unfolding of a function call. The result is obtained by reducing the right-hand side of the corresponding rule (we assume that the considered program P is a global parameter of the calculus). Cost F is attributed to the current cost center cc to account for the function unfolding.

Rule Let adds its associated binding to the heap and proceeds with the evaluation of its main argument. Note that we give the introduced variable a fresh name in order to avoid variable name clashes. In this case, cost H is added to the current cost center cc.

Rule Or non-deterministically reduces an *or* expression to either the first or the second argument. N is attributed to the current cost center to account for a non-deterministic step.

Rule Select corresponds to the evaluation of a case expression whose argument reduces to a constructor-rooted term. In this case, we select the appropriate branch and, then, proceed with the evaluation of the expression in this branch by applying the corresponding matching substitution. In addition to the costs of evaluating the case argument, θ_1, and the selected branch, θ_2, we add cost C to the current cost center cc to account for the pattern matching.

Rule Guess applies when the argument of a flexible case expression reduces to a logical variable. It binds this variable to one of the patterns and proceeds by evaluating the corresponding branch. If there is more than one branch, one of them is chosen non-deterministically. Renaming the pattern variables is necessary to avoid variable name clashes. We also update the heap with the (renamed) logical variables of the pattern. In addition to counting the costs of evaluating the case argument, θ_1, and the selected branch, θ_2, we attribute to the current cost center cc costs V (for determining that y is a logical variable), U (for updating the heap from $y \mapsto y$ to $y \mapsto \rho(p_i)$), B (for binding a logical variable), $n * H$ (for adding n new bindings into the heap) and, if there is more than one branch, N (for performing a non-deterministic step). Note that no cost C is attributed to cost center cc (indeed, cost B is alternative to cost C).

Finally, rule SCC evaluates an scc-expression by reducing the expression e in the context of the new cost center cc'. Accordingly, cost E is added to cost center cc'.

A proof of a judgement corresponds to a derivation sequence using the rules of Figure 2. Given a program P, the *initial configuration* has the form "$cc_{main}, [\,] : main$", where cc_{main} is a distinguished cost center. If the judgement

$$cc_{main}, [\,] : main \Downarrow_\theta \Gamma : v, cc_v$$

holds, we say that *main* evaluates to value v with associated cost θ. The computed *answer* can be extracted from the final heap Γ by a simple process of *dereferencing*.

Obviously, the cost semantics is a conservative extension of the original big-step semantics of [1], since the computation of cost information imposes no restriction on the application of the rules of the semantics.

5   Cost Instrumentation

As mentioned before, implementing an interpreter for the cost semantics of Figure 2 is impractical. It would involve too much overhead to profile any realistic program. Thus, we introduce a transformation to instrument programs in order to compute the symbolic costs:

Definition 1 (cost transformation). *Given a program P, its cost instrumented version $cost(P)$ is obtained as follows: for each program rule*

$$f(x_1, \ldots, x_n) = e$$

$cost(P)$ includes, for each cost center cc in P, one rule of the form

$$f_{cc}(x_1, \ldots, x_n) = F_{cc}(\llbracket e \rrbracket_{cc})$$

where $F_{cc}(e)$ is the identity function on e. Counting the calls to F_{cc} in the proof tree corresponds to the number of F's accumulated in cost center cc. Function $\llbracket\,\rrbracket$ (shown in Figure 3) is used to instrument program expressions; similarly to F_{cc}, functions V_{cc}, U_{cc}, H_{cc}, N_{cc}, C_{cc}, B_{cc}, and E_{cc} are also defined as the identity function on their argument.

Observe that the transformed program contains as many variants of each function of the original program as different cost centers. Semantically, all these variants are equivalent; the only difference is that we obtain the costs of the computation by counting the calls to the different cost center identity functions (like F_{cc}).

Program instrumentation is mainly performed by function $[\![\ ]\!]_{cc}$, where cc denotes the current cost center. We informally explain how the transformation proceeds by a case distinction on the expression, e, in a call of the form $[\![e]\!]_{cc}$:

- If e is a variable, a call to function V_{cc} is added to attribute cost V to cost center cc.
- If $e = c(\overline{x_n})$ is a constructor-rooted term, we add a new argument to store the current cost center. This is necessary to attribute cost U to the appropriate cost center (i.e., to the cost center of the computed value, see Figure 2).
- A call to a function $f(\overline{x_n})$ is translated to a call to the function variant corresponding to cost center cc.
- If $e = (let\ x = e_1\ in\ e_2)$ is a let expression, a call to function H_{cc} is always added to attribute cost H to cost center cc. Additionally, if the binding is neither a logical variable nor a constructor-rooted term, the cost center cc_i, $1 \le i \le k$, of the computed value is determined (by means of an auxiliary function $update$, see Figure 3) and a call to U_{cc_i} is added to attribute cost U to that cost center.

$$[\![x]\!]_{cc} = V_{cc}(x)$$
$$[\![c(x_1,\ldots,x_n)]\!]_{cc} = c(cc, x_1,\ldots,x_n)$$
$$[\![f(x_1,\ldots,x_n)]\!]_{cc} = f_{cc}(x_1,\ldots,x_n)$$

$$[\![let\ x = e'\ in\ e]\!]_{cc} = H_{cc}\left(\begin{array}{ll} let\ x = x\ in\ [\![e]\!]_{cc}) & if\ e' = x \\ let\ x = [\![e']\!]_{cc}\ in\ [\![e]\!]_{cc} & if\ e' = c(\overline{y_n}) \\ let\ x = update([\![e']\!]_{cc})\ in\ [\![e]\!]_{cc} & otherwise \end{array} \right)$$

$$[\![e_1\ or\ e_2]\!]_{cc} = N_{cc}([\![e_1]\!]_{cc}\ or\ [\![e_2]\!]_{cc})$$

$$[\![case\ x\ of\ \{\overline{p_k \to e_k}\}]\!]_{cc} = case\ [\![x]\!]_{cc}\ of\ \{p'_k \to C_{cc}([\![e_k]\!]_{cc})\}$$
$$where\ p'_i = c(cc', \overline{y_n})\ for\ all\ p_i = c(\overline{y_n})$$

$$[\![fcase\ x\ of\ \{\overline{p_k \to e_k}\}]\!]_{cc}$$
$$= if\ isVar(x)$$
$$then\ V_{cc}(U_{cc}(B_{cc}(\theta_N(fcase\ [\![x]\!]_{cc}\ of\ \{p'_k \to |p_k| * H_{cc}([\![e_k]\!]_{cc})\}))))$$
$$else\ fcase\ [\![x]\!]_{cc}\ of\ \{p'_k \to C_{cc}([\![e_k]\!]_{cc})\}$$
$$where\ p'_i = c(cc, \overline{y_n})\ for\ all\ p_i = c(\overline{y_n})\ and\ \theta_N(e) = \left\{ \begin{array}{ll} e & if\ k = 1 \\ N_{cc}(e) & if\ k > 1 \end{array} \right.$$

$$[\![scc(cc', e)]\!]_{cc} = E_{cc'}([\![e]\!]_{cc'})$$

Here, $|p|$ denotes the arity of pattern p, i.e., $|p| = n$ if $p = c(\overline{x_n})$, and the auxiliary function $update$ is used to attribute cost U to the cost center of the computed value:

$$update(x) = case\ x\ of\ \{c_k(cc_k, \overline{x_{n_k}}) \to U_{cc_k}(c_k(cc_k, \overline{x_{n_k}}))\}$$

where $c_1,\ldots,c_k$ are the program constructors.

Fig. 3. Cost transformation $[\![\ ]\!]_{cc}$ for instrumenting expressions

- If $e = (e_1 \text{ or } e_2)$ is a disjunction, a call to N_{cc} is added to attribute N to cost center cc.
- If $e = case \; x \; of \; \{\overline{p_k \to e_k}\}$ is a rigid case expression, we recursively transform both the case argument and the expression of each branch, where a call to C_{cc} is added to attribute cost C to cost center cc. Observe that the cost center, cc', of the patterns is not used (it is only needed in the auxiliary function $update$).
- If $e = fcase \; x \; of \; \{\overline{p_k \to e_k}\}$ is a flexible case expression, a run-time test (function $is\,Var$) is needed to determine whether the argument evaluates to a logical variable or not. This function can be found, e.g., in the library Unsafe of PAKCS. If it does not evaluate to a logical variable, we proceed as in the previous case. Otherwise, we add calls to functions V_{cc}, U_{cc}, B_{cc}, and N_{cc} (if $k > 1$). Also, in each case branch, calls to H_{cc} are added to attribute the size of the pattern to cost center cc. Here, we use $n * H_{cc}$ as a shorthand for writing n nested calls to H_{cc} (in particular, $0 * H_{cc}$ means that no call to H_{cc} is written).
- Finally, if $e = scc(cc', e')$ is an scc-expression, a call to function $E_{cc'}$ is added. More importantly, we update the current cost center to cc' in the recursive transformation of e'.

Derivations with the standard semantics (i.e., without cost centers) are denoted by $([\,] : main \Downarrow \Gamma_c : v)$. Given a heap Γ, we denote by Γ_c the set of bindings $x \mapsto e'$ such that $x \xmapsto{cc} e$ belongs to Γ, where $e' = e$ if e is a logical variable, $e' = \llbracket e \rrbracket_{cc}$ if $e = c(\overline{x_n})$, or $e' = update(\llbracket e \rrbracket_{cc})$ otherwise. Also, in order to make explicit the output of the instrumented program with the standard semantics, we write $([\,] : main \Downarrow^\theta \Gamma_c : v)$, where θ records the set of calls to cost functions (e.g., H_{cc}, F_{cc}).

The correctness of our program instrumentation is stated as follows (the proof can be found in [5]):

Theorem 1 (correctness). *Let P be a program and $cost(P)$ be its cost instrumented version. Then,*

$$(cc_{main}, [\,] : main \Downarrow_\theta \Gamma : v, cc) \; in \; P \; iff \; ([\,] : main_{cc_{main}} \Downarrow^\theta \Gamma_c : v') \; in \; cost(P)$$

where $v = v'$ (if they are variables) or $v = c(\overline{x_n})$ and $v' = c(cc, \overline{x_n})$.

As an alternative to the transformation presented in this section, we could also instrument programs by *partial evaluation* [11], i.e., the partial evaluation of the cost semantics of Section 4 w.r.t. a source program P should return an instrumented program which is equivalent to $cost(P)$. However, this approach requires both an implementation of the instrumented semantics as well as an optimal partial evaluator for the considered language (in order to obtain a reasonable instrumented program, rather than a slight specialization of the cost semantics). Thus, we preferred to introduce a direct transformation.

Now, we illustrate our cost transformation by means of a simple example. Consider, for instance, the following definition for function len:

```
len(x) = fcase x of { Nil          → Z
                    ; Cons(y,ys) → let w = scc("b",len(ys))
                                   in S(w) }
```

Then, the corresponding instrumented definition for the cost center "a" is the following:

```
len_a(x) =
  F_a(if isVar(x)
          then V_a(U_a(B_a(N_a(fcase V_a(x) of
              { Nil(cc) → Z(a)
              ; Cons(cc,y,ys) → H_a(H_a(H_a(let w = update(len_b(ys))
                                            in S(a,w))))
              } ))))
          else fcase V_a(x) of
              { Nil(cc) → Z(a)
              ; Cons(cc,y,ys) → C_a(H_a(let w = update(len_b(ys))
                                        in S(a,w)))
              }
       )
```

where the auxiliary function *update* is defined as follows:

```
update(x) = case x of { Z(cc)   → U_cc(Z(cc))
                      ; S(cc,x) → U_cc(S(cc,x)) }
```

6   Implementation

The main purpose of profiling programs is to increase run-time efficiency. However, in practice, it is important to obtain symbolic profiling information as well as measuring run times. As discussed before, we want to provide cost centers for both kinds of profiling in order to be able to analyze arbitrary sub-computations independently of the defined functions. For the formal introduction of costs and correctness proofs, symbolic costs are the appropriate means. Therefore, we introduced a program transformation dealing with symbolic costs. However, the presented program transformation can easily be extended for measuring run times and distribute them through cost centers. In this section, we first present our approach to measure run times and function calls (Sect. 6.1) and, then, describe the extensions to obtain symbolic profiling (Sect. 6.2).

6.1   Measuring Run Times

When trying to measure actual run times, the crucial point is to alter the run time behavior of the examined program *as little as possible*. If the program instrumented for profiling runs 50% slower or worse, one profiles the process of profiling rather than the program execution. Because of this, measuring actual run times is a matter of low-level programming and, thus, highly depending on the actual language implementation.

Our approach is specific to the Curry implementation PAKCS [10]. In this programming environment, Curry programs are compiled by transforming flat programs (cf. Section 2) to SICStus Prolog (see [3] for details about this transformation). Note, however, that in contrast to Section 2 the programs are not necessarily normalized. In order to provide low-level profiling for PAKCS, we instrument the program with the profiling mechanisms offered by SICStus Prolog. Fortunately, SICStus Prolog features low-level profiling instruments which create an overhead of approximately 22%. The Prolog tools provide precise measuring of the number of predicate and clause calls. For measuring run time, a number of synthetic units is given which is computed according to [7].

The main challenge was to introduce the cost centers into Prolog profiling. Luckily, we found a way to do this *without* further slowing down the execution of the program being profiled. The only overhead we introduce is code duplication, since we introduce a different version of each function for each cost center, as in the program transformation described above. Thus, for the program

```
main = SCC "len" (length (SCC "list" (enumFromTo 1 10)))
```

function main does not call a function length but a variant with the name "length{len}" and also a function named "enumFromTo{list}". Gathering all run times for functions with the attachment {cc}, one gets the run time belonging to that cost center. An obvious optimization is to eliminate unreachable functions like length{list} in the example.

6.2   Extension for Symbolic Profiling

Our approach to symbolic profiling exactly represents the idea described in Section 5 above. For each cost, we introduce a new function, e.g., var_lookup for cost V. There are variations of these functions for the different cost centers, e.g., var_lookup{list} like in Section 6.1. After the execution of the transformed program, we simply count each call to var_lookup{list} to get the sum of costs V attributed to the cost center list.

The advantage of this method is its simplicity. The demands to use our transformation for profiling with any implementation of Curry are not very high. The run-time system must only be able to count the number of calls to a certain function which is easy to implement. The disadvantage is the considerable (but still reasonable) slowdown as we are not only introducing new functions but also new function *calls*. Nevertheless, this overhead does not influence the computation of symbolic costs.

The overhead introduced by the additional function calls is also the reason why our profiler generates different programs for run-time profiling and symbolic profiling. Since the program transformed for symbolic profiling is more than a magnitude slower than the original program, measuring run times in the program transformed for symbolic profiling would lead to results that are not strictly related to the performance of the original program.

It is worthwhile to note that, although the program transformation of Fig. 3 is equivalent to the cost semantics of Fig. 2 for *particular computations* (as stated in Theorem 1), there is one important difference:

> *While the cost semantics is don't-care non-deterministic, the instrumented programs accumulate all costs according to the search strategy.*

For instance, the cost for a failing derivation is also accumulated in the cost of the results computed afterwards. Furthermore, completely failing computations also have an associated cost while no proof tree (and thus no costs) can be constructed in the big-step semantics. From a practical point of view, this is an advantage of the program transformation over the cost semantics, since the cost of failing derivations is relevant in the presence of non-deterministic functions.

7   Using the Profiler

In this section we present how our profiler can be used to improve the runtime of Curry programs by means of a larger example. We want to implement an algorithm solving the following problem:

> An *alphabet* is given by the algebraic datatype
>
> ```
> data Letter = A | B | ... | Y | Z
> type Word = [Letter]
> type Alphabet = [Letter]
> ```
>
> *Words* are defined as sequences of letters and (sub-)alphabets as sets (implemented as lists) of letters. Define a function `sameUsedAlphabet` that takes two words as input and, if both words use the same sub-alphabet, yields this sub-alphabet as its result.

The basic idea of an algorithm for solving this problem could be the following:

- Extract the sub-alphabets used by each string by means of removing double occurrences of letters (`rmDups`).
- Check whether the two sub-alphabets are permutations of each other (`isPerm`), otherwise fail.
- Return the sub-alphabet of the first word.

A possible implementation of these functions in Curry could be the following:

```
rmDups [] = []
rmDups (x:xs) = if elem x (rmDups xs) then rmDups xs
                                      else x:rmDups xs
```

Thus, an element is kept in the list if it is not an element of the remaining list.

```
isPerm []      []  = success
isPerm (x:xs) ys | eqWord (zs++[x]++us) ys = isPerm xs (zs++us)
```

```
    where zs,us free

eqWord [] [] = success
eqWord (x:xs) (y:ys) | eqLetter x y = eqWord xs ys

eqLetter A A = success
...
eqLetter Z Z = success
```

In the implementation of isPerm, we exploit the logical features of Curry. The function isPerm is applied to two lists. We successively delete the elements of the first list from the second list until both lists are empty. For deleting an element from the second list, we use the append function (++) as a relation by applying it to logical variables. When the expression (zs++[x]++us) is compared with ys by the function eqWord, the logical variable zs is bound to the part of ys in front of x and us to the part behind x. The list not containing x is zs++us which is recursively compared with xs.

The functions eqWord and eqLetter define unification for letters and words. In Curry this unification is generalized to arbitrary data types by means of strict equality (=:=) [6]. Our implementation also provides profiling information for this extension. For simplicity, we do not present the technically expensive details of this extension in this paper and define specific functions for the unification of words and letters in this example.

Finally, we combine all these functions to solve the problem by means of the function sameUsedAlphabet:

```
sameUsedAlphabet :: [Letter] -> [Letter] -> [Letter]
sameUsedAlphabet str1 str2
    | isPerm (rmDups str1) (rmDups str2) = rmDups str1
```

Testing sameUsedAlphabet for short words is reasonably efficient. Unfortunately, our algorithm does not scale well for longer words. For instance, the application of sameUsedAlphabet to a word containing all letters of the alphabet does not terminate within one hour.

To find the source of this inefficiency, we use our profiler. We add two cost centers "perm" and "rmDups" as follows:

```
rmDups xs = SCC "rmDups" (rmDups' xs)
rmDups' [] = []
rmDups' (x:xs) = if elem x (rmDups' xs) then rmDups' xs
                                        else x:rmDups' xs

sameUsedAlphabet :: Word -> Word -> Alphabet
sameUsedAlphabet str1 str2
    | SCC "perm" (isPerm (rmDups str1) (rmDups str2)) = rmDups str1
```

Profiling some applications of `sameUsedAlphabet`, we obtain the following measurements for function unfoldings and heap allocations (we do not present the other kinds of costs since they do not provide more information here):

sameUsedAlphabet applied to	"perm"		"rmDups"	
	F	H	F	H
[A,B] [B,A]	39	18	148	159
[A,B,C,D,E,F] [F,E,D,C,B,A]	237	166	3881	3924
[A,B,C,D,E,F] [F,E,D,C,B,A,F,E,D,C,B,A]	237	166	127643	128316

An analysis of these profiling results yields the following conclusions:

- The costs for `rmDups` are much higher than the costs for `perm`.
- The costs for `perm` only depend on the sub-alphabet of the words, not on the size of the word.
- The costs for `rmDups` grow exponentially in the size of the word.

Without using the profiler, we might have blamed the inefficiency to the logical part of the program (i.e., the use of the potentially inefficient constraint `isPerm`). However, thanks to the information gathered by the profiler, we know that we should focus on the code of `rmDups` to optimize our program. In fact, during the recursion of `rmDups` we compute the result of `rmDups xs` twice, which yields exponential runtime. By simply introducing a `let` binding for this result, we obtain a much more efficient version of `rmDups`:

```
rmDups [] = []
rmDups (x:xs) = let ys = rmDups xs in
                if elem x ys then ys else x:ys
```

8   Related Work and Conclusions

The approaches closest to our work are [14] and [2]. On the one hand, [14] presents a formal specification of the attribution of execution costs to cost centers by means of an appropriate cost-augmented semantics in the context of lazy functional programs. A significant difference from our work is that our flat representation of programs provides for logical features (like non-determinism) and that we also present a formal transformation to instrument source programs. On the other hand, [2] introduces a symbolic profiling scheme for functional logic languages. However, the approach of [2] does not consider *sharing* (an essential component of lazy languages) and, thus, it is not an appropriate basis for the development of profiling tools for current implementations of lazy functional logic languages. Furthermore, we introduced a program transformation that allows us to compute symbolic costs with a reasonable overhead. Finally, in the context of the PAKCS environment for Curry, we showed how actual run times can also be computed by reusing the SICStus Prolog profiler.

References

1. E. Albert, M. Hanus, F. Huch, J. Oliver, and G. Vidal. Operational Semantics for Declarative Multi-Paradigm Languages. *Journal of Symbolic Computation*, 2005. To appear.
2. E. Albert and G. Vidal. Symbolic Profiling of Multi-Paradigm Declarative Languages. In *Proc. of Int'l Workshop on Logic-based Program Synthesis and Transformation (LOPSTR'01)*, pages 148–167. Springer LNCS 2372, 2002.
3. S. Antoy and M. Hanus. Compiling Multi-Paradigm Declarative Programs into Prolog. In *Proc. of the Int'l Workshop on Frontiers of Combining Systems (FroCoS'2000)*, pages 171–185. Springer LNCS 1794, 2000.
4. H.P. Barendregt. *The Lambda Calculus—Its Syntax and Semantics*. Elsevier, 1984.
5. B. Braßel, M. Hanus, F. Huch, J. Silva, and G. Vidal. Run-Time Profiling of Functional Logic Programs. Technical report, DSIC, Technical University of Valencia, 2005. Available at: http://www.dsic.upv.es/users/elp/german/papers.html.
6. M. Hanus (ed.). Curry: An Integrated Functional Logic Language. Available at: http://www.informatik.uni-kiel.de/~curry/.
7. M. Gorlick and C. Kesselman. Timing Prolog Programs without Clock. In *Proc. of the 4th Symposium on Logic Programming (SLP'87)*, pages 426–434, 1987.
8. M. Hanus. A Unified Computation Model for Functional and Logic Programming. In *Proc. of the 24th ACM Symp. on Principles of Programming Languages (POPL'97)*, pages 80–93. ACM, New York, 1997.
9. M. Hanus and C. Prehofer. Higher-Order Narrowing with Definitional Trees. *Journal of Functional Programming*, 9(1):33–75, 1999.
10. M. Hanus (ed.), S. Antoy, M. Engelke, K. Höppner, J. Koj, P. Niederau, R. Sadre, and F. Steiner. PAKCS 1.6.0: The Portland Aachen Kiel Curry System—User Manual. Technical report, University of Kiel, Germany, 2004.
11. N.D. Jones, C.K. Gomard, and P. Sestoft. *Partial Evaluation and Automatic Program Generation*. Prentice-Hall, Englewood Cliffs, NJ, 1993.
12. J. Launchbury. A Natural Semantics for Lazy Evaluation. In *Proc. of the ACM Symp. on Principles of Programming Languages (POPL'93)*, pages 144–154. ACM Press, 1993.
13. F. López-Fraguas and J. Sánchez-Hernández. TOY: A Multiparadigm Declarative System. In *Proc. of the 10th Int'l Conf. on Rewriting Techniques and Applications (RTA'99)*, pages 244–247. Springer LNCS 1631, 1999.
14. P.M. Sansom and S.L. Peyton-Jones. Formally Based Profiling for Higher-Order Functional Languages. *ACM Transactions on Programming Languages and Systems*, 19(2):334–385, 1997.

Constructive Specifications for Compositional Units

Kung-Kiu Lau[1], Alberto Momigliano[2], and Mario Ornaghi[2]

[1] School of Computer Science, The University of Manchester,
Manchester M13 9PL, United Kingdom
kung-kiu@cs.man.ac.uk
[2] Dipartimento di Scienze dell'Informazione,
Universita' degli studi di Milano,
Via Comelico 39/41, 20135 Milano, Italy
{momiglia, ornaghi}@dsi.unimi.it

Abstract. In previous work, we have introduced a model-theoretic semantics for compositional units, i.e. reusable units that can be used for compositional program development. Such units contain open (logic) programs and our model-theoretic semantics characterizes their correctness and the correctness of their composition. However, for real-world software development, compositional units should be inter-operable, i.e. they should accept programs in different languages. To cater for this, our model-theoretic semantics needs to be used in conjunction with suitable semantics for behaviours and interfaces. In this paper we describe one possible approach based on constructive specifications.

1   Introduction

A reusable program unit, or a compositional unit, contains code that can be composed with other units, to yield a desired behavior. To be widely reusable, a unit should be open, i.e., not completely defined. The undefined parts become defined as a result of composition. Examples of open units are generic modules with import/export sections in modular languages, generic ADT's [7] and frameworks in OO design [6]. In the context of Logic Programming, open programs have been proposed as open units, due to their compositional properties [2]. Units should be only specified by an interface specification and context dependencies [17], and we need rules for composing and decomposing interface specifications and to compare them, that is, to state whether interface specification S_1 meets or entails interface specification S_2. These properties allow us to combine top-down and bottom-up development.

In all this, the problem context plays an underpinning role. Indeed, context dependencies and specifications have their proper meaning only in the problem context and the latter plays a fundamental aspect in comparing specifications and to prove program properties. We have considered the role of the problem context w.r.t. compositionality in our previous work [10]. We have introduced a model-theoretic semantics for the correctness of open programs and we have studied how to combine programs, contexts and specifications into compositional units of interface specifications and code.

Compositional units should be *inter-operable*, i.e. (pure) logic programs in such units should be able to inter-operate with programs in different languages. For this,

S. Etalle(Ed.): LOPSTR 2004, LNCS 3573, pp. 198–214, 2005.

a model-theoretic semantics does not suffice. Inter-operation involves properties that are not explicit in the model-theoretic specifications, such as, for example, input and output modes in a logic program. Properties of this kind should be *explicit* in the interface specification of a unit. In this paper we propose a notion of constructive interface specifications, which can be consistently used with the model-theoretic one – classical model theory still remaining the basic semantics. This allows us to make explicit modes and other computational behaviours that are relevant for the correct composition of programs, but are not apparent in a purely model-theoretic approach. The advantage of a formalisation of these aspects is that we get both a precise *semantics* and a *compositional calculus*. The latter allows us to reason about interface specifications and to derive *correct* unit compositions, possibly using automatic theorem provers.

2   Program Units and Their Composition

In this section we give an informal overview of our approach to program units and their composition. We define a *program unit* as a triple $U = \langle \Sigma, C, Prog \rangle$, where Σ is a many-sorted signature, C is a class of Σ-models and *Prog* is a collection of programs. We call U a *program unit* (PU) to avoid confusion with compositional units (CU) introduced in our previous work [10]. The class C is called the *context* of U. It may be defined formally (as, e.g., in CU's) or informally (as we will do in the examples), with the purpose of *specifying the meaning of the procedures used in the unit, in terms of the problem domain*. We distinguish between *imported, exported and hidden* procedures. The imported procedures are assumed to be supplied by external units. For each exported procedure p, *Prog* contains a *program* implementing p, hidden in U, and a set of (public) *interfaces* p : I_1, ..., p : I_k, that refer to when and how p can be correctly composed with procedures imported from external units.

Example 1. The *context section* of the following program unit *LG* specifies the problem domain of labeled graphs. The ADT *List*(V) (lists with elements from V) is included to define predicates on paths. For example, the definition of $x \xrightarrow{a^n} y$ (x *is linked to* y *by* n *consecutive arcs with label* a) uses $at : [V, Nat, List(V)]$, defined in *List*(V) ($at(v,i,l)$ means that v occurs at position i in list l). The meaning of the imported and exported procedures is defined by the specifications $S_{\texttt{arc}}$, $S_{\texttt{conn}}$, $S_{\texttt{path}}$, using the context signature and the concrete data types of the implementation language, such as int in $S_{\texttt{conn}}$; $repr_{Nat}(i,n)$ means that the integer i represents the natural number n. We have used a many-sorted Prolog, to shrink the gap between the context and the implementation level for the sorts V, L, *List*(V).

Program unit *LG*;
Context. SIGNATURE: V, L : sort; $\_ \xrightarrow{\quad} \_ : [V, L, V]$; INCLUDES: *List*$(V)$;
INTERPRETATIONS: For each graph, C contains an interpretation where V and L are the sets of nodes and labels, and $x \xrightarrow{a} y$ holds iff there is an arc from x to y with label a.
$$x \xrightarrow{a^n} y \leftrightarrow \exists p.\, at(x,0,p) \wedge at(y,n,p) \wedge \forall u,v,i.\, at(u,i,p) \wedge at(v,s(i),p) \rightarrow (u \xrightarrow{a} v)$$
IMPORT: $S_{\texttt{arc}:[V,L,V]} : \texttt{arc}(x,a,x') \leftrightarrow (x \xrightarrow{a} x')$.
EXPORT: $S_{\texttt{path}:[List(V)]} : \texttt{path}(p) \leftrightarrow \forall x,x',i.\, at(x,i,p) \wedge at(x',s(i),p) \rightarrow \exists a.\, x \xrightarrow{a} x'$.
$\qquad\quad S_{\texttt{conn}:[V,L,V,\texttt{int}]} : repr_{Nat}(i,n) \rightarrow (\texttt{conn}(x,a,y,i) \leftrightarrow (x \xrightarrow{a^n} y))$

Programs.

path : P1 $(\forall x, y. (\exists a. ?\mathtt{arc}(x^+, a^-, y^+)) \vee T(\neg \exists a. \mathtt{arc}(x, a, y)))$
$\qquad \rightarrow (\forall p. ?\mathtt{path}(p^+) \vee T\neg\mathtt{path}(p));$

path : P2 $T(\exists n. \forall p. \mathtt{path}(p) \rightarrow length(p) \leq n) \wedge (\exists s. \forall!x, a, y \in s. ?\mathtt{arc}(x^-, a^-, y^-))$
$\qquad \rightarrow \exists s'. \forall!p \in s'. ?\mathtt{path}(p^-);$

IMPL : $\mathtt{path}([]).$
$\qquad \mathtt{path}([\_]).$
$\qquad \mathtt{path}([\mathtt{X}, \mathtt{Y}|\mathtt{R}]) : -\mathtt{arc}(\mathtt{X}, \_, \mathtt{Y}), \mathtt{path}([\mathtt{Y}|\mathtt{R}]).$

conn : C1 $(\forall x, a. \exists y. !\mathtt{arc}(x^+, a^+, y^-))$
$\qquad \rightarrow (\forall x, a, i. T(i \geq 0) \rightarrow \exists y. !\mathtt{conn}(x^+, a^+, y^-, i^+))$

IMPL : $\mathtt{conn}(\mathtt{X}, \_, \mathtt{X}, 0).$
$\qquad \mathtt{conn}(\mathtt{X}, \mathtt{A}, \mathtt{Y}, \mathtt{I}) : -\mathtt{I} > 0, \mathtt{J} \text{ is } \mathtt{I} - 1, \mathtt{arc}(\mathtt{X}, \mathtt{A}, \mathtt{Z}), \mathtt{conn}(\mathtt{Z}, \mathtt{A}, \mathtt{Y}, \mathtt{J}).$

We call $S_{\mathtt{arc}}$, $S_{\mathtt{conn}}$, $S_{\mathtt{path}}$ *model-theoretic specifications*, to distinguish them from *constructive specifications* of the *interfaces* of the procedures implemented in the *program* section. By conn : C1 we mean that conn *realizes the interface* specified by C1. Similarly for path : P1 and path : P2.

We have used moded call statements, such as $?path(p^-)$, where '$-$' denotes the output mode and '?' the query mode. They will be explained later in the paragraph introducing behaviours. Interfaces are interpreted according to the *constructive semantics* that we are now going to informally introduce. To reuse LG, an external unit Q has to fix the interpretation of the open symbols V, L and $\_ \xrightarrow{\ \ } \_$, to represent the set of the nodes, labels of a specific graph and to implement the procedure arc. We want to guarantee that the program implementing arc correctly composes with the programs imported from LG. To this end, in [10], we have considered a notion of model theoretic interfaces and correctness. For example, $LG.\mathtt{path} : S_{\mathtt{arc}} \rightarrow S_{\mathtt{path}}$ is a model theoretic interface for $LG.\mathtt{path}$ and its (model theoretic) correctness means that $S_{\mathtt{path}}$ is true in the minimum Herbrand model (MHM) of $LG.\mathtt{path}$, whenever $LG.\mathtt{path}$ is composed with a program $Q.\mathtt{arc}$ with a MHM satisfying $S_{\mathtt{arc}}$. This entails that from $LG.\mathtt{path} : S_{\mathtt{arc}} \rightarrow S_{\mathtt{path}}$ and $Q.\mathtt{arc} : true \rightarrow S_{\mathtt{arc}}$ we can infer $Q.\mathtt{arc} \circ_{\mathtt{arc}} LG.\mathtt{path} : true \rightarrow S_{path}$. By $\circ_{\mathtt{arc}}$ we denote the *import composition* with respect to arc, performed at the program level when the unit (LG) importing arc includes or is included in a unit (Q) exporting arc. For logic programs, $\circ_{\mathtt{arc}}$ is the union, although renaming may be needed.

As the above discussion shows, model theoretic interfaces have a simple declarative semantics and simple composition rules. However, they do not take into account computational aspects that are relevant for correct program reuse. For example, the interface $LG.\mathtt{path} : S_{\mathtt{arc}} \rightarrow S_{\mathtt{path}}$ cannot distinguish the following different uses of $P.\mathtt{path}$:

a) If $Q.\mathtt{arc}$ *decides* $\exists a. arc(x, a, y)$ for every pair x, y of nodes of a graph g, we can use $Q.\mathtt{arc} \circ_{\mathtt{arc}} LG.\mathtt{path}$ to decide $\mathtt{path}(p)$, for every ground sequence p of nodes.
b) If g has no infinite paths and via $Q_{\mathtt{arc}}$ we can obtain a finite *enumeration* of all the arcs of g, then $Q.\mathtt{arc} \circ_{\mathtt{arc}} LG.\mathtt{path}$ can be used to enumerate all the paths in g.

Interfaces based on *constructive specifications* make this kind of computational aspects explicit, while preserving the declarativeness of model-theoretic specifications. For example, interfaces P1and P2 correspond to uses a) and b). Here we give an informal account of constructive specifications and their role in procedure composition, by explaining the interfaces of the procedures of LG.

Interfaces and specifications. The interface P1 of LG.path is an *implication* $I_{P1} \rightarrow$ E_{P1}, where I_{P1} is a specification for the imported procedure arc and E_{P1} is a specification for the exported procedure path. The meaning is that LG.path realizes the behaviour specified by E_{P1}, whenever LG is composed with a unit Q containing a program Q.arc realizing I_{P1}. More precisely, after the composition, we get a richer program unit $LG + Q$, where Q.arc $\circ_{arc} LG$.path realizes E_{P1}. Thus, *interfaces model unit composition at the program level.* I_{P1} is a *universal specification*. It is *realized* iff the main sub-formula $(\exists a. \; ?arc(x^+, a^-, y^+)) \vee T(\neg \exists a. \; arc(x, a, y))$ is realized for all the ground substitutions $x = t_1, y = t_2$ of the universally quantified variables. The main sub-formula is an *existential specification*. An existential specification E is built by means of $\wedge, \vee, \exists$, starting from *moded call statements* (such as $?arc(x^+, a^-, y^+)$) and T-*formulas* (such as $T(\neg \exists a. \; arc(x, a, y))$). A ground instance $E\sigma$ of E is *realized by a program unit U* iff it is realized by the *behaviour* of U, *observed* using the moded call statements of E.

Behaviours. To explain realizability, we have to consider moded call statements and behaviours. In the moded call statement $?arc(x^+, a^-, y^+)$ of P1, parameters x, y have *input mode* '+', parameter a has *output mode* '−'and arc has *query mode* '?'. Input and output modes have the usual meaning [4]: a call $arc(t_1, A, t_2)$ works properly if t_1, t_2 are ground and the (possible) variables of A will be instantiated by the answer substitution. In particular, the query $: -arc(t_1, A, t_2)$ is admitted, with A a variable. The query mode $?arc$ signifies that the set $A = a_1, \dots, A = a_k, \dots$ of *all the answers* can be obtained by backtracking. We represent the corresponding *behaviour* $\mathcal{B}_{arc}$ by the *b-formulas* (behaviour formulas) $arc(t_1, a_1, t_2), \dots, arc(t_1, a_k, t_2), \dots$; if after n answers backtracking fails, we put the b-formula $T(\forall a. \; \neg a = a_1 \wedge \dots \neg a = a_n \rightarrow \neg arc(t_1, a, t_2))$ in $\mathcal{B}_{arc}$ (if $n = 0$, $\mathcal{B}_{arc} = \{T(\forall a. \; \neg arc(t_1, a, t_2))\}$). The use of T for representing failure will be explained very soon.

Realizability of existential specifications. The formal definition of $\mathcal{B} \models E$, i.e. when behaviour $\mathcal{B}$ realizes specification E is given in Def. 1. Note that realizability is *constructive*: a realization of $A \vee B$ allows us to decide which disjunct holds and a realization of $\exists x. \; A(x)$ to obtain an answer $x = t$. For example, $(\exists a. \; arc(t_1, a, t_2)) \vee T(\neg \exists a. \; arc(t_1, a, t_2))$ is realized by $\mathcal{B}_{arc}$, as follows. If $arc(t_1, a_1, t_2) \in \mathcal{B}_{arc}$, then the disjunct $\exists a. \; arc(t_1, a, t_2)$ is realized, with answer $a = a_1$. If no answers exist, then $T(\forall a. \; \neg arc(t_1, a, t_2)) \in \mathcal{B}_{arc}$. Therefore the disjunct $T(\neg \exists a. \; arc(t_1, a, t_2))$ is realized by the truth of $\neg \exists a. \; arc(t_1, a, t_2)$.

T-formulas. We have used T in a disjunction of the form $H \vee T(F)$, to deal with finite failure: if the attempt of realizing H fails, we conclude that F is true, but we do not require any further information. In this sense, T corresponds to the *classical truth operator* of [15]. T-formulas can be also used as pre-conditions, not requiring any computation. For example, $T(\exists n. \; \forall p. \; path(p) \rightarrow length(p) \leq n)$ in P2 requires that all the paths of the current graph have length limited by a fixed n, but it does not require to compute n. Another use of T is illustrated by the bounded quantification $\forall! x \in s. \; A(x)$

used in P2, which abbreviates $(\forall x.\, A(x) \vee T(\neg A(x))) \wedge (\forall x.\, T(member(x,s)) \leftrightarrow A(x))$ [1]. Let s be $[t_1,\ldots,t_n]$. Then a behaviour $\mathcal{B}$ realizes $\forall! x \in s.\, A(x)$ iff it realizes $A(t_1)$, ..., $A(t_n)$ and $T(x \neq t_1 \wedge \cdots \wedge x \neq t_n \rightarrow \neg A(x))$. Similarly the notation $\exists! x.\, A(x)$ abbreviates $\exists x.\, A(x) \wedge T(\forall x, y.\, A(x) \wedge A(y) \rightarrow x = y)$.

Different kinds of interfaces. According to the informal explanations above, one can see that P1 corresponds to use a). Its import part I_{P1} and export part E_{P1} specify *decision behaviours*. P2 corresponds to use b). Its import and export parts specify *enumeration behaviours*. Import and export parts of C1 specify *selection behaviours*: if for every node x and label a, Q_{arc} selects a y such that $x \xrightarrow{a} y$, then for every node x, label a and integer $i \geq 0$, $LG.\mathrm{conn}$ selects an y such that $x \xrightarrow{a^i} y$. Here, !arc is the *selection mode*. It means that by means of a call to arc we get an answer (selected by the program), but backtracking is forbidden or it may not work properly. *Functional behaviours* are a special case of selection behaviours, where the selected output is also unique. Decision, enumeration, selection and functional behaviours are the most common. Of course, a complex specification may mix them.

Composition calculus. Finally, we have a *calculus* to compose procedures according to their interfaces, while preserving realizability. The composition calculus is explained in Sect. 5.1. We conclude our informal overview with an example, which shows the application of the calculus and introduces *bridge proofs*, namely proofs that allow us to link interfaces in case they do not match exactly. When we include a unit, the context is included with possible renaming and *closures*, i.e. instantiations of open symbols, as illustrated in the next example. Then procedures may be selectively included. We may *hide* them (when appropriate) via the operator #. We may also use local (hidden) bridge programs generated when building bridge proofs.

Example 2. The unit IT implements an iterator of a generic binary operation
Program Unit IT.   Context. Contains Nat, a generic domain D and a binary operation $\cdot : [D,D] \rightarrow D$ with left unit $\mathbf{u} : D$. Defines $x^0 = \mathbf{u}$, $x^{(n+1)} = x^n \cdot x$.
IMPORT: $S_{\mathrm{unit}:[D]} : \mathrm{unit}(x) \leftrightarrow x = \mathbf{u}$; $S_{\mathrm{op}:[D,D,D]} : \mathrm{op}(x,a,y) \leftrightarrow y = x \cdot a$;
EXPORT: $S_{\mathrm{iter}:[D,\mathrm{int},D]} : repr_{Nat}(i,n) \rightarrow (\mathrm{iter}(x,i,z) \leftrightarrow z = x^n)$.
Programs.

iter : IT $(\exists x.\, !\mathrm{unit}(x^-)) \wedge (\forall x, a.\, \exists y.\, !\mathrm{op}(x^+, a^+, y^-))$
$\rightarrow (\forall x, i.\, T(i \geq 0) \rightarrow \exists! z.\, \mathrm{iter}(x^+, i^+, z^-))$;
    IMPL: iter(X,0,U) : −unit(U).
    iter(X,I,U) : −I > 0, H is I − 1, iter(X,H,V), op(V,X,U).

In the unit LG, $LG.\mathrm{conn}$ is tail recursive and $\mathrm{conn}(x,a,y,n)$ is defined as $x \xrightarrow{a^n} y$. If we include IT into LG and we take the sets V of nodes and L of labels as D, we may interpret each pair $(x, x \cdot a)$ as an arc $x \xrightarrow{a} x \cdot a$ and we can prove $x \xrightarrow{a^n} y \leftrightarrow y = x \cdot a^n$. Thus we can (re)use $LG.\mathrm{conn}$ to compute iter in a tail-recursive way, as follows.
Program Unit $LGIT$ EXTENDS LG, INCLUDES IT.
CLOSE: $V := D$; $L := D$; $x \xrightarrow{a} y \leftrightarrow y = x \cdot a$;

---

[1] With quantifiers such as $\forall! x, a, y \in s$. in P2, s is a list of triples.

THM: $i \geq 0 \rightarrow (\mathtt{iter}(x,i,z) \leftrightarrow \mathtt{conn}(\mathbf{u},x,z,i))$; $\mathtt{op}(x,a,y) \leftrightarrow \mathtt{arc}(x,a,y)$.

Programs.

$\mathtt{iter}: \#\mathrm{IT} \quad (\exists x. \ !\#\mathtt{unit}(x^-)) \wedge (\forall x,a,i. \ T(i \geq 0) \rightarrow \exists y. \ !\#\mathtt{conn}(x^+,a^+,y^-,i^+))$
$\qquad\qquad \rightarrow (\forall x,i. \ T(i \geq 0) \rightarrow \exists!z. \ !\mathtt{iter}(x^+,i^+,z^-)):$

$\qquad$ IMPL: $\mathtt{iter}(X,I,Y): -\#\mathtt{unit}(U), \#\mathtt{conn}(U,X,Y,I)$.

$\mathtt{iter}: \mathrm{IT} \quad (\exists x. \ !\mathtt{unit}(x^-)) \wedge (\forall x,a. \ \exists y. \ !\mathtt{op}(x^+,a^+,y^-))$
$\qquad\qquad \rightarrow (\forall x,i. \ T(i \geq 0) \rightarrow \exists!z. \ !\mathtt{iter}(x^+,i^+,z^-))$

$\qquad$ IMPL: $(\mathrm{rn}[\mathtt{unit}/\#\mathtt{unit}] \mid (\mathrm{rn}[\mathtt{op}/\#\mathtt{arc}] \circ_{\#\mathtt{arc}} LG.\#\mathtt{conn})) \circ_{\#\mathtt{conn},\#\mathtt{unit}} (\mathtt{iter}: \#\mathrm{IT})$.

Program $\mathtt{iter}: \#\mathrm{IT}$ is a *local bridge program* ($\#\mathrm{IT}$ is a local specification, hidden by #). The clause implementing $\mathtt{iter}: \#\mathrm{IT}$ has been derived from the following *bridge proof* $\mathrm{pr}(\#lm1)$ and corresponds to lemma $bd1$.

$$
\cfrac{
\cfrac{\cfrac{\cfrac{I_{\#\mathrm{IT}}}{\mathrm{rn}[]: \exists x. \ !\#\mathtt{unit}(x^-)}\mathrm{rn}, \wedge E_1}{}\quad
\cfrac{\cfrac{T(i \geq 0) \quad I_{\#\mathrm{IT}}}{\mathrm{rn}[]: \exists y. \ !\#\mathtt{conn}(u^+,x^+,y^-,i^+)}\mathrm{rn}, \wedge E_2, \forall E, \rightarrow E}{}\quad
\cfrac{\cfrac{T(i \geq 0) \quad !\#\mathtt{unit}(u^-) \quad !\#\mathtt{conn}(u^+,x^+,y^-,i^+)}{(\mathtt{iter}:\#\mathrm{IT}): !\mathtt{iter}(x^+,i^+,y^-)}bd1}{\cfrac{(\mathtt{iter}:\#\mathrm{IT}): \exists!z. \ !\mathtt{iter}(x^+,i^+,z^-)}{(\mathtt{iter}:\#\mathrm{IT}): \exists!z. \ !\mathtt{iter}(x^+,i^+,z^-)}\exists!I}\circ\exists E}
{(\mathtt{iter}:\#\mathrm{IT}): \exists!z. \ !\mathtt{iter}(x^+,i^+,z^-)}\circ\exists E, \rightarrow I, \forall I, \rightarrow I}
{(\mathtt{iter}:\#\mathrm{IT}): I_{\#\mathrm{IT}} \rightarrow E_{\mathrm{IT}}}
$$

$!\mathtt{iter}$'s mode follows from $!\#\mathtt{conn}$ and modes $+, -$ are treated as usual in logic programs. $I_{\#\mathrm{IT}}$ and E_{IT} denote the import and export parts of the interface $\#\mathrm{IT}$ of $LGIT$ (the export part coincides with the one of IT). The unicity T-formula needed in $\exists!I$ is inherited from LG. The empty renaming $\mathrm{rn}[]$ is generated by the rule rn. For homogeneous programs (as in our example), $\mathrm{rn}[]$ works as the identity for import composition. For heterogeneous programs, it corresponds to a "communication channel". $\circ\exists E$ is a derived rule and gives rise to $\mathrm{rn}[] \circ (\mathtt{iter}:\#\mathrm{IT})$, equal to $(\mathtt{iter}:\#\mathrm{IT})$ [2]. The composite program implementing $LGIT.\mathtt{iter}$ is obtained by the following *composition proof*.

$$
\cfrac{
\cfrac{\cfrac{I_{\#\mathrm{IT}}}{\mathrm{rn}[\mathtt{unit}/\#\mathtt{unit}]: \exists x. \ !\#\mathtt{unit}(x^-)}\mathrm{rn}, \wedge E_1 \quad
\cfrac{\mathrm{rn}[\mathtt{op}/\#\mathtt{arc}]: I_{\#\mathrm{C}1} \quad \cfrac{\cfrac{I_{\mathrm{IT}}}{LG.\#\mathtt{conn}: I_{\#\mathrm{C}1} \rightarrow E_{\#\mathrm{C}1}[\mathrm{pr}(LG)]}\mathrm{rn}, \wedge E_2}{\rightarrow E}}{\mathrm{rn}[\mathtt{op}/\#\mathtt{arc}] \circ_{\#\mathtt{arc}} LG.\#\mathtt{conn}: E_{\#\mathrm{C}1}}}
{\mathrm{rn}[\mathtt{unit}/\#\mathtt{unit}] \mid (\mathrm{rn}[\mathtt{op}/\#\mathtt{arc}] \circ_{\#\mathtt{arc}} LG.\#\mathtt{conn}): I_{\#\mathrm{IT}}}\mid_1, \mid_2, \wedge I \quad
\cfrac{(\mathtt{iter}:\#\mathrm{IT}): I_{\#\mathrm{IT}} \rightarrow E_{\mathrm{IT}}[\mathrm{pr}(\#lm1)]}{}\rightarrow E,}
{(\mathrm{rn}[\mathtt{unit}/\#\mathtt{unit}] \mid (\mathrm{rn}[\mathtt{op}/\#\mathtt{arc}] \circ_{\#\mathtt{arc}} LG.\#\mathtt{conn})) \circ_{\#\mathtt{conn},\#\mathtt{unit}} (\mathtt{iter}:\#\mathrm{IT}): I_{\mathrm{IT}} \rightarrow E_{\mathrm{IT}}}\rightarrow I
$$

$I_{\#\mathrm{C}1}$ and $E_{\#\mathrm{C}1}$ denote the import and export parts of interface $\#\mathrm{C}1$ (included from LG and hidden by $LGIT$). The *hiding renaming* $\mathrm{rn}[\mathtt{unit}/\#\mathtt{unit}]$ generates the clause $\#\mathtt{unit}(X): -\mathtt{unit}(X)$ (# preserves the model theoretic semantics). $\mathrm{rn}[\mathtt{op}/\#\mathtt{arc}]$ is not a purely hiding renaming. It requires to prove $\mathtt{op}(x,y,z) \leftrightarrow \mathtt{arc}(x,y,z)$ in the context and generates $\#\mathtt{arc}(X,Y,Z): -\mathtt{op}(X,Y,Z)$. The operation $\mid$ is parallel program composition. $LGIT$ *extends* IT and $LGIT.\mathtt{iter}$ *correctly overrides* $IT.\mathtt{iter}$ (the exported $\mathtt{iter}$ programs implement the same interface).

---

[2] Importing $\#\mathtt{conn}$ from an heterogeneous LG, the communication channel $(\mathrm{rn}[] \circ_{\#\mathtt{conn}} (\mathtt{iter}: \#\mathrm{IT}))$ would be generated.

3   Behaviours and Program Composition

In this section, we define *behaviours* and we discuss the rationale behind them. A *behaviour* represents the knowledge obtained from an *observation* of a program unit by calling some of its procedures. The observer may be a human or another procedure. A call is characterized by the observed *call statement* C and by the *activation substitution* α, indicating the values observed for the variables of C when the call is activated. For conciseness, we do not consider negation, i.e., C is an atom. We call $C\alpha$ an *activation*. The (call corresponding to an) activation $C\alpha$ starts a computation, which may succeed, fail, yield an error or loop. According to the case, we define the *answer of* $C\alpha$ as follows:

- If the computation started by $C\alpha$ yields an error or loops, we do not have any answers.
- If the computation started by $C\alpha$ succeeds, we get an *answer substitution* β, indicating the values returned for the variables of $C\alpha$, if any.
- If the computation started by $C\alpha$ fails, we get the *negative answer* NO.

To consider backtracking, we use an *observation index*. The same index is only used when a call is repeated (by backtracking) to obtain a new answer. Otherwise, different observations have different index. Thus we define observation sequences and their components as follows (components underline backtracking).

- An *observation sequence* S is a sequence of *observations* of the form $\langle c : C\alpha, \beta \rangle$, where $C\alpha$ is an activation with observation index c and β is its answer
- the *component* with index c of S is the sequence $S[c]$ obtained by deleting all the observations of S with index different from c.

Example 3. Let us consider the composite procedure sum $\circ_{\text{sum}}$ prod:

$$\begin{aligned}
&\text{sum}: \quad \text{sum}(X, 0, X). \\
&\qquad\qquad \text{sum}(X, s(Y), s(Z)) :- \text{sum}(X, Y, Z). \\
&\text{prod}: \text{prod}(X, 0, 0). \\
&\qquad\qquad \text{prod}(X, s(Y), Z) \quad :- \text{prod}(X, Y, P), \text{sum}(P, X, Z).
\end{aligned}$$

If prod observes the call statement sum(P, X, Z) in the computation of prod$(s(0), s(s(0)), 0)$, it obtains the following sequence S with components $S[1]$, $S[2]$:

$$\begin{aligned}
S \ &= \ \langle 1 : sum(0, s(0), v_0), v_0 = s(0) \rangle, \langle 2 : sum(s(0), s(0), 0), \text{NO} \rangle, \\
&\qquad \langle 1 : sum(0, s(0), v_0), \text{NO} \rangle \\
S[1] &= \ \langle 1 : sum(0, s(0), v_0), v_0 = s(0) \rangle, \langle 1 : sum(0, s(0), v_0), \text{NO} \rangle \\
S[2] &= \ \langle 2 : sum(s(0), s(0), 0), \text{NO} \rangle
\end{aligned}$$

The following property is required (and assumed) in our approach.

Property 3.1. Let $S[c] = \langle c : C\alpha, \beta_1 \rangle, \ldots, \langle c : C\alpha, \beta_n \rangle$ be a component of an observation sequence S. If β_n is NO, then $\langle c : C\alpha, \beta_n \rangle$ is the last observation with observation index c occurring in S.

Property 3.1 codifies the fact that backtracking halts when the answer NO is reached. We define the *behaviour* $\mathcal{B}_{S[c]}$ of a component $S[c]$ as the following set of *b*-formulae:

- An atom A belongs to $\mathcal{B}_{S[c]}$ iff $S[c]$ contains an observation $\langle c : C\alpha, \beta \rangle$ s.t. $A = C\alpha\beta$.
- $T(\forall y.\ y \neq t_1 \wedge \cdots \wedge y \neq t_h \rightarrow \neg C\alpha)$ belongs to $\mathcal{B}_{S[c]}$ iff the last answer of $S[c]$ is NO and $t_1, \ldots, t_h$ are all the ground terms associated with the open variables y of $C\alpha$ by the answer substitutions of $S[c]$.

We define the *behaviour* $\mathcal{B}_S$ associated with an observation sequence S as the union of the behaviours of its components.

Example 4. The behaviours corresponding to the observation sequences of Ex. 3 are:
$$\mathcal{B}_{S[1]} = \{sum(0, s(0), s(0)), T(\forall x.\ x \neq s(0) \rightarrow \neg sum(0, s(0), x))\}$$
$$\mathcal{B}_{S[2]} = \{T(\neg sum(s(0), s(0), 0))\}$$
$$\mathcal{B}_S\ \ = \mathcal{B}_{S[1]} \cup \mathcal{B}_{S[2]}$$

Now we link behaviours and unit composition at the program level. A procedure p exported by P *depends* on a set π of import procedures of P iff every procedure called by the program implementing p belongs to π. By $P : \pi \Rightarrow \delta$ we mean that δ is the set of the export procedures, π is a set of import procedures and the procedures of δ depend on π. If $P : \emptyset \Rightarrow \delta$, P is a *closed program unit*, i.e., every and each program does not need other imported procedures to run. Program composition occurs when the contexts of two units have been merged. We can model this stage by two C-units $P = \langle \Sigma, C, Prog_1 \rangle$ and $Q = \langle \Sigma, C, Prog_2 \rangle$ with a common context C, which specifies *the import, export and hidden procedures of both $Prog_1$ and $Prog_2$*. That is, a set of C-units is a set of separate program units with a common context C. C-units can be composed by *restriction*, *parallel* and *import composition*, yielding new C-units, as follows:

> *Restriction.* The *restriction* $R.\delta$ of R to a subset δ of the exported procedures is the C-unit where those procedures and related interfaces not in δ have been deleted.
> *Parallel composition.* The parallel composition $R \mid S$ is defined only if $R : \pi_1 \Rightarrow \delta_1$, $S : \pi_2 \Rightarrow \delta_2$, and $(\pi_1 \cup \pi_2) \cap (\delta_1 \cup \delta_2) = \emptyset$. The resulting C-unit contains and exports $R.\delta_1$ and $S.\delta_2$, i.e.: $R \mid S : \pi_1 \cup \pi_2 \Rightarrow \delta_1 \cup \delta_2$. The (possible) shared procedures must have the same interfaces and implementations. We have: $R \mid S = S \mid R$.
> *Import composition.* The import composition $R \circ_\gamma S$ is defined only if $R : \pi_1 \Rightarrow \delta_1 \cup \gamma$, $S : \pi_2 \cup \gamma \Rightarrow \delta_2$ and $(\pi_1 \cup \pi_2) \cap (\delta_1 \cup \delta_2) = \emptyset$. The resulting C-unit exports $R.\delta_1$ and the procedures $R.\gamma$ are locally composed with $S.\delta_2$, so that they no longer depend on γ, i.e.: $R \circ_\gamma S : \pi_1 \cup \pi_2 \Rightarrow \delta_1 \cup \delta_2$. We have: $R \circ_{\gamma_1} (S \circ_{\gamma_2} T) = (R \circ_{\gamma_1} S) \circ_{\gamma_2} T$ and, if $R \mid S$ is defined, $R \circ_{\gamma_1} (S \circ_{\gamma_2} T) = (R \mid S) \circ_{\gamma_1 \cup \gamma_2} T$.

Example 5. We consider C-units $P = \langle \Sigma, C, Prog \rangle$ containing logic programs. Within P, we associate the axioms $Ax(\mathrm{p}) = Ocomp(\mathrm{p}) \cup CET(\mathrm{p})$ with the program-clauses implementing a procedure $P.\mathrm{p}$, where $Ocomp(\mathrm{p})$ is the open completion of (the clauses implementing) p [11] and $CET(\mathrm{p})$ is Clark's Equality Theory for p [12]. The operation $P \mid Q$ is defined if the general conditions introduced above for composition are satisfied and $Ax(\delta_1 \cup \delta_2) = Ax(\delta_1) \cup Ax(\delta_2)$. The resulting C-unit contains and exports the programs for $\delta_1 \cup \delta_2$. Operation $P \circ_\gamma Q$ is defined if the general conditions introduced above for composition are satisfied and $Ax(\delta_1 \cup \gamma \cup \delta_2) = Ax(\delta_1 \cup \gamma) \cup Ax(\delta_2)$. The resulting C-unit contains the programs for $\delta_1 \cup \gamma \cup \delta_2$, hides γ and exports $\delta_1 \cup \delta_2$. The hidden procedures γ are used locally by δ_2. Going back to Ex. 3, if *SUM* is the closed unit exporting sum and *PROD* the one importing the latter and exporting prod, the import composition $SUM.\text{sum} \circ_{\text{sum}} PROD.\text{prod} : \emptyset \Rightarrow \text{prod}$ is defined and satisfies the above requirements. As we have seen, if we are only using Prolog programs, it suffices to put the various programs together, in the same name space. Hiding may be performed, e.g., by renaming. If we are using heterogeneous programs, we need also an environment supporting the communication among them. This is necessary for import composition.

Let $P \circ_\gamma Q : \emptyset \Rightarrow \delta$ be a C-unit. We can build an observation sequence S_E by means of calls to δ. We call S_E an *experiment for* $P \circ_\gamma Q$. While doing the experiment S_E, we observe the calls performed by Q on γ. We obtain an observation sequence S_I, with a behaviour $\mathcal{B}_{S_I}$. We say that S_I is an *interface observation sequence* and $\mathcal{B}_{S_I}$ is an *interface behaviour* for $P \circ_\gamma Q$. We can abstract from the "server" unit P by introducing generic behaviours and "oracles".

A *generic b-formula* is a ground procedure-atom (i.e., built by a procedure symbol) or a T-formula of the form $T(\forall x. \neq t_1 \wedge \cdots \wedge x \neq t_n \rightarrow \neg A)$, where A is a procedure-atom with variables x. A *generic behaviour* is a consistent set $\mathcal{B}$ of generic b-formulae. $\mathcal{B}$ is an *import behaviour for* Q if the atoms of $\mathcal{B}$ contain only import procedures of Q. We now introduce $\mathcal{B}$-oracles ($\mathcal{B}[o]$): when an activation $C\alpha$ is performed with observation index c, a $\mathcal{B}$-oracle $\mathcal{B}[o]$ yields one of the following answers:

- $\langle c : C\alpha, \beta \rangle$, if there is an atom $A \in \mathcal{B}$ such that $A = C\alpha\beta$, or
- $\langle c : C\alpha, \text{NO} \rangle$, if $\mathcal{B}$ contains $T(\forall y. \, y \neq t_1 \wedge \cdots \wedge y \neq t_n \rightarrow \neg C\alpha)$ and all the possible answers to $C\alpha$ have been given in previous steps, or
- the computation aborts, if none of the previous cases holds.

If there are different possible answers, the oracle makes a choice. It is only obliged to be *fair* on backtracking, that is, if an answer of an activation $C\alpha$ can be chosen, it will be. An oracle $\mathcal{B}[o]$ for a finite behaviour $\mathcal{B}$ can (in principle) be implemented and composed with other programs. To simulate moded procedures, an oracle may be moded. A *moded oracle* $\mathcal{B}[o_\mu]$ has a set μ of moded call statements and aborts if a call is activated that is not allowed by μ.

Example 6. Let P be a C-unit containing logic programs and $\mathcal{B}$ be an import behaviour for P. A $\mathcal{B}$-oracle is a logic program that contains every atom $A \in \mathcal{B}$ as a fact and suitable clauses that abort the program when required. For example, the following program is an oracle for the behaviour $\mathcal{B}$ of Ex. 3.

```
sum(0, s(0), s(0)).
sum(s(0), s(0), s(s(0))).
sum(X, Y, Z) : − not((X == 0, Y == s(0))),
              not((X == s(0), Y == s(0), Z == s(s(0)))), abort.
```

Different oracles are obtained by changing the order of the facts and allowing possible repetitions. As an example of another kind of programming language style, we can consider program units containing imperative style procedures. If we only allow input-output procedures, the modes will always be of the kind $!p(x^+ ; y^\downarrow)$. In the context, a model-theoretic specification S_p specifies p as a predicate. By the input mode x^+, we declare that x are value parameters. By $y^\downarrow$ we denote the *reference mode* (var-parameters in Pascal). In an activation, reference parameters can be only replaced by variables. Oracles can be defined as follows: when a computation performs a call to an imported procedure q, we provide the result by a table-look-up mechanism, where the table contains a finite part of $\mathcal{B}$. By the selection mode !, only the first answer is considered; the computation aborts if no answer is found or the activation is not allowed by $!p(x^+ ; y^\downarrow)$. That is, the oracle is moded.

If $\mathcal{J}$ is an interface behaviour of $P \circ_\gamma Q$ observed by an experiment S, then there is an oracle o_P such that $\mathcal{J}[o_P] \circ_\gamma Q$ replicates exactly the computation of $P \circ_\gamma Q$. However, a different oracle o' may yield a different computation of $\mathcal{J}[o'] \circ_\gamma Q$. We assume that Q is behaviourally stable (b-stable), i.e., we assume that for every o' there is an experiment S' for $\mathcal{J}[o'] \circ_\gamma Q$ with the same observed behaviour ($\mathcal{B}_{S'} \supseteq \mathcal{B}_S$ suffices). B-stability of Q means that it is able to cooperate with external units (simulated by the oracles) independently from the backtracking details, such as order or repetitions of the answers. We believe b-stability should be a property of high-level program units, because this enhances their re-usability. In the next section we will consider b-stability with respect to the moded import behaviours that realize their specification.

4   Behaviour Specifications and Their Realization

A *constructive specification* is a Σ-formula given by the following syntax, where *BF* stands for b-formulas (atoms built by a procedure symbol) and *TF* for *T*-formulas (of the form $T(F)$, where F is any Σ-formula):

$$\begin{aligned}
&\textit{Basic specifications } BS ::= BF \mid TF.\\
&\textit{Existential specifications } ES ::= BS \mid ES \wedge ES \mid ES \vee ES \mid \exists x.\, ES.\\
&\textit{Universal specifications } US ::= ES \mid US \wedge US \mid \forall x.\, US.\\
&\textit{Interfaces } IC ::= US \mid US \rightarrow IC \mid IC \wedge IC \mid \forall x.\, IC.
\end{aligned}$$

Universal specifications are a description of behaviours that are realized (exported) or used (imported) by a program unit. Interfaces relate imported and exported behaviours and model correct unit composition. They will be explained in the next section. Here, we consider universal specifications and their realization by closed C-units within a signature Σ. For behaviours of closed programs we assume that data are *reachable* (i.e., representable by ground Σ-terms). The partial model theoretic correctness of programs is assumed, to ensure the truth (in C) of the observed b-formulas. Thus a *behaviour correct in C is a set $\mathcal{B}$ of b-formulas of the signature Σ, such that $C \models \mathcal{B}$.*

The *behaviour semantics* of universal specifications is given by the *realization* relation $\Vdash$. We write $P \Vdash H$ to denote that a C-unit P realizes a specification H. This means that H is realized by the observable behaviour of P, in the way informally explained in Sect. 2. We firstly define realizability by correct behaviours, considered as sets of b-formulas true in C. Then we define it by program units.

Definition 1 (Behaviour Realizability). *Let $\mathcal{B}$ be a behaviour correct in C and E a ground instance of an ES. Then $\mathcal{B} \Vdash E$ iff one of the following clauses applies:*
Basis. *For a T-formula $T(F)$, $\mathcal{B} \Vdash T(F)$ iff $C \models F$.*
For a b-formula B, $\mathcal{B} \Vdash B$ iff $B \in \mathcal{B}$.

Step. *According to the cases, we have:*

- $\mathcal{B} \models F \wedge G$ *iff* $\mathcal{B} \models F$ *and* $\mathcal{B} \models G$.
- $\mathcal{B} \models F \vee G$ *iff* $\mathcal{B} \models F$ *or* $\mathcal{B} \models G$.
- $\mathcal{B} \models \exists x.\ F(x)$ *iff there is a ground term t such that* $\mathcal{B} \models F(t)$.
- $\mathcal{B} \models \forall x.\ F(x)$ *iff* $\mathcal{B} \models F(t)$, *for every ground term t.*

Theorem 1. *Let $\mathcal{B}$ be a correct behaviour and U an US. $\mathcal{B} \models U$ entails $C \models U$.*

That is, the realized formulas are true in the context (assuming reachability). In the previous definition, behaviours may be infinite. Behaviors of observation sequences are finite. The following theorem can be easily proved.

Theorem 2. *Let E be an ES and $\mathcal{B} \models E$. Then there is a finite $\mathcal{B}' \subseteq \mathcal{B}$ s.t. $\mathcal{B}' \models E$.*

A realization of a universal specification U is, in general, infinite. It can be seen as the unions of the finite realizations of the existential instances of U.

Definition 2 (Inst(U)). *The set $Inst(U)$ of the instances of a ground universal specification U is the smallest subset of formulas satisfying the following clauses:*

- *if U is an ES, then $U \in Inst(U)$;*
- *if t is a ground term and $F \in Inst(H(t))$, then $F \in Inst(\forall x.\ H(x))$;*
- *if $F \in Inst(H)$ and $G \in Inst(K)$, then $F \wedge G \in Inst(H \wedge K)$.*
- *If U is open, $Inst(U)$ is the union of the $Inst(U\sigma)$, where σ is a grounding substitution.*

Theorem 3. *Let U be a ground universal specification and $\mathcal{B}$ be a behaviour. $\mathcal{B} \models U$ iff for every instance $E \in Inst(U)$ there is a finite $\mathcal{B}' \subseteq \mathcal{B}$ s.t. $\mathcal{B}' \models E$.*

Now we can consider realizability by program units. Since T-formulas do not require any realization, the (possible) procedure symbols occurring in them do not require computations. We say that they are *hidden* by T, or *inactive*; non-hidden occurrences are called *active*. A specification S is an *export specification* for a closed program unit $P : \emptyset \Rightarrow \delta$ iff the active call statements of S have procedure symbols from δ. Program realizability is defined starting from finite experiments. Let E be a ground export existential specification for P. We say that P *realizes E with a (finite) experiment S*, written $P \models_S E$, iff S is a finite experiment for P such that $\mathcal{B}_S \models E$. For a universal specification U, we need to validate the various instances $I \in Inst(U)$ by U-*moded experiments*, namely experiments that apply moded call statements from U.

Definition 3 (Program Realizability of US). *Let U be an export universal specification for a closed C-unit P. $P \models U$ iff for every instance $I \in Inst(U)$ there is an U-moded experiment S s.t. $P \models_S I$.*

Export US are specifications for closed program units. In particular, decision, enumeration, selection and functional behaviours can be specified as explained in Sect. 2. We can use a universal specification U also as an assumption on the expected import behaviuor of an open unit. In this case, U states the following *collaboration agreement*:

a client unit Q is assumed to apply only moded call statements of U, while a server unit P is assumed to answer without loop or abort errors, when it is called according to the modes declared in U. Concerning the server side (the client side will be considered in the next section), we require correct moding, as the past history is needed to properly treat the call index i.

Definition 4 (Correct Moding). *Let U be an export universal specification for a closed C-unit P. U is correctly moded with respect to P iff every U-moded experiment S for P can be continued into an experiment $S, \langle i : C\alpha, ans \rangle$, whenever the activation $i : C\alpha$ is legal with respect to the modes of U and the past history S.*

5 Interfaces

Interfaces allow us to specify open program units and their clients relations. To properly abstract from moded server units, we introduce U-*moded $\mathcal{J}$-oracles* $\mathcal{J}[o_U]$, where $\mathcal{J}$ is a possibly infinite [3] behaviour, U is a universal specification and o_U is a moded oracle with moded call statements from U. An experiment S for $\mathcal{J}[o_U]$ is obtained through the answers chosen by o_U and $\mathcal{J}[o_U] \models U$ is defined as in Def. 3. We assume *fairness* (if $\mathcal{J}$ contains an answer for a call statement $i : ?C\alpha$, this answer will be chosen by o_U) and *correct moding* (U is correctly moded with respect to o_U, i.e., each legal continuation of an experiment is answered by o_U).

For every server program unit P realizing U there are a behaviour $\mathcal{J}$ and an U-moded oracle o_U, such that the experiments of P coincide with those of $\mathcal{J}[o_U]$. We use $\mathcal{J}[o_U]$ as abstractions of server units and we introduce the semantics of interfaces. We proceed gradually. We say that $U \to V$ is a *simple interface* if U, V are universal specifications. U must be an *import specification*, that is a specification with only import-active call statements. It is an assumption on the possible import behaviours. V must be an *export specification*, that is a specification with only export-active call statements. It states the expected export behaviour.

Definition 5 (Realizability for Simple Interfaces). *Let Q be a C-unit and $U \to V$ a simple interface. $Q \models U \to V$ iff U is an import specification, V an export specification and for every import oracle $\mathcal{J}[o_U]$ such that $\mathcal{J}[o_U] \models U$, it holds $\mathcal{J}[o_U] \circ_U Q \models V$.*

This definition of realisability requires b-stability (see Sect. 3) with respect to the behaviours realizing U (we may choose, for a behaviour $\mathcal{J}$, any oracle o_U). The compositional meaning of simple interfaces is given by the following theorem.

Theorem 4. *Let P be a C-unit such that $P \models U$ and U correctly moded with respect to P and let Q be a C unit such that $Q \models U \to V$, for a simple interface $U \to V$. Then $P \circ_U Q \models H$.*

Simple interfaces represent simple composition rules, where the import behaviour U has to be realized by the server unit as a whole. It may be useful to choose server units

---

[3] We could consider only finite behaviours, but this would complicate our treatment.

incrementally, by building intermediate open units. To this aim, we allow conjunctions and right-nested implications. For example, the interfaces $U \to (V \to H)$ allows us to choose a server unit for U and delay the choice of the unit for V.

Definition 6 (Realizability for Interfaces). *Let Q be a C-unit and I be an IC. We inductively define* realizability, *as follows:*

B*asis. I is a universal specification. Realizability is defined as in the previous section.*
Step. According to the cases:

- *I is $U \to H$. We proceed by a secondary induction on H. The* base case *coincides with simple interfaces. The* step case *is as follows:*
  - H *is* $V \to K$. $Q \mathrel{|\joinrel\Vdash} U \to (V \to K)$ *iff* U, V *are universal import specifications for Q and $Q \mathrel{|\joinrel\Vdash} U \wedge V \to K$.*
  - H *is* $H_1 \wedge H_2$. $Q \mathrel{|\joinrel\Vdash} U \to (H_1 \wedge H_2)$ *iff U is a universal import specification for Q, $Q \mathrel{|\joinrel\Vdash} U \to H_1$ and $Q \mathrel{|\joinrel\Vdash} U \to H_2$.*
  - H *is* $U \to \forall x. H(x)$. $Q \mathrel{|\joinrel\Vdash} U \to \forall x. H(x)$ *iff U is a universal import specification for Q and $Q \mathrel{|\joinrel\Vdash} U \to H(t)$, for every ground term t.*
- *I is $H \wedge K$. $Q \mathrel{|\joinrel\Vdash} H \wedge K$ iff $Q \mathrel{|\joinrel\Vdash} H$ and $Q \mathrel{|\joinrel\Vdash} K$.*
- *I is $\forall x. H(x)$. $Q \mathrel{|\joinrel\Vdash} \forall x. H(x)$ iff $Q \mathrel{|\joinrel\Vdash} H(t)$ for every ground t.*

Composition proofs, bridge proofs and correct modes. The compositional meaning of interfaces is given by the rules of the compositional calculus shown in Sect. 5.1. By these rules, we can correctly compose C-units at the program level. Our syntax distinguishes universal specifications and interfaces. Correspondingly, we have two kinds of proofs. A proof that applies only the renaming rule rn and the rules for $\to$, $\wedge$, $\forall$ to interfaces is called a *composition proof*. It allows us to compose units whose interfaces match via (possible) renaming. If this level of "exact" matching fails, then we de-structure the universal specifications used in the interfaces and we try to re-structure them in a different form, by means of the other rules and possible "bridge lemmas", such as $bdl1$ in Ex. 2. Proofs of this kind are called *bridge proofs*. Correct modes are required to prove the validity theorem (Thm. 5). They are preserved by composition proofs, but might be destroyed by the bridge proofs. For example, a (trivial) unit containing the procedure $p(a)$ realizes $\exists x. \, !p(x^-)$. If we apply the $\vee I_2$-rule without restrictions, we prove that it realizes $\exists x. \, !p(x^-) \vee \exists x. \, !q(x^-)$. But $: -q(X)$ fails, while it should succeed by mode !. Thus correct moding should be always checked in bridge proofs. Fortunately, there are universal specifications that are correctly moded independently from the implementation details. Specifications of this kind are called *correctly moded* (with respect to any unit P). They have the following property: for every instance $E \in Inst(U)$, every finite behaviour $\mathcal{B}$ such that $\mathcal{B} \mathrel{|\joinrel\Vdash} E$, and every moded oracle o_U (applying the modes of U), there is an observation sequence S for $\mathcal{B}[o_U]$ such that $\mathcal{B}[o] \mathrel{|\joinrel\Vdash}_S E$. There are *syntactical sufficient conditions* for correct moding (omitted here). For example, $A \vee T(F)$ is correctly moded if so is A and it has the query mode (modes of complex formulas are determined starting from those in call statements).

Bidirectional interfaces. In our syntax, interfaces model *unidirectional composition*. If we enlarge the syntax by allowing interfaces of the form $(H \to K) \to R$, we can model *bidirectional composition*. We have not yet completed the analysis of this case, so we only briefly comment on it, by considering the simpler case $(U \to V) \to W$, with U, V, W universal specifications. The active procedures that occur positively (namely in U and W) must be export procedures, while the ones occurring negatively (namely in V) must be import procedures. Moreover, the export procedures of U must not depend on the import procedures of V. In this case, the interface correctly specifies a bidirectional collaboration, as follows. We say that $Q \models (U \to V) \to W$ iff $Q \models U$ and $Q \models V \to W$. A server unit P has to realize $U \to V$. We want to get a bidirectional composition $\circ_{U \to V}$ such that $P \circ_{U \to V} Q \models W$. Under our hypotheses, we can say: $P \circ_{U \to V} Q = (Q \circ_U P) \circ_V Q$. That is, P uses the behaviour for U exported by Q to realize the behaviour for V needed by Q. Q uses this behaviour to realize W.

5.1   The Compositional Calculus

In this section we present a possible compositional calculus, where proof-trees are in the style of natural deduction. The root of a proof-tree is of the form $P : A$, where P is a logic program and A is a constructive specification. $P : A$ is the *consequence* of the proof tree. Assumptions are specifications. The rules are shown next.

$$\frac{H_1, \ldots, H_n}{P : T(F)} \, \text{tt}(L) \qquad \frac{H_1, \ldots, H_n}{P : A} \, \text{pr}(L) \qquad \frac{false}{P : A} \, \text{ff} \qquad \frac{H_1, \ldots, H_n}{\text{rn}[\rho] : \rho \, H_i} \, \text{rn} \qquad \frac{P_i : A}{P_1 \mid P_2 : A} \, |_i$$

$$\frac{P : A_1 \qquad P : A_2}{P : A_1 \wedge A_2} \, \wedge I \qquad \frac{P : A_1 \wedge A_2}{P : A_i} \, \wedge E_i \qquad \frac{P : A_i}{P : A_1 \vee A_2} \, \vee I_i \qquad \frac{A_1 \vee A_2 \qquad \overset{[A_1] \quad [A_2]}{\overset{\vdots \quad \vdots}{P : C \quad P : C}}}{P : C} \, \vee E$$

$$\frac{P : A(t)}{P : \exists x. A(x)} \, \exists I \qquad \frac{\exists x. A(x) \qquad \overset{[A(a)]}{\overset{\vdots}{P : C}}}{P : C} \, \exists E \qquad \frac{\overset{[A]}{\overset{\vdots}{P : B}}}{P : A \to B} \to I \qquad \frac{P : A \qquad Q : A \to B}{P \circ_A Q : B} \to E$$

$$\frac{P : A(a)}{P : \forall x. A(x)} \, \forall I \qquad \frac{P : \forall x. A(x)}{P : A(t)} \, \forall E$$

The rules apply to C-units at the program level. The program rule $\text{pr}(L_j)$ allows us to use an already proven pr-*"lemma"* L_j about a unit P. It is also possible to introduce knowledge from the problem context by the rule $\text{tt}(L_k)$, indicating a tt-*"lemma"* L_k, proving $C \models H_1 \wedge \cdots \wedge H_n \to F$. Lemmas (in particular tt-lemmas) are not necessarily developed in the compositional calculus, but may use any system consistent with classical logic, or they may be informal. Rule rn encodes renaming, which may be needed for hiding or bridging purposes (see Ex. 2). The application of rn is systematically enforced by our calculus (programs do not occur in the assumptions, but are needed in the consequences). The idea is that renaming correspond to "communication channels". The way of forcing renaming is preliminary and needs to be further experimented. The other rules are similar to the ones of intuitionistic predicate logic. The usual provisos apply. We require also that the involved formulas are constructive specifications in the syntax given in Sect. 4. This entails, in particular, that the assumptions may only be universal specifications and that the rules for $\vee, \exists$ can be only applied to existential specifications. To deal with assumptions, we enlarge our definition of interface and allow interface sequents $\Gamma \Rightarrow K$, where Γ is a set of interfaces that are universal specifications:

Definition 7 (Realizability for Interface Sequents). *Let* $\Gamma \Rightarrow K$ *be an interface sequent for a C-unit P. We say that P realizes* $\Gamma \Rightarrow K$, *written* $P \parallel\!\!= \Gamma \Rightarrow K$, *iff for every grounding* Σ*-substitution* σ, $P \parallel\!\!= (\wedge(\Gamma) \to K)\sigma$.

The following theorem states the validity of the calculus. The proof considers separately the bridge proofs, which structure and de-structure universal specifications and the composition proofs, which structure and de-structure the interfaces. For the bridge proofs, the preservation of correct moding ought to be checked.

Theorem 5 (Validity). *Consider a proof-tree with assumptions* Γ *and consequence* P : H. *If the (possibly informal)* tt*-lemmas and* pr*-lemmas are correct, then* $P \parallel\!\!= \Gamma \Rightarrow H$.

6   Discussion

Constructive specifications make explicit aspects that are important for correct composition. They are based on correct modes and on a constructive semantics. This semantics is not alternative, but complementary to our previous model-theoretic approach [10]: the reference semantics still remains classical model theory and constructive logic is used to obtain more expressive interface specifications. The idea of using constructive logic to specify interfaces has been influenced by [16], even if we use a different semantics. The semantics and the calculus explained here are a first step and have been inspired by the *collection semantics* introduced in [13, 14] to prove constructivity results for intermediate first order systems. The T-operator for formulas that are not constructively evaluated comes from [15]. The use of distinguished levels for the problem context and for programs and their interfaces, as well as the possibility of using different programming languages is similar to the Larch specification language [8], although in the latter constructive logic is not used. We next outline some improvements to our work.

Constructive proofs bridging not exactly coinciding specifications are, in general, simpler than the proofs needed to derive programs from scratch. A study of proof strategies oriented to module composition and reuse would be interesting.

Behaviours with closed formulae allow us to capture input-output modes with ground results and the query mode. A possible improvement, as far as logic programs are concerned, is to consider open b-formulas, as e.g. in [1], to capture more general kinds of modes and compositions, including open answers.

The restriction to correctly moded universal specifications guarantees that a constructive evaluation of the export specifications of a server program unit P can be obtained by a client unit Q, by querying P. This explains also our restricted syntax. For example, we do not allow a disjunction such as $(\forall x. A(x)) \vee (\forall x. B(x))$. Indeed, to state that $(A(t)$ holds for all the ground terms t), or $(B(t)$ does), a (possibly) infinite computation is needed. On the other hand, if we know that, say, $\forall x.\ A(x)$ holds, we can use this information by inserting it in the behaviour. In this way, is possible to use any first order formula as a constructive specification. The price to pay is that we have to introduce in behaviours the knowledge needed to trace constructive evaluations, along the lines of [13]. The advantage of a restricted syntax is that it adapts to the operational semantics of any kind of programs, with the only requirement that the model theoretic meaning of the procedures and functions is to be specified in the context.

Nevertheless, it is useful to investigate possible extensions, related to other kinds of module operations. In particular, it would be useful to extend ∘ to bidirectional collaboration of program units. This corresponds to the use of implications of the form $(A \to B) \to C$. From a first partial analysis of this case (see the discussion in Sect. 5), it seems that it can be treated without altering the general lines of our approach. In this way we get a notion of interface that has similarities to the one discussed in [3].

The requirement of b-stability is suited to relatively complete programs, while it may not work for small pieces of code. In this case a lower level of abstraction is required. It can be introduced by a different definition of the behaviour associated to observation sequences and experiments. We believe that an analysis of different levels of abstraction is interesting and potentially fruitful. In particular, it would be interesting to consider behaviours as multisets to exploit the use of linear logic programming techniques [9] to express properties of program units that consume resources and to consider their geometry of collaboration.

In this paper we have concentrated on the definition of behaviour semantics and we have devised a first composition calculus. We have a validity result. It is difficult to even define completeness, due to the presence of modes and the fact that we want to deal with heterogeneous systems. The next step is to experimentally check our ideas and our calculus in real examples, e.g. addressing case studies of formal specification.

References

1. A. Bossi, M. Gabbrielli, G. Levi, and M.C. Meo. A compositional semantics for logic programs. *Theoretical Computer Science*, 122:3–47, 1994.
2. M. Bugliesi, E. Lamma, and P. Mello. Modularity in logic programming. *J. Logic Programming*, 19-20:443–502, 1994. Special issue: Ten years of logic programming.
3. L. de Alfaro and T. Henzinger. Interface Theories for Component-based Design Proc. of EMSOFT 2001, LNCS 2211, pp. 148–165, Springer Verlag, 2001.
4. S.K. Debray. Static Inference of Modes and Data Dependencies in Logic Programs, ACM Transactions on Programming Languages and Systems, 11(3):418–450, 1989.
5. Y. Deville. *Logic Programming. Systematic Program Development.* Addison-Wesley, 1990.
6. D.F. D'Souza and A.C. Wills. *Objects, Components, and Frameworks with UML: The Catalysis Approach.* Addison-Wesley, 1999.
7. H. Ehrig and B. Mahr. *Fundamentals of Algebraic Specification 2.* Springer-Verlag, 1989.
8. J.V. Guttag and J.J. Horning. *Larch: Languages and Tools for Formal Specification.* Springer-Verlag, 1993.
9. J. Hodas and D. Miller. Logic Programming in a Fragment of Intuitionistic Linear Logic. *Information and Computation*, 110(2):327–365, 1994.

10. K.-K. Lau and M. Ornaghi. Specifying Compositional Units for Correct Program Development in Computational Logic. *Program Development in Computational Logic: A Decade of Research Advances in Logic-Based Program Development*, LNCS, vol 3049, pp. 1–29, 2004
11. K.-K. Lau, M. Ornaghi, and S.-Å. Tärnlund. Steadfast logic programs. *J. Logic Programming*, 38(3):259–294, March 1999.
12. J.W. Lloyd. *Foundations of Logic Programming*. 2nd ed., Springer-Verlag, 1987.
13. P. Miglioli, M. Ornaghi. A logically justified model of computation I , II *Fundamenta Informaticae*, 4(1): 151-172, 4(2): 277-342 , 1981.
14. P. Miglioli, U. Moscato, M. Ornaghi. Constructive theories with abstract data types for program synthesis In D.G. Skordev, editor, *Mathematical Logic and its Applications*, pages 293–302. Plenum Press, 1987.
15. P. Miglioli, U. Moscato, M. Ornaghi and G. Usberti. A Constructivism based on classical truth *Notre Dame Journal of Formal Logic*, 30(1):67–90, 1989.
16. D. Miller. A logical analysis of modules in logic programming. *JLP*, 6(1-2):79–108, 1989.
17. C. Szyperski, D. Gruntz, and S. Murer. *Component Software: Beyond Object-Oriented Programming*. Addison-Wesley, second edition, 2002.

Input-Termination of Logic Programs

M.R.K. Krishna Rao

Information and Computer Science Department,
King Fahd University of Petroleum and Minerals,
Dhahran 31261, Saudi Arabia
krishna@ccse.kfupm.edu.sa

Abstract. In this paper, we study termination properties of input-consuming derivations of moded logic programs. Input-consuming derivations can be used to model the behavior of logic programs using dynamic scheduling and employing constructs such as delay declarations. A class of logic programs called linear bounded programs is introduced and input-termination of these programs is investigated. It is proved that linear bounded programs have only input-consuming LD-derivations (i.e., under Prolog's selection) of finite length. An attempt is then made to extend this result to all input-consuming derivations (not ncessarily under Prolog's selection). Through a counterexample, it is shown that the above result does not hold for the whole class of linear bounded programs under arbitrary selection. However, it is proved that simply-moded linear bounded programs have only input-consuming derivations of finite length, i.e., simply-moded linear bounded programs are input-terminating with dynamic scheduling. This class contains many programs like append, delete, insert, reverse, permute, count, listsum, listproduct, insertion-sort, quick-sort on lists, various tree traversal programs and addition, multiplication, factorial, power on natural numbers. Further, it is decidable whether a given logic program is linear bounded or not, in contrast to the notions of acceptable and recurrent programs.

1 Introduction

Termination is an important property of imperative as well as declarative programs and proving termination is one of the main steps in arriving at a sound methodology and for proving the correctness of programs. Recently, termination of logic programs has attracted a lot of attention and many approaches are reported in the literature — see a.o. [3-7,9-16,18-22].

In this paper, we study termination of moded programs under dynamic scheduling. In particular, input-termination of logic programs is investigated. Input-termination was introduced by Smaus [20] and further studied by Bossi et.al. [6, 7]. They defined a few classes of input terminating programs using notions of level mappings and models. The main disadvantage of these classes is that it is undecidable whether a given program belongs to these classes. This undecidability is not surprising as the termination problem is undecidable and

S. Etalle(Ed.): LOPSTR 2004, LNCS 3573, pp. 215–230, 2005.

the classes introduced in [6, 7] give necessary and sufficient conditions for input-termination.

In this paper, we introduce a class of logic programs called linear bounded programs and prove that every linear bounded program is input-terminating under Prolog's selection rule. It is proved that simply-moded linear bounded programs are input-terminating under arbitrary selection rules. A simple counterexample is provided to show that a linear bounded program (if it is not simply-moded) can have an infinite input-consuming derivation under an arbitrary selection rule.

The notion of linear bounded programs is purely syntactic and it is decidable whether a given program is linear bounded or not. The class of linear bounded programs is rich enough to include many natural programs like, append, delete, insert, reverse, permute, count, listsum, listproduct, insertion-sort, quick-sort on lists, various tree traversal programs and addition, multiplication, factorial, power on natural numbers. Unlike the recent approaches like that of Lagoon et.al. [16], the notion of linear bounded programs does not use types. This simplicity together with the decidability and expressive power (to include many natural programs) makes the class of linear bounded programs very interesting.

The rest of the paper is organized as follows. The next section gives preliminary definitions needed later and section 3 defines linear bounded programs and proves the decidability result. Section 4 proves that all input-consuming LD-derivations of linear bounded programs are of finite length and Section 5 proves that all input-consuming derivations of simply-moded linear bounded programs are of finite length, even under arbitrary selection rules.

2   Preliminaries

We assume that the reader is familiar with logic programming concepts and follow the notations of Lloyd [17] and Apt [1].

Definition 1. A *mode* m of an n-ary predicate p is a function from $\{1, \cdots, n\}$ to the set $\{in,\ out\}$. The set $in(p) = \{i \leq n \mid m(i) = in\}$ is the set of input positions of p and $out(p) = \{o \leq n \mid m(o) = out\}$ is the set of output positions of p.

A moded program is a logic program with each predicate having a unique mode associated with it. In the rest of the paper, we assume that the moding information of all the predicates is available. However, this does not mean that the programmer has to supply this information as there are many techniques available in the literature (e.g., [8]) for deriving moding information from a given logic program.

Remark 1. It may be noted that some predicates may be used in different modes in a single program. We use different subscripts to a predicate to differentiate between different modings (usages).

Notation: In the following, $p(\mathbf{s}; \mathbf{t})$ denotes an atom with a sequence $\mathbf{s}$ of input terms and a sequence $\mathbf{t}$ of output terms. Without loss of generality, we assume that input positions of a predicate precede its output positions.

Definition 2. A moded program P is *simply-moded* [2] if each clause in it is simply-moded. A clause $p_0(\mathbf{s_0}; \mathbf{t_0}) \leftarrow p_1(\mathbf{s_1}; \mathbf{t_1}), \cdots, p_k(\mathbf{s_k}; \mathbf{t_k})$ is simply-moded if the following conditions are satisfied:

1. $\mathbf{t_1}, \cdots, \mathbf{t_k}$ is a linear sequence of variables,
2. $Var(\mathbf{s_0}) \cap (Var(\mathbf{t_1}), \cup \cdots \cup Var(\mathbf{t_k})) = \emptyset$ and
3. $Var(\mathbf{s_i}) \cap (Var(\mathbf{t_i}), \cup \cdots \cup Var(\mathbf{t_k})) = \emptyset$ for each $i \in [1, k]$.

A query $\leftarrow p_1(\mathbf{s_1}; \mathbf{t_1}), \cdots, p_k(\mathbf{s_k}; \mathbf{t_k})$ is simply-moded if conditions 1 and 3 are satisfied.

The following definitions from Smaus [20] defines the notion of input termination.

Definition 3. A derivation step for a program P is a pair $\langle Q, \theta \rangle; \langle R, \theta\sigma \rangle$, where $Q = Q_1, p(\mathbf{s}; \mathbf{t}), Q_2$ and $R = Q_1, B, Q_2$ are queries; θ is a substitution; $p(\mathbf{u}; \mathbf{v}) \leftarrow B$ is a renamed variant of a clause in P and σ is an MGU of $p(\mathbf{s}; \mathbf{t})$ and $p(\mathbf{u}; \mathbf{v})$. A *derivation step is input-consuming if* $dom(\sigma) \cap vars(\mathbf{s}\theta) = \emptyset$. *An input-consuming derivation is a sequence of input-consuming derivation steps.*

Definition 4. A program P is input-terminating over a set S of queries if all input-consuming derivations of P starting from every query in S are of finite length.

Input-consuming derivations do not instantiate variables that only occur input positions of the initial query. Input termination implies that all input-consuming derivations are of finite length — the final query in the derivation does not have to be empty.

3   Linear Bounded Programs

In this section, we define the class of linear bounded programs and illustrate the concept with a few examples. The definition is based on the concept of modes and linear predicate inequalities.

Definition 5. For a term t, the *parametric size* $[t]$ of t is defined recursively as follows:

- if t is a variable x then $[t]$ is a linear expression x,
- if t is a constant then $[t]$ is zero,
- if $t = f(t_1, \ldots, t_n)$ then $[t]$ is a linear expression $1 + [t_1] + \cdots + [t_n]$.

The parametric size of a sequence $\mathbf{t}$ of terms $t_1, \cdots, t_n$ is the sum $[t_1] + \cdots + [t_n]$.

For a term t (or a sequence $\mathbf{t}$ of terms), the sum of all constants in its parametric size $[t]$ (or $[\mathbf{t}]$ resp.) is denoted by $[\![t]\!]$ ($[\![\mathbf{t}]\!]$ resp). If t is a ground term, $[t]$ and $[\![t]\!]$ coincide. Essentially, $[\![t]\!]$ is the parametric size of $t\theta$, where θ is a substitution replacing all the variables by constants. In other words, $[\![t]\!]$ is the size of the smallest ground instance of t.

Example 1. *The parametric sizes of terms* a, [ ], [X], [a], [a, b, c], [[ ], [ ], [ ]], [[a], [b], [c]] *are* 0, 0, $X + 1$, 1, 3, 3, 6 *respectively.* □

A nice consequence of the above definition of $[\![t]\!]$ is the following lemma which says that the size of a term never decreases under instantiation (or by an application of a substitution).

Lemma 1. *For every term t and every substitution θ, the size $[\![t\theta]\!]$ of term $t\theta$ is greater than or equal to that of t, i.e., $[\![t\theta]\!] \geq [\![t]\!]$.*

Remark 2. The above notion of parametric size is similar to many termination norms used in the literature (see a.o. [5, 9, 10, 13, 15, 18, 22]). In fact, it is possible to use other norms in its place and yet the results proved in the sequel hold with minor modifications. For pedagogical reasons, we prove our results for the above norm of parametric size.

The following definition introduces the notation $LI(A, I, O)$, which is central to our results. It captures the relation between the sizes of input and output terms of an atom.

Definition 6. Let P be a moded program and I and O be mappings from the set of predicates occurring in P to sets of input positions and output positions satisfying $I(p) \subseteq in(p)$ and $O(p) \subseteq out(p)$ for each predicate p in P. For an atom $A = p(\mathbf{s}; \mathbf{t})$, we denote the linear inequality

$$\sum_{i \in I(p)} [s_i] \geq \sum_{j \in O(p)} [t_j] \tag{1}$$

by $LI(A, I, O)$.

Remark 3. The validity of (linear) inequalities is traditionally defined as the follows: *the inequality* **expression1** $\geq$ **expression2** *is valid if and only if it is valid for all possible assignments of values to variables in it.* In the sequel, we only talk of sizes which are obviously non-negative and hence *the inequality* **expression1** $\geq$ **expression2** *is valid if and only if it is valid for all possible assignments of non-negative values to variables in it.* According to this, $X + 1 > X$ is valid but $X + Y > X$ is not valid because Y can take a zero value and $X + 0$ is not greater than X. Similarly, $2X > X$ is not valid because X can take a zero value. However, both $X + Y \geq X$ and $2X \geq X$ are valid.

The following lemma is a simple consequence of this notion of validity.

Lemma 2. The following holds for any inequality $exp_1 \geq exp_2$.

1. $exp_1 \geq exp_2$ is valid if and only if $exp_1\theta \geq exp_2\theta$ is valid for every substitution θ, and
2. $exp_1 \geq exp_2$ is valid if and only if the constant in exp_2 is less than or equal to the constant in exp_1 and the coefficient of each variable in exp_2 is less than or equal to its coefficient in exp_1.

The following definition captures the call dependencies (and mutual recursion, if any) between predicates in a program.

Definition 7. Let P be a program, p and q be predicates. We say that predicate p *refers to* predicate q in P if there is a clause in P with p in the head and q in the body. We say that p depends on q and write $p \succeq_P q$ if (p, q) is in the reflexive and transitive closure of the relation *refers to*.

Now, we are in a position to define the class of linear bounded programs. Intuitively, any atom $p(\mathbf{s}; \mathbf{t})$ in the least Herbrand model of a linear bounded program (w.r.t. I and O) satisfies the property that the total size of output terms in positions $O(p)$ is bounded by the total size of input terms in positions $I(p)$.

Definition 8. Let P be a moded program and I and O be mappings from the set of predicates occurring in P to sets of input positions and output positions satisfying $I(p) \subseteq in(p)$ and $O(p) \subseteq out(p)$ for each predicate p in P. We say P is *linear bounded w.r.t. I and O* if each clause

$$p_0(\mathbf{s_0}; \mathbf{t_0}) \leftarrow p_1(\mathbf{s_1}; \mathbf{t_1}), \cdots, p_k(\mathbf{s_k}; \mathbf{t_k})$$

$k \geq 0$, in P satisfies the following:

1. $LI(A_1, I, O), \ldots, LI(A_{j-1}, I, O)$ together imply

$$[Iterms(A_0, I)] > [Iterms(A_j, I)]$$

for each $j \geq 1$ such that $p_j \succeq_P p_0$,
2. $LI(A_1, I, O), \ldots, LI(A_k, I, O)$ together imply $LI(A_0, I, O)$, and
3. $Var(\mathbf{s_0}) \cap (Var(\mathbf{t_1}), \cup \cdots \cup Var(\mathbf{t_k})) = \emptyset$

where A_j is the atom $p_j(\mathbf{s_j}; \mathbf{t_j})$ for each $j \geq 0$ and $Iterms(A, I)$ is the sequence of terms occurring in atom A in positions specified by I.
A program P is *linear bounded* if it is linear bounded w.r.t. some mappings I and O.

In the above definition, condition 1 is only applicable to the (mutually) recursive atoms in the body. Conditions 1 and 3 are satisfied by all the programs considered in the sequel.

We illustrate different aspects of our definition through a sequence of examples.

Example 2. Consider the following `reverse` program.

```
moding: app(in,in, out) and rev(in, out).
```

```
app([ ], Ys, Ys) ←
app([X|Xs], Ys, [X|Zs]) ← app(Xs, Ys, Zs)
```

```
rev([ ],[ ]) ←
rev([X|Xs], Zs) ← rev(Xs, Ys), app(Ys, [X], Zs)
```

This program is *linear bounded* w.r.t. the mappings $I(\text{app}) = in(\text{app})$; $I(\text{rev}) = in(\text{rev})$ and $O(\text{app}) = out(\text{app})$; $O(\text{rev}) = out(\text{rev})$. The first clause satisfies the requirements of Definition 8 as $LI(\text{app}([\,], \text{Ys}, \text{Ys}), I, O)$ is $Ys \geq Ys$, which obviously holds. Now consider the second clause.

$$LI(\text{app}(\text{Xs}, \text{Ys}, \text{Zs}), I, O) := Xs + Ys \geq Zs \tag{2}$$

$$LI(\text{app}([\text{X}|\text{Xs}], \text{Ys}, [\text{X}|\text{Zs}]), I, O) := 1 + X + Xs + Ys \geq 1 + X + Zs. \tag{3}$$

It is easy to see that inequality 2 implies inequality 3 satisfying the requirement 2 of Definition 8. The requirement 1 of Definition 8 obviously holds as $1 + X + Xs + Ys > Xs + Ys$.

It is easy to check that the third clause satisfies the requirements of Definition 8. Now consider the fourth clause.

$$LI(\text{rev}(\text{Xs}, \text{Ys}), I, O) := Xs \geq Ys, \tag{4}$$

$$LI(\text{app}(\text{Ys}, [\text{X}], \text{Zs}), I, O) := Ys + 1 + X \geq Zs \tag{5}$$

and for the head `rev([X|Xs], Zs)` of the clause,

$$LI(\text{rev}([\text{X}|\text{Xs}], \text{Zs}), I, O) := 1 + X + Xs \geq Zs. \tag{6}$$

It is easy to see that inequalities 4 and 5 together imply inequality 6 satisfying the requirement 2 of Definition 8. The requirement 1 of Definition 8 obviously holds for the recursive atom $\text{rev}(\text{Xs}, \text{Ys})$ as $1 + X + Xs > Xs$. Hence, `reverse` is a linear bounded program.   □

The above `reverse` program is input recursive (i.e., the set of variables occuring in input positions of any recursive atom is a subset of the set of variables occuring in input positions of the head, for each clause) and simply-moded. Therefore, it is input terminating by the results of [6]. The `quick-sort` program given below is not input recursive and cannot be shown to be input terminating by the results of [6]. The following example shows that `quick-sort` is a linear bounded program and hence input terminating by the results proved in the sequel.

Example 3. Consider the following quick-sort program.

moding: app (in, in, out); part (in, in, out, out) and
        qs (in, out)

$app([\,], Ys, Ys) \leftarrow$
$app([X|Xs], Ys, [X|Zs]) \leftarrow app(Xs, Ys, Zs)$

$part([\,], H, [\,], [\,]) \leftarrow$
$part([X|Xs], H, [X|Ls], Bs) \leftarrow X \leq H, part(Xs, H, Ls, Bs)$
$part([X|Xs], H, Ls, [X|Bs]) \leftarrow X > H, part(Xs, H, Ls, Bs)$

$qs([\,], [\,]) \leftarrow$
$qs([H|L], S) \leftarrow part(L, H, A, B), qs(A, A1), qs(B, B1), app(A1, [H|B1], S)$

This program is *linear bounded* w.r.t. the mappings such that $I(p) = in(p)$ and $O(p) = out(p)$ for each predicate except that $I(\text{part}) = \{1\}$. The third clause satisfies the requirements of Definition 8 as $LI(\text{part}([\,], H, [\,], [\,]), I, O)$ is the inequality $0 \geq 0$. Let us now consider the fourth clause. For the recursive atom $part(Xs, H, Ls, Bs)$, the requirement 1 of Definition 8 holds as $1 + X + Xs > Xs$. We now prove that requirement 2 also holds for this clause.

$$LI(X \leq H, I, O) := X + H \geq 0, \tag{7}$$

$$LI(\text{part}(Xs, H, Ls, Bs), I, O) := Xs \geq Ls + Bs \tag{8}$$

$$LI(\text{part}([X|Xs], H, [X|Ls], Bs), I, O) := 1 + X + Xs \geq 1 + X + Ls + Bs. \tag{9}$$

It is easy to see that inequality 8 implies inequality 9 satisfying the requirement 2 of Def. 8. It can be similarly proved that the fifth clause satisfies the requirements.

It is easy to see that the sixth clause satisfies the requirements of Definition 8. Now consider the last clause.

$$LI(\text{part}(L, H, A, B), I, O) := L \geq A + B, \tag{10}$$

$$LI(\text{qs}(A, A1), I, O) := A \geq A1, \tag{11}$$

$$LI(\text{qs}(B, B1), I, O) := B \geq B1, \tag{12}$$

$$LI(\text{app}(A1, [H|B1], S), I, O) := A1 + 1 + H + B1 \geq S \tag{13}$$

and for the head $qs([H|L], S)$ of the clause, $LI(\text{qs}([H|L], S), I, O)$ is

$$1 + H + L \geq S. \tag{14}$$

It is easy to see that inequalities 10, 11, 12 and 13 together imply inequality 14 satisfying requirement 2 of Definition 8. The requirement 1 of Definition 8 holds for recursive atoms $qs(A, A1)$ and $qs(B, B1)$ as inequality 10 implies $1 + H + L > A$ and $1 + H + L > B$. Therefore, quick-sort is a linear bounded program.   □

The above two program `reverse` and `quick-sort` programs have linear relationships between the input and output. The following example shows that the class of linear bounded programs is rich enough to include programs with non-linear relationships between the input and output.

Example 4. Consider the following `multiplication` program.

    moding: add (in, in, out) and mult (in, in, out)

    add(0, Y, Y) ←
    add(s(X), Y, s(Z)) ← add(X, Y, Z)

    mult(0, Y, 0) ←
    mult(s(X), Y, Z) ← mult(X, Y, Z1), add(Y, Z1, Z)

To prove that this program is *linear bounded*, take I and O as the mappings $I(add) = in(add)$, $O(add) = out(add)$ and $I(mult) = in(mult)$ and $O(mult) = \emptyset$.

The first and third clauses obviously satisfy the requirements of Definition 8 as
$LI(\text{add}(0, Y, Y), I, O)$ is $Y \geq Y$ and $LI(\text{mult}(0, Y, 0), I, O)$ is $Y \geq 0$.

Let us now consider the second clause.

$$LI(\text{add}(X, Y, Z), I, O) := X + Y \geq Z \qquad (15)$$

$$LI(\text{add}(s(X), Y, s(Z)), I, O) := 1 + X + Y \geq 1 + Z. \qquad (16)$$

It is easy to see that inequality 15 implies inequality 16 satisfying the requirement 2 of Definition 8. The requirement 1 of Definition 8 obviously holds as $1 + X + Y > X + Y$.

Let us now consider the fourth clause.

$$LI(\text{mult}(X, Y, Z1), I, O) := X + Y \geq 0 \qquad (17)$$

$$LI(\text{add}(Y, Z1, Z), I, O) := Y + Z1 \geq Z. \qquad (18)$$

and for the head `mult(s(X), Y, Z)` of the clause,

$$LI(\text{mult}(s(X), Y, Z), I, O) := 1 + X + Y \geq 0. \qquad (19)$$

It is easy to see that inequalities 17 and 18 together imply inequality 19 satisfying the requirement 2 of Definition 8 (in fact, inequality 19 is vacuously true, no need to use inequalities 17 and 18). The requirement 1 of Definition 8 obviously holds as $1 + X + Y > X + Y$. Therefore, `multiplication` is a linear bounded program.   □

The best thing about the class of linear bounded programs is that it is decidable whether a given moded program P is linear bounded. We prove this result by first proving that it is decidable whether a given moded program P is linear bounded w.r.t. a given pair of mappings I and O.

Theorem 1. *It is decidable whether a moded program P is linear bounded w.r.t. a given pair of mappings I and O satisfying $I(p) \subseteq in(p)$ and $O(p) \subseteq out(p)$ for each predicate p in P.*

Proof: Follows from the fact that this problem can be reduced to the satisfiability problem of linear inequalities.   □

The verification of linear boundedness of a program w.r.t. a given pair of mappings I and O can be easily automated [11] using the constraint-based approach to termination verification from [10, 22].

Theorem 2. *It is decidable whether a moded program P is linear bounded or not.*

Proof : Since only finitely many choices are possible for I and O, we can check if P is linear bounded w.r.t. at least one such pair of mappings I and O.   □

The significance of this result may be appreciated by noting that the other notions used for proving termination, such as, recurrence and acceptability are undecidable.

4   Termination of Linear Bounded Programs Under Prolog's Selection Rule

In this section, we prove that linear bounded programs only have input-consuming derivations of finite length under Prolog's left-to-right selection rule. We extend this result to arbitrary input-consuming derivations in the next section. A derivation is an input-consuming LD-derivation if the leftmost atom is selected every time and each step is input-consuming.

Theorem 3. Let P be a linear bounded program w.r.t. a pair of mappings I and O. If there is an input-consuming LD-refutation G of $P \cup \{\leftarrow A\}$ with computed answer substitution σ, then $LI(A\sigma, I, O)$ *is valid.*

Proof : Induction on the length l of G. If $l = 1$, there is a unit clause $H \leftarrow$ in P such that $A\sigma \equiv H\sigma$. Since P is a linear bounded program w.r.t. I and O, $LI(H, I, O)$ is valid by the requirement 2 of Definition 8. Now, by Lemma 2, $LI(H\sigma, I, O)$ is valid. Since $A\sigma \equiv H\sigma$, $LI(A\sigma, I, O)$ is also valid.

We now prove that theorem holds for $l = n$ if we assume that theorem holds for all $1 \leq l < n$. Let $H \leftarrow B_1, \cdots, B_k$ be the input clause used in the first LD-resolution step in G. Since P is a linear bounded program w.r.t. I and O, the inequalities $LI(B_1, I, O), \cdots, LI(B_k, I, O)$ together imply the inequality $LI(H, I, O)$ by the requirement 2 of Definition 8. By Lemma 2 it follows that $LI(B_1\sigma, I, O), \cdots, LI(B_k\sigma, I, O)$ together imply $LI(H\sigma, I, O)$. Obviously, for each $i \in [1, k]$, $B_i\sigma$ has an LD-refutation G of length less than n. Therefore, the inequalities $LI(B_1\sigma, I, O), \cdots, LI(B_k\sigma, I, O)$ are valid by the induction hypothesis, and hence $LI(H\sigma, I, O)$ is valid. Since $A\sigma \equiv H\sigma$, $LI(A\sigma, I, O)$ is also valid.   □

It may be noted that the above theorem holds for any SLD-refutation (not just input-consuming LD-refutation). In fact, it shows how linear inequalities capture relevant information about semantics (model used in the notion of acceptability) of linear bounded programs.

The following two theorems show that the recursive calls get smaller and smaller in LD-derivations of linear bounded programs.

Theorem 4. Let P be a linear bounded program w.r.t. a pair of mappings I and O. If $G = Q_0, Q_1, \cdots, Q_n$ is an LD-derivation of $P \cup \{\leftarrow A\}$ with partial computed answer substitution σ such that $Q_n =\leftarrow A', \cdots$ and A' is the first selected atom in G satisfying $rel(A') \succeq_P rel(A)$, then $[Iterms(A\sigma, I)] > [Iterms(A', I)]$.

Proof : Let $H \leftarrow B_1, \cdots, B_k$ be the input clause used in the first LD-resolution step in G. Since none of the atoms selected before A' is in mutual recursion with A, it is clear that $A' \equiv B_j\sigma$ for some $j \in [1, k]$. Since P is a linear bounded program w.r.t. I and O, $LI(B_1\sigma, I, O), \cdots, LI(B_k\sigma, I, O)$ together imply $[Iterms(H\sigma, I)] > [Iterms(B_j\sigma, I)]$ by the requirement 1 of Definition 8. Since we are following Prolog's selection rule, for each $i \in [1, j-1]$, $B_i\sigma$ has an LD-refutation. Therefore, the inequalities $LI(B_1\sigma, I, O), \cdots, LI(B_{j-1}\sigma, I, O)$ are valid by the Theorem 3, and hence $[Iterms(H\sigma, I)] > [Iterms(B_j\sigma, I)]$. Since $A\sigma \equiv H\sigma$ and $A' \equiv B_j\sigma$, it follows that $[Iterms(A\sigma, I)] > [Iterms(A', I)]$. $\square$

Theorem 5. Let P be a linear bounded program w.r.t. a pair of mappings I and O. If $G = Q_0, Q_1, \cdots, Q_n$ is an **input-consuming** LD-derivation of $P \cup \{\leftarrow A\}$ with partial computed answer substitution σ such that $Q_n =\leftarrow A', \cdots$ and A' is the first selected atom in G satisfying $rel(A') \succeq_P rel(A)$, then $[\![Iterms(A, I)]\!] > [\![Iterms(A', I)]\!]$.

Proof : From the above theorem, $[Iterms(A\sigma, I)] > [Iterms(A', I)]$. Since G is an **input-consuming** derivation, input terms of do not get instantiated by G and $Iterms(A\sigma, I) \equiv Iterms(A, I)$. Hence $[Iterms(A, I)] > [Iterms(A', I)]$. By Lemma 2, the constant in $[Iterms(A, I)]$ is greater than the constant in $[Iterms(A', I)]$. Therefore, it is clear from the definition of $[\![.]\!]$ that $[\![Iterms(A, I)]\!] > [\![Iterms(A', I)]\!]$. $\square$

Input termination of linear bounded programs under Prolog's selection rule follows from this theorem.

Theorem 6. If P is a linear bounded program and A is an atom, every **input-consuming** LD-derivation of $P \cup \{\leftarrow A\}$ is of finite length.

Proof : Follows from the above theorem by noetherian induction. $\square$

Example 5. Since programs for multiplication, reverse and quick- sort are linear bounded, they input-terminate under Prolog's selection rule by Theorem 6. $\square$

4.1   Comparison with Related Works

Bossi et.al. [7] defined a class of *simply acceptable* programs using notions of simply local substitutions, simply local models and moded level mappings. Due to lack of space, we do not include definitions of these notions here, but refer interested reader to [7]. The main result on input termination proved in [7] is the following theorem.

Theorem 7. *A simply-moded program is input terminating for all simply-moded queries if and only if it is simply acceptable.*

The relation between Theorems 6 and 7 is the following:

1. Theorem 6 does not require a program to be simply-moded while Theorem 7 requires it to be simply-moded. Therefore, Theorem 6 is applicable to a wider class of programs.
2. On the other hand, Theorem 7 gives a necessary and sufficient condition for input termination (of simply-moded programs) while Theorem 6 gives only a necessary condition for input termination. That's, there are some input terminating programs which are not linear bounded.
3. In view of the above point, the class of simply acceptable programs has undecidable membership problem, while membership problem for the class of linear bounded programs is decidable.

5   Input Termination of Linear Bounded Programs

In this section, we prove that all input-consuming derivations of **simply-moded** linear bounded programs (even if we do not follow Prolog's left-to-right selection rule) are of finite length. Since we are now considering arbitrary selection rule, our results in the previous section do not extend to the whole class of linear bounded programs, but only **simply-moded** linear bounded programs.

Taking advantage of the left switching lemma proved in [6], we restrict our attention to input-consuming derivations in which no atom is selected after one of its right neighbors has been selected. That is, if atom A_j is selected from the query $\leftarrow A_1, \cdots, A_n$, the atoms $A_1, \cdots, A_{j-1}$ will never be selected in the rest of the derivation.

Our proof technique is to show that corresponding to every atom B selected in an input-consuming derivation of $P \cup \{\leftarrow A\}$ under an arbitrary selection rule, there is a selected atom $B\theta$ in some input-consuming derivation of $P_{aug} \cup \{\leftarrow A\}$ under Prolog's left-to-right selection rule, for some substitution θ, where P_{aug} is a linear bounded program obtained by adding a few unit clauses to P. This ensures finiteness of all input-consuming derivations, because LD-derivations are of finite length by the results of Section 4.

Definition 9. Let P be a moded program and p be a predicate in it with m input positions and n output positions. The dummy clause for p (denoted by $DC(p)$) is defined as the unit clause

$$p(X_1, \cdots, X_m, \diamond_1, \cdots, \diamond_n) \leftarrow,$$

where $X_1, \cdots, X_m$ are distinct variables and $\diamond_1, \cdots, \diamond_n$ are fresh constants not occurring in P. The augmented program P_{aug} of P is defined as $P \cup \{DC(p) \mid p$ is a predicate in $P\}$.

The following lemma shows that P_{aug} is linear bounded whenever P is.

Lemma 3. If a program P is linear bounded w.r.t. I and O, P_{aug} is linear bounded w.r.t. I and O as well.

Proof: Each dummy clause is linear bounded w.r.t. I and O as the output terms are all constants (whose size is defined as 0), i.e., $[\diamond_1, \cdots, \diamond_n] = 0$. Each clause in P is already linear bounded w.r.t. I and O. Therefore, P_{aug} is linear bounded w.r.t. I and O. □

The following theorem shows that corresponding to every step in an input-consuming derivation of $P \cup \{\leftarrow A\}$ under an arbitrary selection rule, there is a step in some input-consuming derivation of $P_{aug} \cup \{\leftarrow A\}$ under Prolog's selection rule.

Theorem 8. Let P be a linear bounded simply-moded program and $Q_1, \cdots, Q_n, Q_{n+1}$ be an input-consuming derivation of $P \cup \{Q_1\}$ with $A_1, \cdots, A_n$ as the sequence of selected atoms and Q_1 a simply-moded query. Then *there is an input-consuming LD-derivation $AQ_1, \cdots, AQ_m$ of $P_{aug} \cup \{Q_1\}$ such that there is a sequence of integers $1 \leq i_1 < i_2 \cdots < i_n$ and AQ_{i_j} is $\leftarrow A_j\theta_j, PartR_j\theta_j$ when Q_j is $\leftarrow PartL_j, A_j, PartR_j$ for each $j \in [1, n]$ and each θ_i substitutes dummy constants for some variables occurring only in input positions of $A_j, PartR_j$.*
Proof: Induction on n.

Basis: $n = 1$. Let Q_1 be $\leftarrow PartL_1, A_1, PartR_1$. We obtain an input-consuming LD-derivation $AQ_1, \cdots, AQ_{i_1}$ of $P_{aug} \cup \{Q_1\}$ by resolving all the atoms in $PartL_1$ with dummy unit clauses. This is possible because Q_1 is simply-moded and all the output terms in it are distinct variables and hence atoms in $PartL_1$ unify with dummy clauses containing constants in output positions. Obviously, AQ_{i_1} is $\leftarrow A_1\theta_1, PartR_1\theta_1$, where θ_1 is a substitution replacing output variables in $PartL_1$ by dummy constants. Theses variables occur only in input positions of $A_1, PartR_1$, since Q_1 is simply-moded.

Induction step: Assuming that the theorem holds for $n = k$, we prove that it holds for $n = k + 1$.

By induction hypothesis, AQ_{i_k} is $\leftarrow A_k\theta_k, PartR_k\theta_k$, and Q_k is $\leftarrow PartL_k, A_k, PartR_k$. Let $H \leftarrow Body$ be the input clause resolved with A_k and σ be the mgu that does not bind input variables of A_k. Now, Q_{k+1} is $\leftarrow PartL_k, Body\sigma, PartR_k\sigma$ and can be written as $\leftarrow PartL_{k+1}, A_{k+1}, PartR_{k+1}$ such that[1] A_{k+1} is in $Body\sigma$ or $PartR_k\sigma$.

---

[1] Here, we restrict our attention to input-consuming derivations in which no atom is selected after one of its right neighbors has been selected, taking advantage of the left switching lemma proved in [6].

We extend the input-consuming LD-derivation $AQ_1, \cdots, AQ_{i_k}$ of $P_{aug} \cup \{Q_1\}$ by resolving $A_k\theta_k$ with the above input clause. It is easy to see that the mgu is $\sigma\theta_k$ and AQ_{i_k+1} is $\leftarrow Body\sigma\theta_k, PartR_k\theta_k\sigma$. Since the domain of σ is output variable and that of θ_k is input variables, $\sigma\theta_k = \theta_k\sigma$ and AQ_{i_k+1} can be written as $\leftarrow Body\sigma\theta_k, PartR_k\sigma\theta_k$. As A_{k+1} is in $Body\sigma$ or $PartR_k\sigma$, it is clear that $A_{k+1}\theta_k$ is in AQ_{i_k+1}.

Since P_{aug} and Q_1 are simply-moded, every query in any derivation of $P_{aug} \cup \{Q_1\}$ is simply-moded and the output terms are distinct variables, making it possible to resolve any atom with a dummy clause. We further extend the input-consuming LD-derivation of $AQ_1, \cdots, AQ_{i_k}, AQ_{i_k+1}$ of $P_{aug} \cup \{Q_1\}$ to $AQ_1, \cdots, AQ_{i_k}, AQ_{i_k+1}, \cdots, AQ_{i_{k+1}}$ by resolving all the atoms on the left of $A_{k+1}\theta_k$ with dummy clauses and get $AQ_{k+1} = \leftarrow A_{k+1}\theta_{k+1}, PartR_{k+1}\theta_{k+1}$. □

The following example demonstrates the need for dummy clauses.

Example 6. Consider append program with moding: app(in, in, out) and a simply-moded query $\leftarrow$ app(X, [1, 2, 3], Y), app([1, 2, 3], Y, Z). There is no input-consuming LD-derivation for this query (because the leftmost atom is not instantiated enough). However, we have an input-consuming derivation of length 4 for this query when we select the rightmost atom.

When we add dummy clause app(X, Y, $\diamond_1$) $\leftarrow$, we get an input-consuming LD-derivation of length 5 for the above query. □

Now, we are in a position to prove the main theorem of the paper.

Theorem 9. Let P be a linear bounded simply-moded program and Q be a simply-moded query. Then, *all the input-consuming derivations of $P \cup \{Q\}$ are of finite length.*
Proof: By the above theorem, if $P \cup \{Q\}$ has an infinite input-consuming derivation it $P_{aug} \cup \{Q\}$ has an infinite input-consuming LD-derivation. However, by Theorem 6, all the input-consuming LD-derivations of $P_{aug} \cup \{Q\}$ are of finite length as P_{aug} is a linear bounded program. □

The following example shows that this result does not hold for the whole class of linear bounded programs.

Example 7. Consider the program obtained by replacing the last clause of quick-sort by the following 3 clauses (with moding doub(in, out) for the new predicate).

qs([H|L], S) $\leftarrow$ part(L, H, A, B), doub([H|L], A), qs(A, A1), qs(B, B1),
$\qquad\qquad\qquad\qquad$ app(A1, [H|B1], S)
doub([ ], [ ]) $\leftarrow$
doub([H|L], [H, H|R]) $\leftarrow$ doub(L, R)

Note that, this program is not simply-moded (variable A occurs twice in output positions).

This program is linear bounded w.r.t. I and O such that $I(p) = in(p)$ and $O(p) = out(p)$ for each predicate except that $I(\mathtt{part}) = \{1\}$ and $O(\mathtt{doub}) = \emptyset$. However, it has an infinite input-consuming derivation starting from query $\leftarrow \mathtt{qs}([1], X)$, in which $\mathtt{partition}$ atoms are never selected, but $\mathtt{double}$ and $\mathtt{quick\text{-}sort}$ atoms are selected. This infinite derivation has recursive atoms $\mathtt{qs}([1], X), \mathtt{qs}([1, 1], A), \mathtt{qs}([1, 1, 1, 1], A'), \cdots$ selected.

Note that this program is input-terminating under Prolog's selection rule because $\mathtt{part(L,H,A,B)}$, $\mathtt{doub([H|L], A)}$ will never succeed.   □

The class of linear bounded programs is rich enough to include many programs like append, delete, insert, reverse, permute, count, listsum, listproduct, insertion-sort, quick-sort on lists, various tree traversal programs and addition, multiplication, factorial, power on natural numbers. One little surprise is that the following merge-sort is not linear bounded. However a specialized version of it is linear bounded.

Example 8. Consider the following program for merge-sort.

```
moding: split (in, out, out); merge (in, in, out) and
        ms (in, out)
```

$$\mathtt{split}([\,],[\,],[\,]) \leftarrow$$
$$\mathtt{split}([X|Xs],[X|As],Bs) \leftarrow \mathtt{split}(Xs, Bs, As)$$

$$\mathtt{merge}([\,],Ys,Ys) \leftarrow$$
$$\mathtt{merge}(Xs,[\,],Xs) \leftarrow$$
$$\mathtt{merge}([X|Xs],[Y|Ys],[X|Zs]) \leftarrow X \leq Y, \mathtt{merge}(Xs,[Y|Ys],Zs)$$
$$\mathtt{merge}([X|Xs],[Y|Ys],[Y|Zs]) \leftarrow X > Y, \mathtt{merge}([X|Xs],Ys,Zs)$$

$$\mathtt{ms}([\,],[\,]) \leftarrow$$
$$\mathtt{ms}([X],[X]) \leftarrow$$
$$\mathtt{ms}([X1,X2|L],S) \leftarrow \mathtt{split}([X1,X2|L],A,B), \mathtt{ms}(A,A1), \mathtt{ms}(B,B1),$$
$$\mathtt{merge}(A1,B1,S)$$

Subprograms defining $\mathtt{split}$ and $\mathtt{merge}$ are linear bounded w.r.t. I and O such that $I(p) = in(p)$ and $O(p) = out(p)$ for each predicate. However, we cannot prove that ms is linear bounded because $2 + X1 + X2 + L \geq A + B$ does not imply $2 + X1 + X2 + L > A$ and $2 + X1 + X2 + L > B$ for recursive atoms $\mathtt{ms(A,A1)}$, $\mathtt{ms(B,B1)}$.   □

This is the price we pay for having a definition which is purely syntactic. However, purely syntactic definitions have many advantages, like decidability in our case. The following specialized version of merge-sort is linear bounded.

Example 9. Consider the program for merge-sort obtained by replacing the last clause with the following.

$$\mathtt{ms}([X1,X2|L],S) \leftarrow \mathtt{split}(L,A,B), \mathtt{ms}([X1|A],A1), \mathtt{ms}([X2|B],B1),$$
$$\mathtt{merge}(A1,B1,S)$$

This program is linear bounded as the inequality $LI(\mathtt{split}(\mathtt{L},\mathtt{A},\mathtt{B}), I, O)$, i.e., $L \geq A+B$ implies $2+X1+X2+L > 1+X1+A$ and $2+X1+X2+L > 1+X2+B$ for the two recursive atoms $\mathtt{ms(A,A1)}$, $\mathtt{ms(B,B1)}$. □

5.1   Comparison with Related Works

Bossi, Rossi and Etalle [6] defined classes of *quasi recurrent* and *input-recursive* programs and proved the following theorem on input termination.

Theorem 10. *A simply-moded input-recursive program is input terminating if and only if it is quasi recurrent.*

The main restriction in these programs is that (mutual) recursive atoms cannot have any local variables in input positions. Many programs like quick-sort do not satisfy this requirement.

The relation between Theorems 9 and 10 is similar to the between Theorems 6 and 7. Theorem 9 is applicable to a much wider class of programs than Theorem 10. The membership problem of the class of linear bounded programs is decidable, while that of the class of quasi recurrent programs is undecidable. Theorem 10 gives a necessary and sufficient condition for input termination (albiet for a small class of programs) while Theorem 9 gives only a necessary condition for input termination.

6   Conclusion

In this paper, we study input termination of logic programs. We introduce a class of logic programs called linear bounded programs and prove that linear bounded programs only have input-consuming derivations of finite length under Prolog's selection rule. The result also holds for arbitrary selection rules if we consider simply-moded linear bounded programs. Further,

1. the class of linear bounded programs is rich enough to include many natural programs like append, delete, insert, reverse, permute, count, listsum, list-product, insertion-sort, quick-sort on lists, various tree traversal programs and addition, multiplication, factorial, power on natural numbers, and
2. it is decidable whether a given logic program is linear bounded or not,
3. the notion of linear bounded programs uses very simple concepts like mod-ing and linear inequalities, and does not involve types, level mappings and models.

This combination of simplicity, expressive power and decidability makes the class of linear bounded programs very appealing.

Acknowledgement: The author would like to sincerely thank Danny De Schreye for his helpful comments on the paper.

References

1. K. R. Apt. 1990. Introduction to Logic Programming. In J. van Leeuwen, editor, Handbook of Theoretical Computer Science, volume B: Formal Models and Semantics, pages 495-574.
2. K. R. Apt and I. Luitjes. 1995. Verification of logic programs with delay declarations. Proc. of AMAST'95, LNCS 936, 66-90. Springer-Verlag.
3. K. R. Apt and D. Pedreschi. 1993. Reasoning about termination of pure prolog programs. Information and Computation 106, 109-157.
4. M. Bezem. 1992. Characterizing termination of logic programs with level mappings. Journal of Logic Programming 15, 1/2, 79-98.
5. A. Bossi, N. Cocco, and M. Fabris. 1994. Norms on Terms and their use in Proving Universal Termination of a Logic Program. Theoretical Computer Science 124:297-328.
6. A. Bossi, S. Etalle, and S. Rossi. 2002. Properties of input-consuming derivations. Theory and Practice of Logic Programming, 2, 125-154.
7. A. Bossi, S. Etalle, S. Rossi, and J.G. Smaus. 2004. Termination of simply-moded logic programs with dynamic scheduling. ACM Trans. Comput. Log. 15(3):470-507.
8. S. K. Debray and D. S. Warren. 1988. Automatic mode inference for logic programs. J. Logic Programming 5, pp. 207-229.
9. S. Decorte, D. De Schreye and M. Fabris. 1993. Automatic inference of norms: a missing link in automatic termination analysis, ILPS'93, Lecture Notes in Computer Science 526, pp. 420-436.
10. S. Decorte, D. De Schreye, and H. Vandecasteele. 1999. Constraint-based termination analysis of logic programs. ACM Trans. Program. Lang. Syst. 21(6):1137-1195.
11. D. De Schreye. 2004. Personal communication.
12. D. De Schreye and S. Decorte. 1994. Termination of logic programs: The never-ending story. Journal of Logic Programming, 19/20:199-260.
13. S. Genaim, M. Codish, J. Gallagher, V. Lagoon. 2002. Combining Norms to Prove Termination. VMCAI 2002, Lecture Notes in Computer Science 2294, pp. 126-138.
14. M.R.K. Krishna Rao, D. Kapur, R.K. Shyamasundar. 1998. Transformational Methodology for Proving Termination of Logic Programs. Journal of Log. Program. 34(1): 1-41.
15. N. lindenstrauss and Y. Sagiv. 1997. Automatic termination analysis of logic programs, ICLP'1997, pp. 63-77.
16. V. Lagoon, F. Mesnard, P. Stuckey. 2003. Termination Analysis with Types Is More Accurate. ICLP 2003, Lecture Notes in Computer Science 2916, pp. 254-268.
17. J. W. Lloyd. 1987. Foundations of Logic Programming. SpringerVerlag.
18. F. Mesnard and S. Ruggieri. 2003. On proving left termination of constraint logic programs. ACM Transactions on Computational Logic, 4(2):1-26.
19. L. Plümer (1990), *Termination proofs for logic programs*, Ph. D. thesis, University of Dortmund, Also appeared as Lecture Notes in Computer Science 446, Springer-Verlag.
20. J.-G. Smaus. 1999. Proving termination of input-consuming logic programs. Proc. of ICLP'99, pp. 335-349.
21. J.-G. Smaus, P.M. Hill, A. King: 2001. Verifying Termination and Error-Freedom of Logic Programs with block Declarations. Theory and Practice of Logic Programming 1(4): 447-486.
22. K. Verschaetse and D. De Schreye. 1991. Deriving Termination Proofs for Logic Programs, Using Abstract Procedures. Proc. of ICLP'91, pp. 301-315.

On Termination of Binary CLP Programs

Alexander Serebrenik[1] and Fred Mesnard[2]

[1] Laboratory of Quality of Software (LaQuSo), T.U.Eindhoven,
HG 5.71, Den Dolech 2, P.O.Box 513,
5600 MB Eindhoven, The Netherlands
A.Serebrenik@laquso.com
[2] IREMIA, Université de La Réunion, France
fred@univ-reunion.fr

Abstract. Termination of binary CLP programs has recently become an important question in the termination analysis community. The reason for this is due to the fact that some of the recent approaches to termination of logic programs abstract the input program to a binary CLP program and conclude termination of the input program from termination of the abstracted program. In this paper we introduce a class of binary CLP programs such that their termination can be proved by using linear level mappings. We show that membership to this class is decidable and present a decision procedure. Further, we extend this class to programs such that their termination proofs require a combination of linear functions. In particular we consider as level mappings tuples of linear functions and piecewise linear functions.

1 Introduction

Termination is well-known to be one of the crucial properties of software verification. Logic programming with its strong theoretical basis lends itself easily to termination analysis as witnessed by a very intensive research in the area. Some of the recent approaches to termination [4, 10, 13] proceed in two steps. First, a logic program is abstracted to a $CLP(\mathcal{N})$-program, $i.e.$ logic program extended with constraint solving over the domain of natural numbers $\mathcal{N}$. Second, the $CLP(\mathcal{N})$-program is approximated by a $binary$ $CLP(\mathcal{N})$ program, $i.e.$, a set of clauses of the form $p(\tilde{x}) \leftarrow c, q(\tilde{y})$, where c is a CLP-constraint and p, q are user-defined predicates.

In this paper we study decidability of termination for binary $CLP(\mathcal{C})$ programs. In general, it depends on the constraint domain $\mathcal{C}$. On the one hand, Devienne et al. [6] have established undecidability of termination for one-clause binary $CLP(\mathcal{H})$ programs, where $\mathcal{H}$ is the domain of Herbrand terms. Similar results can be obtained for other CLP languages such as $CLP(\mathcal{N})$ and $CLP(\mathcal{Q})$. On the other hand, Datalog, $i.e.$, logic programming language with no function symbols, provides an example of a constraint programming language such that termination is decidable for it.

S. Etalle(Ed.): LOPSTR 2004, LNCS 3573, pp. 231–244, 2005.

For constraint domains with the undecidable termination property, we are interested in subclasses of binary programs such that termination is decidable for these subclasses. A trivial example of such a subclass is the subclass of non-recursive binary programs. After the preliminary remarks of Section 2, in Section 3 we present our main result, namely a non-trivial subclass of terminating binary CLP($\mathcal{C}$) programs such that membership to this subclass is decidable if $\mathcal{C}$ is $\mathcal{Q}$, $\mathcal{Q}^+$ or $\mathcal{R}$. Intuitively, this is the class of binary CLP programs such that there exists a linear function decreasing while traversing the clauses. Two extensions of this class are discussed in Section 4.

2   Preliminaries

2.1   Constraint Logic Programming

We adhere to the definitions of [8]. For sake of completeness we recapitulate them briefly. A constraint domain $\mathcal{C}$ is a tuple $(\Sigma_\mathcal{C}, \mathcal{L}_\mathcal{C}, \mathcal{D}_\mathcal{C}, \mathcal{T}_\mathcal{C}, solv_\mathcal{C})$. The *domain signature* $\Sigma_\mathcal{C}$ is a pair $(F_\mathcal{C}, \Pi_\mathcal{C})$, where $F_\mathcal{C}$ is the set of function symbols and $\Pi_\mathcal{C}$ is the set of predicate symbols. The class of constraints $\mathcal{L}_\mathcal{C}$ is a set of first order formulae closed under conjunction and existential quantification. The domain of computation $\mathcal{D}_\mathcal{C}$ is the intended interpretation of constraints over a set $D_\mathcal{C}$. The constraint theory $\mathcal{T}_\mathcal{C}$ describes the logical semantics of the constraints. Finally, the constraint solver $solv_\mathcal{C}$ maps each formula in $\mathcal{L}_\mathcal{C}$ to $\{true, false, unknown\}$, such that for any $c \in \mathcal{L}_\mathcal{C}$, $solv_\mathcal{C}(c) = false$ implies $\mathcal{T}_\mathcal{C} \models \neg\exists c$, and $solv_\mathcal{C}(c) = true$ implies $\mathcal{T}_\mathcal{C} \models \exists c$. A constraint solver is called *complete* if it only returns *true* or *false*. A constraint domain with a complete solver is called *ideal*. A constraint logic programming language over an ideal domain is also called *ideal*.

We consider the following ideal constraint domains:

- $\mathcal{N}$. The predicate symbols are $=$ and $\geq$, the function symbols are 0, 1, and $+$. The constraint theory $\mathcal{T}_\mathcal{N}$ is the theory of Presburger arithmetic, known to be decidable. It should be noted that constraints produced by the abstraction techniques of [4, 10, 13] can be expressed in Presburger arithmetic.
- $\mathcal{Q}$ and $\mathcal{R}$. The predicate symbols are as above, the function symbols are 0, 1, $+$, $-$, $*$, and $/$, however only linear constraints are admitted. $\mathcal{Q}^+$ and $\mathcal{R}^+$ restrict $\mathcal{Q}$ and $\mathcal{R}$ to non-negative numbers.

Given a program P, we define Π_P as the set of user-defined predicate symbols appearing in P. Syntactic objects are viewed modulo renaming of variables. In this paper we restrict our attention to binary programs. We assume that binary rules are in *flat* form: $p(\tilde{x}) \leftarrow c, q(\tilde{y})$, with $\tilde{x} \cap \tilde{y} = \varnothing$ (where $\varnothing$ denotes the empty set and $\tilde{x}$ a tuple of *distinct* variables). Flat facts and flat queries are defined accordingly. An *atomic query* is a flat query of the form $c, q(\tilde{y})$ where $q \in \Pi_P$.

A $\mathcal{C}$-interpretation for a CLP($\mathcal{C}$) program P is an interpretation on the domain signature $(F_\mathcal{C}, \Pi_\mathcal{C} \cup \Pi_P)$ that agrees with the domain of computation $\mathcal{D}_\mathcal{C}$ on the interpretation of the symbols in $\Sigma_\mathcal{C}$. Given a CLP($\mathcal{C}$)-program P, the $\mathcal{C}$-base $B_P^\mathcal{C}$ is defined as $\{p(d_1, \ldots, d_n) \mid p \in \Pi_P, (d_1, \ldots, d_n) \in (D_\mathcal{C})^n\}$. A $\mathcal{C}$-

interpretation can be regarded as a subset of the $\mathcal{C}$-base. A $\mathcal{C}$-model of a program P is a $\mathcal{C}$-interpretation of P that is also a model of P.

A *valuation* θ is a function that maps all variables to $D_\mathcal{C}$. For an interpretation J and a formula φ we write $J \models_\theta \varphi$ if $\theta(\varphi)$ is valid with respect to J. For a query Q of the form (c, A), we define $ground_\mathcal{C}(Q) = \{\theta(A)|D_\mathcal{C} \models_\theta c\}$. For a rule, we define $ground_\mathcal{C}((A \leftarrow c, B)) = \{\theta(A \leftarrow B)|D_\mathcal{C} \models_\theta c\}$. Similarly, for a program P, $ground_\mathcal{C}(P)$ is the set of ground $\mathcal{C}$-instances of the rules of P.

2.2   Termination Analysis

In this subsection we present briefly a number of notions related to termination analysis. First of all, we say that a CLP($\mathcal{C}$) program P and a query Q *left-terminate* if every derivation of Q with respect to P via the leftmost selection rule is finite.

One key concept in many (theoretical) approaches lies in the use of *level mappings*, *i.e.*, mappings from ground atoms to natural numbers. We slightly extend this traditional definition and map the elements of the $\mathcal{C}$-base to a well-founded set. We prefer to talk about a general well-founded set rather than about the set of the naturals, in order to be able to consider functions to $\mathcal{R}^+$ and $(\mathcal{R}^+)^m$. Recall that a well-founded set is a partially ordered set $(S, \rhd)$ such that there is no infinitely decreasing chain $s_1 \rhd s_2 \rhd \dots$ of elements of S. Formally, a *level mapping* for a constraint domain $\mathcal{C}$ is a function $|\cdot| : \mathcal{C}\text{-base} \to S$. It is well-known that termination of a CLP program can be characterised by means of level mappings. The following definition is taken from [14].

Definition 1. *Let* $|\cdot| : \mathcal{C}\text{-base} \to S$ *be a level mapping, and* I *be a* $\mathcal{C}$-interpretation*. A CLP($\mathcal{C}$) program P is* acceptable *by* $|\cdot|$ *and* I *if* I *is a* $\mathcal{C}$-model of P, *and for every* $A \leftarrow B_1, \dots, B_n$ *in* $ground_\mathcal{C}(P)$, *for* $i \in [1, n]$, $I \models B_1, \dots, B_{i-1}$ *implies* $|A| \rhd |B_i|$. *A query Q is* acceptable *by* $|\cdot|$ *and* I *if there exists* $k \in S$ *such that for every* $A_1, \dots, A_n$ *in* $ground_\mathcal{C}(Q)$, *for* $i \in [1, n]$, $I \models A_1, \dots, A_{i-1}$ *implies* $k \rhd |A_i|$.

For binary programs and atomic queries, model and queries can be eliminated from the previous definition (see Lemma 1 and Proposition 1). By doing so we can obtain a notion similar to *recurrency*. Originally the notion of recurrency has been introduced in [1] to characterise termination of ground queries to logic programs for all selection rules. For constraint logic programming we introduce the following definition:

Definition 2. *Let P be a binary CLP($\mathcal{C}$) program, and* $|\cdot| : \mathcal{C}\text{-base} \to S$ *be a level mapping. P is called* recurrent *with respect to* $|\cdot|$ *if for every* $A \leftarrow B \in ground_\mathcal{C}(P)$, $|A| \rhd |B|$ *holds.*

The following lemma states that for binary programs the notions of acceptability and recurrency coincide.

Lemma 1. *Let P be a binary CLP($\mathcal{C}$) program and* $|\cdot| : \mathcal{C}\text{-base} \to S$ *be a level mapping. Then, P is acceptable by* $|\cdot|$ *and the $\mathcal{C}$-base if and only if P is recurrent with respect to* $|\cdot|$.

The relationship between acceptability and termination for ideal CLP languages can be expressed by the following theorems:

Theorem 1. *([14]) Let CLP(C) be an ideal CLP language. If a program P and a query Q are both acceptable by some level mapping $|\cdot|$ and a C-model I then they left terminate.*

From here on we consider only ideal constraint logic programming languages. This assumption is quite common in termination analysis for CLP. For binary programs one can use Lemma 1 and replace acceptability with respect to a level mapping and a model by recurrency with respect to a level mapping.

Observe that we do not need to introduce the corresponding notion of recurrency for queries. Instead, in order to take care of the atomic query Q we extend the corresponding binary program P by a clause $q \leftarrow Q$, where q is a *fresh* predicate symbol, i.e., $q \notin \Pi_P, q \notin \Pi_C$. The basic idea is that recurrency of $P \cup \{q \leftarrow Q\}$ implies termination of Q with respect to P. Formally, the following proposition holds.

Proposition 1. *Let P be a binary CLP(C) program, Q be an atomic query, and q be a fresh predicate symbol as above. If $P \cup \{q \leftarrow Q\}$ is recurrent with respect to a level mapping $|\cdot|$ then Q terminates with respect to P.*

2.3   Linear Programming

In this subsection we recall briefly some basic notions of linear programming (see [16] for instance) to be applied in Section 3.1. Essentially, linear programming aims at finding the extremum of a linear function of positive numbers, so called the *objective function*, given that a system of linear inequalities on these variables holds. Formally, a minimising linear programming problem can be expressed as follows: *minimise $\tilde{c}\tilde{x}^T$ subject to $A\tilde{x}^T \geq \tilde{b}^T$ and $\tilde{x} \geq 0$*, where $\tilde{x}$ is a vector of variables, $\tilde{c}$ expresses the objective function, the superscript ^{T} denotes a transposed of a vector, and $A\tilde{x}^T \geq \tilde{b}^T$ denotes the system of linear constraints. For every minimising linear programming problem over the rationals or the reals, there exists a maximising linear programming problem, called *dual*, such that an optimal solution to one problem ensures the existence of an optimal solution to the other and that the optimal values of the objective functions are equal. This statement is known as *the duality theorem*. Given a minimising linear programming problem as above, the dual linear programming problem has the following form: *maximise $\tilde{y}\tilde{b}^T$ subject to $\tilde{y}A^T \leq \tilde{c}$ and $\tilde{y} \geq 0$*.

3   Llm-Recurrent Programs

In this section we consider a special subclass of binary programs and atomic queries. In particular, we are interested in programs and queries that can be analysed by means of linear level mappings. Let C be $\mathcal{N}$ or $\mathcal{Z}$ or $\mathcal{Q}^+$ or $\mathcal{Q}$ or $\mathcal{R}$. As a range for a level mapping in this section we take $(\mathcal{R}^+, \rhd)$, where $x \rhd y$ holds if $x \geq y + 1$.

Definition 3. *A level mapping* $| \cdot |$: $\mathcal{C}$-*base* $\rightarrow \mathcal{R}^+$ *is called* linear *if for any n-ary predicate symbol p, there exist real numbers* μ_p^i, $0 \leq i \leq n$, *such that for any atom* $p(e_1, \ldots, e_n) \in \mathcal{C}$-base, $|p(e_1, \ldots, e_n)| = max(0, \mu_p^0 + \sum_{i=1}^{n} \mu_p^i e_i)$.

Using the notion of a linear level mapping we can define the class of programs we are going to study.

Definition 4. *Let P be a binary flat CLP($\mathcal{C}$) program. We say that P is* llm-recurrent *if there exists a linear level mapping* $| \cdot |$ *such that P is recurrent with respect to it.*

Example 1. Consider the following program: $\mathrm{p(X)} \leftarrow \mathrm{X} \leq 72, \mathrm{Y} = \mathrm{X} + 1, \mathrm{p(Y)}$. This program is llm-recurrent with respect to $|\mathrm{p(x)}| = max(0, 73 - \mathrm{x})$.   □

In the next subsection we quickly review the algorithm of Sohn and Van Gelder [18] that aims at checking the existence of a linear level mapping such that P is llm-recurrent with respect to it. This will allow us to show that llm-recurrency is decidable for $\mathcal{Q}$ and $\mathcal{R}$.

3.1   The Algorithm SVG

Sohn and Van Gelder [18] have proposed the following algorithm (SVG) as a sufficient condition for termination. SVG examines each recursive user-defined predicate symbol p of a CLP($\mathcal{Q}^+$) program in turn (the precise order does not matter) and try to find a level mapping for $p(x_1, \ldots, x_n)$ symbolically defined as $|p(\tilde{x})| = \mu_0 + \sum_{1 \leq i \leq n} \mu_i x_i$ where $\mu_i \geq 0$ for all i. For sake of simplicity, we assume that the program is only *directly* recursive. By this we mean that if there exist sequences of predicates $p = r_0, r_1, \ldots, r_n = q$ and $q = r_n, r_{n+1}, \ldots, r_m = p$ such that for all i, $r_i(\tilde{x}) \leftarrow c(\tilde{x}, \tilde{y}), r_{i+1}(\tilde{y})$ is a clause in P, then p is identical to q. Moreover, we may safely ignore the constant μ_0.

For every rule r, say $p(\tilde{x}_0) \leftarrow c, p(\tilde{x}_k)$, we assume that the constraint c is satisfiable, already projected onto $\tilde{x}_0 \cup \tilde{x}_k$, only contains inequalities of the form $e_1 \geq e_2$, with e_1 and e_2 being arithmetical expressions over $\tilde{x}_0 \cup \tilde{x}_k$ and constants. For such a rule recurrency requires that c implies $\sum_{1 \leq i \leq n} \mu_i x_i^0 - \sum_{1 \leq i \leq n} \mu_i x_i^k \geq 1$, where $\tilde{x}_0$ is the vector $(x_1^0, \ldots, x_n^0)$ and $\tilde{x}_k$ is the vector $(x_1^k, \ldots, x_n^k)$. In other words, such a binary rule gives rise to the following *pseudo*[1] linear programming problem

$$minimise \ \theta = \tilde{\mu}(\tilde{x}_0 - \tilde{x}_k) \ subject \ to \ c, \ \tilde{x}_0 \geq 0, \ \tilde{x}_k \geq 0 \qquad (1)$$

where $\tilde{\mu}$ is the vector $(\mu_1, \ldots, \mu_n)$. A level mapping $|\cdot|$ ensuring recurrency exists (at least for this clause) if $\theta^* \geq 1$ where θ^* denotes the minimum of the objective function. Because of the symbolic constants $\tilde{\mu}$, (1) is *not* a linear programming problem. The idea of Sohn and Van Gelder is to consider its dual form:

$$maximise \ \eta = \beta \tilde{y} \ subject \ to \ A\tilde{y} \leq (\mu_1, \ldots, \mu_n, -\mu_1, \ldots, -\mu_n), \ \tilde{y} \geq 0 \qquad (2)$$

---

[1] because *symbolic* parameters appear in the objective function.

where β and A are automatically derived while switching to the dual form of (1) and $\tilde{y}$ is the vector of dual variables. By the duality theorem of linear programming, we have $\theta^* = \eta^*$. Now, the authors observe that $\tilde{\mu}$ appears linearly in the dual problem (it is not true for (1)) because no μ_i appears in A. Hence the constraints of (2) can be rewritten, by adding $\eta \geq 1$, $\tilde{y} \geq 0$, as a set of linear inequations, denoted S_r. If the conjunction $S_p = \wedge_k S_r$ (for each clause defining p) is satisfiable, then there exists a linear level mapping for p ensuring recurrency.

Example 2. We consider the $\mathrm{CLP}(\mathcal{Q}^+)$ program P:

$$p(X_1, X_2) \leftarrow X_1 + 2 * X_2 \geq 3 * X_3 + 4 * X_4 + 1, p(X_3, X_4).$$

The first step is the pseudo-linear program: *minimise* $\theta = a(x_1 - x_3) + b(x_2 - x_4)$ *subject to* $x_1, x_2, x_3, x_4 \geq 0, x_1 + 2x_2 \geq 3x_3 + 4x_4 + 1$. We get: *minimise* $\theta = [a\ b\ -a\ -b]\,[x_1\ x_2\ x_3\ x_4]^T$ *subject to* $A\,[x_1\ x_2\ x_3\ x_4]^T \geq [0\ 0\ 0\ 1]^T$, where

$$A \text{ is } \begin{bmatrix} 1 & 0 & 0 & 0 \\ 0 & 1 & 0 & 0 \\ 0 & 0 & 1 & 0 \\ 0 & 0 & 0 & 1 \\ 1 & 2 & -3 & -4 \end{bmatrix}.$$ The dual form is: *maximise* $\eta = [0\ 0\ 0\ 0\ 1]\,[y_1\ y_2\ y_3\ y_4\ y_5]^T$

subject to $A^T\,[y_1\ y_2\ y_3\ y_4\ y_5]^T \leq [a\ b\ -a\ -b]^T$ *and* $y_1, y_2, y_3, y_4, y_5 \geq 0$. The parameters a and b now appear linearly, they will be considered as new variables and we have: *maximise* $\eta = [0\ 0\ 0\ 0\ 1\ 0\ 0]\,[y_1\ y_2\ y_3\ y_4\ y_5\ a\ b]^T$ *subject to*

$$\begin{bmatrix} 1 & 0 & 0 & 0 & 1 & -1 & 0 \\ 0 & 1 & 0 & 0 & 2 & 0 & -1 \\ 0 & 0 & 1 & 0 & -3 & 1 & 0 \\ 0 & 0 & 0 & 1 & -4 & 0 & 1 \end{bmatrix} \begin{bmatrix} y_1 \\ y_2 \\ y_3 \\ y_4 \\ y_5 \\ a \\ b \end{bmatrix} \leq \begin{bmatrix} 0 \\ 0 \\ 0 \\ 0 \end{bmatrix} \text{ and } y_1, y_2, y_3, y_4, y_5, a, b \geq 0.$$ As the system

S_p (where $\eta = y_5$):

$$\begin{cases} y_5 & \geq 1 \\ y_1 + y_5 - a & \leq 0 \\ y_2 + 2y_5 - b & \leq 0 \\ y_3 - 3y_5 + a & \leq 0 \\ y_4 - 4y_5 + b & \leq 0 \\ y_1, y_2, y_3, y_4, y_5, a, b \geq 0 \end{cases}$$

is satisfiable, we conclude that there exists a linear level mapping ensuring recurrency of P. $\square$

So SVG is basically an efficient procedure for deciding in $\mathcal{R}$ (or any other domain such that the duality theorem holds for it) the formula $\exists \tilde{\mu}\,\forall \tilde{x} \cup \tilde{y}[c(\tilde{x}, \tilde{y}) \to \tilde{\mu}\tilde{x} \geq 1 + \tilde{\mu}\tilde{y}]$ corresponding to the rule $p(\tilde{x}) \leftarrow c(\tilde{x}, \tilde{y}), p(\tilde{y})$. It produces a linear constraint (the system S_p in our example) such that satisfiability of this constraint is *equivalent* to a positive answer for the decision problem.

3.2   Verifying llm-Recurrency with SVG

To prove llm-recurrency, we need to find a function satisfying Definition 3, *i.e.*, for every predicate p we are looking for a vector $\tilde{\mu}_p$, such that $max(0, \mu_p^0 + \sum_{i=1}^n \mu_p^i e_i)$ decreases while traversing the rules. Hence, we extend SVG to decide the existence of $\tilde{\mu}$ such that for each renamed apart rule $p(\tilde{x}) \leftarrow c(\tilde{x}, \tilde{y}), q(\tilde{y}) \in P$, we have: $\forall \tilde{x} \cup \tilde{y} \; \{c(\tilde{x}, \tilde{y}) \rightarrow [\tilde{\mu}_p \tilde{x} \geq 1 + \tilde{\mu}_q \tilde{y} \wedge \tilde{\mu}_q \tilde{y} \geq 0]\}$. We compute the equivalent constraint corresponding to each rule, and satisfiability of their conjunction is equivalent to llm-recurrency.

Note that for a ground atom $p(\tilde{e})$ we may have $\tilde{\mu}_p \tilde{e} < 0$. But as $|p(\tilde{e})|$ is defined by $max(0, \tilde{\mu}_p \tilde{e})$, we have $|p(\tilde{e})| = 0$. Observe also that $\tilde{\mu}_p \tilde{e} < 0$ may hold only for atoms $p(\tilde{e})$ such that $c(\tilde{e}, \tilde{y})$ is unsatisfiable for all $\tilde{y}$, *i.e.*, atoms with computation of depth 1. The explanation above justifies the following decidability result.

Theorem 2. *SVG is a decision procedure for llm-recurrency of binary constraint logic programs over $\mathcal{Q}^+, \mathcal{Q}$ and $\mathcal{R}$.*

Example 3. Example 2, continued. We need to find $\mu_p(x, y) = ax + by$ such that

$$ax_1 + bx_2 \geq ax_3 + bx_4 + 1 \; and \; ax_3 + bx_4 \geq 0$$
$$subject \; to \; x_1, x_2, x_3, x_4 \geq 0, x_1 + 2x_2 \geq 3x_3 + 4x_4 + 1$$

One of such solutions is $a = 1, b = 2$ leading to the following linear level mapping $|p(x, y)| = max(0, x + 2y)$. Since constraints solving is done over $\mathcal{Q}^+$ we can further simplify this definition to $|p(x, y)| = x + 2y$.   □

Observe that although SVG is not necessarily complete for binary constraint logic programs over $\mathcal{N}$ or $\mathcal{Z}$, it is still a sound way to prove termination of programs over these domains. Indeed, by considering a CLP($\mathcal{N}$) program as a CLP($\mathcal{Q}$) program we enlarge the domain. Hence, if the program terminates over $\mathcal{Q}$ it also terminates over $\mathcal{N}$. The following example illustrates that the converse is not necessarily true.

Example 4. Consider the program:

$$\texttt{div2(X)} \leftarrow \texttt{X} > 0, 2 * \texttt{Y} = \texttt{X}, \texttt{div2(Y)}.$$

The query $\texttt{X} = 1, \texttt{div2(X)}$ terminates with respect to this program if constraint solving is done over $\mathcal{N}$ or $\mathcal{Z}$. This is clearly not the case for $\mathcal{Q}$.   □

To estimate the relative importance of this class of binary CLP($\mathcal{N}$) programs we have considered a number of logic programming examples, abstracted them and binarised as proposed in [4]. The class of llm-recurrent programs turned out to be broad enough to include binary CLP($\mathcal{N}$) programs corresponding to *fluctuates, mergesort, queens*, and *rotate* [2].

4   Extending llm-Recurrency

In this section we present two extensions of the class of llm-recurrent programs. Our first extension has been motivated by a local approach for termination [4, 11], while the second one by the previous study of numerical computations [17].

4.1   Tuples of Linear Functions

The basic idea of our first extension is to consider tuples of linear level mappings. In other words, a level mapping should map any ground atom to an m-tuple of non-negative real numbers, where m is a fixed natural number. As above, we need to guarantee that this set is well-founded. Hence, we combine linear level mappings lexicographically. As a range for tuple-linear level mappings we choose $((\mathcal{R}^+)^m, \rhd)$, where $x \rhd y$ holds if $x = (x_1, \dots, x_m), y = (y_1, \dots, y_m)$ and there exists $1 \le i \le m$ such that for all $j \in [1, i-1]$, $x_j = y_j$ and $x_i \ge y_i + 1$.

Definition 5. *A level mapping* $| \cdot |^m : \mathcal{C}\text{-base} \rightarrow ((\mathcal{R}^+)^m, \rhd)$ *is called tuple-linear if for any atom* $p(e_1, \dots, e_n) \in \mathcal{C}\text{-base}$,

$$|p(e_1, \dots, e_n)| = (max(0, \mu_p^{(0,1)} + \sum_{j=1}^n \mu_p^{(j,1)} e_j), \dots, max(0, \mu_p^{(0,m)} + \sum_{j=1}^n \mu_p^{(j,m)} e_j))$$

where the coefficients $\mu_p^{(j,i)}$ *are real numbers.*

The order relation on tuples is given as the lexicographic order relationship on $\mathcal{R}^+$. Similarly to the definition above we say that a program P is *tuple llm-recurrent* if there exists a tuple-linear level mapping such that P is recurrent with respect to it. Clearly, tuple llm-recurrency implies termination in the same fashion as in Proposition 1.

Example 5. Consider the following binary CLP($\mathcal{Q}^+$) program:

$$mul(\_, Z) \leftarrow Z = 0.$$
$$mul(N, M) \leftarrow N \ge 0, M > 0, M1 = M - 1, mul\_aux(N, M1, M1).$$
$$mul\_aux(X, Y, Z) \leftarrow X > 0, Y > 0, X1 = X, Y1 = Y - 1, Z1 = Z,$$
$$mul\_aux(X1, Y1, Z1).$$
$$mul\_aux(X, Y, Z) \leftarrow X > 0, Y = 0, X1 = X - 1, Y1 = Z, Z1 = Z,$$
$$mul\_aux(X1, Y1, Z1).$$
$$mul\_aux(X, \_, \_) \leftarrow X = 0.$$

This program is not llm-recurrent. Indeed, if it has been llm recurrent, the maximal depth of any derivation of $mul(n, m)$ would be linear in n and m. However, one can see that the maximal depth of such a computation depends on $m * n$.

To show that the multiplication example is tuple llm-recurrent we use the following level mapping: $|mul(n, m)| = (n, m)$, $|mul\_aux(x, y, z)| = (x, y)$. This level mapping is clearly tuple-linear. To prove the recurrency observe that the following inequalities hold:

$$|\texttt{mul}(\texttt{n},\texttt{m})| = (\texttt{n},\texttt{m}) > (\texttt{n},\texttt{m}-1) = |\texttt{mul\_aux}(\texttt{n},\texttt{m1},\texttt{m1})|$$
$$|\texttt{mul\_aux}(\texttt{x},\texttt{y},\texttt{z})| = (\texttt{x},\texttt{y}) > (\texttt{x},\texttt{y}-1) = |\texttt{mul\_aux}(\texttt{x1},\texttt{y1},\texttt{z1})|$$
$$|\texttt{mul\_aux}(\texttt{x},\texttt{y},\texttt{z})| = (\texttt{x},\texttt{y}) > (\texttt{x}-1,\texttt{z}) = |\texttt{mul\_aux}(\texttt{x1},\texttt{y1},\texttt{z1})|$$

An additional example of a program that is tuple llm-recurrent but not llm-recurrent can be obtained by abstracting and binarising *ackermann*.   □

Decidability of llm-recurrency implies:

Theorem 3. *Tuple llm-recurrency is decidable for* $\mathcal{Q}^+$, $\mathcal{Q}$ *and* $\mathcal{R}$.

Proof. Observe that each function of the tuple should decrease at least for one binary clause. Hence, let n_p be the number of binary clauses defining the predicate symbol p, excluding facts. Then m is limited by $max(\{n_p | p \in \varPi_P\})$. Let $\mu^1, \ldots, \mu^m$ be linear functions of the tuple. Then, for each rule $p(\tilde{x}) \leftarrow c, p(\tilde{y})$ with $vars(c) \subseteq \tilde{x} \cup \tilde{y}$, the following should hold:

$$\forall \tilde{x} \cup \tilde{y} \qquad \{c \to [\mu^1(\tilde{x}-\tilde{y}) \geq 1 \wedge \mu^1(\tilde{y}) \geq 0]\} \vee$$
$$\forall \tilde{x} \cup \tilde{y} \qquad \{c \to [\mu^1(\tilde{x}-\tilde{y}) = 0 \wedge \mu^2(\tilde{x}-\tilde{y}) \geq 1 \wedge \mu^2(\tilde{y}) \geq 0]\} \vee$$

$$\cdots$$

$$\forall \tilde{x} \cup \tilde{y} \quad \{c \to [\mu^1(\tilde{x}-\tilde{y}) = \ldots = \mu^{m-1}(\tilde{x}-\tilde{y}) = 0 \wedge \mu^m(\tilde{x}-\tilde{y}) \geq 1 \wedge \mu^m(\tilde{y}) \geq 0]\}$$

Each one of the disjuncts is similar to (1), *i.e.*, can be decided by SVG.   □

Similarly to the previous case while the method outlined above is not necessarily complete for binary constraint logic programs over $\mathcal{N}$ or $\mathcal{Z}$, it is still a sound way to prove termination of programs over these domains.

4.2   Piecewise Linear Level Mappings

The second extension of the class of the llm recurrent programs has been motivated by our previous study of termination of numerical computations [17]. We have suggested to split the domain of an argument into pairwise disjoint cases, called "adornments" and to specialise the program with respect to the adornments. Termination of the specialised program implies termination of the original one. Moreover, this transformation technique allows us to infer a piecewise linear level mapping proving termination of the original program.

Definition 6. *A level mapping* $| \cdot |: \mathcal{C}\text{-base} \to (\mathcal{R}^+, \rhd)$ *is called* piecewise linear *if there exist linear level mappings* $| \cdot |_1, \ldots, | \cdot |_n: \mathcal{C}\text{-base} \to (\mathcal{R}^+, \rhd)$ *such that for all* $A \in \mathcal{C}\text{-base}$ *there exists* i *such that* $| A | = | A |_i$ *and if* $| A | \neq 0$ *this* i *is unique.*

We can also write a piecewise level mapping $|\cdot|$ as follows:

$$|A| = \begin{cases} |A|_1, & |A|_1 \neq 0, \\ \cdots & \cdots \\ |A|_n, & |A|_n \neq 0, \\ 0, & \textit{otherwise} \end{cases}$$

To see that a piecewise linear level mapping generalises Definition 3 observe that any linear level mapping is a piecewise linear level mapping for $n = 1$. A binary CLP($\mathcal{C}$) program P is called *piecewise llm recurrent* if there exists a piecewise linear level mapping such that P is recurrent with respect to it.

Unlike the results presented in Sections 3 and 4.1 at the moment it is not known to us whether piecewise recurrency is decidable. However, we suggest a technique that upon success allows us to prove piecewise recurrency (and hence, termination). Moreover, this technique finds a piecewise level mapping such that the program is recurrent with respect to it. We present the technique by means of example. Consider the following CLP($\mathcal{N}$) program P:

$$q(X) \leftarrow X + X + Y = 50, q(Y).$$

We are interested in showing termination of $S = \{q(X)\}$.

1. First, we identify the reference points with respect to this clause. *Reference points* with respect to a clause $p(\tilde{x}) \leftarrow c(\tilde{x}, \tilde{y}), p(\tilde{y})$ are solutions of $c(\tilde{x}, \tilde{y}), \tilde{x} = \tilde{y}$. If there is no solution over $\mathcal{N}$ ($\mathcal{Z}$) but there exists a solution $\tilde{x}_0$ over $\mathcal{Q}$ take $\lfloor \tilde{x}_0 \rfloor$. For our example, we need to solve $x + x + y = 50, x = y$ which does not have solutions over $\mathcal{N}$ but it has one solution over $\mathcal{Q}$, namely $\frac{50}{3}$. Hence, we take 16 as the reference point.
2. The following step considers collecting the constraints and constructing the adornments. The set of constraints C is defined as the union of the following three sets of inequalities:
   - set of $\tilde{x} \leq \tilde{x}_0$ for every reference point of the form $\tilde{x}_0$;
   - projection of $c(\tilde{x}, \tilde{y})$ on $\tilde{x}$, i.e., $c'(\tilde{x})$ such that $c(\tilde{x}, \tilde{y}) \models c'(\tilde{x})$ and for every $c''(\tilde{x})$, if $c(\tilde{x}, \tilde{y}) \models c''(\tilde{x})$ then $c'(\tilde{x}) \models c''(\tilde{x})$;
   - if the domain is $\mathcal{N}$, $\mathcal{Q}^+$ or $\mathcal{R}^+$, inequalities of the form $\tilde{x} \geq 0$.

   In our case these sets are $\{X \leq 16\}$, $\{X \leq 25\}$, $\{X \geq 0\}$, respectively. In order to compute the set of adornments $\mathcal{A}_q$ we take all possible conjunctions of the elements of C and their negations. For the running example after simplifying the conjunctions, removing inconsistencies with respect to $\mathcal{N}$ and replacing strict inequalities with the non-strict ones, we obtain $\{0 \leq X \leq 16, 17 \leq X \leq 25, X \geq 26\}$. For the sake of simplicity we denote elements of this set $\{\mathsf{a}, \mathsf{b}, \mathsf{c}\}$. In general, if a number of elements in C is k, the maximal number of adornments is 2^k. Note that k is expected to be small, so the size of the set of adornments should not be problematic in practise.
3. Steps 3-8 have been inspired by the technique we used for numerical computations. Hence, here we present the steps briefly and refer to [17] for further details and proofs. For each binary clause r in P add $\bigvee_{c \in \mathcal{A}_p} c(\tilde{x})$ before a

call $p(\tilde{x})$ in the body of r. By the construction above the disjunction is *true*, thus, the transformed program is equivalent to the original one. In our case, the following program is obtained:

$$q(X) \leftarrow X + X + Y = 50, (0 \leq Y \leq 16 \vee 17 \leq Y \leq 25 \vee Y \geq 26), q(Y).$$

4. For each clause, such that the head of the clause, say $p(\tilde{x})$, has a recursive predicate p, add $\bigvee_{c \in \mathcal{A}_p} c(\tilde{x})$ as the first subgoal in its body. As for the previous step, the introduced call is equivalent to *true*, so that the transformation is obviously correct:

$$q(X) \leftarrow (0 \leq X \leq 16 \vee 17 \leq X \leq 25 \vee X \geq 26),$$
$$X + X + Y = 50, (0 \leq Y \leq 16 \vee 17 \leq Y \leq 25 \vee Y \geq 26), q(Y).$$

5. Next, moving to an alternative procedural interpretation of disjunction, for each clause in which we introduced a disjunction in one of the previous two steps, and for each such introduced disjunction we split these disjunctions, introducing a separate clause for each disjunct. For our running example we obtain 9 clauses. In general, every binary clause of the original program can produce $(2^k)^2$ adorned clauses.

   To prepare the next step in the transformation, note that, in the program resulting from step 5, for each rule r and for each recursive predicate p:
   - if a call $p(\tilde{x})$ occurs in r, it is immediately preceded by some adornment,
   - if an atom $p(\tilde{x})$ occurs as the head of r, it is immediately followed by some adornment.

   Moreover, since the elements $\mathcal{A}_p$ partition the domain, conjuncts like $c_i(\tilde{x})$, $p(\tilde{x})$ and $c_j(\tilde{x}), p(\tilde{x})$ for $i \neq j$, are mutually exclusive, as well as the analogous initial parts of the rules. This means that we can now safely rename the different cases apart.

6. Replace each occurrence of $c(\tilde{x}), p(\tilde{x})$ in the body of the clause with $c(\tilde{x})$, $p^c(\tilde{x})$ and each occurrence of a rule $p(\tilde{x}) \leftarrow c(\tilde{x}), Q$ with the corresponding rule $p^c(\tilde{x}) \leftarrow c(\tilde{x}), Q$. Because of the arguments presented above the LD-trees that exist for the given program and for the renamed program are identical, except for the names of the predicates and for a number of failing 1-step derivations (due to entering clauses that fail in their guard in the given program). As a result, both the semantics (up to renaming) and the termination behaviour of the program are preserved.

7. Remove all rules $p(\tilde{x}) \leftarrow c, \dots$ with an inconsistent constraint c. We get:

$$q^a(X) \leftarrow 0 \leq X \leq 16, X + X + Y = 50, 17 \leq Y \leq 25, q^b(Y).$$
$$q^a(X) \leftarrow 0 \leq X \leq 16, X + X + Y = 50, 26 \leq Y, q^c(Y).$$
$$q^b(X) \leftarrow 17 \leq X \leq 25, X + X + Y = 50, 0 \leq Y \leq 16, q^a(Y).$$

which is the *adorned* program, P^a.

8. Next we need to prove termination of the adorned program with respect to the set of adorned queries $S^a = \{0 \leq X \leq 16, q^a(X)\} \cup \{17 \leq X \leq 25, q^b(X)\} \cup \{X \geq 26, q^c(X)\}$. Observe that for every adornment $c, p^c(e_1, \dots, e_n)$ is called

in a computation of a query in S^a with respect to P^a if and only if $p(e_1, \ldots, e_n)$ is called in a computation of the corresponding query in S with respect to P, and c holds for $e_1, \ldots, e_n$. In our particular case termination can be proved by applying SVG. The following is one of the level mappings obtained.

$$|q^{\mathsf{a}}(x)|^{\mathsf{a}} = \begin{cases} 3x + 50 & 0 \leq x \leq 16, \\ 0 & \textit{otherwise} \end{cases}$$
$$|q^{\mathsf{b}}(x)|^{\mathsf{b}} = \begin{cases} 150 - 3x, & 17 \leq x \leq 25, \\ 0 & \textit{otherwise} \end{cases}$$
$$|q^{\mathsf{c}}(x)|^{\mathsf{c}} = 0$$

9. Finally, we combine the linear level mappings found to obtain a piecewise linear level mapping. In our running example we can write the resulting level mapping as

$$|q(x)| = \begin{cases} 3x + 50 & 0 \leq x \leq 16 \\ 150 - 3x & 17 \leq x \leq 25 \\ 0 & x \geq 26 \end{cases}$$

Since this level-mapping exists we conclude termination of our CLP($\mathcal{N}$) program for all queries $c, q(X)$. This would not be the case if a different constraint domain such as $\mathcal{Q}$ have been considered.

Correctness of this transformation follows from [17]:

Theorem 4. *Let P be a binary CLP program, S be a set of atomic CLP-queries, P^a and S^a the adorned program and the set of adorned queries, respectively. Then, all queries in S terminate with respect to P if and only if all queries in S^a terminate with respect to P^a.*

5   Conclusion

We have identified a class of CLP programs such that a linear level mapping is sufficient to prove their termination. We have seen that membership to this class is decidable and suggested a decision technique. We have further extended this class by considering tuples of linear functions. We have seen that membership to this class is also decidable. Finally, we have discussed piecewise level mappings.

The basic idea of identifying decidable and undecidable subsets of logic programs goes back to [5, 6, 15]. We generalise the class of programs considered to constraint logic programming (recall that logic programming can be seen as constraint logic programming over the domain of Herbrand terms). The restriction we pose is not syntactic. We have seen that llm-recurrency is a decidable condition sufficient for termination for all the domains considered. This condition can be automatically verified by cTI [13].

The idea of using mappings to domains more general than the natural numbers originated in early works on termination analysis [7, 9]. Tuple llm recurrency condition can be seen as a particular instance of this framework. Using tuples has been motivated by [4, 11] that do not compare sizes of atoms but sizes of arguments of these atoms. In [4, 11] a local approach to termination has been suggested, *i.e.* termination proof was based on a (locally verified) property of the computation abstraction. We follow a global approach to termination, *i.e.*, require the existence of a function (level mapping) decreasing along all possible computation paths. In their study of the relationship between local approaches and global approaches Codish and Genaim [3] have proposed an efficient technique that can be seen as an indirect way to prove tuple llm recurrency. Following important differences with our work should be stressed. First, Codish and Genaim consider a subclass of binary programs, so called *binary unfoldings*, *i.e.*, sets of binary clauses closed under composition. Second, as basic components of a tuple we use affine functions of sizes of arguments, while [3] is limited to the sizes themselves. The latter restriction does not allow to analyse bounded-increase examples such as Example 1. Finally, in order for the technique to be applicable, binary clauses are further restricted only to contain inequalities between the same argument positions.

A related technique of using two level-mappings has been recently investigated in [12]. The main difference is that Martin and King use the two level mappings separately for two different goals, *i.e.* proving decrease and boundedness, while we use a lexicographic combination of level mappings to achieve both goals at the same time.

The adornments method presented above has been first presented in context of the numerical computations [17] and in its turn is related to the previous work on splitting predicates [18]. This technique can be seen as a variant of multiple specialisation [19]. However, to the best of our knowledge none of the existing specialisation tools considered constraint logic programming.

A number of interesting questions are considered as future work. First of all, we would like to understand whether the adornments technique is complete for piecewise llm recurrent programs. On a more practical side, we would like to implement these extensions in the termination analyser cTI [13] and evaluate our approach experimentally.

References

1. K. R. Apt and M. Bezem. Acyclic programs. *New Generation Computing*, 9(3/4):335–364, 1991.
2. M. Codish. TerminWeb. Collection of benchmarks available at: http://lvs.cs. bgu.ac.il/~mcodish/suexec/terminweb/bin/terminweb.cgi?command=examples.
3. M. Codish and S. Genaim. Proving termination one loop at a time. In A. Serebrenik and F. Mesnard, editors. *Proceedings of the 13th International Workshop on Logic Programming Environments*, Technical report CW 371, Department of Computer Science, K.U.Leuven, pages 48–59, 2003.
4. M. Codish and C. Taboch. A semantic basis for termination analysis of logic programs. *Journal of Logic Programming*, 41(1):103–123, 1999.
5. D. De Schreye, K. Verschaetse, and M. Bruynooghe. A practical technique for detecting non-terminating queries for a restricted class of Horn clauses, using di-

rected, weighted graphs. In D. H. Warren and P. Szeredi, editors, *Logic Programming, Proceedings of the Seventh International Conference*, pages 649–663. MIT Press, 1990.

6. P. Devienne, P. Lebègue, and J.-C. Routier. Halting problem of one binary horn clause is undecidable. In P. Enjalbert, A. Finkel, and K. W. Wagner, editors, *STACS 93, 10th Annual Symposium on Theoretical Aspects of Computer Science, Proceedings.*, volume 665 of *Lecture Notes in Computer Science*, pages 48–57. Springer Verlag, 1993.

7. R. W. Floyd. Assigning meanings to programs. In J. Schwartz, editor, *Mathematical Aspects of Computer Science*, pages 19–32. American Mathematical Society, 1967. Proceedings of Symposium in Applied Mathematics; v. 19.

8. J. Jaffar and M. J. Maher. Constraint logic programming: A survey. *Journal of Logic Programming*, 19/20:503–582, May/July 1994.

9. S. Katz and Z. Manna. A closer look at termination. *Acta Informatica*, 5:333–352, 1975.

10. V. Lagoon, F. Mesnard, and P. J. Stuckey. Termination analysis with types is more accurate. In C. Palamidessi, editor, *Logic Programming, 19th International Conference on Logic Programming*, pages 254–269. Springer Verlag, 2003.

11. N. Lindenstrauss and Y. Sagiv. Automatic termination analysis of logic programs. In L. Naish, editor, *Proceedings of the Fourteenth International Conference on Logic Programming*, pages 63–77. MIT Press, July 1997.

12. J. C. Martin and A. King. On the inference of natural level mappings. In M. Bruynooghe and K.-K. Lau, editors, *Program Development in Computational Logic*, volume 3049 of *Lecture Notes in Computer Science*. Springer Verlag, 2004.

13. F. Mesnard and U. Neumerkel. Applying static analysis techniques for inferring termination conditions of logic programs. In P. Cousot, editor, *Static Analysis, 8th International Symposium, SAS 2001*, volume 2126 of *Lecture Notes in Computer Science*, pages 93–110. Springer Verlag, 2001.

14. F. Mesnard and S. Ruggieri. On proving left termination of constraint logic programs. *ACM Transaction on Computational Logic*, 4(2):207–259, 2003.

15. S. Ruggieri. Decidability of logic program semantics and applications to testing. *Journal of Logic Programming*, 46(1–2):103–137, November/December 2000.

16. A. Schrijver. *Theory of Linear and Integer Programming*. Wiley, 1986.

17. A. Serebrenik and D. De Schreye. Inference of termination conditions for numerical loops in Prolog. *Theory and Practice of Logic Programming*, 2004. to appear.

18. K. Sohn and A. Van Gelder. Termination detection in logic programs using argument sizes. In *Proceedings of the Tenth ACM SIGACT-SIGART-SIGMOD Symposium on Principles of Database Systems*, pages 216–226. ACM Press, 1991.

19. W. Winsborough. Multiple specialization using minimal-function graph semantics. *Journal of Logic Programming*, 13(2/3):259–290, 1992.

From Natural Semantics to Abstract Machines

Mads Sig Ager

BRICS*
Department of Computer Science, University of Aarhus,
IT-parken, Aabogade 34, DK-8200 Aarhus N, Denmark
mads@brics.dk

Abstract. We describe how to construct correct abstract machines from the class of L-attributed natural semantics introduced by Ibraheem and Schmidt at HOOTS 1997. The construction produces stack-based abstract machines where the stack contains evaluation contexts. It is defined directly on the natural semantics rules. We formalize it as an extraction algorithm and we prove that the algorithm produces abstract machines that are equivalent to the original natural semantics. We illustrate the algorithm by extracting abstract machines from natural semantics for call-by-value and call-by-name evaluation of lambda terms.

1   Introduction

Abstract machines have been widely used in the implementation of programming languages [8]. Most of them have been invented from scratch and subsequently been proved to correctly implement the specification of a programming language [12]. Some of them have been derived from the specification of a programming language using some formal system [11, 18]. Most of these derivations use ad hoc derivation steps and are fairly complicated.

In this work we present a simple approach to the construction of correct abstract machines from natural semantics descriptions. At HOOTS 1997 Ibraheem and Schmidt introduced a restricted class of natural semantics called L-attributed natural semantics [13]. The class of L-attributed natural semantics is restricted to have a left-to-right ordering on the premises of each rule ensuring that a proof search using the rules can be performed as left-to-right tree traversals. We observe that for the class of L-attributed natural semantics it is possible to directly extract abstract machines from the natural semantics rules. The extracted machines are stack based and the stack contains evaluation contexts. We formalize this observation as an extraction algorithm and we prove that the algorithm produces abstract machines that are equivalent to the natural semantics.

---

* Basic Research in Computer Science (www.brics.dk), funded by the Danish National Research Foundation.

S. Etalle(Ed.): LOPSTR 2004, LNCS 3573, pp. 245–261, 2005.

The class of L-attributed natural semantics is large, containing for instance semantics for pure functional languages, impure functional languages, and imperative languages. The extraction algorithm makes it possible to mechanically extract abstract machines that are correct by construction from these semantics. We illustrate the extraction algorithm by extracting abstract machines from L-attributed natural semantics for call-by-value and call-by-name evaluation of λ-terms. In an extended version of this article we also illustrate the algorithm by extracting an abstract machine from a natural semantics for call-by-need evaluation of λ-terms [1].

The rest of this article is organized as follows. We first define the class of L-attributed natural semantics (Section 2.1). We next define an algorithm for extracting abstract machines from L-attributed natural semantics (Section 2.2) and prove its correctness (Section 2.3). We then consider applications of the extraction (Section 3). Finally, we consider limitations of the approach (Section 4), review related work (Section 5), and conclude (Section 6).

2   From Natural Semantics to Abstract Machines

We consider operational semantics for languages consisting of terms. Terms are inductively constructed from atomic terms using term constructors. Other than that, the terms are left unspecified. Values and environments are left unspecified.

- $t \in$ Terms,
- $op \in$ Term constructors,
- $v \in$ Values,
- $\rho \in$ Environments,
- $\sigma \in$ Stacks.

We use the notation $v : \sigma$ for the stack σ with the value v added as the top element. We use subscripting (t_i) and primes (t') to distinguish different occurrences of the meta variables.

2.1   L-Attributed Natural Semantics

In this section we present a restricted class of natural semantics called L-attributed natural semantics. The definition below is essentially identical to the definition of Ibraheem and Schmidt [13]. Similar restrictions on the format of natural semantics rules can be found in Hannan and Miller's work on deriving abstract machines from operational semantics using proof-theoretic methods [11].

Definition 1 (L-attributed natural semantics). *A natural semantics is L-attributed if it consists of rules of the form:*

$$\frac{\rho_1 \vdash t_1' \Downarrow v_1 \qquad \rho_2 \vdash t_2' \Downarrow v_2 \qquad \cdots \qquad \rho_m \vdash t_m' \Downarrow v_m}{\rho_0 \vdash op(t_1, \ldots, t_n) \Downarrow v_{m+1}} \tag{R}$$

$$where \quad \rho_i = f_R^{\rho_i}(t_1, \ldots, t_n, \rho_0, \ldots, \rho_{i-1}, v_1, \ldots, v_{i-1})$$
$$t_i' = f_R^{t_i}(t_1, \ldots, t_n, \rho_0, \ldots, \rho_{i-1}, v_1, \ldots, v_{i-1})$$
$$v_{m+1} = f_R^{val}(t_1, \ldots, t_n, \rho_0, \ldots, \rho_m, v_1, \ldots, v_m)$$

for some partial functions $f_R^{\rho_i}$, $f_R^{t_i}$, and f_R^{val} with $1 \le i \le m$.

Rules with no premises ($m = 0$) are called axiom rules and rules with at least one premise ($m > 0$) are called non-axiom rules. The number of premises m of a rule is not related to the number of subterms n of the term in the conclusion of the rule as illustrated by the following examples:

- A semantics for a language of boolean-valued terms might contain a negation term constructor $\neg t$ with one subterm. The natural semantics rule for the evaluation of $\neg t$ would have one premise stating that the subterm t evaluates to a boolean b. The value in the conclusion of the rule would then be $\neg b$. In this case the number of premises equals the number of subterms.
- For a language with *if*-expressions the number of premises will be less than the number of subterms in rules for the *if* term constructor *if t_0 then t_1 else t_2*. There will be one premise for the evaluation of the first subterm t_0 and one premise for the evaluation of either t_1 or t_2.
- A natural semantics for call-by-value evaluation of λ-terms contains a rule for the application term constructor $t_0 t_1$ with two subterms. This rule has three premises: the evaluation of t_0 to a function value, the evaluation of t_1 to an argument value, and the evaluation of the application of the function value to the argument value. In this case the number of premises is greater than the number of subterms.

Compared to Kahn's original definition of natural semantics [14], an L-attributed natural semantics is restricted to working on ternary relations relating a term and an environment to a value. The restriction to ternary relations is not a serious restriction: environments, terms, and values are left unspecified, so all three components can have structure. In Kahn's format, each rule has an unordered collection of premises and the rule may have conditions. The L-attributed rules instead have a left-to-right ordering on the premises. This ordering is captured in the definition by ensuring that each of the environments ρ_i, terms t_i, and values v_i can be computed from the previous environments, terms, and values. Furthermore, the rules do not have explicit conditions. Conditions are encoded as part of the functional dependencies $f_R^{t_i}$, $f_R^{\rho_i}$, and f_R^{val} between environments, terms, and values. Therefore, the functions giving the dependencies are partial functions and a rule only applies if the dependency functions are defined for the given arguments.

Enforcing a left-to-right ordering on the premises of the rules ensures that if the semantics is deterministic, a proof search using the rules can be performed as a single left-to-right depth-first traversal. Therefore, if the semantics is deterministic, the proof search can be implemented as a recursively defined evaluator in a functional language. For the rest of the development in this article we do not assume that the semantics is deterministic.

2.2   Abstract-Machine Extraction

We now show how to extract an abstract machine directly from L-attributed natural semantics rules. The abstract machines we consider are state-transition systems operating on three types of states:

1. Triples $(t, \rho, \sigma)_{\mathcal{E}}$ consisting of a term, an environment, and a stack. States of this form correspond to evaluating the term t in the environment ρ and stack σ.
2. Pairs $(\sigma, v)_{\mathcal{A}}$ consisting of a stack and a value. States of this form correspond to 'applying' the stack σ to the value v.
3. Values v representing the final state of a computation.

Before defining the extraction, we introduce a bit of notation. Given an L-attributed natural semantics rule of the form

$$\frac{\rho_1 \vdash t_1' \Downarrow v_1 \qquad \rho_2 \vdash t_2' \Downarrow v_2 \qquad \cdots \qquad \rho_m \vdash t_m' \Downarrow v_m}{\rho_0 \vdash op(t_1, \ldots, t_n) \Downarrow v_{m+1}} \tag{R}$$

where
$$\rho_i = f_{\mathrm{R}}^{\rho_i}(t_1, \ldots, t_n, \rho_0, \ldots, \rho_{i-1}, v_1, \ldots, v_{i-1})$$
$$t_i' = f_{\mathrm{R}}^{t_i}(t_1, \ldots, t_n, \rho_0, \ldots, \rho_{i-1}, v_1, \ldots, v_{i-1})$$
$$v_{m+1} = f_{\mathrm{R}}^{val}(t_1, \ldots, t_n, \rho_0, \ldots, \rho_m, v_1, \ldots, v_m)$$

for $1 \leq i \leq m$, we define the tuples $\mathrm{R}_j[\overline{t_1}, \ldots, \overline{t_n}, \overline{\rho_0}, \ldots, \overline{\rho_j}, \overline{v_1}, \ldots, \overline{v_{j-1}}]$ for each $1 \leq j \leq m$. The overlining of terms, environments, and values indicates that the terms, environments, and values are only present in the tuple if they are used by dependency functions $f_{\mathrm{R}}^{\rho_k}$ or $f_{\mathrm{R}}^{t_k}$ for $k > j$ or by f_{R}^{val}. A term, environment, or value is used by a later dependency function if the corresponding variable occurs free in the body of one of these functions. For such a tuple, we define the application $f(\overline{t_1}, \ldots, \overline{t_n}, \overline{\rho_0}, \ldots, \overline{\rho_j}, \overline{v_1}, \ldots, \overline{v_{j-1}}, v_j)$ to be the application of the function f to the elements that are actually present in the tuple and a value supplying dummy arguments for the elements not present in the tuple. Supplying dummy arguments makes sense since they will not be used—if they were used, there would be a value corresponding to the overlined variable in the tuple.

With these notational conventions in place, we are ready to define the extraction of an abstract machine from an L-attributed natural semantics.

Definition 2 (Extracted abstract machine). *Given an L-attributed natural semantics where each rule has a distinct name, define the extracted abstract machine consisting of the following transition rules:*

1. *An unload rule to terminate the computation:*

$$(\sigma_0, v)_{\mathcal{A}} \rightarrow v$$

where σ_0 is the empty stack.

2. *For each axiom in the L-attributed natural semantics*

$$\rho \vdash op(t_1, \ldots, t_n) \Downarrow v \tag{R}$$

the rule:

$$(op(t_1, \ldots, t_n), \rho, \sigma)_\mathcal{E} \to (\sigma, v)_\mathcal{A}$$

where $v = f_R^{val}(t_1, \ldots, t_n, \rho)$.

3. *For each non-axiom rule in the L-attributed natural semantics*

$$\frac{\rho_1 \vdash t_1' \Downarrow v_1 \qquad \rho_2 \vdash t_2' \Downarrow v_2 \qquad \cdots \qquad \rho_m \vdash t_m' \Downarrow v_m}{\rho_0 \vdash op(t_1, \ldots, t_n) \Downarrow v_{m+1}} \tag{R}$$

where
$$\rho_i = f_R^{\rho_i}(t_1, \ldots, t_n, \rho_0, \ldots, \rho_{i-1}, v_1, \ldots, v_{i-1})$$
$$t_i' = f_R^{t_i}(t_1, \ldots, t_n, \rho_0, \ldots, \rho_{i-1}, v_1, \ldots, v_{i-1})$$
$$v_{m+1} = f_R^{val}(t_1, \ldots, t_n, \rho_0, \ldots, \rho_m, v_1, \ldots, v_m)$$
for $1 \leq i \leq m$, *the rules:*

– *Initial evaluation rule:*

$$(op(t_1, \ldots, t_n), \rho_0, \sigma)_\mathcal{E} \to (t_1', \rho_1, R_1[\overline{t_1}, \ldots, \overline{t_n}, \overline{\rho_0}, \overline{\rho_1}] : \sigma)_\mathcal{E}$$

where $t_1' = f_R^{t_1}(t_1, \ldots, t_n, \rho_0)$ *and* $\rho_1 = f_R^{\rho_1}(t_1, \ldots, t_n, \rho_0)$.

– *Stack application rules for* $1 \leq i \leq m - 1$:

$$(R_i[\overline{t_1}, \ldots, \overline{t_n}, \overline{\rho_0}, \ldots, \overline{\rho_i}, \overline{v_1}, \ldots, \overline{v_{i-1}}] : \sigma, v_i)_\mathcal{A} \to$$
$$(t_{i+1}', \rho_{i+1}, R_{i+1}[\overline{t_1}, \ldots, \overline{t_n}, \overline{\rho_0}, \ldots, \overline{\rho_{i+1}}, \overline{v_1}, \ldots, \overline{v_i}] : \sigma)_\mathcal{E}$$

where $t_{i+1}' = f_R^{t_{i+1}}(\overline{t_1}, \ldots, \overline{t_n}, \overline{\rho_0}, \ldots, \overline{\rho_i}, \overline{v_1}, \ldots, \overline{v_{i-1}}, v_i)$ *and*
$$\rho_{i+1} = f_R^{\rho_{i+1}}(\overline{t_1}, \ldots, \overline{t_n}, \overline{\rho_0}, \ldots, \overline{\rho_i}, \overline{v_1}, \ldots, \overline{v_{i-1}}, v_i).$$

– *Final stack application rule:*

$$(R_m[\overline{t_1}, \ldots, \overline{t_n}, \overline{\rho_0}, \ldots, \overline{\rho_m}, \overline{v_1}, \ldots, \overline{v_{m-1}}] : \sigma, v_m)_\mathcal{A} \to (\sigma, v_{m+1})_\mathcal{A}$$

where $v_{m+1} = f_R^{val}(\overline{t_1}, \ldots, \overline{t_n}, \overline{\rho_0}, \ldots, \overline{\rho_m}, \overline{v_1}, \ldots, \overline{v_{m-1}}, v_m)$.

The stack introduced by the extraction algorithm is a stack of evaluation contexts. The extraction is therefore a new way of constructing evaluation contexts in the style of Felleisen [9]. (Our previous work on deriving abstract machines by continuation-passing style transforming and defunctionalizing evaluators provided another construction of evaluation contexts as defunctionalized continuations [2, 7].)

2.3   Correctness of the Extraction

The extraction of Definition 2 is partially correct with respect to the original L-attributed natural semantics. The correctness is partial in the sense that we only consider finite derivations, i.e., convergent computations.

Theorem 1 (Equivalence). *An L-attributed natural semantics and the extracted abstract machine are equivalent. For all term constructors op, terms $t_1, \ldots, t_n$, environments ρ, and values v:*

$$\rho \vdash op(t_1, \ldots, t_n) \Downarrow v \Rightarrow (op(t_1, \ldots, t_n), \rho, \sigma_0)_{\mathcal{E}} \rightarrow^* v$$

and

$$(op(t_1, \ldots, t_n), \rho, \sigma_0)_{\mathcal{E}} \rightarrow^k v \Rightarrow \rho \vdash op(t_1, \ldots, t_n) \Downarrow v$$

for some finite $k > 0$, where σ_0 is the empty stack.

In order to prove Theorem 1 we prove two lemmas that each imply one part of the equivalence.

Lemma 1. *For all term constructors op, terms $t_1, \ldots, t_n$, environments ρ, stacks σ, and values v:*

$$\rho \vdash op(t_1, \ldots, t_n) \Downarrow v \Rightarrow (op(t_1, \ldots, t_n), \rho, \sigma)_{\mathcal{E}} \rightarrow^* (\sigma, v)_{\mathcal{A}}.$$

Proof. By induction on the height of the derivation of

$$\rho \vdash op(t_1, \ldots, t_n) \Downarrow v$$

Assume that the last rule used in the derivation was an axiom of the form

$$\rho \vdash op(t_1, \ldots, t_n) \Downarrow v \tag{R}$$

then by definition the extracted abstract machine contains the rule

$$(op(t_1, \ldots, t_n), \rho, \sigma)_{\mathcal{E}} \rightarrow (\sigma, v)_{\mathcal{A}}$$

where $v = f_{\mathrm{R}}^{val}(t_1, \ldots, t_n, \rho_0)$ which is what we needed to show.

Assume that the last rule used in the derivation was a non-axiom rule of the form

$$\frac{\rho_1 \vdash t_1' \Downarrow v_1 \qquad \rho_2 \vdash t_2' \Downarrow v_2 \qquad \cdots \qquad \rho_m \vdash t_m' \Downarrow v_m}{\rho_0 \vdash op(t_1, \ldots, t_n) \Downarrow v_{m+1}} \tag{R}$$

where
$$\begin{aligned}
\rho_i &= f_{\mathrm{R}}^{\rho_i}(t_1, \ldots, t_n, \rho_0, \ldots, \rho_{i-1}, v_1, \ldots, v_{i-1}) \\
t_i' &= f_{\mathrm{R}}^{t_i}(t_1, \ldots, t_n, \rho_0, \ldots, \rho_{i-1}, v_1, \ldots, v_{i-1}) \\
v_{m+1} &= f_{\mathrm{R}}^{val}(t_1, \ldots, t_n, \rho_0, \ldots, \rho_m, v_1, \ldots, v_m).
\end{aligned}$$

By inversion we know that each of the premises holds and therefore by the induction hypothesis for all $1 \leq i \leq m$

$$(t'_i, \rho_i, \sigma)_{\mathcal{E}} \rightarrow^* (\sigma, v_i)_{\mathcal{A}}$$

for all stacks σ. For each $1 \leq j \leq m$, we prove that

$$(op(t_1, \ldots, t_n), \rho_0, \sigma)_{\mathcal{E}} \rightarrow^* (R_j[\overline{t_1}, \ldots, \overline{t_n}, \overline{\rho_0}, \ldots, \overline{\rho_j}, \overline{v_1}, \ldots, \overline{v_{j-1}}] : \sigma, v_j)_{\mathcal{A}}$$

by induction on j.

Base case: $j = 1$ and by definition of the extracted abstract machine there is an initial evaluation rule such that

$$(op(t_1, \ldots, t_n), \rho_0, \sigma)_{\mathcal{E}} \rightarrow (t'_1, \rho_1, R_1[\overline{t_1}, \ldots, \overline{t_n}, \overline{\rho_0}, \overline{\rho_1}] : \sigma)_{\mathcal{E}}.$$

By the outer induction hypothesis on the premises of the L-attributed natural semantics rule, the following derivation exists:

$$(op(t_1, \ldots, t_n), \rho_0, \sigma)_{\mathcal{E}} \rightarrow (t'_1, \rho_1, R_1[\overline{t_1}, \ldots, \overline{t_n}, \overline{\rho_0}, \overline{\rho_1}] : \sigma)_{\mathcal{E}}$$
$$\rightarrow^* (R_1[\overline{t_1}, \ldots, \overline{t_n}, \overline{\rho_0}, \overline{\rho_1}] : \sigma, v_1)_{\mathcal{A}}.$$

Induction case: $j > 1$. By the induction hypothesis on $j - 1$ we can derive

$$(op(t_1, \ldots, t_n), \rho_0, \sigma)_{\mathcal{E}} \rightarrow^* (R_{j-1}[\overline{t_1}, \ldots, \overline{t_n}, \overline{\rho_0}, \ldots, \overline{\rho_{j-1}}, \overline{v_1}, \ldots, \overline{v_{j-2}}] : \sigma, v_{j-1})_{\mathcal{A}}.$$

By definition the extracted abstract machine contains the rule

$$(R_{j-1}[\overline{t_1}, \ldots, \overline{t_n}, \overline{\rho_0}, \ldots, \overline{\rho_{j-1}}, \overline{v_1}, \ldots, \overline{v_{j-2}}] : \sigma, v_{j-1})_{\mathcal{A}} \rightarrow$$
$$(t'_j, \rho_j, R_j[\overline{t_1}, \ldots, \overline{t_n}, \overline{\rho_0}, \ldots, \overline{\rho_j}, \overline{v_1}, \ldots, \overline{v_{j-1}}] : \sigma)_{\mathcal{E}}.$$

By the outer induction hypothesis on the premises of the L-attributed natural semantics rule, the following holds:

$$(t'_j, \rho_j, R_j[\overline{t_1}, \ldots, \overline{t_n}, \overline{\rho_0}, \ldots, \overline{\rho_j}, \overline{v_1}, \ldots, \overline{v_{j-1}}] : \sigma)_{\mathcal{E}} \rightarrow^*$$
$$(R_j[\overline{t_1}, \ldots, \overline{t_n}, \overline{\rho_0}, \ldots, \overline{\rho_j}, \overline{v_1}, \ldots, \overline{v_{j-1}}] : \sigma, v_j)_{\mathcal{A}}.$$

Putting these parts together finishes the subproof.

By what we have just proved with $j = m$ combined with the final stack application rule of the extracted abstract machine we have the following derivation

$$(op(t_1, \ldots, t_n), \rho, \sigma)_{\mathcal{E}} \rightarrow^* (R_m[\overline{t_1}, \ldots, \overline{t_n}, \overline{\rho_0}, \ldots, \overline{\rho_m}, \overline{v_1}, \ldots, \overline{v_{m-1}}] : \sigma, v_m)_{\mathcal{A}}$$
$$\rightarrow (\sigma, v_{m+1})_{\mathcal{A}}$$

which concludes the proof.

Setting $\sigma = \sigma_0$, the empty stack, in Lemma 1 we obtain one direction of Theorem 1.

Lemma 2. *For all term constructors* op, *terms* $t_1, \ldots, t_n$, *environments* ρ, *stacks* σ, *and values* v, *if*

$$(op(t_1, \ldots, t_n), \rho, \sigma)_{\mathcal{E}} \to^k v$$

for a finite $k > 0$ *then*

$$\rho \vdash op(t_1, \ldots, t_n) \Downarrow v'$$

for some value v' *and there exists a prefix of the abstract machine derivation of length* $a < k$ *such that*

$$(op(t_1, \ldots, t_n), \rho, \sigma)_{\mathcal{E}} \to^a (\sigma, v')_{\mathcal{A}}.$$

Proof. By induction on the length k of the derivation.

Base case: $k = 2$. The minimum length of a derivation of the extracted abstract machine is two steps, and the derivation has the form:

$$(op(t_1, \ldots, t_n), \rho, \sigma_0)_{\mathcal{E}} \to (\sigma_0, v)_{\mathcal{A}} \to v$$

where σ_0 is the empty stack. The first step of this derivation is only possible for a rule in the extracted abstract machine that corresponds to an axiom in the L-attributed natural semantics. Since such a rule exists in the extracted abstract machine, the following axiom must be a part of the natural semantics:

$$\rho \vdash op(t_1, \ldots, t_n) \Downarrow v$$

Setting $a = 1$ finishes this case.

Induction case: $k > 2$. Since the number of steps in the abstract-machine derivation is larger than two, the first rule used in the derivation was extracted from a natural semantics rule with $m \geq 1$ premises:

$$\frac{\rho_1 \vdash t_1' \Downarrow v_1 \qquad \rho_2 \vdash t_2' \Downarrow v_2 \qquad \cdots \qquad \rho_m \vdash t_m' \Downarrow v_m}{\rho_0 \vdash op(t_1, \ldots, t_n) \Downarrow v_{m+1}} \quad \text{(R)}$$

where
$$\rho_i = f_R^{\rho_i}(t_1, \ldots, t_n, \rho_0, \ldots, \rho_{i-1}, v_1, \ldots, v_{i-1})$$
$$t_i' = f_R^{t_i}(t_1, \ldots, t_n, \rho_0, \ldots, \rho_{i-1}, v_1, \ldots, v_{i-1})$$
$$v_{m+1} = f_R^{val}(t_1, \ldots, t_n, \rho_0, \ldots, \rho_m, v_1, \ldots, v_m).$$

We start by proving that for all $1 \leq i \leq m$ there exists a prefix of the abstract machine derivation of length $a_i < k - 1$ such that

$$(op(t_1, \ldots, t_n), \rho, \sigma)_{\mathcal{E}} \to^{a_i} (R_i[\overline{t_1}, \ldots, \overline{t_n}, \overline{\rho_0}, \ldots, \overline{\rho_i}, \overline{v_1}, \ldots, \overline{v_{i-1}}] : \sigma, v_i)_{\mathcal{A}}$$

and

$$\rho_i \vdash t_i' \Downarrow v_i$$

for some value v_i. The proof is by induction on i.

Base case: $i = 1$. The derivation of length k has the following form

$$(op(t_1, \ldots, t_n), \rho, \sigma)_\mathcal{E} \to (t_1', \rho_1, R_1[\overline{t_1}, \ldots, \overline{t_n}, \overline{\rho_0}, \overline{\rho_1}] : \sigma)_\mathcal{E} \to^{k-1} v$$

By the outer induction hypothesis on $k - 1$

$$\rho_1 \vdash t_1' \Downarrow v_1$$

and there exists a prefix of the abstract machine derivation of length $p < k - 1$ such that

$$(t_1', \rho_1, R_1[\overline{t_1}, \ldots, \overline{t_n}, \overline{\rho_0}, \overline{\rho_1}] : \sigma)_\mathcal{E} \to^p (R_1[\overline{t_1}, \ldots, \overline{t_n}, \overline{\rho_0}, \overline{\rho_1}] : \sigma, v_1)_\mathcal{A}.$$

Since the stack is non-empty, a final state cannot be reached in less than two steps, so we know that $p < k - 2$. Letting $a_1 = p + 1$ finishes this case.

Inductive case: $i = t + 1$ for some $t \geq 1$. By the induction hypothesis on t

$$(op(t_1, \ldots, t_n), \rho, \sigma)_\mathcal{E} \to^{a_t} (R_t[\overline{t_1}, \ldots, \overline{t_n}, \overline{\rho_0}, \ldots, \overline{\rho_t}, \overline{v_1}, \ldots, \overline{v_{t-1}}] : \sigma, v_t)_\mathcal{A}$$

for some $a_t < k - 1$. By definition, the extracted abstract machine contains the stack application rule

$$(R_t[\overline{t_1}, \ldots, \overline{t_n}, \overline{\rho_0}, \ldots, \overline{\rho_t}, \overline{v_1}, \ldots, \overline{v_{t-1}}] : \sigma, v_t)_\mathcal{A} \to$$
$$(t_{t+1}', \rho_{t+1}, R_{t+1}[\overline{t_1}, \ldots, \overline{t_n}, \overline{\rho_0}, \ldots, \overline{\rho_{t+1}}, \overline{v_1}, \ldots, \overline{v_t}] : \sigma)_\mathcal{E}.$$

We have that

$$(t_{t+1}', \rho_{t+1}, R_{t+1}[\overline{t_1}, \ldots, \overline{t_n}, \overline{\rho_0}, \ldots, \overline{\rho_{t+1}}, \overline{v_1}, \ldots, \overline{v_t}] : \sigma)_\mathcal{E} \to^{k-(a_t+1)} v$$

and by the outer induction hypothesis

$$\rho_{t+1} \vdash t_{t+1}' \Downarrow v_{t+1}$$

for some v_{t+1} and there exists a prefix of the abstract machine derivation of length $p < k - (a_t + 1)$ such that

$$(t_{t+1}', \rho_{t+1}, R_{t+1}[\overline{t_1}, \ldots, \overline{t_n}, \overline{\rho_0}, \ldots, \overline{\rho_{t+1}}, \overline{v_1}, \ldots, \overline{v_t}] : \sigma)_\mathcal{E} \to^p$$
$$(R_{t+1}[\overline{t_1}, \ldots, \overline{t_n}, \overline{\rho_0}, \ldots, \overline{\rho_{t+1}}, \overline{v_1}, \ldots, \overline{v_t}] : \sigma, v_{t+1})_\mathcal{A}$$

Set $a_{t+1} = a_t + p + 1 < k$. Since the stack is non-empty in the configuration after a_{t+1} steps, a final state cannot be reached in less than two steps. Therefore $a_{t+1} < k - 1$ which finishes the case.

We have just proved that for each $1 \leq i \leq m$, $\rho_i \vdash t_i' \Downarrow v_i$. Therefore, we can build a derivation of $\rho_0 \vdash op(t_1, \ldots, t_n) \Downarrow v$ using the natural semantics rule from which the first step in the abstract-machine derivation was extracted. We have also proved that there exists a prefix of the abstract machine derivation of the form

$$(op(t_1, \ldots, t_n), \rho, \sigma)_\mathcal{E} \to^{a_m}$$
$$(R_m[\overline{t_1}, \ldots, \overline{t_n}, \overline{\rho_0}, \ldots, \overline{\rho_m}, \overline{v_1}, \ldots, \overline{v_{m-1}}] : \sigma, v_m)_\mathcal{A}$$

where $a_m < k - 1$. Combining this with the final stack application rule extracted from the natural semantics rule yields the prefix

$$(op(t_1, \ldots, t_n), \rho, \sigma)_{\mathcal{E}} \rightarrow^{a_m+1} (\sigma, v)_{\mathcal{A}}$$

of length $a_m + 1 < k$ which finishes the proof.

Setting $\sigma = \sigma_0$, the empty stack, in Lemma 2 we obtain the second direction of Theorem 1. Therefore, the proof of Theorem 1 is a straightforward corollary of Lemmas 1 and 2.

3   Applications

In Section 2 we have shown that abstract machines can be extracted directly from L-attributed natural semantics. In this section we illustrate this extraction.

3.1   Call-by-Value Evaluation of λ-Terms

We first consider the following standard natural semantics for call-by-value evaluation of λ-terms. Terms are λ-calculus terms: variables x, abstractions $\lambda x.t$, and applications $t_0 t_1$. Values are closures $\langle x, t, \rho \rangle$, which are triples containing a variable, a term, and an environment. An environment ρ is a partial function from variables to values.

$$\rho \vdash x \Downarrow \rho(x) \qquad \text{(VAR)}$$

$$\rho \vdash \lambda x.t \Downarrow \langle x, t, \rho \rangle \qquad \text{(LAM)}$$

$$\frac{\rho \vdash t_0 \Downarrow \langle x, t', \rho' \rangle \qquad \rho \vdash t_1 \Downarrow v' \qquad \rho'[x \mapsto v'] \vdash t' \Downarrow v}{\rho \vdash t_0 t_1 \Downarrow v} \qquad \text{(APP)}$$

This natural semantics is obviously L-attributed: there is a left-to-right ordering of the premises of each rule, and the dependency of later terms, environments, and values on previous terms, environments and values can be easily specified as functions. Therefore, we can apply the extraction of Section 2.2 to obtain an abstract machine. The resulting abstract machine is as follows:

1. Unload rule:

$$(\sigma_0, v)_{\mathcal{A}} \rightarrow v$$

2. Axiom rules:

$$(x, \rho, \sigma)_{\mathcal{E}} \rightarrow (\sigma, \rho(x))_{\mathcal{A}}$$

$$(\lambda x.t, \rho, \sigma)_{\mathcal{E}} \rightarrow (\sigma, \langle x, t, \rho \rangle)_{\mathcal{A}}$$

3. Non-axiom rules:

$$(t_0 \, t_1, \rho, \sigma)_{\mathcal{E}} \rightarrow (t_0, \rho, \text{APP}_1[t_1, \rho] : \sigma)_{\mathcal{E}}$$

$$(\text{APP}_1[t_1, \rho] : \sigma, v_1)_{\mathcal{A}} \rightarrow (t_1, \rho, \text{APP}_2[v_1] : \sigma)_{\mathcal{E}}$$

$$(\text{APP}_2[\langle x, t, \rho' \rangle] : \sigma, v_2)_{\mathcal{A}} \rightarrow (t, \rho'[x \mapsto v_2], \text{APP}_3[] : \sigma)_{\mathcal{E}}$$

$$(\text{APP}_3[] : \sigma, v)_{\mathcal{A}} \rightarrow (\sigma, v)_{\mathcal{A}}$$

We identify this machine as a variant of the CEK machine [10]. The only difference is that the extracted machine pushes an empty evaluation context on the stack in the function application rule. This evaluation context is removed from the stack by the last rule and the value is passed unchanged to the next evaluation context. Our extracted machine is therefore not properly tail-recursive. We are currently extending our extraction to identify when the last evaluation context is empty and the f_{R}^{val} is the 'identity function' that just returns the value of the last premise of a rule. In this case we could avoid adding an evaluation context to the stack and not define the final stack application rule, which would correspond to a tail-call optimization.

3.2 Call-by-Name Evaluation of λ-Terms

The following natural semantics is the standard semantics for call-by-name evaluation of λ-terms. As in Section 3.1, terms are λ-calculus terms: variables x, abstractions $\lambda x.t$, and applications $t_0 \, t_1$. Values are closures $\langle x, t, \rho \rangle$ which are triples containing a variable, a term, and an environment. An environment ρ is a partial function from variables to pairs (t, ρ) consisting of a term and an environment.

$$\frac{\rho(x) = (t, \rho') \qquad \rho' \vdash t \Downarrow v}{\rho \vdash x \Downarrow v} \qquad (\text{VAR})$$

$$\rho \vdash \lambda x.t \Downarrow \langle x, t, \rho \rangle \qquad (\text{LAM})$$

$$\frac{\rho \vdash t_0 \Downarrow \langle x, t, \rho' \rangle \qquad \rho'[x \mapsto (t_1, \rho)] \vdash t \Downarrow v}{\rho \vdash t_0 \, t_1 \Downarrow v} \qquad (\text{APP})$$

This natural semantics is L-attributed. It is easy to see that the LAM and APP rules fit the format of L-attributed natural semantics, but the VAR rule deserves a bit of explanation. The rule has one premise and a condition. Putting it into L-attributed form, we have a rule of the form:

$$\frac{\rho_1 \vdash t_1 \Downarrow v}{\rho_0 \vdash x \Downarrow v} \qquad (\text{VAR'})$$

The condition $\rho(x) = (t, \rho')$ of the VAR rule needs to be captured in the functional dependencies $f_{\text{VAR}}^{t_1}$ and $f_{\text{VAR}'}^{\rho_1}$. The following functions capture the condition:

$$f_{\text{VAR}'}^{t_1}(x, \rho_0) = \begin{cases} t & \text{if } \rho_0(x) = (t, \rho') \\ \text{undefined} & \text{otherwise} \end{cases}$$

$$f_{\text{VAR}'}^{\rho_1}(x, \rho_0) = \begin{cases} \rho' & \text{if } \rho_0(x) = (t, \rho') \\ \text{undefined} & \text{otherwise} \end{cases}$$

If the dependency functions are undefined for some arguments, the condition is not true, and the rule does not apply.

With this explanation, we see that the natural semantics is L-attributed, and we can apply the extraction of Section 2.2 to obtain an abstract machine. The resulting abstract machine is as follows:

1. Unload rule:

$$(\sigma_0, v)_{\mathcal{A}} \to v$$

2. Axiom rules:

$$(\lambda x.t, \rho, \sigma)_{\mathcal{E}} \to (\sigma, \langle x, t, \rho \rangle)_{\mathcal{A}}$$

3. Non-axiom rules:

$$(x, \rho, \sigma)_{\mathcal{E}} \to (t, \rho', \text{VAR}_1[\,] : \sigma)_{\mathcal{E}} \quad \text{if } \rho(x) = (t, \rho')$$

$$(\text{VAR}_1[\,] : \sigma, v)_{\mathcal{A}} \to (\sigma, v)_{\mathcal{A}}$$

$$(t_0\, t_1, \rho, \sigma)_{\mathcal{E}} \to (t_0, \rho, \text{APP}_1[t_1, \rho] : \sigma)_{\mathcal{E}}$$

$$(\text{APP}_1[t, \rho] : \sigma, \langle x, t', \rho' \rangle)_{\mathcal{A}} \to (t', \rho'[x \mapsto (t, \rho)], \text{APP}_2[\,] : \sigma)_{\mathcal{E}}$$

$$(\text{APP}_2[\,] : \sigma, v)_{\mathcal{A}} \to (\sigma, v)_{\mathcal{A}}$$

As in the call-by-value case, the machine is not properly tail recursive. Both the VAR_1 and APP_2 evaluation contexts are empty, and when given a value they both pass it directly to the next evaluation context on the stack. We are currently extending the extraction algorithm to avoid generating these empty evaluation contexts. Such an extension would correspond to a tail-call optimization.

One might hope to obtain the Krivine machine [6] from the call-by-name semantics. However, the extraction always gives two transition relations: an eval transition relation where the left-hand side of the transitions are triples and an apply transition relation where the left-hand side of the transitions are pairs. The Krivine machine only has one transition relation, so we cannot directly obtain it by the extraction of Section 2.2. It is easy to transform the machine obtained into the Krivine machine, but in its current form the extraction does not give it directly.

3.3   Call-by-Need Evaluation of λ-Terms

Launchbury gave a natural semantics for call-by-need evaluation of λ-terms [15] which Sestoft used as the starting point of his derivation of a lazy abstract machine [18]. Before deriving an abstract machine, Sestoft changed the renaming behaviour of Launchbury's natural semantics. Sestoft's revised version of Launchbury's natural semantics is L-attributed and we can therefore apply the extraction algorithm to obtain an abstract machine. The extracted abstract machine is essentially Sestoft's mark 1 machine. Due to lack of space we omit the details which can be found in an extended version of this article [1].

3.4   Other Applications

In Sections 3.1 and 3.2 we have constructed abstract machines from natural semantics for call-by-value and call-by-name evaluation of λ-terms. Many natural semantics fit the format of L-attributed natural semantics. For instance, one can give an L-attributed natural semantics for λ-calculus extended with exceptions, state, and combinations of exceptions and state and therefore stack inspection can be specified with an L-attributed natural semantics [3]. Simple imperative languages can also be given L-attributed natural semantics. From each of these natural semantics, the extraction algorithm yields a correct abstract machine.

4   Limitations

The extraction presented in Section 2.2 has three main limitations:

1. The extraction algorithm is restricted to L-attributed natural semantics, which rules out some natural semantics. For instance, the mini-ML natural semantics of Kahn is not L-attributed because of cyclic dependencies used to model recursive bindings[1] [14].
2. If an L-attributed natural semantics contains multiple rules for the same term, the abstract machine resulting from the extraction is non-deterministic.
3. As explained in Sections 3.1 and 3.2, the extraction algorithm does not give properly tail-recursive abstract machines.

We are currently working on extending both the class of L-attributed natural semantics and the extraction algorithm to address these limitations.

Another limitation of the approach is that we only consider partial correctness in the sense that we only consider convergent computations. In order to address the issue of divergent computations we would have to provide a means

---

[1] Note that this does not mean that recursive bindings cannot be described with an L-attributed natural semantics. Some natural semantics descriptions of recursive bindings are L-attributed while others are not. For instance, Sestoft's L-attributed version of Launchbury's natural semantics for lazy evaluation of λ-terms includes recursive bindings [18].

of reasoning about divergent computations in the framework of natural semantics. Ibraheem and Schmidt considered divergent computations by applying a coinductive interpretation of some of the natural semantics rules [13]. We leave such a generalization for future work.

5   Related Work

Defining natural semantics and abstract machines separately and then proving that they coincide is standard. Most semantics textbooks describe both kinds of semantics and show how to relate them [17, 19]. The goal of our work is to mechanize the extraction of abstract machines from natural semantics so that the extracted abstract machines are correct by construction.

In previous work, we have observed that defunctionalized, continuation-passing style evaluators are transition systems, i.e., abstract machines [2, 3, 4, 5, 7]. Starting from an evaluator written in a functional programming language such as ML [16], we (1) transform the evaluator into continuation-passing style to make its flow of control explicit, and (2) defunctionalize the continuations to make them first order, obtaining a stack of evaluation contexts. The result is the ML-encoding of an abstract machine, and the correctness of the abstract machine is a corollary of the correctness of the original evaluator and of the program transformations. The evaluators are direct encodings of natural semantics:

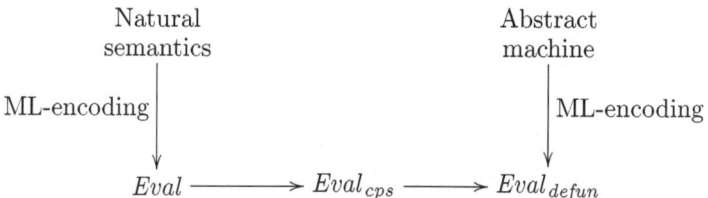

The work presented in this article is a different approach to constructing correct abstract machines from natural-semantics descriptions. We extract a correct abstract machine directly from the natural semantics rules:

$$\text{Natural semantics} \dashrightarrow \text{Abstract machine}$$

The idea of characterizing the left-to-right processing natural semantics in the form of L-attributed natural semantics is due to Ibraheem and Schmidt [13]. The motivation for their definition came from L-attributed grammars. Ibraheem and Schmidt are concerned with reasoning about divergent computations in the framework of natural semantics. To this end, they start from L-attributed natural semantics and generate sets of positive (or convergent) rules and negative (or divergent) rules. Using an inductive interpretation of the positive rules and a coinductive interpretation of the negative rules allows them to reason about divergent computations. In contrast, we only consider convergent computations, and we extract an abstract machine from an L-attributed natural semantics that is equivalent to the natural semantics.

Hannan and Miller derive abstract machines from natural semantics using proof theory [11]. Their derivation consists in encoding a natural semantics in a proof-theoretic meta-language and then carrying out transformations at the meta-language level. In that sense, the work of Hannan and Miller is closely related to our previous work on deriving abstract machine by using standard program transformations on an encoding of a natural semantics in a functional language. One of Hannan and Miller's derivation steps relies on a left-to-right ordering of the premises of the natural semantics rules. This restriction seems to correspond to our present restriction to L-attributed natural semantics. Hannan and Miller derive abstract machines for call-by-name and call-by-value evaluation of λ-terms. Their starting points, called the $\mathcal{N}_0$ and $\mathcal{V}_0$ proof systems, are L-attributed natural semantics. Both natural semantics are very close to the standard ones presented in Sections 3.1 and 3.2. The difference is that λ-terms are de Bruijn encoded, environments are lists of values, and there are explicit rules for looking up an index in an environment. Applying our extraction to these L-attributes natural semantics yields abstract machines that are very similar to the machines extracted in Sections 3.1 and 3.2.

Kahn introduced natural semantics and presented natural semantics for various aspects of programming languages [14]. For instance, he presented a natural semantics for mini-ML which is almost L-attributed: removing the *letrec* construct from the language, the semantics is L-attributed and we can extract an abstract machine directly. The problem with the *letrec* construct is that there is a cyclic dependency between the value of a term and the environment in which the term is evaluated. The environment in which to evaluate the term can therefore not be defined solely as a function of previous terms, environments, and values and therefore the semantics is not L-attributed.

Sestoft derived a lazy abstract machine from Launchbury's natural semantics for call-by-need evaluation of λ-terms [18]. His derivation consists of a number of intuitive steps and a proof of the correctness of each of the steps. As mentioned in Section 3.3 the extraction algorithm presented in this article applies to the natural semantics and the resulting machine is essentially Sestoft's mark 1 machine. Sestoft obtained the mark 1 machine by introducing a stack of evaluation contexts and subsequently proving the correctness of the resulting machine. Our present work shows that such a stack introduction can be applied to a wide range of natural semantics and proves the correctness of the stack introduction algorithm once and for all instead of relying on a correctness proof for each machine. Sestoft only uses the mark 1 machine as a stepping stone, and goes on to introduce environments (besides the stores already present), closures, and variable indices. He proves the correctness of the resulting machines.

6   Conclusion

We have presented a simple and mechanical extraction of correct abstract machines from the class of L-attributed natural semantics introduced by Ibraheem and Schmidt. We have formalized this extraction as an extraction algorithm and proved its correctness. The class of L-attributed natural semantics is large, containing semantics for call-by-value, call-by-name, and call-by-need functional languages, as well as imperative languages. For each L-attributed natural semantics the extraction algorithm produces a correct abstract machine.

Acknowledgements. To Olivier Danvy for his encouragement, fruitful discussions, and useful comments. Thanks are also due to Neil Jones, Julia Lawall, Jan Midtgaard, and the anonymous reviewers for their useful comments.

References

1. Mads Sig Ager. From natural semantics to abstract machines. Technical Report BRICS RS-04-20, Department of Computer Science, University of Aarhus, Aarhus, Denmark, October 2004.
2. Mads Sig Ager, Dariusz Biernacki, Olivier Danvy, and Jan Midtgaard. A functional correspondence between evaluators and abstract machines. In Dale Miller, editor, *Proceedings of the Fifth ACM-SIGPLAN International Conference on Principles and Practice of Declarative Programming*, pages 8–19. ACM Press, 2003.
3. Mads Sig Ager, Olivier Danvy, and Jan Midtgaard. A functional correspondence between monadic evaluators and abstract machines for languages with computational effects. Technical Report BRICS RS-03-35, DAIMI, Department of Computer Science, University of Aarhus, Aarhus, Denmark, November 2003. Presented at the 2nd APPSEM II workshop, Talinn, Estonia, April 2004.
4. Mads Sig Ager, Olivier Danvy, and Jan Midtgaard. A functional correspondence between call-by-need evaluators and lazy abstract machines. *Information Processing Letters*, 90(5):223–232, 2004.
5. Dariusz Biernacki and Olivier Danvy. From interpreter to logic engine by defunctionalization. In Maurice Bruynooghe, editor, *Logic Based Program Synthesis and Transformation, 13th International Symposium, LOPSTR 2003*, number 3018 in Lecture Notes in Computer Science, pages 143–159, Uppsala, Sweden, August 2003. Springer-Verlag.
6. Pierre Crégut. An abstract machine for the normalization of λ-terms. In *Proceedings of the 1990 ACM conference on LISP and functional programming*, pages 333–340. ACM Press, 1990.
7. Olivier Danvy. A rational deconstruction of Landin's SECD machine. Technical Report BRICS RS-03-33, DAIMI, Department of Computer Science, University of Aarhus, Aarhus, Denmark, October 2003.
8. Stephan Diehl, Pieter Hartel, and Peter Sestoft. Abstract machines for programming language implementation. *Future Generation Computer Systems*, 16:739–751, 2000.
9. Matthias Felleisen. *The Calculi of λ-v-CS Conversion: A Syntactic Theory of Control and State in Imperative Higher-Order Programming Languages*. PhD thesis, Department of Computer Science, Indiana University, Bloomington, Indiana, August 1987.
10. Matthias Felleisen and Matthew Flatt. Programming languages and lambda calculi. Unpublished lecture notes.
http://www.ccs.neu.edu/home/matthias/3810-w02/readings.html, 1989-2001.
11. John Hannan and Dale Miller. From operational semantics to abstract machines. *Mathematical Structures in Computer Science*, 2(4):415–459, 1992.

12. Thérèse Hardin, Luc Maranget, and Bruno Pagano. Functional runtime systems within the lambda-sigma calculus. *Journal of Functional Programming*, 1(1):1–100, January 1993.

13. Husain Ibraheem and David A. Schmidt. Adapting big-step semantics to small-step style: Coinductive interpretations and "higher-order" derivations. In Andrew Gordon, Andrew Pitts, and Carolyn Talcott, editors, *Electronic Notes in Theoretical Computer Science*, volume 10. Elsevier, 2000.

14. Gilles Kahn. Natural semantics. In Franz-Josef Brandenburg, Guy Vidal-Naquet, and Martin Wirsing, editors, *Proceedings of the 4th Annual Symposium on Theoretical Aspects of Computer Science*, volume 247 of *Lecture Notes in Computer Science*, pages 22–39, Passau, Germany, February 1987. Springer-Verlag.

15. John Launchbury. A natural semantics for lazy evaluation. In *Proceedings of the 20th ACM SIGPLAN-SIGACT symposium on Principles of programming languages*, pages 144–154. ACM Press, 1993.

16. Robin Milner, Mads Tofte, Robert Harper, and David MacQueen. *The Definition of Standard ML (Revised)*. The MIT Press, 1997.

17. Flemming Nielson and Hanne Riis Nielson. *Semantics with Applications*. John Wiley & Sons, 1992.

18. Peter Sestoft. Deriving a lazy abstract machine. *Journal of Functional Programming*, 7(3):231–264, May 1997.

19. Glynn Winskel. *The Formal Semantics of Programming Languages*. Foundation of Computing Series. The MIT Press, 1993.

Graph-Based Proof Counting and Enumeration with Applications for Program Fragment Synthesis[*]

J.B. Wells[1] and Boris Yakobowski[2]

[1] Heriot-Watt University
http://www.macs.hw.ac.uk/~jbw/
[2] ENS Lyon
http://www.yakobowski.org/

Abstract. For use in earlier approaches to automated module interface adaptation, we seek a restricted form of program synthesis. Given some typing assumptions and a desired result type, we wish to automatically build a number of program fragments of this chosen typing, using functions and values available in the given typing environment. We call this problem *term enumeration*. To solve the problem, we use the Curry-Howard correspondence (propositions-as-types, proofs-as-programs) to transform it into a *proof enumeration* problem for an intuitionistic logic calculus. We formally study proof enumeration and counting in this calculus. We prove that proof counting is solvable and give an algorithm to solve it. This in turn yields a proof enumeration algorithm.

1 Introduction

1.1 Background and Motivation

Researchers have recently expressed interest [7, 8, 1] in type-directed program synthesis that outputs terms of a desired goal typing (i.e., environment of type assumptions and result type) using the values (possibly functions) available in the type environment. These terms are typically wanted for use in simple glue code that adapts one module interface to another, overcoming simple interface differences. There are usually many terms of the goal typing, with many computational behaviors, and only some will satisfy all the user's criteria. To find terms of the goal typing that satisfy all the criteria, it is desirable to systematically enumerate terms of the typing. The enumerated terms can then be filtered [7, 8], possibly with user assistance [1], to find the most suitable ones.

Higher-order typed languages (e.g., the ML family) are suitable for this kind of synthesis. They have expressive type systems that allow specifying precise goals. They also support easily composing and decomposing functions, tuples,

---

[*] Supported by grants: EC FP5/IST/FET IST-2001-33477 "DART", EPSRC GR/L 41545/01, NSF 0113193 (ITR), Sun Microsystems EDUD-7826-990410-US.

S. Etalle(Ed.): LOPSTR 2004, LNCS 3573, pp. 262–277, 2005.

and tagged variants, which can accomplish most of what is needed for the kind of simple interface adaptation we envision.

1.2   Applications

Both the AxML module adaptation approach [7, 8] and work on signature subtyping modulo isomorphisms [1] do whole module adaptation through the use of higher-order ML functors.

In AxML, term enumeration is mainly needed to fill in unspecified holes in adaptation code and the main adaptation work is done by other mechanisms. Term enumeration is useful because an unspecified hole may indicate that the programmer has not thought things through and they might benefit from seeing possible alternatives for filling the hole. This will mainly be useful when the alternatives are small and have somewhat distinct behavior, so a systematic breadth-first enumeration is expected to be best and enumerating many large chunks of code would likely be less useful.

In the work on signature subtyping modulo isomorphisms, requirements for the calculus are quite light: only arrow types (and a subtyping rule) are needed. Typical examples involve applying a functor to a pre-existing module, in order to get a module having the same signature as the result of the functor. For example, we might compose a functor resulting in a map over a given type with a module containing a generic comparison function.

1.3   Possible Approaches to Term Enumeration

Program synthesis such as term enumeration seeks to find functions with some desired behavior, which is similar to library *retrieval*. Closer to our task, some retrieval systems also *compose* functions available in the library (see [8] for discussion), but are not suitable for enumeration. Research on *type inhabitation* [2, 11, 15] is related, but is mostly concerned with the *theoretical* issue of the number of terms in a typing (mainly whether there is at least 1), and the resulting enumeration algorithms are overly inefficient.

The most closely related work is on *proof search*. Although most of this work focuses on yes/no answers to theorem proving queries or on building individual proofs, there has been some work on proof enumeration in various logics [4, 12, 14]. With constructive logics, we can use the Curry-Howard correspondence to generate terms from the proofs of a formula. We follow this approach here.

1.4   Overview

We explain in Sec. 2 that the existing calculus LJT is the most suited to our task and we modify it slightly in Sec. 4 to make the even more suitable LJT^{Enum}. Next, we present in Sec. 5 a graph representation of proofs and use it to show solvability of proof counting. In Sec. 6, we present COUNT, a direct proof counting algorithm, and outline proof enumeration. We then discuss in Sec. 7 the links between proof counting and term enumeration and add proof terms to LJT^{Enum}.

2   Which Calculus for Proof Enumeration?

As already mentioned, proof enumeration is defined as the enumeration of all the proofs of a formula, as opposed to finding only one proof. Using the Curry-Howard correspondence, term enumeration can be reduced to proof enumeration; but for that approach to be usable, there must exist some guaranties on the correspondence. For example, 1-∞ correspondences are unsuitable, because we might have to examine an infinity of proofs to find different program fragments.

In our case, it is important to find a calculus in which the proofs are in bijection with normal λ-terms, or equivalently with the set of normal terms in natural deduction style. Dyckhoff and Pinto [4] provide a survey of various calculi usable for proof enumeration. They argue that *"the appropriate proof-search calculi are those that have not only the syntax-directed features of Gentzen-style sequent calculi but also a natural 1–1 correspondence between the derivations and the real objects of interest, normal natural deductions"* and we agree with their analysis. Unfortunately, calculi having these properties are quite rare.

For example, a sequent calculus such as Gentzen's LJ does not meet the previous criteria. Indeed, due to possible permutations in the proofs, or to the use of cut rules, two proofs can be associated to the same term. In fact, it has been long known that 2 proofs in LJ are "the same", meaning that they are equivalent to the same normal deduction proof in NJ, if they are inter-permutable. As a result, we have to consider cut-free and *permutation-free* calculi.

Historically, the first calculus having those properties is Herbelin's LJT [9]. Proofs in LJT are in bijection with the terms of the simply typed λ-calculus. Later, Herbelin introduced LKT [10], which is based on Gentzen's classical calculus LK, and Pinto and Dyckhoff [14] proposed two other calculi for systems with dependent types. Of all these calculi, LJT is better adapted to our purpose, because the additional features in the three others do not help our task.

The permutation-free property of LJT is achieved by adding in each sequent a special place, called a *stoup*, used to focus the proof. The stoup can either be empty or filled by one variable. Once the stoup is full, deductions can only be made based on its content, and it cannot be emptied easily. The content of the stoup is interpreted as the head variable in the standard λ-calculus.

All the sequents provable in LJ are provable in LJT. The cut-free version of LJT is a sequent calculus which enjoys the subformula property, and is syntax-directed, with few sources of non determinism. LJT also enjoys a cut elimination theorem [9,5], so we can restrict ourselves to considering only cut-free proofs. Finally, as was needed, while the traditional proof terms in LJ correspond to the simply-typed λ-terms, the proof terms in the cut-free version of LJT are in bijection with the simply-typed λ-terms in normal form, so all interesting terms may potentially be found.

3   Mathematical Preliminaries

Given a set E, let $\mathsf{Set}(E)$ be the set of all subsets of E. Let a *multiset* over E be a function from E to $\mathbb{N}$ (the natural numbers); if $\mathcal{M}$ is a multiset, we say that $m \in \mathcal{M}$ iff $\mathcal{M}(m) > 0$. A multiset $\mathcal{M}$ is *finite* iff $\{\, m \mid m \in \mathcal{M} \,\}$ is finite. Let $\mathsf{MSet}(E)$ be the set of all multisets over E. Let $\mathsf{FinMSet}(E)$ be the set of all finite multisets over E. Multiset literals use the same notation as sets.

Multiset union is defined as usual by $(\mathcal{M}_1 \uplus \mathcal{M}_2)(x) = \mathcal{M}_1(x) + \mathcal{M}_2(x)$. A "set-like" multiset union is defined by $(\mathcal{M}_1 \cup \mathcal{M}_2)(x) = \max(\mathcal{M}_1(x), \mathcal{M}_2(x))$. Let $\mathcal{S}$ range over the names Set and MSet. Let $\cup_{\mathsf{Set}} = \cup$ and $\cup_{\mathsf{MSet}} = \uplus$.

We extend the arithmetic operators $+$ and $\times$ and the relation $\leq$ to $\mathbb{N} \cup \{\infty\}$ using the usual arithmetic rules for members of $\mathbb{N}$, and by letting $n + \infty = \infty$, $n \times \infty = \infty$ if $n \neq 0$, $0 \times \infty = 0$, and $n \leq \infty$. Also, as usual let $\Sigma_{x \in \emptyset} v(x) = 0$ and let $\Pi_{x \in \emptyset} v(x) = 1$ for any function v.

Given a set S, a directed graph G over S is a pair (V, E) where $V \subset S$ and $E \subset S \times S$. The elements of V are the vertexes of G, and those of E are the edges of G. Given a graph $G = (V, E)$, let $\mathsf{succ}_G(v) = \{ v' \in V \mid (v, v') \in E \}$. Given two graphs $G_1 = (V_1, E_1)$ and $G_2 = (V_2, E_2)$, let $G_1 \cup G_2$ be $(V_1 \cup V_2, E_1 \cup E_2)$.

We represent mathematical functions as sets of pairs. Let the *domain* of a function f be $\mathsf{Dom}(f) = \{ x \mid (x, y) \in f \}$. To modify functions, we write $f, x : v$ for $(f \setminus \{ (x, y) \mid (x, y) \in f \}) \cup \{ (x, v) \}$.

4   The Calculus LJT^{Enum}

In this section, we present LJT^{Enum}, a slightly modified version of LJT more suitable for term enumeration. The following pseudo-grammars define the syntax.

$$
\begin{aligned}
Q \in \ &\textsf{Propositional-Variables} ::= Q_i \\
X, Y \in \ &\textsf{Basic-Propositions} ::= Q \mid Q[A_1, \ldots, A_n] \\
A, B \in \ &\textsf{Formulas} ::= X \mid A_1 \rightarrow A_2 \mid A_1 \wedge A_2 \mid A_1 \vee A_2 \\
A^? \in \ &\textsf{Stoups} ::= A \mid \bullet \\
\varGamma \in \ &\textsf{Environments}_{\mathsf{MSet}} = \mathsf{FinMSet}(\textsf{Formulas}) \\
s \in \ &\textsf{Sequents}_{\mathsf{MSet}} ::= \varGamma; A^? \vdash B
\end{aligned}
$$

Let also $\textsf{Environments}_{\mathsf{Set}} = \{ \varGamma \in \textsf{Environments}_{\mathsf{MSet}} \mid \forall A \in \textsf{Formulas}, \varGamma(A) \leq 1 \}$. Let $\textsf{Sequents}_{\mathsf{Set}}$ be the subset of $\textsf{Sequents}_{\mathsf{MSet}}$ such that the environment of each sequent is in $\textsf{Environments}_{\mathsf{Set}}$. The symbol $\bullet$ is the empty stoup.

Basic propositions which are not propositional variables are used to encode parameterized ML types, such as list. For example, if int is encoded as A and list as B, int list is encoded as $B[A]$. Note that we do not yet support polymorphism as in $\forall \alpha.\ \alpha$ list. Separate functions for handling int list or bool list must be supplied in the environment.

We present the rules of LJT$_S^{\mathsf{Enum}}$ in Fig. 1, which are basically the cut-free rules of LJT. The rules which add elements in the environment are parameterized by the operation to use. The two systems LJT$_{\mathsf{Set}}^{\mathsf{Enum}}$ and LJT$_{\mathsf{MSet}}^{\mathsf{Enum}}$ prove essentially

Axiom rule

$$\frac{}{\Gamma; X \vdash X} \text{ Ax}$$

Contraction rule

$$\frac{\Gamma \uplus \{A\}; A \vdash B}{\Gamma \uplus \{A\}; \bullet \vdash B} \text{ Cont}(A)$$

Left implication rule

$$\frac{\Gamma; \bullet \vdash A \qquad \Gamma; B \vdash C}{\Gamma; A \to B \vdash C} \text{ Imp}_L$$

Right implication rule

$$\frac{\Gamma \cup_S \{A\}; \bullet \vdash B}{\Gamma; \bullet \vdash A \to B} \text{ Imp}_R$$

Left conjunction rule

$$\frac{\Gamma; A_i \vdash B}{\Gamma; A_1 \wedge A_2 \vdash B} \text{ And}_{L_i}$$

Right conjunction rule

$$\frac{\Gamma; \bullet \vdash A \qquad \Gamma; \bullet \vdash B}{\Gamma; \bullet \vdash A \wedge B} \text{ And}_R$$

Left disjunction rule

$$\frac{\Gamma \cup_S \{A\}; \bullet \vdash C \qquad \Gamma \cup_S \{B\}; \bullet \vdash C}{\Gamma; A \vee B \vdash C} \text{ Or}_L$$

Right disjunction rule

$$\frac{\Gamma; \bullet \vdash A_i}{\Gamma; \bullet \vdash A_1 \vee A_2} \text{ Or}_{R_i}$$

Fig. 1. Rules of $\mathsf{LJT}_S^{\mathsf{Enum}}$ ($i \in \{1, 2\}$)

the same judgements, but with possibly different proof trees. This distinction helps in analyzing the problem of term enumeration and devising our solution. These points will be developed in Secs. 5 and 6.

5   The Proof Counting Problem

In this section, we formally study the problems of proof counting in $\mathsf{LJT}^{\mathsf{Enum}}$. We interpret sequent resolution as a graph problem. From that we prove that finding the number of proofs (which is ∞ if there are an infinite number of proofs) of a sequent is computable.

Let $\mathsf{C}_S(s)$ be the number of proofs of a sequent s in $\mathsf{LJT}_S^{\mathsf{Enum}}$. $\mathsf{C}_{\mathsf{MSet}}(s)$ is strongly related to the number of different terms which can be obtained from the proofs of s; Sec. 7.2 will discuss this. Although apparently less interesting, $\mathsf{C}_{\mathsf{Set}}(s)$ is much easier to compute, and can help in finding $\mathsf{C}_{\mathsf{MSet}}(s)$.

5.1   A Graph Representation of Possible Proofs

We start by defining the notion of applicable rule to a sequent. Let R be the set of rules $\mathsf{R} = \{\text{Ax}, \text{Imp}_L, \text{Imp}_R, \text{And}_{L_1}, \text{And}_{L_2}, \text{And}_R, \text{Or}_L, \text{Or}_{R_1}, \text{Or}_{R_2}, \text{Cont}(A) \mid A \in \mathsf{Formulas}\}$. Let r range over R.

A rule r with conclusion c is *applicable* to a sequent s iff, viewing the basic propositions and formulas in r as meta-variables, there is a substitution σ from these meta-variables to basic propositions or formulas such that $\sigma(c) = s$. If the rule is $\text{Cont}(A)$, the formula A must be the one chosen from the environment Γ. Let $\mathsf{RA}(s)$ be the set of rules applicable to a sequent s. Let the valid sequent/rule pairs be $\mathsf{VP}_S = \{(s, r) \mid s \in \mathsf{Sequents}_S, r \in \mathsf{RA}(s)\}$. Let τ range over VP_S.

Given a sequent s and a rule r applicable to s via a substitution σ, let $\mathsf{Prs}(s, r, i)$ be the ith premise of $\sigma(r)$ if r has at least i premises, using $\cup_S$ as the combining operator on the environment.

Definition 5.1. *Let* $\mathsf{G}_S = (\mathsf{V}_S, \mathsf{E}_S)$ *be the directed graph of all possible sequents and rule uses in* $\mathsf{LJT}_S^{\mathsf{Enum}}$ *defined by:*

- $\mathsf{V}_S = \mathsf{Sequents}_S \cup \mathsf{VP}_S$.
- $\mathsf{E}_{1,S} = \{(s, (s, r)) \mid s \in \mathsf{Sequents}_S,\ r \in \mathsf{RA}(s)\}$.
- $\mathsf{E}_{2,S} = \{((s, r), s', n) \mid n \in \mathbb{N},\ s' = \mathsf{Prs}(s, r, n)\}$.
- $\mathsf{E}_S = \mathsf{E}_{1,S} \cup \mathsf{E}_{2,S}$.

The elements of V_S which are in $\mathsf{Sequents}_S$ are called sequent vertexes. Their outgoing edges (which are in $\mathsf{E}_{1,S}$) go to valid pairs. The elements of V_S which are in VP_S are called rule-use vertexes. Their outgoing edges (which are in $\mathsf{E}_{2,S}$) go to the sequents which are the premises of the rule use. On each outgoing edge we add a number indicating which premise we are considering (needed only when there is more than one premise). An example of part of $\mathsf{G}_{\mathsf{Set}}$ and $\mathsf{G}_{\mathsf{MSet}}$ is provided in Fig. 2.

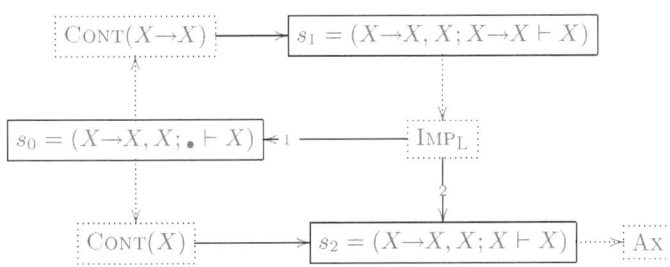

Fig. 2. $\mathsf{G}_{\mathsf{Set}}(s_0) = \mathsf{G}_{\mathsf{MSet}}(s_0)$

The *lowering* of a multiset $\mathcal{M}$ to a "set-like" multiset $\lfloor\mathcal{M}\rfloor$ is defined such that $\lfloor\mathcal{M}\rfloor(x) = \min(1, \mathcal{M}(x))$. Let $\lfloor(\Gamma; A^? \vdash B)\rfloor = (\lfloor\Gamma\rfloor; A^? \vdash B)$, let $\lfloor(s, r)\rfloor = (\lfloor s\rfloor, r)$, let $\lfloor(s, \tau)\rfloor = (\lfloor s\rfloor, \lfloor\tau\rfloor)$, and let $\lfloor(\tau, s, i)\rfloor = (\lfloor\tau\rfloor, \lfloor s\rfloor, i)$. Given any set W, let $\lfloor(W)\rfloor = \{\lfloor w\rfloor \mid w \in W\}$. For graphs, let $\lfloor(V, E)\rfloor = (\lfloor V\rfloor, \lfloor E\rfloor)$. Note that $\lfloor\mathsf{G}_{\mathsf{MSet}}\rfloor = \mathsf{G}_{\mathsf{Set}}$.

A graph $g = (V, E)$ is an S-*subgraph* iff $V \subseteq \mathsf{V}_S$, $E \subseteq \mathsf{E}_S$, and $s, \tau \in V$ whenever $(s, \tau) \in E$ or $(\tau, s, i) \in E$. An S-subgraph $g = (V, E)$ is *valid* iff for every $\tau = (s, r) \in V$ where r has n premises, $(\tau, \mathsf{Prs}(s, r, i), i) \in E$ for $1 \le i \le n$.

Given a sequent s, let $\mathsf{G}_S(s)$ be the subgraph of G_S containing all the sequent and rule-use vertexes reachable from s. From a practical viewpoint, $\mathsf{G}_S(s)$ is the largest subgraph of G_S that a procedure attempting to find proofs of s should have to consider. It is worth noting that in the general case, $\mathsf{G}_{\mathsf{Set}}(s)$ and $\mathsf{G}_{\mathsf{MSet}}(s)$ may be cyclic graphs (e.g., in Fig. 2). Note that $\lfloor\mathsf{G}_{\mathsf{MSet}}(s)\rfloor = \mathsf{G}_{\mathsf{Set}}(\lfloor s\rfloor)$ and $\mathsf{raise}(s, \mathsf{G}_{\mathsf{Set}}(\lfloor s\rfloor)) = \mathsf{G}_{\mathsf{MSet}}(s)$.

Lemma 5.2 (Finiteness). $\mathsf{G}_{\mathsf{Set}}(s)$ *is always finite.* $\mathsf{G}_{\mathsf{MSet}}(s)$ *can be infinite.*

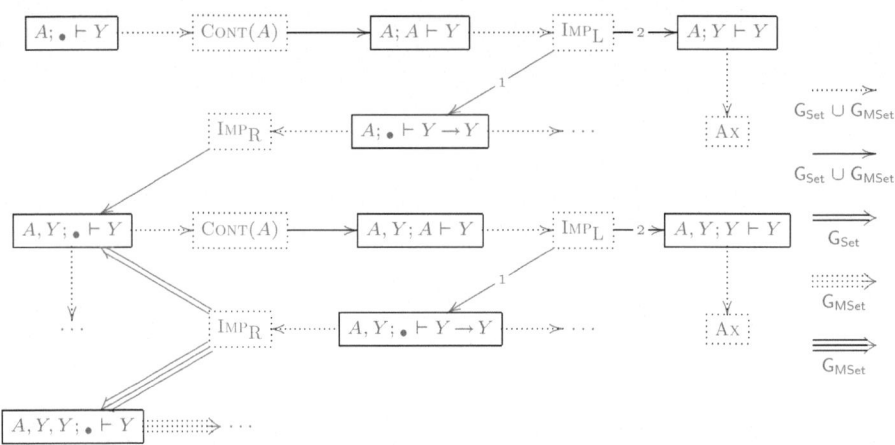

Fig. 3. A subgraph of $\mathsf{G}_{\mathsf{MSet}}(A; \bullet \vdash Y)$ and $\mathsf{G}_{\mathsf{Set}}(A; \bullet \vdash Y)$ with $A = (Y \to Y) \to Y$

Proof. When environments are sets, it is a direct consequence of the fact that $\mathsf{LJT}^{\mathsf{Enum}}$ enjoys the subformula property. When environments are multisets, a sufficient condition for the graph to be infinite is to have in the context a function taking as an argument a function, or a disjunction. We can then find a derivation branch in which a formula can be added an arbitrary number of times in the environment, making the graph infinite. See for example Fig. 3.   □

5.2   Proof Trees and Their Relationship with the Graph

We now define a structure which captures exactly one proof of a sequent.

Definition 5.3 (Proof trees). *Let proof trees be given by this pseudo-grammar:*

$$T \in \mathsf{ProofTree} ::= \tau(T_1, \ldots, T_n)$$

Let $\mathsf{Seq}(s, r) = s$ *and let* $\mathsf{Seq}(\tau(T_1, \ldots, T_n)) = \mathsf{Seq}(\tau)$. *A particular proof tree* $T = (s, r)(T_1, \ldots, T_n)$ *is an* S-*proof tree iff (1)* $s \in \mathsf{Sequents}_\mathsf{S}$, *(2)* $r \in \mathsf{RA}(s)$, *and (3)* r *has* n *premises and for* $1 \leq i \leq n$ *it holds that* T_i *is an* S-*proof tree such that* $\mathsf{Seq}(T_i) = \mathsf{Pr}_\mathsf{S}(s, r, i)$. *We henceforth consider only* S-*proof trees.*

We recursively fold an S-proof tree into a S-valid subgraph of $\mathsf{G}_\mathsf{S}(s)$ by:

$$
\begin{aligned}
\mathsf{Fold}_\mathsf{S}&((s, r)(T_1, \ldots, T_n)) \\
&= (\{s, (s, r)\} \cup \{\mathsf{Seq}(T_i) \mid 1 \leq i \leq n\}, \\
&\quad\quad \{(s, (s, r))\} \cup \{((s, r), \mathsf{Seq}(T_i), i) \mid 1 \leq i \leq n\}) \\
&\quad \cup (\textstyle\bigcup_{1 \leq i \leq n} \mathsf{Fold}_\mathsf{S}(T_i))
\end{aligned}
$$

To allow lowering MSet-proof trees to Set-proof trees, let $\lfloor \tau(T_1, \ldots, T_n) \rfloor = \lfloor \tau \rfloor (\lfloor T_1 \rfloor, \ldots, \lfloor T_n \rfloor)$. Similarly, a Set-proof tree T can be raised to an MSet-proof tree T' such that $\lfloor \mathsf{Seq}(T') \rfloor = \mathsf{Seq}(T)$:

$$\mathsf{raise}(s, (\lfloor s \rfloor, r)(T_1, \ldots, T_n))$$
$$= (s, r)(\mathsf{raise}(\mathsf{Pr}_{\mathsf{MSet}}(s, r, 1), T_1), \ldots, \mathsf{raise}(\mathsf{Pr}_{\mathsf{MSet}}(s, r, n), T_n))$$

An S-proof tree T is *acyclic* iff $\mathsf{Fold}_S(T)$ is acyclic. Given an acyclic S-proof tree T, there are only a finite number (possibly more than 1) of S-proof trees T' such that $\mathsf{Fold}_S(T') = \mathsf{Fold}_S(T)$. Given a sequent s for which $\mathsf{G}_S(s)$ is finite, it is possible to count the number of acyclic S-proof trees for s, by a simple brute force enumeration (there are only a finite possible number of them).

An S-proof tree T is *cyclic* iff $\mathsf{Fold}_S(T)$ is cyclic. Given a cyclic S-proof tree T, there are an infinite number of S-proof trees T' such that $\mathsf{Fold}_S(T') = \mathsf{Fold}_S(T)$. This follows from the fact that in a cyclic S-proof tree, the proof of some sequent s depends on a smaller proof of s. Thus, each time we find a proof of s, we can build a new, bigger (with respect to the height of the proof tree) proof of s, by unfolding the proof already found.

The raising of an acyclic Set-proof tree is an acyclic MSet-proof tree, and the lowering of a cyclic MSet-proof tree is a cyclic Set-proof tree. But the lowering of an acyclic MSet-proof tree can be a cyclic Set-proof tree. Similarly, the raisng of a cyclic Set-proof tree can be an acyclic MSet-proof tree. Fig. 3 shows part of an example of the last two points.

5.3   Proof Counting

Lemma 5.4. *Let s be a sequent.*

- *There are the same number of $\mathsf{LJT}_S^{\mathsf{Enum}}$ proofs of s and S-proof trees for s.*
- *Suppose $\mathsf{G}_S(s)$ is finite. If there is no cyclic S-proof tree for s, then the number of S-proof trees for s is finite; otherwise it is infinite.*
- *Suppose $\mathsf{G}_S(s)$ is infinite. If there is no cyclic S-proof tree for s, then the number of S-proofs of s can be either finite or infinite; otherwise it is infinite.*

Lemma 5.5. *Given an MSet-sequent s, if there exists an infinity of acyclic MSet-proof trees for s, then there exists a cyclic Set-proof tree for $\lfloor s \rfloor$.*

Proof. We say that a proof tree is of height n iff its longest path goes through n sequent nodes. Let N be the number of Set-sequent nodes in $\mathsf{G}_{\mathsf{Set}}(\lfloor s \rfloor)$.

We first prove that there exists an MSet-proof tree T for s of height greater than N. For this, construct a (possibly infinite in branching and number of nodes) tree BT ("big tree") by unfolding the graph $\mathsf{G}_{\mathsf{MSet}}(s)$ starting from s into a tree, choosing some arbitrary order for the rule-use children of a sequent node, and making all sequent nodes at depth N (not counting rule-use nodes and with the root sequent node at depth 1) into leaves and adding no further children beyond depth N. By construction, all MSet-proof trees of s of height less than N can be seen to be "embedded" in BT.

Now we observe that BT is finitely branching. For every sequent s' occurring in BT, there are a finite number of rule uses that can use other sequents to prove s'. This is so because R is finite except for rules of the form $\mathrm{CONT}(A)$, and at most a finite number of those can apply to s' because the environment Γ of s' can mention only a finite number of distinct formulas.

Now, by König's lemma, BT contains a finite number of nodes. As a consequence, there are only a finite number of distinct MSet-proof trees embedded in BT. Thus T exists and has height $m > N$.

The Set-proof tree $\lfloor T \rfloor$ has the same height as T, so $\lfloor T \rfloor$ has at least one path of length m. Along this path, some Set-sequent nodes must be repeated in $\mathsf{Fold}_{\mathsf{Set}}(\lfloor T \rfloor)$, and thus $\lfloor T \rfloor$ is a cyclic Set-proof tree for $\lfloor s \rfloor$.   □

Theorem 5.6. *Let $s \in \mathsf{Sequents}_{\mathsf{MSet}}$. Then all of the following statements hold:*

- $\mathsf{C}_{\mathsf{Set}}(\lfloor s \rfloor) \leq \mathsf{C}_{\mathsf{MSet}}(s)$.
- $\mathsf{C}_{\mathsf{Set}}(\lfloor s \rfloor) = \infty \iff \mathsf{C}_{\mathsf{MSet}}(s) = \infty$.
- $\mathsf{C}_{\mathsf{Set}}(\lfloor s \rfloor) = 0 \iff \mathsf{C}_{\mathsf{MSet}}(s) = 0$.

Proof. The first point is easy: for each Set-proof tree T for $\lfloor s \rfloor$, $\mathsf{raise}(s, T)$ is a MSet-proof tree for s, and raise is injective. This also proves that $\mathsf{C}_{\mathsf{Set}}(\lfloor s \rfloor) = \infty \Rightarrow \mathsf{C}_{\mathsf{MSet}}(s) = \infty$ and $\mathsf{C}_{\mathsf{MSet}}(s) = 0 \Rightarrow \mathsf{C}_{\mathsf{Set}}(\lfloor s \rfloor) = 0$.

Next, suppose that $\mathsf{C}_{\mathsf{Set}}(\lfloor s \rfloor) = 0$. If there was an MSet-proof tree T for s, then $\lfloor T \rfloor$ would be a Set-proof tree for $\lfloor s \rfloor$ and we would have $\mathsf{C}_{\mathsf{Set}}(\lfloor s \rfloor) \neq 0$. Absurd.

Finally suppose that $\mathsf{C}_{\mathsf{MSet}}(s) = \infty$. There are two cases: (1) There is a cyclic MSet-proof tree T for s. Then $\lfloor T \rfloor$ is a cyclic Set-proof tree for $\lfloor s \rfloor$; (2) There are no cyclic MSet-proof trees for s. By Lemma 5.4, it means there are an infinite number of acyclic MSet-proof trees for s. Then by Lemma 5.5, there is a cyclic Set-proof tree for $\lfloor s \rfloor$. In both cases, by Lemma 5.4, $\mathsf{C}_{\mathsf{Set}}(\lfloor s \rfloor) = \infty$.   □

Theorem 5.7. *Proof counting is computable for $\mathsf{LJT}_{\mathsf{Set}}^{\mathsf{Enum}}$ and $\mathsf{LJT}_{\mathsf{MSet}}^{\mathsf{Enum}}$.*

Proof. The following algorithm COUNTNAIVE counts the proofs of a sequent s:

1. Build $\mathsf{G}_{\mathsf{Set}}(s)$; by Lemma 5.2, it is finite.
2. Search for a cyclic Set-proof tree for s. For this, use the same exhaustive enumeration as when searching for acyclic ones, but stop as soon as a cyclic one is found. If a cyclic Set-proof tree is found, then return $\infty = \mathsf{C}_{\mathsf{MSet}}(s) = \mathsf{C}_{\mathsf{Set}}(s)$ (by Theorem 5.6).
3. Otherwise $\mathsf{C}_{\mathsf{MSet}}(s)$ and $\mathsf{C}_{\mathsf{Set}}(s)$ are finite, by Theorem 5.6. If we are searching for $\mathsf{C}_{\mathsf{Set}}(s)$, return the number of Set-proof trees for s found by the exhaustive enumeration in the previous step.
4. Otherwise, we are searching for $\mathsf{C}_{\mathsf{MSet}}(s)$. Build a restricted (and finite) subgraph g of $\mathsf{G}_{\mathsf{MSet}}(s)$ containing all the foldings of the MSet-proof trees for s. For this, start at s and do a breadth-first exploration. At each new node s' visited, check whether or not it is provable, by finding the number of proofs of $\lfloor s' \rfloor$ in $\mathsf{G}_{\mathsf{Set}}(s)$, which is the number of Set-proof trees for $\lfloor s' \rfloor$ (indeed, $\mathsf{G}_{\mathsf{Set}}(\lfloor s' \rfloor) \subseteq \mathsf{G}_{\mathsf{Set}}(s)$ and thus cannot contain a cyclic Set-proof tree). If $\lfloor s' \rfloor$ is unprovable, so is s' by Theorem 5.6; do not explore its successors. Because there are no arbitrarily large acyclic MSet-proof trees for s (by Lemma 5.5), g is finite and this process terminates.
5. Find the number of MSet-proof trees for s whose foldings are in g by exhaustive enumeration. By construction, it is $\mathsf{C}_{\mathsf{MSet}}(s)$.   □

5.4   The Generality of the Idea

Our approach (using G_{Set} to study G_{MSet}) resembles a static analysis where instead of considering the number of times a formula is present in the environment, we consider only its presence or absence. That property is interesting because provability does not depend on duplicate formulas in the environment. In our case, proof counting is also compatible with our simplifying hypothesis (because $C_{Set}(s) = \infty \Rightarrow C_{MSet}(s) = \infty$). This idea is quite general because it is usable in every calculus in which the environment only increases.

6   An Algorithm for Counting and Enumerating Proofs in LJT^{Enum}

The algorithm COUNTNAIVE could theoretically be used to find the number of proofs of a sequent. Unfortunately, it is overly inefficient. In this section we propose COUNT, a more efficient algorithm to compute $C_S(s)$. We also link proof counting to proof enumeration.

6.1   Underlying Ideas

The main inefficiency of COUNTNAIVE is that it does not exploit the inductive structure of proof trees. Indeed, the number of proofs of a sequent vertex is the sum of the number of proofs of its successors, and the number of proofs of a rule-use vertex is the product of the number of proofs of its successors. That simple definition cannot be trivially computed, because a proof for a sequent s can use inside itself another proof of s; instead we must explicitly check for loops. As a consequence, instead of returning $C_S(s)$, we return equations verified by $C_S(s')$, for all the s' in $G_S(s)$.

Consider for example Fig. 2. The equations verified by $C_S(s_0)$, $C_S(s_1)$ and $C_S(s_2)$ are:

$$C_S(s_0) = C_S(s_1) + C_S(s_2)$$
$$C_S(s_1) = C_S(s_0) \cdot C_S(s_2)$$
$$C_S(s_2) = 1$$

Afterward, this set of equations must be solved, using standard mathematical reasoning. But we are only interested in the smallest solutions. Indeed, consider the system $C_S(s) = C_S(s')$, $C_S(s') = C_S(s)$. All the solutions $C_S(s) = C_S(s') = k$ are mathematically acceptable, but only the solution $C_S(s) = C_S(s') = 0$ counts the valid finite proof trees (none in this case).

Formally, these are polynomial equations over $\mathbb{N} \cup \{\infty\}$. An algorithm for finding the smallest solution of such systems of polynomial equations has already been given by Zaionc [15].

6.2   Formal Description of the Algorithm Count

An exploration of a sequent s is complete when all the subgraphs of $G_S(s)$ which could possibly lead to finding a proof have been considered. A complete exploration of $G_{MSet}(s)$ is not always possible, because it can be infinite. For this reason, we suppose the existence of a procedure ORACLE which in the case of $\mathcal{S} = \mathsf{MSet}$ can calculate and return the value of $C_{\mathsf{Set}}(s)$ (justified by Theorem 5.6), although if $C_{\mathsf{Set}}(s) = \infty$ we may deliberately continue exploring $G_{\mathsf{MSet}}(s)$ when enumerating proofs instead of just counting. We can also use the oracle to deliberately cut off the search early when we have enumerated enough proofs.

We also suppose the existence of an algorithm SOLVE which takes as input a system of polynomials over $\mathbb{N} \cup \{\infty\}$, and returns as result the least solution of the system; the result should be a function from the variables used in the polynomials to their values in the solution.

In order to find $C_{\mathcal{S}}(s)$, the algorithm COUNTSEQUENT presented below first gathers polynomial equations verified by the sequents present in $G_{\mathcal{S}}(s)$ and then uses SOLVE to solve the resulting system. In the polynomials, for each sequent $s' \in G_{\mathcal{S}}(s)$ we use the variable $c_{s'}$ to stand for $C_{\mathcal{S}}(s')$.

COUNTSEQUENT$(\mathcal{S}, R, s)$
1   **if** $c_s \in \mathsf{Dom}(R)$ **then return** R
2   **match** ORACLE$(\mathcal{S}, s)$ **with**
3 | $0 \Rightarrow$ **return** $\{(c_s, 0)\} \cup R$
4 | $\infty \Rightarrow$ **return** $\{(c_s, \infty)\} \cup R$
5   $v \leftarrow \sum_{\tau \in \mathsf{succ}_{G_{\mathcal{S}}}(s)} \prod_{s' \in \mathsf{succ}_{G_{\mathcal{S}}}(\tau)} c_{s'}$
6   $R' \leftarrow \{(c_s, v)\} \cup R$
7   $L \leftarrow \{ s' \mid s' \in \mathsf{succ}_{G_{\mathcal{S}}}(\tau), \tau \in \mathsf{succ}_{G_{\mathcal{S}}}(s) \}$
8   **return** COUNTSET$(\mathcal{S}, R', L)$

COUNTSET$(\mathcal{S}, R, L)$
1   **match** L **with**
2 | $\emptyset \Rightarrow$ **return** R
3 | $\{s\} \cup L' \Rightarrow$
4        $R' \leftarrow$ COUNTSEQUENT$(\mathcal{S}, R, s)$
5   **return** COUNTSET$(\mathcal{S}, R', L')$

COUNT$(\mathcal{S}, s)$
1   $R \leftarrow$ COUNTSEQUENT$(\mathcal{S}, \emptyset, s)$
2   **return** $(\mathrm{SOLVE}(R))(c_s)$

With a correctly choosen oracle, the algorithm always terminates. Following the results from Sec. 5, valid oracles would be:

– The function which always answers "No answer" in the Set case; termination is guaranteed by the finiteness of $G_{\mathcal{S}}(s)$ anyway.
– COUNT called with $\mathcal{S} = \mathsf{Set}$ in the MSet case. This follows from Theorem 5.6.

COUNT$(\mathcal{S}, s)$ returns exactly $C_{\mathcal{S}}(s)$ given a valid oracle as described just above. Otherwise, if ORACLE$(\mathcal{S}, s)$ is always a lower bound on $C_{\mathcal{S}}(s)$ (or "No answer"), COUNT$(C_{\mathcal{S}}, s)$ is a lower bound on $C_{\mathcal{S}}(s)$ (but termination may fail).

To check the feasibility of our proof counting algorithm, we have built a completely working implementation. We present in Fig. 5 (p. 277) its output on an example. After each sequent, the number of proofs of that sequent is indicated. Unlike the examples presented in Sec. 5, which were hand-made, this example is automatically[1] generated.

Our implementation uses various improvements over the algorithm presented here. For example, once a count of 0 is found in calculating a product, we do not explore the other sequents whose counts are the other factors in the product. Also, instead of calling SOLVE on the whole set of equations, is is more efficient to call it on all the strongly connected components of the equations, which can be found while exploring the graph in COUNTSEQUENT.

---

[1] With some manual annotations added to get a better graph layout.

6.3   Links Between Proof Counting and Proof Enumeration

Exhaustive proof enumeration in G_S could be done by a breadth-first traversal of G_S to find proof trees, but that is inefficient. In particular, some infinite subparts of G_S do not lead to the finding of a proof. Our approach using proof counting is more efficient. We stop exploring a branch whenever we find out that it contains 0 solutions, and we use the more efficient computation of $C_{Set}(s)$ to help when computing $C_{MSet}(s)$. Of course, if there are an infinite number of solutions, only a finite number of them can ever be enumerated.

7   Proof Terms

In this section, we assign proof terms to proofs in LJT^{Enum}. We also discuss the links between the number of different terms which can be found from the proofs of a sequent s and $C_{MSet}(s)$.

7.1   The Assignment of Proofs to $\overline{\lambda}$-Expressions

Proofs of LJT are assigned to terms of a calculus called the $\overline{\lambda}$-calculus. Compared with Herbelin's [10], our presentation is much shorter because in our cut-free calculus we only need terms in normal form. We call our restricted version of the $\overline{\lambda}$-calculus the $\overline{\lambda}'$-calculus.

In the $\overline{\lambda}'$-calculus, the usual application constructor between terms is transformed into an application constructor between a variable and a list of arguments. So there are two sorts of $\overline{\lambda}'$-expressions: $\overline{\lambda}'$-terms and lists of arguments, defined by the following pseudo-grammars where $i \in \{1, 2\}$ and $j \in \mathbb{N}$:

$$x, y \in \quad \text{Variables} ::= x_j$$
$$t, u \in \quad \overline{\lambda}'\text{-Terms} ::= (x\ l) \mid (\lambda x.t) \mid \langle t_1, t_2 \rangle \mid \text{inj}_i(t)$$
$$l \in \text{Argument-Lists} ::= [] \mid [\langle (x_1)t_1 | (x_2)t_2 \rangle] \mid [\langle x, y \rangle t] \mid [t :: l] \mid [\pi_i :: l]$$

As usual, $[]$ is the empty list of arguments, and $[t :: l]$ is the list resulting from the addition of t at the beginning of l. We abbreviate $(x\ [])$ by x.

Solely to aid the reader's understanding of the meaning of $\overline{\lambda}'$-terms, we will relate them to terms of the λ-calculus extended with pairs and tagged variants. We define the extended λ-terms by this pseudo-grammar where $i \in \{1, 2\}$:

$$\hat{t} \in \lambda\text{-Terms} ::= x \mid \lambda x.\hat{t} \mid \hat{t_1}\,\hat{t_2} \mid \langle \hat{t_1}, \hat{t_2} \rangle \mid \text{inj}_i(\hat{t}) \mid \pi_i(\hat{t}) \mid \text{let } x, y = \hat{t} \text{ in } \hat{u} \mid$$
$$\text{case } \hat{t} \text{ of } \text{inj}_1(x) \Rightarrow \hat{t_1}, \text{inj}_2(x) \Rightarrow \hat{t_2}$$

Now we translate $\overline{\lambda}'$-terms into extended λ-terms:

$$
\begin{array}{ll}
(x\ l)^* = \varphi(x, l) & \varphi(\hat{t}, []) = \hat{t} \\
(\lambda x.t)^* = \lambda x.t^* & \varphi(\hat{t}, [u :: l]) = \varphi(\hat{t}\,u^*, l) \\
\langle t_1, t_2 \rangle^* = \langle t_1^*, t_2^* \rangle & \varphi(\hat{t}, [\pi_i :: l]) = \varphi(\pi_i(\hat{t}), l) \\
& \varphi(\hat{t}, [\langle x, y \rangle u]) = \text{let } x, y = \hat{t} \text{ in } \hat{u} \\
(\text{inj}_i(t))^* = \text{inj}_i(t^*) & \varphi(\hat{t}, [\langle (x_1)t_1 | (x_2)t_2 \rangle]) = \\
& \quad \text{case } \hat{t} \text{ of } \text{inj}_1(x) \Rightarrow t_1^*, \text{inj}_2(x) \Rightarrow t_2^*
\end{array}
$$

Applicative contexts formation rules   Terms formation rules

$$\frac{}{\Sigma;.:X \vdash [\,]:X}\ \text{Ax} \qquad\qquad \frac{\Sigma,x:A;.:A \vdash l:B}{\Sigma,x:A;\bullet \vdash (x\ l):B}\ \text{Cont}(x:A)$$

$$\frac{\Sigma;\bullet \vdash u:A \quad \Sigma;.:B \vdash l:C}{\Sigma;.:A \to B \vdash [u::l]:C}\ \text{Imp}_L \qquad \frac{\Sigma,x:A;\bullet \vdash u:B}{\Sigma;\bullet \vdash \lambda x.u:A \to B}\ \text{Imp}_R$$

$$\frac{\Sigma;.:A_i \vdash l:B}{\Sigma;.:A_1 \wedge A_2 \vdash [\pi_i::l]:B}\ \text{And}_{L_i} \qquad \frac{\Sigma;\bullet \vdash t:A \quad \Sigma;\bullet \vdash u:B}{\Sigma;\bullet \vdash \langle t,u \rangle:A \wedge B}\ \text{And}_R$$

$$\frac{\Sigma,x:A;\bullet \vdash t:C \quad \Sigma,y:B;\bullet \vdash u:C}{\Sigma;.:A \vee B \vdash [\langle(x)t|(y)u\rangle]:C}\ \text{Or}_L \qquad \frac{\Sigma;\bullet \vdash u:A_i}{\Sigma;\bullet \vdash \text{inj}_i(u):A_1 \vee A_2}\ \text{Or}_{R_i}$$

Fig. 4. Proof terms for the rules of $\mathsf{LJT}^{\mathsf{Enum}}_{\mathsf{Term}}(i \in \{1,2\})$

Let a *named environment* be a partial function from variables to formulas, and let Σ range over named-environments.

The rules of $\mathsf{LJT}^{\mathsf{Enum}}$ with the corresponding proof terms, which we call $\mathsf{LJT}^{\mathsf{Enum}}_{\mathsf{Term}}$, are given in Fig. 4.

Formulas in the goal are associated to a $\overline{\lambda}'$-expression. By construction, goals of rules in which the stoup is empty are $\overline{\lambda}'$-terms while those in which the stoup is full are lists of arguments waiting to be applied. Formulas which are in the stoup are not associated to a $\overline{\lambda}'$-expression, as is indicated by the notation ". : A".

7.2   Number of Different Proof Terms

Given a sequent s, there are strong ties between $\mathsf{C}_{\mathsf{MSet}}(s)$ and the number of different $\overline{\lambda}$-terms up to α-conversion which can be built from the proofs of s. In fact, the only source of difference is that $\mathsf{C}_{\mathsf{MSet}}(s)$ does not capture multiple uses of CONT on propositions which occur multiple times in the context, with different variable names.

From there, it is easy to devise a proof counting and enumerating algorithm for $\mathsf{LJT}^{\mathsf{Enum}}_{\mathsf{Term}}$: in $\mathsf{G}_{\mathsf{MSet}}$, just duplicate n times the edge between s and $(s,\ \text{Cont}(A))$ if A appears n times in the environment of s. All the results and theorems applicable to $\mathsf{G}_{\mathsf{MSet}}$ remain true with that modification. As a result, proof enumeration is no more difficult in $\mathsf{LJT}^{\mathsf{Enum}}_{\mathsf{Term}}$ than in $\mathsf{LJT}^{\mathsf{Enum}}$.

8   Related Work

Dyckhoff and Pinto propose a confluent rewriting relation $\prec$ on the structure of cut-free proofs in LJ [6]. The normal forms of the proofs in LJ w.r.t. to $\prec$ are in 1-1 correspondence with normal natural deductions in NJ. That solution would not have been suitable for our purpose however, because we could easily have ended up finding an important number of proofs in LJ which would all have corresponded to the same normal proof in NJ.

Howe proposes two mechanisms to efficiently add an history to a sequent proof in LJT, in order to avoid loops in the proof [12]. One of these mechanisms has been added to our implementation of COUNT.

Pinto presents a mechanism to define names for proof-witnesses of formulae and thus to use Gentzen's cut-rule in logic programming [13]. Because using the cut-rule can make some proofs exponentially shorter, it should be possible to discover terms which are much more efficient from a computational standpoint than those we can generate using a cut-free calculus. Devising an exhaustive term enumeration procedure for such a calculus would be an interesting task.

Ben-Yelles [2], Hindley [11], Zaionc [15], Broda and Damas [3] propose various algorithms to solve the problem of type inhabitation in the simply typed λ-calculus. Zaionc's approach is somewhat similar to our own, using fixpoints on polynomials. Broda and Damas propose a tool for studying inhabitation of simple types. In all four cases only simple types are considered.

9   Conclusion

9.1   Summary of Contributions

We have presented COUNT, a proof counting algorithm for the LJT^{Enum} calculus of intuitionistic logic. The idea is reusable for any calculus in which the environment of assumptions only increases (e.g., Gentzen's LJ). Using COUNT and the Curry-Howard correspondence, we have implemented an algorithm which effectively builds all the possible program fragments of a given typing.

We believe our approach to proof counting and enumeration is the first that has the following properties. First, we use the easier solution for assumption *sets* to build a more efficient solution for *multisets*, which is closer to our motivating goal of term enumeration. Second, our method works directly on logical-deduction style sequent derivations as normally used in proof search (i.e., L-systems with left-introduction rules instead of right-elimination rules), while earlier approaches instead count λ-terms in normal forms. Third, our method uses a graph representation of all proofs which seems essential for practicality.

9.2   Future Work

Let us mention some promising ways to extend the expressiveness of our program fragments synthesizer. First, to better handle ML languages, adding some support for polymorphism would be useful; but this will break the syntax-directed property of the calculus, and probably the finiteness of $G_{Set}(s)$.

Ideally, we would also support full algebraic datatypes. We partially achieve this goal in that the method in this paper handles parametric types (e.g., the type constructor list as used in the type int list in Standard ML), provided the environment has functions to build and use them.

Furthermore, the addition of fully general sum types to model inductive datatypes, as well as of recursion, could also be interesting. This could be done for example using recursive propositions. However, a potential pitfall to avoid is generating "dead code" or predictably non-terminating functions.

Finally, while theoretically sound, the OR_L rule generates a huge number of λ-term which are extensionally equal. It is possible to rule out the less inefficient ones after they have been produced, but we are also investigating the possibility of pruning them during an earlier phase of the search.

Acknowledgements. We are grateful to Christian Haack, Daniel Hirschkoff, and the anonymous referees for their helpful comments on earlier versions.

References

[1] M. V. Aponte, R. Di Cosmo, C. Dubois, B. Yakobowski. Signature subtyping modulo type isomorphisms. In preparation, 2004.

[2] C.-B. Ben-Yelles. *Type-assignment in the lambda-calculus; syntax and semantics.* PhD thesis, Mathematics Dept., University of Wales Swansea, UK, 1979.

[3] S. Broda, L. Damas. On the structure of normal λ-terms having a certain type. In *7th Workshop on Logic, Language, Information and Computation (WoLLIC 2000)*, Brazil, 2000.

[4] R. Dyckhoff. Proof search in constructive logics. In *Logic Colloquium '97*, 1998.

[5] R. Dyckhoff, L. Pinto. Cut-elimination and a permutation-free sequent calculus for intuitionistic logic. *Studia Logica*, 60(1), 1998.

[6] R. Dyckhoff, L. Pinto. Permutability of proofs in intuitionistic sequent calculi. *Theoret. Comput. Sci.*, 212(1–2), 1999.

[7] C. Haack. *Foundations for a tool for the automatic adaptation of software components based on semantic specifications.* PhD thesis, Kansas State University, 2001.

[8] C. Haack, B. Howard, A. Stoughton, J. B. Wells. Fully automatic adaptation of software components based on semantic specifications. In *Algebraic Methodology & Softw. Tech., 9th Int'l Conf., AMAST 2002, Proc.*, vol. 2422 of *LNCS*. Springer-Verlag, 2002.

[9] H. Herbelin. A λ-calculus structure isomorphic to Gentzen-style sequent calculus structure. In *Proc. Conf. Computer Science Logic*, vol. 933 of *LNCS*. Springer-Verlag, 1994.

[10] H. Herbelin. A λ-calculus structure isomorphic to Gentzen-style sequent calculus structure. Available at http://coq.inria.fr/~herbelin/LAMBDA-BAR-FULL.dvi.gz, 1994.

[11] J. R. Hindley. *Basic Simple Type Theory*, vol. 42 of *Cambridge Tracts in Theoretical Computer Science*. Cambridge University Press, 1997.

[12] J. M. Howe. *Proof Search Issues In Some Non-Classical Logics*. PhD thesis, University of St Andrews, 1998.

[13] L. Pinto. Cut formulae and logic programming. In R. Dyckhoff, ed., *Extensions of Logic Programming: Proc. of the 4th International Workshop ELP'93*. Springer-Verlag, 1994.

[14] L. Pinto, R. Dyckhoff. Sequent calculi for the normal terms of the $\lambda\Pi$ and $\lambda\Pi\Sigma$ calculi. In D. Galmiche, ed., *Electronic Notes in Theoretical Computer Science*, vol. 17. Elsevier, 2000.

[15] M. Zaionc. Fixpoint technique for counting terms in typed lambda calculus. Technical Report 95-20, State University of New York, 1995.

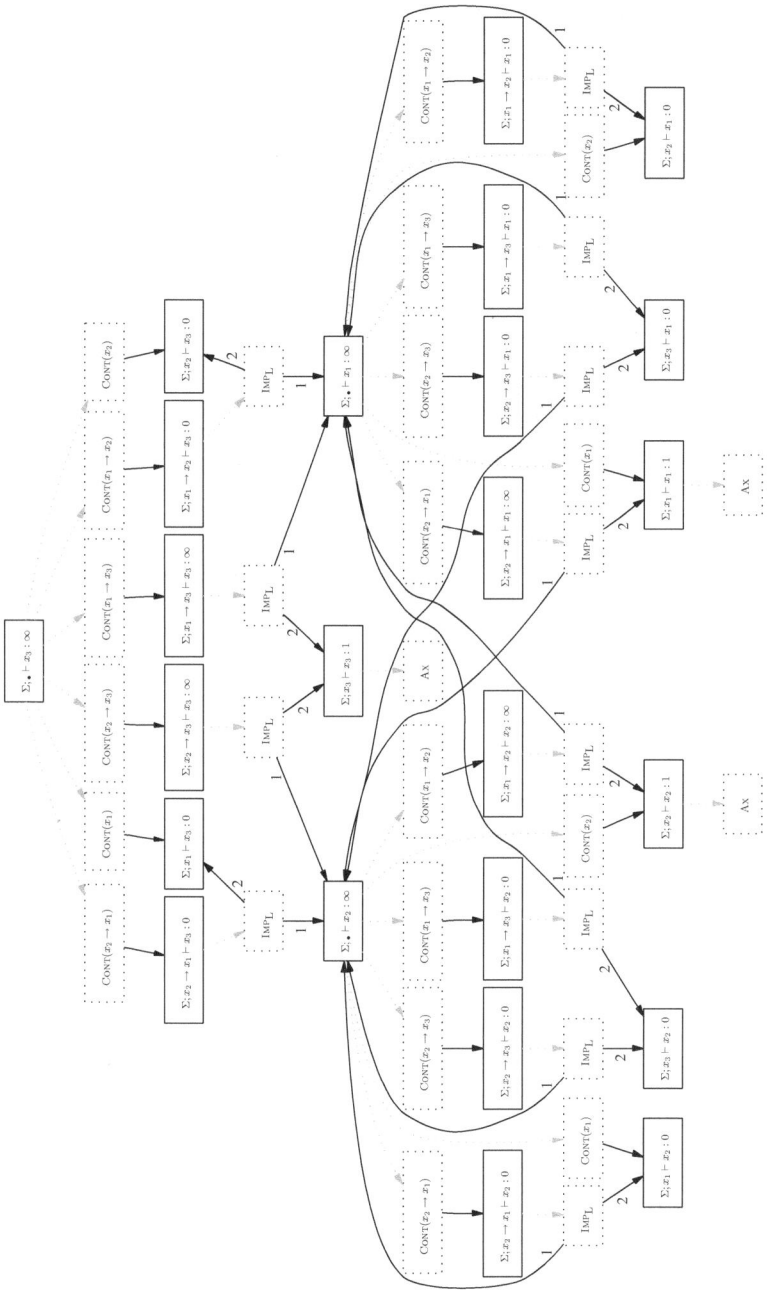

Fig. 5. $\mathsf{G}_{\mathsf{Set}}(\Sigma; \bullet \vdash x_3) = \mathsf{G}_{\mathsf{MSet}}(\Sigma; \bullet \vdash x_3)$ with $\Sigma = \{x_1, x_2, x_1 \to x_2, x_2 \to x_1, x_1 \to x_3, x_2 \to x_3\}$

Author Index

Lecture Notes in Computer Science

For information about Vols. 1–3462

please contact your bookseller or Springer